SAT UPDATE: CHANGES TO SCORE-REPORTING POLICY

The College Board has decided to make important changes to their SAT score-reporting policy. The following information will tell you everything you need to know about these new changes and how you can use them to your advantage!

WHAT CHANGED?

The new SAT score-reporting policy gives you the ability to select which scores by sitting date (test date) that you wish to send to colleges. This is a completely **optional** feature, and was first available during the **March 2009** SAT test administration. You can use this new score-reporting feature on any score report you plan on sending, and you can send one, several, or all of your test scores to a college on a single report—with no difference in cost!

For those who choose not to use this feature, all scores will be sent automatically.

It's important to note that only scores from an entire SAT exam can be sent to schools—you can not select individual test sections from exams you've taken at different times. Please visit the official College Board website at www.collegeboard.com for complete details.

HOW DOES THIS CHANGE AFFECT ME?

This new policy gives you a real boost of empowerment in the college admissions process. It gives you more control over what colleges see and lets you show schools the SAT score that you feel best represents your test-taking ability. Since choosing to send sectional scores from different testing dates is not an option, you should make sure that you are well prepared for each and every SAT exam you take!

Although you should be aware of the score-reporting requirements of each college that you plan on applying to, the bottom line is that **this score-reporting change is good news for students**—use it to lower your anxiety and stress-level as you prepare for test day!

STAY ON TOP OF THE LATEST SAT DEVELOPMENTS

You can depend on Kaplan to provide you with the most accurate, up-to-the-minute test information. You can get updates by visiting us at **kaptest.com/SAT.**

Good Luck!

SAT® ADVANCED

Second Edition

RELATED TITLES FOR COLLEGE-BOUND STUDENTS

COLLEGE ADMISSIONS AND FINANCIAL AID

TEST PREPARATION

SAT® ADVANCED

Second Edition

The Staff of Kaplan Test Prep and Admissions

PUBLISHING

New York

© 2010 by Kaplan, Inc.

Published by Kaplan Publishing, a division of Kaplan, Inc.
1 Liberty Plaza, 24th Floor
New York, NY 10006

Printed in the United States of America

10 9 8 7 6 5 4 3 2 1

ISBN-13: 978-1-4195-5340-0

Kaplan Publishing books are available at special quantity discounts to use for sales promotions, employee premiums, or educational purposes. For more information or to order books, please call the Simon & Schuster special sales department at 866-506-1949.

Table of Contents

PART THREE: WRITING

AVAILABLE ONLINE

FOR ANY TEST CHANGES OR LATE-BREAKING DEVELOPMENTS

KAPTEST.COM/PUBLISHING

The material in this book is up-to-date at the time of publication. However, the College Board may have instituted changes in the test after this book was published. Be sure to carefully read the materials you receive when you register for the test. If there are any important late-breaking developments—or any changes or corrections to the Kaplan test preparation materials in this book—we will post that information online at **kaptest.com/publishing.**

FEEDBACK AND COMMENTS

KAPLANSURVEYS.COM/BOOKS

We'd love to hear your comments and suggestions about this book. We invite you to fill out our online survey form at **kaplansurveys.com/books.** Your feedback is extremely helpful as we continue to develop high-quality resources to meet your needs.

THE PERFECT SCORE

AIMING FOR 2400

If you've bought this book, you must think you've got the right stuff to take on the toughest stuff the SAT Advanced can dish out. Kudos to you! Confidence and ambition are invaluable to upper-echelon SAT performance.

But it doesn't stop there. It takes the right mix of determination, preparation, and moxie to launch you into the SAT stratosphere.

That's where we come in. Over the years, we've taught thousands of students like you. And we realize that most SAT books aren't really written with high scorers like you in mind. Rather than the standard review of concepts you've already mastered, mixed with strategies for questions you can knock off in seconds, this book targets the especially tricky concepts and tough questions that stand between the good score you know you can get and the great score you're aiming for. We'll move fast and push you hard to raise your score as high as it can go.

But what is it with this quest for a perfect score? No college requires a perfect score on the SAT. Getting a perfect score on the SAT won't guarantee success in all your future endeavors. It probably won't make you the center of attention at parties. And if you've ever had an unrequited crush, it most likely won't make that past or present object of your affections realize what a fool he or she has been. The only thing a perfect score—or even a very high score—will get you is a strong chance to get into the school of your dreams. However, that's no small thing.

We understand your quest for perfection. We salute your desire for a top score. We find your goal to be perfectly laudable, and we think we have written the perfect book for you.

HOW TO USE THIS BOOK

We should warn you up front: This book is not for the faint of heart. It is comprised exclusively of the toughest material you're likely to see on the SAT and the strategies designed for cracking the tough stuff.

If you want a more fundamental introduction to the SAT and practice with questions ranging from easy to difficult, we recommend that you work your way through some of our more traditional test prep materials, such as *SAT Strategies, Practice, and Review* or *SAT Premier*. And if you find any deficiencies in your SAT knowledge base as you go through this book, you should get your hands on one or more of these books.

Basically, we are assuming that you already have some other SAT test prep materials in the form of Practice Tests, such as those found in the books we've just mentioned. This is because the best course of test preparation for a high scorer like yourself involves a combination of taking real or simulated SATs under testlike conditions and studying the tips and techniques for acing the hard questions, which is what this book is all about.

This book is divided into six sections. Section One, Inside the SAT, gives you an overview of the SAT, plus a review of Kaplan's proven multiple-choice strategies. Section Two, Critical Reading, shows you how to handle the hardest Long and Short Reading Passages, with a special focus on difficult Narrative, Science, and Paired Passages. This section also gives you the best strategies for difficult Sentence Completion questions, including tough two-blankers, hard vocabulary, and more.

Section Three gives you the help you need to ace the SAT Writing Section. We start by looking at the Essay section, and identifying exactly what it takes to get a great score. We'll show you, step-by-step, how to turn a "so-so" essay into a top-scoring one. You'll become an expert as you work with sample essays, reader analyses, and practice prompts. Then we'll turn to the Writing Multiple-Choice questions, and show you how to score the most points in the least time on Identifying Sentence Errors, Improving Sentences, and Improving Paragraphs. Plus, you'll find out what to expect from this new section.

The first Math section, Section Four, SAT Advanced Math—The Basics, introduces you to the tricky nature of difficult math questions, and reveals our most effective strategies for handling the toughest math questions, whatever their format. Section Five deals with the trickiest "straight math" questions found on the SAT—that is, the really tough questions that are not word problems. The final Math section, SAT Math Word Problems, deals with ugly SAT Math word problems of every stripe, size, and flavor. We also give you 100 Essential Math Concepts in an appendix at the end of this book.

Each of the "Strategy" chapters in the book—chapters 4, 7, 9, 12, and 15—concludes with a recap of all our favorite advanced-level strategies for handling the different SAT question types. Finally, at the end of every section is a practice set of questions that allows you to apply the tips and strategies you've just been studying, along with detailed answer explanations for every question. Unlike the practice sets found in our other books, these are composed of only the most difficult questions.

You can either work your way through the sections in the order presented, or jump right into the section that gives you the most trouble. You'll notice that the habits and thought processes of top test takers are highlighted throughout the book, as are our favorite strategy tips. Study these thoroughly, and strive to make these effective techniques your own.

No matter what you do, try not to overload. Remember that this is dense, complicated material and not representative of the range of difficulty you'll see on test day. One thing is for sure: if you can ace this stuff, the real thing will be a breeze.

Have fun, and good luck!

Part One

INSIDE THE SAT

CHAPTER 1: ABOUT THE SAT

THE TEST BREAKDOWN

The SAT is 3 hours and 45 minutes long, and there are two 10-minute breaks. The exam is mostly multiple-choice, and it's divided into three Math, three Critical Reading, and three Writing sections. There is also an experimental section, but we will discuss that section later. The essay section is always first. The multiple-choice sections can appear in *any order* on test day. The order is random, and your test will be different from that of the person sitting next to you.

Each section of the SAT is scored on a 200–800 point scale. The three scores are then added together to get your cumulative score. You can now get a perfect score of 2400. This book is designed for the Advanced test taker.

FORMAT AND TIME

The SAT topic areas are divided into nine sections. (Actually, there will be ten sections on the test, but one of them is a 25-minute experimental section that won't count. You won't know which section that is, however, so you'll have to work through all sections alike.) Here's how they break down.

MATH SECTION (70 MINUTES)

There are two kinds of questions on the Math section: **Regular Math** questions, which are straightforward multiple-choice questions; and **Grid-Ins,** which require you to write your response in a little grid. Both types of question test the same math concepts—they're just in different formats. There are two 25-minute sections and one 20-minute section.

CRITICAL READING SECTION (70 MINUTES)

The Critical Reading section contains three types of questions. **Sentence Completions** test your ability to see how the parts of a sentence relate to each other. They are basic fill-in-the-blank questions—with either one blank or two. **Short Reading Comprehension** questions test your ability to understand a very brief passage, and **Long Reading Comprehension** questions test your know-how with a longer text. For the Reading Comprehension questions, you are asked about such things as the main idea, contextual references, and vocabulary. There are two 25-minute sections and one 20-minute section.

WRITING SECTION (60 MINUTES)

The Writing section is broken into two parts: a **written essay** (that *you* write), and multiple-choice questions in **Identifying Sentence Errors, Improving Sentences,** and **Improving Paragraphs.** Both sections are meant to test your grasp of grammar, identifying sentence errors, and vocabulary.

The Essay assignment is the very first section on the test. You'll have 25 minutes to write the essay. You'll have 25 minutes for one multiple-choice section, and one 10-minute section.

SAT REGISTRATION

There are a few different ways to register for the SAT exam. You will want to check the College Board website at collegeboard.com for complete information about registering for the SAT and for the most up-to-date information concerning changes in dates, fees, etc. You should try to register early to secure the time you want at the test center of your choice and to avoid late registration fees.

REGISTER BY MAIL, ONLINE, OR TELEPHONE

- To register for the SAT by mail, you'll need to get a *Registration Bulletin* from your high school guidance counselor and follow the instructions within.

- You can also register online at collegeboard.com/sat/html/satform.html. The website contains easy, step-by-step instructions for electronically submitting your registration. Not all students are eligible to register online; read the instructions and requirements carefully.

- Students with disabilities can call (609) 771-7137 (TTY: (609) 882-4118) or contact the College Board SSD Office by email at ssd@info.collegeboard.org for more information.

- The basic fee for the SAT is $45 in the United States. This price includes reports for you, your high school, and up to four colleges and scholarship programs. There are additional fees for late registration, standby testing, international processing, changing test centers or test dates, rush reporting, and for additional services and products.

- The SAT is administered on select Saturdays during the school year. Sunday testing is available for students who cannot take the Saturday test because of religious observances.

- You will receive an admission ticket at least a week before the test. The ticket confirms your registration at a specified date and at a specified test center. Make sure to bring it, and proper identification, with you to the test center. Some acceptable forms of identification include photo IDs, such as a driver's license, a school identification card, or a valid passport. Unacceptable forms of identification include a Social Security card, credit card, or birth certificate.

- Check with the College Board for all the latest information on the test. Every effort is made to keep the information in this book up-to-date, but changes may occur after the book is published.

- You might be wondering whether to take the SAT, ACT, or both. For more information on the ACT, go to the ACT website at act.org.

- SAT scores will be available online approximately three weeks after the test. If you can't wait that long, you can get your scores eight days earlier with Scores by Web or Scores by Phone. Please visit collegeboard.com for more information.

CHAPTER 2: SAT STRATEGY OVERVIEW

Now that you know some basics about how the test is set up, you can approach the multiple-choice questions with a plan. Having a plan is the key to success on the SAT. Here's the basic Kaplan plan of attack. We'll go into more detailed, tough-question strategies in subsequent chapters. We'll also take an in-depth look at the new Essay strategies to ensure you get a top score. For now, though, get these strategies down cold.

1. Think about the question first.
2. Pace yourself.
3. Know when a question is supposed to be easy or hard.
4. Move around within a section.
5. Be a good guesser.
6. Be a good gridder.
7. Two-minute warning: locate quick points.

GENERAL SAT STRATEGIES

1. THINK ABOUT THE QUESTION FIRST

The people who write the SAT put distracters among the answer choices. Distracters are answer choices that look right, but aren't. If you jump into the answer choices without thinking about what you're looking for, you're more likely to fall for a trap. So always think about the question for a couple of seconds before you look at the answers.

2. PACE YOURSELF

The SAT gives you a lot of questions to answer in a short period of time. To get through a whole section, you can't spend too much time on any one question. Keep moving through the test at a good speed. If you run into a hard question, circle it in your test booklet, skip it, and come back to it later if you have time.

The questions also get harder as you move through a problem set. Ideally, you can work through the easy problems at a faster pace and use a little more of your time for the harder ones that come at the end of the set.

3. Know When a Question Is Supposed to Be Easy or Hard

The SAT will have its multiple-choice questions arranged in order of difficulty. Here's a breakdown:

		Arranged Easiest to Hardest?
Math	Regular Math	Yes
	Grid-Ins	Yes
Critical Reading	Sentence Completions	Yes
	Short Reading Comprehension	No
	Long Reading Comprehension	No
Writing	Essay	N/A
	Identifying Sentence Errors	No
	Improving Sentences	No
	Improving Paragraphs	No

As you can see, all question sets in Math are arranged in order of difficulty, as are sentence completions in Critical Reading. As you work through a set that is organized this way, *be aware of where you are in a set*. When working on the easy problems, you can generally trust your first impulse—the obvious answer is likely to be right. As you get to the end of the set, you need to be more suspicious of "obvious" answers, because the answer should not come easily. If it does, look at the problem again because the obvious answer is likely to be wrong. It may be one of those distracters—a wrong answer choice meant to trick you.

Hard SAT questions are usually tough for two reasons:

1. Their answers are not immediately obvious.

2. The questions do not ask for information in a straightforward way.

Here's an easy question:

Known for their devotion, dogs were often used as symbols of _____ in Medieval and Renaissance painting.

(A) breakfast
(B) tidal waves
(C) fidelity
(D) campfires
(E) toothpaste

The correct answer, *fidelity* (C), probably lunged right out at you. This question would be at the beginning of a problem set. Easy questions are purposely designed to be easy, and their answer choices are purposely obvious.

Here is virtually the same question, made hard:

Known for their _____, dogs were often used as symbols of _____ in Medieval and Renaissance painting.

(A) dispassion . . bawdiness
(B) fidelity . . aloofness
(C) monogamy . . parsimony
(D) parity . . diplomacy
(E) loyalty . . faithfulness

This question would be at the end of a problem set. This time the answer is harder to find. For one thing, the answer choices are far more difficult. In addition, the sentence contains two blanks.

The correct answer is (E). Did you fall for (B) because the first word is *fidelity*? (B) is a good example of a distracter.

4. MOVE AROUND WITHIN A SECTION

On a test at school, you probably spend more time on the hard questions than you do on the easy ones, since hard questions are usually worth more points. *Do not do this on the SAT.*

Easy problems are worth as many points as tough problems, so do the easy problems first. Don't rush through the easy problems just to get to the hard ones. When you run into questions that look tough, circle them in your test booklet and skip them for the time being. (Make sure you skip them on your answer grid too.)

Then, if you have time, go back to them *after* you have answered the easier ones. Sometimes, after you have answered some easier questions, troublesome questions can get easier too.

5. BE A GOOD GUESSER

The SAT administrators say there is a penalty for guessing on the SAT. This is not true. There is only a "wrong answer penalty": if you guess WRONG, you get penalized. Here's how the wrong answer penalty works:

- If you get an answer wrong on multiple-choice questions, which have five answer choices, you lose one-quarter point. These fractions of points are meant to offset the points you might get "accidentally" by guessing the correct answer.

- If you get an answer wrong on a Grid-In Math question, for which you write in your own answers, you lose NOTHING.

- If you can eliminate one or more wrong answers, you turn the odds in your favor, and you will actually come out ahead by guessing.

Take a look at this question:

> After spending countless hours helping the needy children in their community, the basketball players were as recognized for their acts of _____ as they were for their slam dunks.
>
> (A) breakfast
> (B) tidal waves
> (C) charity
> (D) campfires
> (E) toothpaste

Chances are, you recognized that choice (A), *breakfast*, was wrong. You then looked at the next answer choice, and then the next one, and so on, eliminating wrong answers to find the correct answer. This process is usually the best way to work through multiple-choice SAT questions. If you still don't know the right answer, but can eliminate one or more wrong answers, *you should guess.*

6. BE A GOOD GRIDDER

Don't make mistakes filling out your answer grid. When time is short, it's easy to get confused skipping around a section and going back and forth between your test book and your grid. If you misgrid a *single* question, you can misgrid several others before realizing your error—if you realize it at all. You can lose a *ton* of points this way.

To avoid mistakes on the answer grid:

- Always circle the answers you choose. Circling your answers in the test book makes it easier to check your grid against your book.

- Grid five or more answers at once. Don't transfer your answers to the grid after every question. Transfer your answers after every five questions, or in the Critical Reading section, at the end of each reading passage. That way, you won't keep breaking your concentration to mark the grid. You'll save time and improve accuracy.

  Important Exception:
  When time is running out at the end of a section, start gridding one by one so you don't get caught at the end with ungridded answers.

- Circle the questions you skip. Put a big circle in your test book around the number of any questions you skip, so they'll be easy to locate when you return to them. Also, if you realize later that you accidentally skipped a box on the grid, you can more easily check your grid against your book to see where you went wrong.

- Write in your booklet. Take notes, circle hard questions, underline things, etc. Proctors collect booklets at the end of each testing session, but the booklets are not examined or reused.

7. TWO-MINUTE WARNING: LOCATE QUICK POINTS

When you start to run out of time, locate and answer any of the quick points that remain. For example, some Critical Reading questions will ask you to identify the meaning of a particular word in the passage. These can be done at the last minute, even if you haven't read the passage.

Since a great way to prepare yourself for the SAT is to practice answering testlike questions, this book gives you hundreds of sample problems to work on, the toughest you'll see on the exam. We'll detail the strongest strategies for cracking the hardest Critical Reading, Writing, and Math questions around. You *can* get a 2400 on the SAT!

Part Two

CRITICAL READING

CHAPTER 3: THE READING COMPREHENSION CHALLENGE

- Learn Kaplan's Five-Step Method for Reading Comprehension.

- Practice the five Kaplan Reading Principles for working with Reading Comprehension.

- Get to know the Reading Comprehension question types.

If you're already a top scorer, you may find Reading Comprehension easy, like browsing through an article in your favorite magazine, and then having a pleasant chat about its contents with one of your more intellectual friends. Right. Most SAT takers, even high scorers, have trouble with Reading Comprehension. The passages are usually on subjects you know nothing about, and the questions are either impossibly broad or way too picky.

Before we jump into strategies, let's discuss a few facts. The test features two types of Reading Comprehension: Short and Long. The Short passages are single paragraphs of about 100 words and are followed by just a few questions. The Long passages range from 450 to over 800 words and are followed by anywhere from 6 to 12 questions. Don't let these distinctions fool you—Reading Comprehension is Reading Comprehension. Short and Long passages are written in the same style, cover the same topics, and present the same types of questions. Best of all, you can use the same strategies to handle both.

How can you improve your performance on Reading Comprehension? As with all the other SAT question types, practice helps. However, there's something much more helpful that you can do right now if you want to improve your Reading Comprehension performance. Let's say that again, in bold this time, in case you missed it.

ONE THING YOU CAN DO TO IMPROVE IN SAT READING COMPREHENSION

Learn how to spend less time reading the passage and more time researching the questions and attacking the answer choices.

> An Advanced test taker manages time wisely, especially when tackling tough passages.

Time management is a critical issue in SAT Reading Comprehension. Most students spend far too much time reading the passage and not enough time researching the passage for the answers to specific questions, attacking the answer choices, and choosing the best response. To help you manage your time more efficiently, Kaplan has developed the following approach.

ATTACKING SAT READING COMPREHENSION STRATEGICALLY

Step 1: When you first encounter the passage, read enough of it to figure out the author's "Big Idea" and get a general sense of how the passage is organized.

Step 2: Analyze the question; if a question seems hard, go back to it after you've answered the other questions in the set.

Step 3: As necessary, go back into the passage to locate the answer to a specific question.

Step 4: Put the answer in your own words.

Step 5: Attack the answer choices, and choose the one that comes closest to the answer you found.

This is the approach that you should internalize as you work through the Reading Comprehension passages in this book.

THE METHOD IN ACTION

Here's an example of a typical Short Reading Comprehension passage:

> Recent research indicates that dreams may be the result of random electrical activity in the brain during sleep. These electrical impulses stimulate a series of unrelated sensations and images which our analytic forebrain then struggles to
> (5) form into a coherent narrative. Although the images stimulated by this random activity may not in themselves be meaningful, the way in which we form them into a whole may be quite

revealing, just as the way we interpret random ink blot pictures
can expose something about our unconscious selves. Ink blot
(10) tests and dream analysis have been common techniques used
by psychiatrists for decades, and it now appears that the mechanisms behind both of these may be closely related.

1. According to the author, the "unrelated sensations and images" (lines 3–4)

   (A) stem from ink blot pictures

   (B) are likely not intrinsically meaningful

   (C) lend themselves easily to a coherent narrative

   (D) create a struggle within the unconscious self

   (E) have been a popular analytic technique for decades

Let's see how the Five-Step Method can help you to quickly home in on the right answer.

STEP 1: READ FOR THE "BIG IDEA"

The passage provide lots of details, but the Big Idea is that our brains create random images in our
sleep, and the way in which we interpret these images says something about us.

STEP 2: ANALYZE THE QUESTION

The question is asking about a very specific part of the passage. In fact, you are given a line number.

STEP 3: GO BACK INTO THE PASSAGE

When you go back to the passage, you read that the sensations and images are stimulated by electrical
impulses. The passage also states that the images don't have much meaning in themselves, although
our interpretations of the images can be revealing.

STEP 4: PUT THE ANSWER IN YOUR OWN WORDS

It's tough to make an exact prediction on an open-ended question like this one, but you can
summarize in your mind the author's point of view: "Dreamers force the images into some kind of
order, and that effort reveals something about the dreamers."

STEP 5: ATTACK THE ANSWER CHOICES

(B) nicely matches the passage. In fact, the author later writes, "The images stimulated by this
random activity may not in themselves be meaningful."

Take a look at the other choices. (A) is a distortion; although the author compares dreams and ink
blot pictures, he doesn't say that one causes the other. (C) doesn't fit because of the word *easily*. The
author says that people "struggle" to form a coherent narrative. (D) is outside the scope of the passage.
The author doesn't ever use the phrase "unconscious self," so we don't know the author's thoughts in

this area. (E) is tempting, but also wrong. The *analysis* of dreams has long been a popular technique, but it makes no sense to say that the images and sensations themselves are a popular technique.

Now try your hand on this question, using steps 2–5. (The answer appears on page 19.)

2. The author of this passage would be most likely to agree with which of the following statements about ink blot tests and dream analysis?

(A) Both techniques are probably more effective than was previously believed.

(B) Although dream analysis is a more recent development than ink blot tests, it is also less reliable.

(C) The techniques both seek to find information that people unconsciously provide about themselves through the way in which they interpret random events.

(D) Both methods can be used to reveal a coherent narrative in seemingly random events.

(E) Neither technique is inherently meaningful, though we may create meaning through the way in which we interpret the techniques.

WORKING WITH THE PASSAGE

Now let's take a closer look at reading effectively on the SAT.

Step 1: When you first encounter the passage, read enough of it to figure out the author's Big Idea and get a general sense of how the passage is organized.

How you approach reading the passage may vary depending on how difficult the passage is and whether you are running into time trouble. For instance, when you're not running into time trouble and the passage itself doesn't present serious obstacles, you'll want to read the entire passage. Here are some reading principles that will allow you to do so with maximum efficiency:

> An Advanced test taker follows the Kaplan Reading Principles in order to focus and save time.

Principle 1: Focus on the author.

Principle 2: Don't sweat the details.

Principle 3: Read the first third closely.

Principle 4: Note paragraph topics and make a road map.

Principle 5: Stop to sum up.

Notice that Principles 3 and 4 are more relevant to Long passages, while 1, 2, and 5 apply to all passage types.

Let's try out these reading principles on the following Long Reading Comprehension passage.

ANSWER, PLEASE

The answer to question 2 on page 18 is (C).

The following passage is excerpted from the catalog of a museum exhibition on arms and armor. The passage provides examples of the connections between art and weaponry throughout the ages.

From the beginning, arms and art were essential and interrelated elements in the life of mankind. Weapons for the hunt were necessary tools in the daily struggle for survival. Art, meanwhile, seems to have begun primarily as
(5) hunting magic. By painting images of game animals on cave walls and carving them on spear-throwers and arrow straighteners, hunters attempted to use supernatural means to secure an abundant supply of meat and hides for food and clothing.
(10) Since arms were literally a matter of life and death, either as weapons designed to kill or as armor designed to protect, it was crucial that they be constructed for maximum effect and with the greatest technical efficiency; in many cases this process also resulted in functional beauty.
(15) To further enhance the aesthetic and ideological values of arms—and to increase their cachet as status symbols—arms of all periods were embellished with a wide range of designs in every technique known to the decorative arts.
In classical antiquity, too, there was a close relationship
(20) between art and arms. The patron deity of the arts in ancient Greece, for instance, was Pallas Athena, who was represented as helmeted, armored, and carrying a shield and a spear. Significantly, there was also one among the Olympian gods who worked with his hands at a human
(25) craft, the divine smith Hephaestos—known as Vulcan to the Romans—who not only created dazzling jewelry for the goddesses but also manufactured impenetrable and splendidly decorated armor for the god of war Ares, or Mars, as well as for the mortal hero Achilles.
(30) Evidence of the artistry brought to weapons in ancient times is abundant. In *The Iliad*, Homer describes the shield of Achilles as a mirror of the world "in imperishable bronze, some tin, and precious gold and silver." When Mycenae was excavated in 1875 by Heinrich Schliemann,
(35) he found swords and daggers decorated with superb multi-

colored inlays in the technique vividly described by Homer. They were of such artistic finesse that they would have met with the approval even of Hephaestos.

(40) Under the influence of Christianity, the idea of the divine craftsman was transformed into a human figure: the legendary Wayland the Smith. Wayland worked in gold as well as in steel, fashioning jewels so temptingly beautiful as to sway the virtue of princesses, and forging sword blades painstakingly wrought from interwoven strands of iron and steel. The craft

(45) of the smith was believed to hold a powerful magic, and the prestige of even the greatest of Celtic or Germanic heroes was enhanced if they were apprenticed to smiths.

For centuries master craftsmen remained nameless, but when awakening artistic self-esteem in the Renaissance let

(50) artists step out of the shadows of anonymity, the greatest names, such as Leonardo da Vinci, Hans Holbein, Albrecht Dürer, and Benvenuto Cellini, were found quite matter-of-factly among those of designers and manufacturers of arms.

PRINCIPLE 1: FOCUS ON THE AUTHOR

SAT Reading Comprehension tests your understanding of what the author is thinking and doing. Therefore, your focus as you read must be always on the author. The test writers may want you to draw conclusions about why the passage is organized the way it is and what the author's purpose is in writing it.

INSIDE YOUR BRAIN:

"Okay, this passage doesn't seem so bad. It appears to be about the relationship between art and weaponry in human history. In fact, the italicized information tells me that much, and also tells me that the passage was written for an art catalog. The author's tone is descriptive and neutral."

This is a good way to begin. Get the gist of the author's tone and his or her purpose in writing the passage.

PRINCIPLE 2: DON'T SWEAT THE DETAILS

Details are in the passage only to illustrate what the author is thinking or doing. Therefore, read over details quickly. Trying to comprehend all of the content is a waste of time. Always boil down the passage to its basics.

INSIDE YOUR BRAIN:

"'. . . Pallas Athena, who was represented as . . . In The Iliad, *Homer describes . . . . When Mycenae was excavated . . . .' These are details. I don't need to memorize them. They might ask me questions about them later, but that's okay, because I can always go back to the passage."*

It's okay to recognize details. Just don't obsess over them.

PRINCIPLE 3: READ THE FIRST THIRD CLOSELY

When you're reading Long Reading Comprehension passages, you should read the first third more closely than the rest of the passage. Why? Because the passage's topic is revealed here, and—quite often—so is the author's purpose, as well as his or her attitude toward the subject. This is what you want to know to get a sense of the "Big Picture."

INSIDE YOUR BRAIN:

"'Since the beginning of mankind, art and weaponry have been very closely allied human activities.' The very first sentence here gives me the Big Idea of the whole passage. The rest of this paragraph applies this Big Idea to prehistoric man. The second discusses how a wide range of decorative arts were used in each period and how art could even make weaponry a status symbol."

Good. Recognizing the topic and supporting details is key to understanding the passage.

PRINCIPLE 4: NOTE PARAGRAPH TOPICS AND MAKE A ROAD MAP

Paragraphs are the fundamental building blocks of a passage. For Short passages, you have only one paragraph to keep track of; but things get much more complicated with the Long passages. Therefore, as you read Long passages, you should take note of paragraph topics and make a mental road map. Ask yourself: "What's the point of this paragraph? How does it fit into the overall structure of the passage?"

INSIDE YOUR BRAIN:

"The first paragraph discusses art and weaponry in the stone age and subsequent paragraphs carry this discussion up through the Renaissance (¶1: the stone age, ¶2: background, general about each period, ¶¶3 and 4: classical antiquity, ¶5: early Christianity, ¶6: the Renaissance)."

PRINCIPLE 5: STOP TO SUM UP

After you've read through the passage, take a moment to think about how the passage was put together. Sum up the main idea of the passage in your own words.

INSIDE YOUR BRAIN:

"The passage was amazingly straightforward. It's about the close relationship between art and weaponry throughout history. It carries this discussion up through the Renaissance."

That's a clear, concise summary of the passage.

All the work that you've done to read and understand the passage in Step 1 will serve you well as you attack the questions in Steps 2–5.

WORKING WITH THE QUESTIONS

As soon as you've read through the passage, you're ready to focus on the questions. Understanding the different types of Reading Comprehension questions can help you cut down on the amount of time you spend answering them. Each type of question calls for a slightly different plan of attack. Let's take a look at the different types of Reading Comprehension questions.

"BIG PICTURE" QUESTIONS

Big Picture questions relate to the passage as a whole. They may ask about the main idea or primary purpose of the passage. You should be able to answer these questions based on your initial reading of the passage.

Correct answers to Reading Comprehension questions tend to be fairly inconspicuous, while incorrect answers always contain some sort of wording that makes them definitely wrong. Therefore, the process of elimination is essential on this question type.

WHAT DOES THIS MEAN TO ME?

You should concentrate your efforts on attacking and eliminating wrong answer choices. Common wrong answer choices to Big Picture questions include those that:

- Don't relate to the main idea of the passage
- Contradict the passage
- Are too specific (deal with just one part of the passage)
- Are too general (go beyond the scope of the passage)
- Are too extreme

> An Advanced test taker has the Big Picture—the author's main idea and purpose—in mind before attacking the questions.

Keeping this in mind, let's review the passage again and give this Big Picture question a try.

The following passage is excerpted from the catalog of a museum exhibition on arms and armor. The passage provides examples of the connections between art and weaponry throughout the ages.

From the beginning, arms and art were essential and interrelated elements in the life of mankind. Weapons for the hunt were necessary tools in the daily struggle for survival. Art, meanwhile, seems to have begun primarily as
(5) hunting magic. By painting images of game animals on cave walls and carving them on spear-throwers and arrow straighteners, hunters attempted to use supernatural means to secure an abundant supply of meat and hides for food and clothing.

(10) Since arms were literally a matter of life and death, either as weapons designed to kill or as armor designed to protect, it was crucial that they be constructed for maximum effect and with the greatest technical efficiency; in many cases this process also resulted in functional beauty.

(15) To further enhance the aesthetic and ideological values of arms—and to increase their cachet as status symbols— arms of all periods were embellished with a wide range of designs in every technique known to the decorative arts.

In classical antiquity, too, there was a close relation-
(20) ship between art and arms. The patron deity of the arts in ancient Greece, for instance, was Pallas Athena, who was represented as helmeted, armored, and carrying a shield and a spear. Significantly, there was also one among the Olympian gods who worked with his hands at a human
(25) craft, the divine smith Hephaestos—known as Vulcan to the Romans—who not only created dazzling jewelry for the goddesses but also manufactured impenetrable and splendidly decorated armor for the god of war Ares, or Mars, as well as for the mortal hero Achilles.

(30) Evidence of the artistry brought to weapons in ancient times is abundant. In *The Iliad*, Homer describes the shield of Achilles as a mirror of the world "in imperishable bronze, some tin, and precious gold and silver." When Mycenae was excavated in 1875 by Heinrich Schliemann,
(35) he found swords and daggers decorated with superb multi-colored inlays in the technique vividly described by Homer. They were of such artistic finesse that they would have met with the approval even of Hephaestos.

Under the influence of Christianity, the idea of the divine
(40) craftsman was transformed into a human figure: the legendary Wayland the Smith. Wayland worked in gold as well as in steel, fashioning jewels so temptingly beautiful as to sway the virtue of princesses, and forging sword blades painstakingly wrought from interwoven strands of iron and steel. The craft
(45) of the smith was believed to hold a powerful magic, and the prestige of even the greatest of Celtic or Germanic heroes was enhanced if they were apprenticed to smiths.

For centuries master craftsmen remained nameless, but when awakening artistic self-esteem in the Renaissance let
(50) artists step out of the shadows of anonymity, the greatest names, such as Leonardo da Vinci, Hans Holbein, Albrecht Dürer, and Benvenuto Cellini, were found quite matter-of-factly among those of designers and manufacturers of arms.

1. The central purpose of the passage is to

    (A) compare the relative importance of art and of arms-making in various eras

    (B) describe the high level of artistry brought to arms-making throughout history

    (C) show how the influence of Christianity affected the practice of arms-making

    (D) analyze the interplay between Renaissance ideals of beauty and function in the design of arms

    (E) trace the artistic growth of arms-making artisans throughout human history

This is a classic Big Picture question stem, one that you'll see often on the SAT. The answer should be summed up by the purpose and main idea of the passage.

(B) gives the most accurate paraphrase of the passage. (A) is wrong because the passage never says or implies that art and arms-making were more or less important in one era than in another. (C) is too narrow; the influence of Christianity is mentioned as one chapter in a lengthy history. (D) is also too specific; the Renaissance is only mentioned in the final paragraph. And (E) is off because the passage is about the relationship between arms-making and artistry, not the "artistic growth" of arms-making artisans.

DETAIL QUESTIONS

Detail questions ask about a specific part of the passage. On these questions, you may have to go back into the passage to research the answer.

The key is to know where to look for the answer. Also note that common wrong answer choices to Detail questions include those that:

- Refer to the wrong part of the passage—in other words, they don't answer the question being asked
- Use wording similar to the passage, but distort what was said
- Contradict the passage
- Go outside the scope of the passage, stating things that aren't said
- Use extreme wording

FUNCTION QUESTIONS

Function questions ask you about the function of a word, phrase, sentence, or paragraph. You need to put yourself in the author's shoes and identify *why* the author wrote the passage the way he or she did.

STRATEGY HIGHLIGHT

To answer this Big Picture question, we relied on our paraphrase of the passage's topic and scope. You may have also eliminated choices that were too specific or outside the scope of the passage.

STRATEGY TIP

The correct answers to Detail questions will almost always be paraphrases of information found in the passage.

Take a look at the following question. Refer to the passage as necessary to find the answer.

2. It is most likely that the author mentions Pallas Athena (line 21) and Hephaestos (line 25) in order to demonstrate

    (A) the close association between the tools of war and the arts

    (B) the difference between human and divine arts

    (C) the classical ideals of beauty and craftsmanship

    (D) the notion of artists as divinely inspired

    (E) the technical advances in the artistry of weapon-making

STRATEGY TIP

Reading just the sentence that contains the line reference may not be sufficient; you may have to read a few lines before and after the reference to get a sense of the context.

This Function question gives us a line reference, so to answer the question we can go directly to the cited lines. Rereading the sentence before the referenced line will point to the best answer. "In classical antiquity, too, there was a close relationship between art and arms" (lines 19–20). Athena and Hephaestos are then used as examples of the connection between weaponry and the arts, so (A) is the correct answer.

Choice (B) isn't right because the paragraph isn't about divine arts. You can eliminate (C) because not enough description of Athena's weaponry is provided to qualify as a demonstration of the classical ideals of beauty and craftsmanship. (D) is out because the examples have nothing to do with artists being inspired. And finally, (E) is completely off base, as the paragraph in question has nothing to do with "technical advances."

INFERENCE QUESTIONS

Inference questions can deal with either the Big Picture or details in the passage, but because of the way they are worded, they present a unique challenge for test takers. This is because Inference questions require you to conclude something that is not explicitly stated in the passage. To some extent, they require you to "read between the lines."

STRATEGY HIGHLIGHT

We were able to paraphrase the cited lines, which helped us identify the correct choice. We also used elimination strategies to get rid of choices that contradicted or went beyond the scope of the passage.

An Advanced test taker draws reasonable inferences that are within the scope of the passage.

We'll talk more about Inference questions in a later section, but let's try one that fits with this passage.

3. In lines 15–18, the author implies that arms were decorated as a way of

(A) lending legitimacy to the causes for which wars were fought

(B) distinguishing them from purely ceremonial objects

(C) enhancing their effectiveness in battle

(D) identifying strategic military alliances

(E) suggesting the importance of those who possessed them

The word *implies* in the question stem signals that this is an Inference question, and you may need to think outside the passage a bit in order to find the answer.

This question asks you to make an inference from information in the passage: why were arms decorated in ancient times? Lines 15–18 give several reasons: it enhanced their aesthetic and ideological value, and made them more valuable as status symbols. (E) captures the second of these ideas: decorating arms helped suggest the status or importance of the arms-bearer.

(A) is too broad: arms decorating couldn't really make a war seem more legitimate. (B) distorts the passage: distinguishing arms from purely ceremonial objects (vases, statues, etc.) doesn't seem to have been a problem. (C) is simply not mentioned, nor is (D).

VOCABULARY-IN-CONTEXT QUESTIONS

Vocabulary-in-Context questions ask you about the usage of a single word. You won't need to define the word, but you'll need to glean the meaning of the word from context.

An Advanced test taker predicts the answer before checking out the answer choices to nail Vocabulary-in-Context questions.

Here's our recommended method for handling Vocabulary-in-Context questions:

Step 1: Read the sentence through, looking for clues.

Step 2: Predict a word that could replace the vocabulary word.

Step 3: Check the answer choices for a word that matches.

Step 4: Plug your selection into the sentence to make sure it makes sense.

4. In line 8, *secure* most nearly means

    (A) create

    (B) make safe

    (C) obtain

    (D) guard

    (E) attach

This is a straightforward Vocabulary-in-Context question, so the first thing to do is go back to the passage and do a little research. According to lines 7–9, "Hunters attempted to use supernatural means to secure an abundant supply of meat and hides for food and clothing." In other words, they were trying to obtain a supply, so (C) is correct.

It doesn't make sense that they would (A) create a supply of animals. (B) and (D) don't work because the sentence is not about making safe or guarding the supply; it's about getting it in the first place. Finally, (E) makes no sense; why would anyone attach a supply of animals?

Now that you've got the overview, let's go on to some hard—really hard—passages and look at what makes them hard. In the next chapter, we'll examine the different passage types and give you strategies to crack the toughest ones.

STRATEGY HIGHLIGHT

We used the Sentence Completion strategy of predicting a replacement for the word in this question to get this one right. (See chapter six.)

CHAPTER 4: STRATEGIES FOR TOUGH READING COMPREHENSION

> - Find out what makes hard Reading Comprehension passages hard, and how to handle them.
>
> - Get to know the four Reading Comprehension passage types.
>
> - Tackle extra-hard Science and Narrative passages.
>
> - Learn the secrets of Paired passages.
>
> - Learn what makes Reading Comprehension questions hard, and how to handle them.

WHAT MAKES HARD READING COMPREHENSION PASSAGES HARD?

Some Reading Comprehension passages are born bad. The vocabulary is grueling, the sentence structure is torturous, and the tone, scope, and focus are nowhere to be found. In fact, you're not even sure that it's in English.

Give up? Not if you want that 2400, you don't. In this section, we'll talk about how to deal with tough passages of all kinds. We'll also review certain passage types that many test takers find difficult and give you special strategies to help you tackle them.

THE PASSAGE TYPES

As you may already know, both Long and Short SAT Reading Comprehension passages come in four flavors: Humanities, Social Science, Science, and Narrative. Usually Humanities and Social Science passages are manageable, though we'll take a look at a tough one on the next page. The passage types that tend to strike the most fear into the hearts of high school students everywhere are the tag team of Science and Narrative. Most students dread one or the other of these types. To apply some gross stereotypes, Physics Club members usually eat Science passages for breakfast, but a few dense fiction paragraphs will send them running for the solace of their bug collections. English major types will incisively pick through the most complex Narrative passages with a quick glance, but the merest hint of a chemistry symbol may induce sweating, gasping, and a tendency to quote soliloquies from *Hamlet*.

Whatever your preferences, you can't afford to ignore any passage type if you want to do your best. We'll start off by looking at a tough Short Social Sciences Reading Comprehension passage. Next, we'll take a look at an approach that can help you with any type of hard passage, and we'll talk you through it step-by-step. We'll then tackle a hard Science and a hard Narrative passage together. Finally, we'll confront one other passage type that tends to send test takers into a panic: the Paired passages.

TOUGH SOCIAL SCIENCES AND HUMANITIES

As we noted earlier, Social Science and Humanities passages are usually fairly straightforward. When they do get tough, it's usually because they discuss very abstract topics. Here's an example of a challenging Social Sciences Short Reading Comp passage:

> Immanuel Kant (1724–1804) is often considered the father of modern philosophy, partially based on his contributions to (some would say establishment of) the branch of inquiry known as epistemology, which—in the words of
> (5) Kant—seeks to answer the question, "What can we know?" For Kant, the area of the knowable is limited to that which can be tested empirically—in short to scientific and mathematical truths. Any judgment that seeks to extend beyond this circumscription is termed *transcendental*, and it is a
> (10) tempting but dangerous error to consider a transcendental judgment true knowledge. Though many subsequent philosophers would later disagree (one group of American writers proudly adopted the term "Transcendentalist" as a badge of honor), it is telling that much of this debate took
> (15) place using the ideas and terminology invented by Kant.

This passage covers some very abstract ideas and provides very few concrete facts to help you orient yourself. Don't let that stop you! Remember that you don't need to understand every single sentence fully in order to get a great score on the test. In fact, your first read through should be quick and should just allow you to get a basic, broad picture. Here, for example, you should note simply that:

- Immanual Kant was a big deal.

- He was interested in the question "What can we know?"

- He used the term *transcendental*.

Now let's take a look at a question.

1. Based on the passage, Kant considered "transcendental judgments"

    (A) more important than scientific and mathematical truths
    (B) a badge of honor
    (C) not an example of the truly knowable
    (D) the aim of the field of epistemology
    (E) the highest form of knowledge

Since the passage was so dense, you may not have gotten a sense of what the phrase "transcendental knowledge" means. That's okay—just go back to the passage and reread the sentences in which the term appears. There we find that Kant thought that "it is a tempting but dangerous error to consider a transcendental judgment true knowledge." So transcendental judgments are not true knowledge. You could even ignore the rest of the passage and still identify (C) as correct! All the other choices are positive, and Kant seems to have a negative opinion of transcendental judgments.

The most important lesson here is that you don't need to understand the entire passage to answer questions correctly.

> Savvy test takers know that hard passages are usually paired with easier questions.

ATTACKING DIFFICULT LONG PASSAGES: THE APPROACH

You can almost always manage to get through an entire Short Reading Comprehension passage. In most instances, you'll also want to read most Long Reading Comprehension passages straight through. But if you are running into time trouble, or if the passage is extraordinarily dense and hard to get through, you'll want to try a different approach.

When the going gets tough, here's what we recommend: Read the first third of the passage carefully, then read the first sentence of each subsequent paragraph and the last sentence of the passage. As with all passages, focus on the Big Picture, not the details. Apply the following reading principles:

- Read with the author in mind. Ask yourself, "What is the author trying to convey? Why is the passage structured as it is?"

- Even in the first third that you will be reading in its entirety, focus on the Big Idea(s), not the supporting details.

If you're still unsure about the main idea from the first third of the passage, pay close attention to the last sentence of the passage; this is where many authors tie together the loose ends and clarify the main idea of the passage.

An Advanced test taker reads hard passages selectively, focusing on topic sentences and the sections that provide the most relevant information.

SCIENCE PASSAGES

Let's try this approach on a tough Science passage.

The following passage was excerpted from a geology text book.

The basic theory of plate tectonics recognizes two ways in which continental margins can grow seaward. Where two plates move away from a midocean rift that separates them, the continental margins on those plates are said to be passive.

(5)   Such continental margins grow slowly from the accumulation of riverborne sediments and from the carbonate skeletons of marine organisms. Since most sequences of such accretions, or miogeoclinal deposits, are undeformed, passive margins are not associated with mountain building.

(10)   Along active margins continents tend to grow much faster. At an active margin an oceanic plate plunges under a continental plate, fragments of which then adhere to the continental margin. The process is met with extensive volcanism and mountain-building. A classic example is the

(15)   Andes of the west coast of South America.

In the original plate-tectonic model, western North America was described as being initially passive and then active. It was assumed that the continent grew to a limited extent along this margin as oceanic rocks accreted in places

(20)   such as the Coast Ranges of California. The model was successful in explaining such disparate features as the Franciscan rocks of the California Coast Ranges, created by subduction, and the granite rocks of the Sierra Nevada that originated in volcanoes.

(25)   The basic plate-tectonic reconstruction of the geologic history of western North America remains unchanged in the light of microplate tectonics, but the details are radically changed. It is now clear that much more crust was added to North America in the Mesozoic era than can be accounted for

(30)   by volcanism and by the simple accretion of sediments.

Further, some adjacent terranes are not genetically related, as
would be expected from simple plate tectonics, but have
almost certainly traveled great distances from entirely different parts of the world.

What makes this passage hard? A quick glance will show you that it's an esoteric, difficult topic
with its own unique lingo and a mass of technical details. Now's the time for all you science-phobes
to take a deep breath. Hang on, and we'll talk you through it.

> An Advanced test taker approaches Science passages with a clear head and isn't
> phased by technical vocabulary.

The first third:

This passage has four paragraphs, so let's read the first two carefully. In Paragraph 1, the first line gives
us the topic: the basic theory of plate tectonics. This theory, we're told, "recognizes two ways in which
continental margins can grow seaward." The phrase "two ways" is key here; it tells us that we should
be looking out for a comparison or contrast. The paragraph goes on to describe one of the two ways,
a mechanism known as passive margins. There are many details about passive margins, but we can let
those pass for now and move on.

In Paragraph 2, the author describes the other way that continental margins can grow, and that's
along active margins. We're told what actually happens at active margins, the results of such activity
(volcanoes and mountains), and an example of these results (the Andes). Take in what you can, but
don't obsess over the details.

The first sentence of each subsequent paragraph:

The beginning of Paragraph 3 talks about "the original model," which is a clue that we'll probably
get information about some kind of new model. In this sentence, we find that western North
America was seen as first passive, then active. We can move on to the next paragraph with
confidence, assuming that the rest of Paragraph 3 consists of details to support the first sentence.

Paragraph 4 begins with more information about the plate-tectonic model of western North
America. Here we're told that the basic reconstruction of geologic history remains the same, but
the details are radically different, in the light of something called "microplate tectonics."

The last sentence of the passage:

In this case, the last sentence gives further detail about the plate-tectonics of western North
America. From this detail, we get the gist that information about "microplate tectonics" is

undermining the credibility of the basic theory of plate tectonics. Did you miss this? The sentence explains that adjacent terranes (whatever they are) aren't genetically related as would be expected from simple plate tectonics.

Often an author will conclude a passage with a rousing send-off summary, which can be very useful when you attack the questions. Even when the final sentence isn't so blatantly helpful, you can usually get some good information.

What do we have?

The author's purpose is to describe the basic theory of plate tectonics. Passive and active margins are discussed. Microplate tectonics are introduced, and it seems that the basic theory of plate tectonics falls short of explaining all the phenomena of growing continental margins.

Not so bad, considering that we didn't even read the whole passage. Let's reread the passage and try some questions.

The following passage was excerpted from a geology textbook.

The basic theory of plate tectonics recognizes two ways in which continental margins can grow seaward. Where two plates move away from a midocean rift that separates them, the continental margins on those plates are said to be pas-

(5)   sive. Such continental margins grow slowly from the accumulation of riverborne sediments and from the carbonate skeletons of marine organisms. Since most sequences of such accretions, or miogeoclinal deposits, are undeformed, passive margins are not associated with mountain building.

(10)   Along active margins continents tend to grow much faster. At an active margin an oceanic plate plunges under a continental plate, fragments of which then adhere to the continental margin. The process is met with extensive volcanism and mountain-building. A classic example is the

(15)   Andes of the west coast of South America.

In the original plate-tectonic model western North America was described as being initially passive and then active. It was assumed that the continent grew to a limited extent along this margin as oceanic rocks accreted in places

(20)   such as the Coast Ranges of California. The model was successful in explaining such disparate features as the Franciscan rocks of the California Coast Ranges, created by subduction, and the granite rocks of the Sierra Nevada that originated in volcanoes.

(25)   The basic plate-tectonic reconstruction of the geologic history of western North America remains unchanged in the light of microplate tectonics, but the details are radically changed. It is now clear that much more crust was added to

North America in the Mesozoic era than can be accounted for
(30) by volcanism and by the simple accretion of sediments.
Further, some adjacent terranes are not genetically related, as
would be expected from simple plate tectonics, but have
almost certainly traveled great distances from entirely different parts of the world.

1. Which one of the following best expresses the main idea of the passage?

   (A) The margin of the west coast of North America developed through a combination of active and passive mechanisms.

   (B) The growth of continental margins is only partially explained by the basic theory of plate tectonics.

   (C) Continental margins can grow seaward in two ways, through sedimentation or volcanism.

   (D) The introduction of microplate tectonics poses a fundamental challenge to the existing theory of how continental margins are formed.

   (E) Continental margins grow more rapidly along active margins than along passive margins.

Here's a classic Big Picture question. In our quick summary, we said that while the basic theory of plate tectonics explains much about the growth of continental margins, the fourth paragraph suggests that it cannot fully explain certain geologic details. Choice (B) best captures this idea, and it's correct.

Choices (A) and (E) both represent true statements, but they're details from the passage, not the passage's main idea. Choice (C) distorts the notion of the two ways that continental margins can grow. We don't know that sedimentation and volcanism are the two ways, and even if we did, this is too specific to be the main point of the passage.

And choice (D) is incorrect because it's too extreme. The first sentence of Paragraph 4 states that the basic plate tectonic theory remains unchanged in the light of microplate tectonics; it's the details that are radically changed, not the basic theory.

2. The author mentions the Franciscan rocks of the California Coast Ranges in order to make which of the following points?

   (A) The basic theory of plate tectonics accounts for a wide variety of geologic features.

   (B) The original plate tectonic model falls short of explaining such features.

   (C) Subduction processes are responsible for the majority of the geologic features found along the west coast of North America.

   (D) Passive margins can take on many geologic forms.

   (E) The concept of microplate tectonics was first introduced to account for such phenomena.

In our quick reading of the passage, we missed this detail about the Franciscan rocks. No matter; we can simply scan the passage for the detail, then read the lines around it to get the answer. Scan for the phrase Franciscan rocks. You'll find it there toward the end of Paragraph 3. Read that sentence and you'll find that the Franciscan rocks are an example of a geologic feature that is successfully explained by the model discussed in the topic sentence of that paragraph—i.e., the original plate-tectonic model. Choice (A) is an excellent paraphrase of just what we're looking for.

Choice (B) is wrong because it directly contradicts Paragraph 3; the problems with the basic plate-tectonic model are discussed in Paragraph 4, a paragraph in which the California Coast Ranges are never mentioned. (C) is a distortion of the facts. We don't know if subduction processes are responsible for the majority of the west coast's geologic features. We're told only that they're responsible for some, such as the Coast Ranges. (D) is wrong because the Coast Ranges were formed by local subduction processes, according to Paragraph 3, not by the actions of passive margins. The concept of microplate tectonics was introduced to account for phenomena that the basic model couldn't explain. But the Coast Ranges are features that the basic model can account for, so (E) is incorrect.

> An Advanced test taker knows that the key to answering most Science passage questions is simply locating the answer in the passage and then finding a paraphrase of that answer among the answer choices.

3. Which one of the following does the author mention as evidence for the inadequacy of the original plate-tectonic model to describe the formation of continental margins?

    (A) Accreted rock formations have been found along some continental margins where there are granite mountains farther inland.
    (B) Sediments and fragments from the depths of the ocean accumulate along continental margins.
    (C) Large pieces of the earth's crust that appear to be completely unrelated are found in the same area today.
    (D) Undeformed miogeoclinal deposits are usually not linked to mountain-building.
    (E) Oceanic plates drop beneath continental plates along active margins.

To answer this Detail question, go straight to the final paragraph. That's where the inadequacy of the plate-tectonic model is finally discussed. There we're told that genetically distinct pieces of the earth's crust are found in the same area, a fact that the original plate-tectonic model can't explain. (C) gets at this issue.

The original plate tectonic model can account for (A)—see the description of the California Coast Ranges in the third paragraph. (B), (D), and (E) are true statements—see the first and second paragraphs—but none of these statements has a direct bearing on the issue of the inadequacy of the original plate-tectonic model, which is discussed only in the final paragraph.

> An Advanced test taker realizes that she doesn't have to completely understand everything in an SAT Science passage in order to answer all the questions correctly.

NARRATIVE PASSAGES

On the SAT, you will encounter at least one Narrative passage. Narratives are like stories. Sometimes they come from memoirs and reminiscences; other times they come from works of fiction. In either case, your goal is to figure out the main point of the story.

Narrative passages can appear as Paired passages or as stand-alone passages in any Reading Comprehension section.

For those of you who haven't voluntarily read a work of fiction since *Charlotte's Web,* we'll take it nice and slow.

Narrative passages are pretty similar to other passages. You still see Big Picture, Detail, and Vocabulary-in-Context questions, and you still want to read for structure. There is one important difference, though.

THE BIG IDEA IN A NARRATIVE PASSAGE

In Narrative passages, the Big Idea is a little different from other passages. The test maker wants you to understand why people do what they do or why people feel a particular way.

To figure out the author's opinion in a Narrative passage, you may have to read between the lines or draw conclusions from what is not stated. With a Narrative passage, you will most likely get several questions that ask you to infer or surmise the characters' opinions or intentions. This is actually easier than it sounds.

> An Advanced test taker reads Narrative passages with an eye toward characters' personalities and motivations.

READING FOR INFERENCES—THREE QUESTIONS TO ASK YOURSELF

As you read a Narrative passage, Short or Long, you should ask yourself three questions:

1. Who are the characters and how does the author describe them?

- What do the characters want?
- What are the characters doing?
- Can you think of adjectives to describe each character?

2. What do the characters think of each other, or themselves?

- Do they like each other? Hate each other?
- Why does each character make a particular decision or take a particular course of action?
- What do these decisions or actions tell you about a character?

3. What's the "point" of the story?

- What are the "turning points" in the passage?
- Is there a "moral" to the story?

Keep these questions in mind as you read this tough Long Narrative passage.

> *The following passage, excerpted from a Victorian novel first published in 1871, focuses on the reactions by two male characters, Mr. Casaubon and Sir Chettam, to the upcoming marriage of Mr. Casaubon to a woman that both men courted.*

Mr. Casaubon, as might be expected, spent a great deal of his time at the Grange in these weeks, and the hindrance which courtship occasioned to the progress of his great work—the Key to all Mythologies—naturally made him

(5) look forward the more eagerly to the happy termination of courtship. But he had deliberately incurred the hindrance, having made up his mind that it was now time for him to adorn his life with the graces of female companionship, to irradiate the gloom which fatigue was apt to hang over the

(10) intervals of studious labor with the play of female fancy, and to secure in this, his culminating age, the solace of female tending for his declining years. Hence he determined to abandon himself to the stream of feeling, and perhaps was surprised to find what an exceedingly shallow rill it was. As

(15) in droughty regions baptism by immersion could only be performed symbolically, Mr. Casaubon found that sprinkling was the utmost approach to a plunge which his stream

would afford him; and he concluded that the poets had
much exaggerated the force of masculine passion.

(20)   Nevertheless, he observed with pleasure that Miss Brooke
showed an ardent submissive affection which promised to
fulfill his most agreeable previsions of marriage. It had once
or twice crossed his mind that possibly there was some deficiency in Dorothea to account for the moderation of his

(25)   abandonment; but he was unable to discern the deficiency,
or to figure to himself a woman who would have pleased
him better; so that there was clearly no reason to fall back
upon but the exaggerations of human tradition.

It was wonderful to Sir James Chettam how well he

(30)   continued to like going to the Grange after he had once
encountered the difficulty of seeing Dorothea for the first
time in the light of a woman who was engaged to another
man. Of course the forked lightning seemed to pass
through him when he first approached her, and he

(35)   remained conscious throughout the interview of hiding
uneasiness; but, good as he was, it must be owned that his
uneasiness was less than it would have been if he had
thought his rival a brilliant and desirable match. He had no
sense of being eclipsed by Mr. Casaubon; he was only

(40)   shocked that Dorothea was under a melancholy illusion,
and his mortification lost some of its bitterness by being
mingled with compassion.

Nevertheless, while Sir James said to himself that he had
completely resigned her, since with the perversity of a

(45)   Desdemona she had not affected a proposed match that
was clearly suitable and according to nature, he could not
yet be quite passive under the idea of her engagement to
Mr. Casaubon.

MIDDLEMARCH: THE RECAP

If you're a literature fan, you may have recognized this as a selection from *Middlemarch* by
George Eliot. If not, don't worry. As with the other SAT Reading Comprehension passage types,
you don't need any outside knowledge to do well.

We start out with a short italicized blurb, which gives us some good clues about the content of the
selection. From the blurb, we know that we'll have three main characters: a young woman, her
fiancé, and the fiancé's rival.

Let's break down the passage in terms of these three main characters, and ask the first two of our
three Narrative passage questions.

Who are the characters and how does the author describe them? What do the characters think of each other, or themselves?

Mr. Casaubon: This character is Dorothea's fiancé. He has decided to become engaged because he believes that it is the correct time in his life to do so, yet he finds himself lacking in passion. He wonders whether it's Dorothea's fault that he isn't more passionate toward her, but concludes that romance is an exaggerated notion.

Dorothea Brooke: We don't know much about her, except with regard to her relationship to the two men. She shows "an ardent submissive affection" to Mr. Casaubon. From Sir James's perspective, she has made a mistake by becoming engaged to Mr. Casaubon, and the match is not suitable.

Sir James Chettam: Sir James believes that Mr. Casaubon is not a worthy rival for Dorothea's affections. He is clearly smitten by Dorothea and is "not quite passive" about the engagement. Finally, we can address the third Narrative question:

What's the "point" of the story?

The passage focuses on the different views of the characters toward the recent engagement. We get a great deal of information about Mr. Casaubon's thoughts and feelings, some details on Sir James's feelings, and very little knowledge about Dorothea's perspective on the matter.

The passage paints a picture of a struggle that is about to occur. We aren't told what happens next, but we get a sense of foreboding, based on the feelings of the two rivals.

This passage has a great deal of flowery language and some tough vocabulary, but when you break it down, it has the same plot line that you might find on your favorite soap opera or TV drama. Let's look at the passage again and check out the questions.

> *The following passage, excerpted from a Victorian novel first published in 1871, focuses on the reactions by two male characters, Mr. Casaubon and Sir Chettam, to the upcoming marriage of Mr. Casaubon to a woman that both men courted.*

> Mr. Casaubon, as might be expected, spent a great deal of his time at the Grange in these weeks, and the hindrance which courtship occasioned to the progress of his great work—the Key to all Mythologies—naturally made him
> (5) look forward the more eagerly to the happy termination of courtship. But he had deliberately incurred the hindrance, having made up his mind that it was now time for him to adorn his life with the graces of female companionship, to irradiate the gloom which fatigue was apt to hang over the
> (10) intervals of studious labor with the play of female fancy, and to secure in this, his culminating age, the solace of female tending for his declining years. Hence he determined to abandon himself to the stream of feeling, and perhaps was

surprised to find what an exceedingly shallow rill it was. As

(15) in droughty regions baptism by immersion could only be
performed symbolically, Mr. Casaubon found that sprinkling was the utmost approach to a plunge which his stream
would afford him; and he concluded that the poets had
much exaggerated the force of masculine passion.

(20) Nevertheless, he observed with pleasure that Miss Brooke
showed an ardent submissive affection which promised to
fulfill his most agreeable previsions of marriage. It had once
or twice crossed his mind that possibly there was some deficiency in Dorothea to account for the moderation of his

(25) abandonment; but he was unable to discern the deficiency,
or to figure to himself a woman who would have pleased
him better; so that there was clearly no reason to fall back
upon but the exaggerations of human tradition.

It was wonderful to Sir James Chettam how well he

(30) continued to like going to the Grange after he had once
encountered the difficulty of seeing Dorothea for the first
time in the light of a woman who was engaged to another
man. Of course the forked lightning seemed to pass
through him when he first approached her, and he

(35) remained conscious throughout the interview of hiding
uneasiness; but, good as he was, it must be owned that his
uneasiness was less than it would have been if he had
thought his rival a brilliant and desirable match. He had no
sense of being eclipsed by Mr. Casaubon; he was only

(40) shocked that Dorothea was under a melancholy illusion,
and his mortification lost some of its bitterness by being
mingled with compassion.

Nevertheless, while Sir James said to himself that he had
completely resigned her, since with the perversity of a

(45) Desdemona she had not affected a proposed match that
was clearly suitable and according to nature, he could not
yet be quite passive under the idea of her engagement to
Mr. Casaubon.

1. In line 12, *tending* most nearly means

   (A) inclination

   (B) care

   (C) leaning

   (D) love

   (E) aptitude

This is a tough section of the passage, but you just need to decode the language in order to get
this Vocabulary-in-Context question right. Read the lines surrounding the word *tending* to get the

gist of what's going on. Mr. Casaubon feels he should get married because he wants "the solace of female tending for his declining years." In other words, he wants a wife to take care of him as he gets older. (Doesn't sound like much fun for Dorothea!) In fact, *care* is the correct answer choice here.

Notice that (A), (C), and (E) all relate to another meaning of *tending*—to have a tendency. (D) misses the point of the sentence. Casaubon is looking for someone to take care of him, not necessarily someone to love him.

2. Mr. Casaubon concludes that his lack of deep feeling for Dorothea derives from

    (A) Dorothea's own hidden deficiencies
    (B) his advancing age
    (C) the gloom and fatigue of studious labor
    (D) the distractions of his profession
    (E) overstated descriptions of romantic passion

Plunging back into Mr. Casaubon's thoughts, we find that he spends quite a bit of energy musing about his lack of passion for Dorothea. We need to forge our way to the very end of the long first paragraph to discern his justification for this lack: "there was clearly no reason to fall back upon but the exaggerations of human tradition." Choice (E) paraphrases this nicely, capturing the idea that the fault is not in Mr. Casaubon, but in overstated descriptions of what passion should be.

As for the other choices, Mr. Casaubon discusses his thoughts that his lack of passion may be Dorothea's fault, choice (A), but rejects this theory. (B), (C), and (D) are all cited as reasons that Mr. Casaubon should find a wife, but none figure into his lack of passion. Choice (E) is correct.

3. According to the passage, which of the following is true about Sir James's reaction to Dorothea's engagement?

    (A) He felt sympathy for Dorothea in spite of his opposition to her decision.
    (B) He was unhappy but reconciled to the situation.
    (C) He was unsure about the suitability of the proposed union.
    (D) He opposed the engagement but felt daunted by his rival's qualities.
    (E) His discomfort was lessened after he spoke with Dorothea.

The last two paragraphs deal with Sir James's thoughts about Dorothea's engagement. We learn that Sir James is uneasy, but not as uneasy as he would be if he thought Mr. Casaubon a worthy rival. He's not happy about the engagement, but the end of the second paragraph tells us that he has compassion for her despite his disapproval of the match. This is echoed in choice (A), the correct answer.

We know that Sir James is not reconciled to the situation, choice (B), and choice (C) misses the point that Sir James in not at all unsure about the engagement—he feels it's a lousy match. The passage states specifically that he doesn't think that his rival is "a brilliant or desirable match," so (D) is out. Finally, there's no mention of his discomfort lessening after speaking with Dorothea, choice (E).

PAIRED PASSAGES—THE FACTS

Paired passages are two passages written by different authors who deal with related issues from different points of view. These can appear in both Short and Long form. Your goal in reading these passages is to determine where the authors agree—and where they disagree. We'll take a look at how to do this in a minute.

Long Paired passages often appear in the 20-minute Critical Reading section, though they occasionally crop up in the earlier sections. Short Paired passages can appear in any Critical Reading section.

PAIRED PASSAGES—THE METHOD

The questions that accompany Paired passages fall into the following categories:

- Questions about Passage 1
- Questions about Passage 2
- Compare and Contrast questions about both passages

Here's our method for attacking Paired passages:

Step 1: Read Passage 1 and answer accompanying questions.

Step 2: Read Passage 2 and answer accompanying questions.

Step 3: Answer Compare and Contrast questions.

> An Advanced test taker first treats Paired passages separately, then compares and contrasts the two passages.

Remember that you should use this method for both Short and Long Reading Comprehension passages. It lets you attack the questions for each passage while that passage is still fresh in your mind. This will help you avoid wrong answer choices that refer to the wrong passage.

Try this method as you tackle this pair of passages.

1. ATTACK PASSAGE 1 AND ITS QUESTIONS

The following two passages, excerpted from the works of two prominent social observers, were written a little more than one century apart. The first, from Alexis de Tocqueville's Democracy in America, *was first published in 1835, while the second, adapted from Aldous Huxley's* Brave New World Revisited, *was published in 1958.*

Passage 1

When men are no longer united amongst themselves by firm and lasting ties, it is impossible to obtain the cooperation of any great number of them, unless you can persuade every man whose concurrence you require that this private
(5)   interest obliges him voluntarily to unite his exertions to the exertions of all the rest. This can only be habitually and conveniently effected by means of a newspaper; nothing but a newspaper can drop the same thought into a thousand minds at the same moment. A newspaper is an adviser who
(10)   does not require to be sought, but who comes of his own accord, and talks to you briefly every day of the common weal, without distracting you from your private affairs.

Newspapers therefore become more necessary in proportion as men become more equal, and individualism more to
(15)   be feared. To suppose that they only serve to protect freedom would be to diminish their importance: they maintain civilization. I shall not deny that in democratic countries newspapers frequently lead the citizens to launch together in very ill-digested schemes; but if there were no newspapers
(20)   there would be no common activity. The evil which they produce is therefore much less than that which they cure.

The effect of a newspaper is not only to suggest the same purpose to a great number of persons, but also to furnish means for executing in common the designs which
(25)   they may have singly conceived. The principal citizens who inhabit an aristocratic country discern each other from afar; and if they wish to unite their forces, they move towards each other, drawing a multitude of men after them. It frequently happens, on the contrary, in democratic coun-
(30)   tries, that a great number of men who wish or who want to combine cannot accomplish it, because as they are very insignificant and lost amidst the crowd, they cannot see, and know not where to find, one another. A newspaper then takes up the notion or the feeling which had occurred
(35)   simultaneously, but singly, to each of them. All are then

immediately guided towards this beacon; and these wandering minds, which had long sought each other in darkness, at length meet and unite.

Now move on to the first question.

1. The author of Passage 1 would most likely agree with all of the following statements EXCEPT

    (A) Newspapers are necessary for the proper functioning of democracy.

    (B) Individualism poses a danger in a democratic society.

    (C) Newspapers can cause the public to act in foolhardy ways.

    (D) Aristocratic nations find it difficult to unite the masses in common activity.

    (E) Newspapers allow like-minded people to seek out and find one another.

This EXCEPT/NOT question allows us to focus on Passage 1. We'll be talking more about this sometimes-tricky question type in the next section, but for now, all you need to know is that you should eliminate choices that agree with the passage.

Choices (A), (B), and (C) can all be found in the text of the second paragraph of Passage 1. Each is part of de Tocqueville's argument, so he would certainly agree with these statements. Choice (E) is a paraphrase of the author's argument in the third paragraph.

We're left with choice (D). Since this answer choice discusses aristocratic nations, we should look to see where they are discussed, which is in the second sentence of Paragraph 3. There, de Tocqueville states that in such countries, principal citizens, i.e., fellow aristocrats, discern each other from afar, and draw the multitudes together as they please, which directly contradicts this answer choice. So (D) is the correct answer.

2. ATTACK PASSAGE 2 AND ITS QUESTIONS

After you have answered all the questions that refer to Passage 1, you can move on to Passage 2.

Passage 2

The early advocates of universal literacy and a free press
(40) envisaged only two possibilities: the propaganda might be true, or it might be false. They did not foresee what in fact has happened, above all in our Western capitalist democracies—the development of a vast mass communications industry, concerned in the main neither with the true nor
(45) the false, but with the unreal, the more or less totally irrelevant. In a word, they failed to take into account man's almost infinite appetite for distractions.

In the past people never got a chance of fully satisfying this appetite. They might long for distractions, but the dis-
(50) tractions were not provided. For conditions even remotely

comparable to those now prevailing we must return to
imperial Rome, where the populace was kept in good
humor by frequent, gratuitous fights, from recitations of
Virgil to all-out boxing, from concerts to military reviews

(55) and public executions. But even in Rome there was nothing
like the non-stop distractions now provided by newspapers
and magazines, by radio, television and the cinema.

Only the vigilant can maintain their liberties, and only
those who are constantly and intelligently on the spot can

(60) hope to govern themselves effectively by democratic procedures. A society, most of whose members spend a great
part of their time, not on the spot, not here and now and in
the calculable future, but somewhere else, in the irrelevant
other worlds of sport and soap opera, of mythology and

(65) metaphysical fantasy, will find it hard to resist the
encroachments of these who would manipulate and control
it. The dictators of the future will doubtless learn to combine the art and science of manipulation with the non-stop
distractions which, in the West, are now threatening to

(70) drown in a sea of irrelevance the information and rational
argument essential to the maintenance of individual liberty
and the survival of democratic institutions.

2. The author of Passage 2 refers to imperial Rome in order to

(A) illustrate the types of distractions that enjoy popularity in a nondemocratic society

(B) suggest that the public distractions of that period pale in comparison to those
of today

(C) cite a source of inspiration for the mass communications industry of the modern era

(D) note the wide diversity of entertainments that were available to people many
centuries ago

(E) intimate that the public distractions of that era led to the fall of the Roman empire

This question focuses on the second paragraph of the Huxley passage. In an attempt to illustrate
the number and types of distractions available to modern people, Huxley cites entertainments
available in ancient Rome. He then explains that these are barely comparable to "the non-stop
distractions now provided . . ." This is best paraphrased by choice (B).

The other choices are misrepresentations of the author's intent, as in (A) and (D), or distortions
that go beyond the scope of the argument, as in (C) and (E).

3. MOVE ON TO THE COMBO QUESTIONS

Once you've handled all the questions that focus on Passage 2, you can attack the questions that
ask you to compare and contrast the passages.

3. Both authors would most likely agree with which of the following statements?

   (A) Newspapers help people to act together in their common interests.

   (B) The maintenance of democracy requires an informed citizenry.

   (C) Newspapers function most effectively in democratic states.

   (D) A free press guarantees a free and open democracy.

   (E) Newspapers provide a pleasant distraction from private concerns.

This question asks you to test a number of statements against both authors' arguments.

Starting with choice (A), de Tocqueville would certainly agree with this statement, but we can't draw a clear inference on Huxley's views on the subject.

Choice (B) is supported by de Tocqueville's entire argument and by the last line of Huxley's passage, so it looks good.

Choice (C) isn't supported by either passage, since de Tocqueville doesn't discuss the effectiveness of newspapers in nondemocratic societies, and Huxley doesn't talk in detail about newspapers.

Choice (D) is too strong. The word *guarantee* sends the statement beyond the scope of either passage.

Choice (E) is a distortion of Huxley's views on distraction, and it's incorrect.

So choice (B) is the correct answer.

4. Huxley would most likely respond to the observations made in Passage 1 by pointing out that

   (A) de Tocqueville's faith in newspapers and their usefulness in a democracy was entirely misplaced

   (B) despite de Tocqueville's claims to the contrary, individualism is not more to be feared as men become more equal

   (C) what was useful to the functioning of democracy in de Tocqueville's day no longer applied to Western capitalist democracies

   (D) de Tocqueville could not have predicted that magazines, radio, television, and cinema would come to drown out the useful information provided by newspapers

   (E) de Tocqueville did not live long enough to witness evolution of mass media into its modern form

The first paragraph of Passage 2 almost seems like a response to de Tocqueville's passage. There, Huxley addresses earlier theorists who advocated a free press and states that these thinkers didn't foresee the developments that would accompany the modern mass communications industry. This is best represented in choice (E), the correct answer. Choice (A) is too strong, (B) is nowhere discussed in the Huxley passage, and (C) is a distortion. So is (D); according to Huxley, newspapers are of a piece with, and just as bad as, magazines, radio, television, and cinema—see lines 55–57.

WHAT MAKES HARD READING COMPREHENSION QUESTIONS HARD?

Hard Reading Comprehension questions can come in many guises, from inscrutable Big Picture queries to picayune requests for obscure details. In this section, we'd like to give you some practice with two especially thorny question types: EXCEPT/NOT and Inference.

ATTACKING EXCEPT/NOT QUESTIONS

You saw one of these tricky questions in the Paired passage section. EXCEPT and NOT questions are among the toughest of all SAT Reading Comprehension questions. This is because these questions require you to go to the answer choices and find information in the passage that will verify all of the answer choices EXCEPT the correct answer—that is, the one answer that's NOT true. In other words, you're looking for the one answer that's wrong.

Because these questions are so tricky and confusing, the test maker is obliged to tip you off by putting EXCEPT or NOT in caps. Watch out for these words, and you'll avoid careless errors.

Try this example.

> *In the following, a social scientist reflects on the disparate cultural influences on the Gullah, an island-dwelling people.*

Before the recent encroachments of tourism and commercialization, the culture of the Gullah communities on the Sea Islands off the southeast coast of the United States retained a unique identity derived partially from the Islands' history as
(5) an area reserved for freed slaves after the Civil War. As an almost exclusively black community, the Gullah preserved African traditions concerning family structure and religious practices. At the same time, as a community of ex-slaves, the residents retained several facets of the Southern life they had
(10) left behind. This mixture provided a heritage that until recently was strong enough to sustain a vital culture.

As Patricia Jones-Jackson has pointed out, the basic unit of social life on the Sea Islands, as in West Africa, is the extended family. Since many islands are sectioned off into
(15) family communities, kinship ties are important to one's acceptance into the social structure. Membership in the extended family also affects property rights. In the traditional Gullah system, family members do not normally buy land from one another, but acquire it by an unwritten con-
(20) tract known as "heir's land." Rules pertaining to marriage seem to be at least as broad in scope. Common-law marriages are considered as legitimate as marriages recorded by contract under law. Indeed, the infrequent occurrence of

divorce and separation within the Sea Island communities
(25) demonstrates the strong cohesion of Gullah marital and
      familial institutions.
          Unlike the laws and customs relating to family structure,
      the religious practices of the Sea Islanders, on the surface at
      least, bespeak a U.S. heritage. Depending on the village, a
(30) Baptist or Methodist church acts as an essential social insti-
      tution. Yet, in contrast to the dualistic body-soul approach
      to the individual found in Christian teaching, the Gullah
      believe that a person has an earthly body, a soul that
      returns upon death to the Divine Kingdom, and a separate
(35) spiritual entity that can remain on Earth and influence the
      lives of those still living. This belief in a "body spirit" is
      prevalent among West African peoples, according to Jones-
      Jackson. She also notes the African influences on the inter-
      action between the minister and the congregation: The
(40) prayers and sermons "embody a classical, Ciceronian
      rhetorical style and employ sophistic ornaments capable of
      divinely inspiring and passionately persuading a congrega-
      tion to respond with raucous and joyous replies."

Passage recap:

Let's do a quick review, which should help us answer the questions that follow.

The topic of the passage is the society of the Gullah, especially their customs. The author wishes to show that Gullah heritage is a mixture of African and U.S. cultures.

Paragraph 1 is an introduction to the Gullah and why their identity is unique. Paragraph 2 covers aspects of Gullah culture that are obviously of African origin. Paragraph 3 describes how religious customs of the Gullah seem to be of U.S. origin, but also reveal their African heritage.

1. According to the passage, all of the following aspects of the culture of the Sea Islanders show the influence of African traditions EXCEPT the

    (A) family structure
    (B) conception of the afterlife
    (C) method of acquiring land
    (D) style used in prayers and sermons
    (E) importance of the churches as social institutions

Again, the real key to getting EXCEPT/NOT questions right is reading the question. Once you know what you're trying to eliminate, you're halfway there.

The second tricky part of EXCEPT/NOT questions is that they can take longer to answer than the average question. On a Detail question like this one, you often need to go back, read through the text and verify each wrong answer choice so that you can eliminate it. Let's try this now. Just to be clear, we're checking each choice to see if it's an aspect of Sea Island culture that shows an African influence.

> An Advanced test taker often skips a question that looks difficult, going back to it only after answering all the other questions in the set.

The first sentence of Paragraph 2 offers the extended family as an example of West African influence on Gullah social life, so (A) is out.

In Paragraph 3, we're told that the Gullah conception of the "body spirit" is similar to a West African belief, choice (B).

As for choice (C), we're told in Paragraph 2 that membership in the extended family, itself an African element, affects property rights.

Choice (D) is mentioned as an African influence by Jones-Jackson in the third paragraph.

This leaves us with choice (E). In the third paragraph, the author cites the role of Baptist and Methodist churches as "essential social institutions." Inferably, the social role of the churches is an American, not an African, element of the culture. Choice (E) is correct.

> An Advanced test taker doesn't make careless mistakes on EXCEPT/NOT questions.

ATTACKING INFERENCE QUESTIONS

You've already had some practice with Inference questions, and you probably have a pretty good idea of how to manage inferences. However, you'll need to stay on your toes as you work your way through Inference questions on tough passages. Let's review some basic principles.

Inferences are conclusions you reach that are hinted at, but not directly stated in the passage. They often require you to "read between the lines"—although sometimes a question will ask you to "infer" something that is directly stated (although with different wording than the correct answer choice) in the passage.

Inference tips:

- Always look for evidence in the passage to support an inference.
- Don't go too far. SAT inferences tend to be straightforward and consistent with the overall idea of the passage.

An Advanced test taker always chooses an inference that is supported by evidence in the passage.

Here is that passage again along with two Inference questions for you to try.

In the following, a social scientist reflects on the disparate cultural influences on the Gullah, an island-dwelling people.

Before the recent encroachments of tourism and commercialization, the culture of the Gullah communities on the Sea Islands off the southeast coast of the United States retained a unique identity derived partially from the Islands' history as
(5) an area reserved for freed slaves after the Civil War. As an almost exclusively black community, the Gullah preserved African traditions concerning family structure and religious practices. At the same time, as a community of ex-slaves, the residents retained several facets of the Southern life they had
(10) left behind. This mixture provided a heritage which until recently was strong enough to sustain a vital culture.

As Patricia Jones-Jackson has pointed out, the basic unit of social life on the Sea Islands, as in West Africa, is the extended family. Since many islands are sectioned off into
(15) family communities, kinship ties are important to one's acceptance into the social structure. Membership in the extended family also affects property rights. In the traditional Gullah system, family members do not normally buy land from one another, but acquire it by an unwritten con-
(20) tract known as "heir's land." Rules pertaining to marriage seem to be at least as broad in scope. Common-law marriages are considered as legitimate as marriages recorded by contract under law. Indeed, the infrequent occurrence of divorce and separation within the Sea Island communities
(25) demonstrates the strong cohesion of Gullah marital and familial institutions.

Unlike the laws and customs relating to family structure, the religious practices of the Sea Islanders, on the surface at least, bespeak a U.S. heritage. Depending on the village, a
(30) Baptist or Methodist church acts as an essential social institution. Yet, in contrast to the dualistic body-soul approach to the individual found in Christian teaching, the Gullah believe that a person has an earthly body, a soul that returns upon death to the Divine Kingdom, and a separate

(35) spiritual entity that can remain on Earth and influence the
lives of those still living. This belief in a "body spirit" is
prevalent among West African peoples, according to Jones-
Jackson. She also notes the African influences on the interaction between the minister and the congregation: The
(40) prayers and sermons "embody a classical, Ciceronian
rhetorical style and employ sophistic ornaments capable of
divinely inspiring and passionately persuading a congregation to respond with raucous and joyous replies."

1. It can be inferred that the institution of "heir's land" allows the transfer of property under
   the terms of

   (A) a formal grant by the government

   (B) a marriage settlement between families

   (C) an oral agreement among family members

   (D) a written deed of ownership

   (E) an alteration of communal rights

To get a handle on this Inference question, you should begin by scanning the paragraph for
information on "heir's land," which can be found in the middle of the second paragraph. That's
where you'll find the evidence to support your inference.

The author states that "heir's land" is a way for family members to acquire land through an
"unwritten contract," without paying for it. Any contract is by its nature an agreement, and since
this kind of agreement is not on paper, it follows that it is orally communicated, choice (C). This is
a straightforward, consistent inference that stays within the scope of the passage.

Choice (A) is outside the scope. There's no reference to government grants with regard to "heir's
land." Choice (B) distorts the passage by linking "heir's land," which operates within families,
to marriage settlements that take place between families. The fact that "heir's land" is defined
as an unwritten contract eliminates choice (D). Finally, no alterations in communal rights are
mentioned, disposing of choice (E).

2. On the basis of information supplied by the passage, which of the following would most
   likely resemble a social experience of a Sea Islander?

   (A) Dividing property in a divorce settlement under court supervision

   (B) Being required to sell one's home because it lies in the path of a new highway

   (C) Growing up in a communal household composed of unrelated adults

   (D) Learning how to play a traditional song on a centuries-old instrument

   (E) Being given employment by a relative on the basis of one's standing in the family

This is a tough Inference question that asks you to apply knowledge in the passage. Let's begin by
looking for a social experience that parallels one described, probably in more general terms, in the

passage. The second paragraph notes the importance of family ties and illustrates this by discussing how family members can acquire land through these ties. This is similar to acquiring a job, or any other benefit, through family connections. Note that you don't need to find evidence that the Sea Islanders get jobs this way. The point is that choice (E) is logically similar to an experience of the Sea Islanders, and this choice is a reasonable inference.

Choice (A) is out because of the reference to court supervision. There's no direct mention of courts and other government institutions in the passage. Choice (B) is certainly not like anything in traditional Gullah life; it might be like an experience that has occurred since the "encroachments of tourism and commercialization," except that we're never told what these encroachments have been. Choice (C) relates to the importance of family units, but it's the extended family that's important to the Gullah, while choice (C) involves unrelated adults. Choice (D) comes out of left field and can't be substantiated.

TOUGH READING COMPREHENSION: STRATEGY RECAP

GREAT ADVICE FOR ANY PASSAGE

How to Attack SAT Reading Comprehension Strategically

Step 1: When you first encounter the passage, read enough of it to figure out the author's Big Idea and get a general sense of how the passage is organized.

Step 2: Read the question. If a question seems hard, go back to it after you've answered the other questions in the set.

Step 3: As necessary, go back into the passage to locate the answer to a specific question.

Step 4: Put the answer in your own words; the correct answer will most often be a paraphrase of what's stated in the passage.

Step 5: Attack the answer choices, and choose the one that comes closest to the answer you found.

Five Principles for Reading Comprehension

Principle 1: Focus on the author.

Principle 2: Don't sweat the details.

Principle 3: Read the first third closely.

Principle 4: Note paragraph topics and make a road map.

Principle 5: Stop to sum up.

EXTRA-GREAT ADVICE FOR TOUGH PASSAGES

If the passage is long and/or the subject matter is difficult to get through, read the **first third** of the passage carefully, then read the **first sentence of each subsequent paragraph** and **the last sentence of the passage.** As with all passages, focus on the Big Picture, not the details. Apply the following reading principles:

- Read with the author in mind. Ask yourself, "What is the author trying to convey? Why is the passage structured the way it is?"

- Even in the first third, focus on the Big Idea(s), not the supporting details.

- If you're still unsure about the main idea from the first third of the passage, pay close attention to the last sentence of the passage; this is where many authors tie together the loose ends and clarify the main idea of the passage.

HOW TO READ TOUGH NARRATIVE PASSAGES

As you read a Narrative passage, you should ask yourself three questions:

1. Who are the characters and how does the author describe them?

- What do the characters want?
- What are the characters doing?
- Can you think of adjectives to describe each character?

2. What do the characters think of each other, or themselves?

- Do they like each other? Hate each other?
- Why does each character make a particular decision or take a particular course of action?
- What do these decisions or actions tell you about a character?

3. What's the "point" of the story?

- What are the "turning points" in the passage?
- Is there a "moral" to the story?

HOW TO HANDLE PAIRED PASSAGES

Step 1: Read Passage 1 and answer accompanying questions.

Step 2: Read Passage 2 and answer accompanying questions.

Step 3: Answer Compare and Contrast questions.

THE QUESTION TYPES REVISITED

Big Picture questions ask about the main idea or primary purpose of the passage. You should be able to answer these questions based on your initial reading of the passage. You should concentrate your efforts on attacking and eliminating wrong answer choices. These include answer choices that are too specific, dealing with only one part of the passage; answer choices that are too broad, going beyond the scope of the passage; or answer choices that are too strongly worded, containing language that's too extreme to properly describe the passage.

Detail questions ask about a specific part of the passage. On these questions, you may have to go back into the passage to research the answer. The correct answer to a Detail question will almost always be a **paraphrase** of information found in the passage. Wrong answers to Detail questions, on the other hand, will usually do one of the following: they don't answer the question—i.e., they refer to a part of the passage different than that which the question addresses; they use language that's too extreme; they contradict or go beyond the scope of the passage, making claims that are not supported by the passage.

Vocabulary-in-Context questions ask you about the usage of a single word. You won't need to define the word, but you'll need to infer the meaning of the word from context. You can treat these questions as if they were Sentence Completion questions and employ the following method:

Step 1: Read the sentence, looking for clues.

Step 2: Predict a word that could replace the vocabulary word.

Step 3: Check the answer choices for a word that matches.

Step 4: Plug your selection into the sentence to make sure it makes sense.

Inference questions ask you to draw conclusions that are hinted at, but not directly stated, in the passage. They often require you to "read between the lines."

Always look for evidence in the passage to support an inference, and don't go too far. SAT inferences tend to be straightforward and consistent with the overall idea of the passage.

EXCEPT/NOT questions require you to go to the answer choices and find information in the passage that will verify all of the answer choices EXCEPT the correct answer, the one answer that's NOT true. In other words, you're trying to find the one answer that's wrong.

Now that you've has a taste of the tough passages and questions and how to deal with them, you can try your hand at some more tough practice passages in the next chapter.

CHAPTER 5: READING COMPREHENSION PRACTICE SETS AND EXPLANATIONS

The passages below are followed by questions based on their content; questions following a pair of related passages may also be based on the relationship between the paired passages. Answer the questions on the basis of what is <u>stated</u> or <u>implied</u> in the passages and in any introductory material that may be provided.

PRACTICE SET 1: SHORT PASSAGES

Questions 1–2 are based on the following passage.

In eighteenth-century Britain, two subgenres of satire flourished. Writers modeled one type on the elegant, deftly mocking satires and epistles of the Roman poet Horace (first century B.C.E.). The
(5) spirit of Horatian satire was especially evident in the works of Alexander Pope. The second type was Juvenalian satire, characterized by what the Roman poet Juvenal (early second century C.E.) called his *saeva indignatio*, or "savage rage." It was
(10) Jonathan Swift who incarnated this spirit. In such works as *Gulliver's Travels* and "A Modest Proposal," Swift mounted devastating attacks on what he deemed abuses in politics, literature, government, and science.

1. Based on the passage, the author of the passage would characterize the work of Alexander Pope (line 6) as

   (A) fiercely critical
   (B) tragically overlooked
   (C) slavishly imitative
   (D) elegantly satirical
   (E) mockingly comical

2. As used in the passage, *mounted* (line 12) most nearly means

   (A) climbed
   (B) ascended
   (C) boarded
   (D) supported
   (E) presented

Questions 3–4 are based on the following passage.

Although few Americans would deny the many advantages of our democratic system, recent developments betray a disappointing lack of interest in its preservation. It is a lamentable fact that
(5) voter participation in national elections sometimes represents fewer than half of registered voters. This failure of so many to exercise their franchise means that, in a closely contested election, a "majority" of votes for a candidate may actually
(10) represent fewer than 25 percent of eligible voters in the population. A second worrisome sign is the adoption of recall provisions by many states. In some cases, a well-organized but small minority of voters can force a governor in office to face a new
(15) election before his or her term expires.

3. The writer uses quotation marks around the word *majority* (line 9) in order to

(A) show that few Americans have shown an interest in preserving the democratic system of their country

(B) suggest that such a proportion represents a surprisingly low percentage of potential voters

(C) imply that such an election should not be recognized as legitimate

(D) emphasize that a candidate can be elected only by a majority of those who cast a vote

(E) argue for the necessity of an alternate means of holding elections

4. Based on the passage, the author would most likely agree that

(A) the prohibition of recall provisions would ensure the preservation of democracy

(B) most elected politicians have received votes from only 25 percent of eligible voters

(C) participating in elections is an important component of preserving America's democratic system

(D) the low numbers of voters at recent elections casts doubt on the value that Americans place in the American democratic system

(E) a governor forced from office by recall has likely displeased a majority of his or her voters

Questions 5–6 are based on the following passage.

Vascular cambium, a layer of cells located between the heartwood and the bark of a tree plays a pivotal role in the tree's life. The innermost layer of vascular cambium, made up of xylem cells, is
(5) the primary distribution mechanism of water and minerals from the roots to the rest of a tree, while another layer made up of phloem cells conducts food. Interestingly, it is the xylem cells that eventually contribute to the girth of a tree by becoming
(10) the heartwood, the hard central part of the tree—a process reflected in the derivation of the word xylem from the Greek *xylon*, meaning wood.

5. As used in the passage, *pivotal* (line 3) most nearly means

(A) essential

(B) rotating

(C) noteworthy

(D) round

(E) important

6. The author cites the Greek word *xylon* (line 12) in order to

(A) illustrate the extent to which biological terms are based on classical languages

(B) emphasize the importance of the heartwood in supporting a tree

(C) help explain the function of xylem in circulating vitamins and minerals

(D) draw a distinction between the xylem that becomes heartwood and the phloem that does not

(E) emphasize the role of xylem in forming heartwood

Questions 7–8 are based on the following passage.

The comedy of manners reached its height in mid-seventeenth century France and England. In France, the most outstanding playwright of the genre was Molière, whose comedies mocked the
(5) social pretensions and moral hypocrisy of both the court circle and the middle class, while in England, Restoration dramatists such as William Wycherley and William Congreve took their cue from Molière. Cynical, witty, and epigrammatic by
(10) turns, Restoration plays were as popular under King Charles II as the dramas of Shakespeare and his contemporaries had been nearly a century earlier. However, it was the foibles of society, rather than the fortunes of kings and heroes, that
(15) became their principal theme.

7. The author would most likely agree that

(A) the plays of Shakespeare and his contemporaries focused largely on heroic and royal subjects

(B) Molière was the most innovative of the Restoration dramatists

(C) the comedy of manners was primarily popular both in France and in England, though for different reasons

(D) the French court circle and middle class could be well described as both witty and cynical

(E) Restoration plays are the finest of examples of English drama

8. The phrase "took their cue from Molière" (lines 8–9) conveys that that Restoration playwrights

(A) hoped to achieve the same level of success as Molière

(B) were influenced by Molière in their artistic aims

(C) depended on Molière for thematic inspiration

(D) likely studied with Molière to learn his techniques

(E) modeled each of their plays on works by Molière

Questions 9–10 are based on the following passage.

Redshift is the condition in which the frequency of light when observed is lower than its frequency when it was emitted. Since red light has the lowest frequency of all observable electromagnetic radia-
(5) tion, this shift towards the lower end of the spectrum is referred to as redshift. It occurs when the distance between the sound source and observer is constantly increasing, elongating the period of the light waves and thus lowering their frequency from
(10) the perspective of the observer, not unlike the changing pitch of a siren moving past a stationary observer. In the case of redshift, however, the implications are profound—the large redshift observed for sources far away from our galaxy lends credence
(15) to the model of a constantly expanding universe.

9. The author cites a siren (line 11) as an example of

   (A) another light source which seems to be lower than it truly is

   (B) electromagnetic radiation that is probably familiar to the reader

   (C) an expanding distance between a source and its observer

   (D) evidence that observers cannot trust their senses to provide accurate data

   (E) an observed frequency that is lower than that frequency when emitted

10. The author would most likely describe the condition of redshift as

    (A) a fascinating, though little understood phenomenon

    (B) a useful clue about the nature of the universe

    (C) without parallel in our daily experience

    (D) disproof of the assertion that the universe is constantly expanding

    (E) an explanation of a commonly experienced phenomenon of sound

Questions 11–12 are based on the following passage.

Mr. Nioche wore a glossy wig of an unnatural color which overhung his little meek, white, vacant face, and left it hardly more expressive than the unfeatured block upon which these articles are
(5) displayed in the barber's window. He was an exquisite image of shabby gentility. His scant ill-made coat, desperately brushed, his darned gloves, his highly polished boots, his rusty, shapely hat, told the story of a person who had "had losses"
(10) and who clung to the spirit of nice habits even though the letter had been hopelessly effaced. Among other things Mr. Nioche had lost courage. Adversity had not only ruined him, it had frightened him, and he was evidently going through his
(15) remnant of life on tiptoe, for fear of waking up the hostile fates.

11. The description of Mr. Nioche's coat as "desperately brushed" (line 7) serves to

    (A) emphasize that Mr. Nioche endeavored to avoid confrontation

    (B) imply that Mr. Nioche worked to maintain an image of prosperity

    (C) convey the highly fashionable impression created by Mr. Nioche's appearance

    (D) mock the ridiculous concerns which preoccupied Mr. Nioche

    (E) imply that Mr. Nioche was a victim of desperate poverty

12. Based on the passage, it seems most likely that Mr. Nioche

    (A) was once successful, but has since encountered misfortunes

    (B) was once meek, but became bolder because of adversity

    (C) was once a barber, but has since switched professions

    (D) was once concerned with his appearance, but later found it unimportant

    (E) was once handsome, but became less so due to hardship

Questions 13–16 are based on the following passages.

Passage 1

Historically, sailors and farmers have been especially interested in forecasting the weather since their livelihoods depend so directly on its conditions. Over time, close observation of the natural
(5) world revealed to these groups a number of accurate keys to forecasting. For instance, people living near the seacoast have often hung seaweed or kelp outside their houses. The plants act as primitive hygrometers, shriveling during dry, fine-weather
(10) spells, and becoming swollen and damp in the moist air that portends rain. Pine cones have long served a similar function—their scales typically open out in dry weather but contract in humid air, a reliable sign that rain is imminent.

Passage 2

(15)   Although people have attempted to predict the
weather for centuries, it was not until the 1920s
that the science of large-scale forecasting got its
start, due in no small measure to the efforts of
Lewis Richardson, a British meteorologist.
(20) Richardson believed that the key to accurate forecasting was to measure temperature, humidity,
air pressure, and wind simultaneously at evenly
spaced "grid points" throughout the world.
Richardson's method was sound, but it was only
(25) with the advent of supercomputers several decades
later that the billions of calculations necessary for
accurate, large-scale forecasts became feasible.

13. Based on Passage 1, it seems most likely that a
     hygrometer (line 9) measures

     (A) wind speed

     (B) temperature

     (C) air humidity

     (D) rainfall

     (E) ocean conditions

14. As used in Passage 2, *sound* (line 24) most
     nearly means

     (A) noisy

     (B) valid

     (C) excellent

     (D) normal

     (E) practical

15. The author of Passage 1 would most likely
     react to the statement in Passage 2 that "people
     have attempted to predict the weather for
     centuries" (lines 15–16) by stating that such
     attempts were

     (A) resourceful and helpful

     (B) admirable but unsuccessful

     (C) ambitious and groundbreaking

     (D) beneficial but incomplete

     (E) superstitious but informative

16. Based on Passage 2, Richardson would regard
     the attempts described in Passage 1 to predict
     the weather as

     (A) foolish and largely without scientific basis

     (B) likely to provide incorrect predictions
          since these attempts considered irrel-
          evant factors

     (C) unsurprising, given that the people who
          employed these techniques depended on
          weather conditions for their livelihood

     (D) highly admirable, though unlikely to suc-
          ceed primarily because of the primitive
          nature of the hygrometers employed

     (E) unlikely to succeed completely, since
          these attempts provided so little data

Questions 17–20 are based on the following passages.

Passage 1

Teaching writing to students is a matter of providing them with a proper understanding of the
cognitive process by which competent writers
compose. This process may be modeled by an
(5) instructor to illustrate the logical flow of thought
in a skilled writer's mind as he or she develops a
composition. By becoming familiar with these
stages and learning to emulate them, a basic writer
can gradually master the skill of writing. Because
(10) these writers will only learn to write correctly by
understanding and mastering these structures of
writing, cognitive scientists and educational theorists must continue their present investigation into
the process of writing and develop classroom
(15) exercises that teach this process to students.

Passage 2

Much attention has been focused on the plight of
the "basic," or struggling, writer. Several composition theorists, in their quest for quick solutions to
these writers' dilemma, have overlooked that
(20) thought and writing cannot be free of the social
contexts in which communication take place. Each
of us belongs to multiple communities—family,
peers, friends—and each of these communities

demands a different mode of communication. A
(25) student who is considered a "basic" writer may excel
in other spheres of communication. We must help
such a student to channel existing communication
skills into new modes, rather than ask them to start
from scratch and learn an entirely new, entirely arti-
(30) ficial method of thought and communication.

17. As used in Passage 1, the phrase "structures of writing" (lines 11–12) refers to

    (A) the organization of a finished piece of writing

    (B) instructional methods used to teach writing

    (C) modes of communication present in all social communities

    (D) the composition process employed by skilled writers

    (E) investigations by educational theorists and cognitive scientists

18. According to the author of Passage 2, effective writing instruction must

    (A) help students communicate with their families, peers, and friends

    (B) teach the composition process employed by skilled writers

    (C) acknowledge the existence of other modes of communication

    (D) seek to adapt existing social bonds into new communities

    (E) instill a new method of thought, rather than simply present rules of composition

19. The authors of both passages agree on the merit of writing instruction that

    (A) channels communication skills from other social settings

    (B) presents the composition process of a skilled writer

    (C) is based on research by cognitive scientists

    (D) avoids artificial methods of thought and communication

    (E) is tailored to the needs of "basic" writers

20. The author of Passage 2 suggests that the "classroom exercises" (lines 14–15) mentioned in Passage 1

    (A) are unlikely to succeed

    (B) should model for students the process of skilled composition

    (C) best meet the needs of "basic" writers

    (D) fail to make use of existing communication skills

    (E) often fail to help students to communicate in other social settings

PRACTICE SET 2: LONG PASSAGES

> The passages below are followed by questions based on their content; questions following a pair of related passages may also be based on the relationship between the paired passages. Answer the questions on the basis of what is <u>stated</u> or <u>implied</u> in the passages and in any introductory material that may be provided.

Questions 21–26 are based on the following passage.

The following passage, which examines a debate on possible linkages between the American Populist movement and Joseph McCarthy's anti-communist crusade of the 1950s, has been excerpted from a political science journal.

Historians have long known that there were two sides to the Populist movement of the 1890s: a progressive side, embodying the protests of farmers against big business, and a darker side, marked by a

(5) distrust of Easterners, immigrants, and intellectuals. In the 1950s, one school of U.S. social thinkers constructed a parallel between this dark side of Populism and the contemporary anti-communist crusade spearheaded by Wisconsin Senator Joseph

(10) McCarthy, which attacked liberalism, Eastern intellectuals, and civil liberties in general. To Seymour Martin Lipset, McCarthyism represented "the sour dregs of Populism"; to Edward Shils, McCarthyism, like Populism, exemplified "the ambiguous

(15) American impulse toward 'direct democracy.'"

Noting that McCarthyism and Populism had both found their strongest support in the agrarian Midwest, Lipset argued that voters who backed agrarian protest movements during earlier eco-

(20) nomic crises had supported McCarthy in the post-World War II period of prosperity. "It would be interesting to know," Lipset wrote, "what percentage of those who supported the isolationist but progressive Bob La Follette in Wisconsin now

(25) backs McCarthy." But, in the eyes of these writers, the appeal of McCarthyism extended beyond the agrarian base of Populism to include urban groups such as industrial workers. Lipset claimed that "the lower classes, especially the workers," had backed

(30) McCarthy. In a more sweeping fashion, Lewis Feuer claimed that "it was the American lower classes…who gave their overwhelming support to the attacks in recent years on civil liberties."

Writing a few years later, political scientist

(35) Michael Paul Rogin challenged these superficially plausible notions, contending that they merely embodied the writers' own assumptions about the supposed intolerance of lower class groups, rather than a valid interpretation of McCarthyism. Rogin

(40) critically examined their assertions by the simple method of testing them against the evidence. He tested Lipset's claims about the continuity of McCarthyism and earlier agrarian protest movements by breaking down statewide voting statistics

(45) on a county-by-county and precinct-by-precinct basis. He found that Wisconsin counties that had voted strongly for Progressives before World War II did not support McCarthy; McCarthy's support was concentrated in his home region and in ethnic

(50) German areas that had been traditionally conservative. The old Progressive vote had in fact gone to McCarthy's opponents, the Democrats.

To test Lipset's generalizations about McCarthy's support among lower-class groups, Rogin attempted

(55) to determine whether industrial workers had, in fact, backed McCarthy. Correlating income and employment statistics with voting records, Rogin found that the greater the employment in industry in a given Wisconsin county, the lower was

(60) McCarthy's share of the vote. Rogin concluded that the thesis of "McCarthyism as Populism" should be judged "not as the product of science but as a…venture into conservative political theory."

21. The author would probably assert that Populism and McCarthyism

   (A) were basically similar

   (B) were completely opposite in character

   (C) were responses to, respectively, agrarian and industrial conditions

   (D) were essentially dissimilar movements that shared some common features

   (E) each had both a progressive and a darker side

22. It can be inferred that Rogin's most serious criticism of Lipset, Feuer, and Shils's methodology would probably be that they

    (A) reached incorrect conclusions about McCarthy

    (B) equated support for McCarthyism with anti-intellectualism

    (C) placed too much emphasis on the dual character of Populism

    (D) failed to examine the evidence that could support or weaken their conclusions

    (E) offered a theory that could not easily be tested

23. Rogin studied the class character of Wisconsin voters in order to

    I. challenge the idea that less affluent socioeconomic groups supported McCarthy

    II. explain the underlying causes of the links between Populism and McCarthyism

    III. account for important changes in voting patterns during the twentieth century

    (A) I only

    (B) III only

    (C) I and II only

    (D) I and III only

    (E) I, II, and III

24. It can be inferred that both Lipset and Rogin made which of the following assumptions about voter support for McCarthy?

    (A) The voting patterns of industrial workers are representative of lower-class political preferences.

    (B) Industrial workers usually vote for conservative political candidates.

    (C) Supporters of McCarthy were almost exclusively of lower-class origin.

    (D) Lower-class voters generally tend to vote in favor of civil rights measures.

    (E) Voters in Midwestern counties are typical of American voters elsewhere.

25. According to the passage, Rogin concluded that the writings of Lipset, Shils, and Feuer

    (A) intentionally distorted historical evidence

    (B) were flawed by political presuppositions

    (C) lent support to attacks on civil liberties

    (D) took an overly statistical approach to historical evidence

    (E) were marked by an anti-intellectual bias

26. The author is primarily concerned with

    (A) comparing positions in a political debate

    (B) advocating the use of statistical methods in historical research

    (C) examining the similarities between two political movements

    (D) explaining why historical conclusions should be revised according to later revelations

    (E) discoveries describing an instance of flawed historical analysis

Questions 27–35 are based on the following passage.

The following passage is excerpted from a major scientific journal.

The transformer is an essential component of modern electric power systems. Simply put, it can convert electricity with a low current and a high voltage into electricity with a high current and low

(5) voltage (and vice versa) with almost no loss of energy. The conversion is important because electric power is transmitted most efficiently at high voltages but is best generated and used at low voltages. Were it not for transformers, the distance separating

(10) generators from consumers would have to be minimized, many households and industries would require their own power stations, and electricity would be a much less practical form of energy.

In addition to its role in electric power systems,

(15) the transformer is an integral component of many things that run on electricity. Desk lamps, battery chargers, toy trains, and television sets all rely on transformers to cut or boost voltage. In all its multiplicity of applications, the transformer can range

(20) from tiny assemblies the size of a pea to behemoths weighing 500 tons or more. The principles that govern the function of electrical transformers are the same regardless of form or application.

The English physicist Michael Faraday discovered

(25) the basic action of the transformer during his pioneering investigations of electricity in 1831. Some fifty years later, the advent of a practical transformer, containing all the essential elements of the modern instrument, revolutionized the infant elec-

(30) tric lighting industry. By the turn of the century, alternating-current power systems had been universally adopted and the transformer had assumed a key role in electrical transmission and distribution.

Yet the transformer's tale does not end in 1900.

(35) Today's transformers can handle 500 times the power and 15 times the voltage of their turn-of-the-century ancestors; the weight per unit of power has dropped by a factor of ten and efficiency typically exceeds 99 percent. These advances

(40) reflect the marriage of theoretical inquiry and engineering that first elucidated and then exploited the phenomena governing transformer action.

Faraday's investigations were inspired by the Danish physicist Hans Christian Oersted, who had

(45) shown in 1820 that an electric current flowing through a conducting material creates a magnetic field around the conductor. At the time, Oersted's discovery was considered remarkable, since electricity and magnetism were thought to be separate

(50) and unrelated forces. If an electric current could generate a magnetic field, it seemed likely that a magnetic field could give rise to an electric current.

In 1831, Faraday demonstrated that in order for a magnetic field to induce a current in a conduc-

(55) tor, the field must be changing. Faraday caused the strength of the field to fluctuate by making and breaking the electric circuit generating the field; the same effect can be achieved with a current whose direction alternates in time. This fasci-

(60) nating interaction of electricity and magnetism came to be known as electromagnetic induction.

27. According to the passage, the first practical transformer was developed in

(A) 1820

(B) 1831

(C) 1860

(D) 1881

(E) 1900

28. The passage suggests that advances in the efficiency of the transformer are

(A) based solely on Faraday's discovery of electromagnetic induction

(B) due to a combination of engineering and theoretical curiosity

(C) continuing to occur at an ever accelerated pace

(D) most likely at a peak that cannot be surpassed

(E) found in transformers that weigh 500 tons or more

29. According to the passage, Oersted's discovery regarding the production of a magnetic field is considered remarkable because

    (A) the transformer had not yet been universally adopted

    (B) Faraday had already demonstrated that this was impossible

    (C) scientists believed that there was no relationship between electricity and magnetism

    (D) it contradicted the established principles of electromagnetism

    (E) it proved that a magnetic field could generate electricity

30. In line 32, *assumed* most nearly means

    (A) presupposed

    (B) understood

    (C) feigned

    (D) taken

    (E) borrowed

31. Which of the following is NOT true of transformers today as compared to the first transformers?

    (A) They comprise the same basic components.

    (B) They are lighter in weight.

    (C) They are many times more powerful.

    (D) They operate at a much lower voltage.

    (E) They are almost completely efficient.

32. According to the passage, Oersted's discovery proved that

    (A) magnetism and electricity are unrelated forces

    (B) a magnetic field can induce an electric current

    (C) all materials that conduct electricity are magnetic

    (D) electricity can be transported over long distances

    (E) an electric current can create a magnetic field

33. According to the passage, one function of the transformer is to

    (A) convert electricity into the high voltages most useful for transmission

    (B) create the magnetic fields used in industry

    (C) minimize the distance between generators and consumers

    (D) protect electric power systems from energy loss

    (E) transform electrical energy into a magnetic field

34. Which of the following statements is best supported by the passage?

    (A) Faraday was the first to show how an electric current can induce a magnetic field.

    (B) Oersted was the first to utilize transformers in a practical application, by using them to power electric lights.

    (C) Faraday invented the first practical transformer.

    (D) Oersted coined the term *electromagnetic induction*.

    (E) Faraday demonstrated that when a magnetic field is changing, it can produce an electric current in a conducting material.

35. According to the passage, electricity would be a much less practical form of energy if there were no transformers because

   (A) generating electricity would become much more expensive

   (B) there would be no dependable source of electric power

   (C) generators would have to be built close to the consumers they supply

   (D) industries and households would have to be supplied with the same power

   (E) household appliances would have to operate with a low voltage

Questions 36–47 are based on the following passage.

The following excerpt, taken from a novel first published in 1965, describes the narrator's time spent at Magdalen College—part of England's Oxford University system—during the period shortly after WW II, and his first experiences upon graduation.

I went to Oxford in 1948. In my second year at Magdalen, soon after a long vacation during which I hardly saw my parents, my father had to fly out to India. He took my mother with him. Their
(5) plane crashed, a high-octane pyre, in a thunderstorm some forty miles east of Karachi. After the first shock I felt an almost immediate sense of relief, of freedom. My only other close relation, my mother's brother, farmed in Rhodesia, so I had no
(10) family to trammel what I regarded as my real self. I may have been weak on filial charity, but I was strong on the discipline in vogue.

At least, along with a group of fellow odd men out at Magdalen, I thought I was strong in the dis-
(15) cipline. We formed a small club called Les Hommes Révoltés, drank very dry sherry, and (as a protest against those shabby duffle-coated last years of the forties) wore dark-grey suits and black ties for our meetings; we argued about
(20) essences and existences and called a certain kind of inconsequential behaviour "existentialist." Less enlightened people would have called it capricious

or just plain selfish; but we didn't realize that the heroes, or anti-heroes, of the French existentialist
(25) novels we read were not supposed to be realistic. We tried to imitate them, mistaking metaphorical descriptions of complex modes of feeling for straightforward prescriptions of behaviour. We duly felt the right anguishes. Most of us, true to
(30) the eternal dandyism of Oxford, simply wanted to look different. In our club, we did.

I acquired expensive habits and affected manners. I got a third-class degree and a first-class illusion: that I was a poet. But nothing could have been less
(35) poetic than my pseudo-aristocratic, seeing-through-all boredom with life in general and with making a living in particular. I was too green to know that all cynicism masks a failure to cope—an impotence, in short; and that to despise all effort is the greatest
(40) effort of all. But I did absorb a small dose of one permanently useful thing, Oxford's greatest gift to civilized life: Socratic honesty. It showed me, very intermittently, that it is not enough to revolt against one's past. One day I was outrageously bitter among
(45) some friends about the Army; back in my own rooms later it suddenly struck me that just because I said with impunity things that would have apoplexed my dead father, I was still no less under his influence. The truth was that I was not a cynic
(50) by nature; only by revolt. I had got away from what I hated, but I hadn't found where I loved, and so I pretended there was nowhere to love.

Handsomely equipped to fail, I went out into the world. My father hadn't kept Financial
(55) Prudence among his armoury of essential words; he ran a ridiculously large account at Ladbroke's and his mess bills always reached staggering proportions, because he liked to be popular and in place of charm had to dispense alcohol. What
(60) remained of his money when the lawyers and tax men had had their cuts yielded not nearly enough for me to live on. But every kind of job I looked at—the Foreign Service, the Civil, the Colonial, the banks, commerce, advertising—was
(65) transpierceable at a glance. I went to several interviews and since I didn't feel obliged to show the eager enthusiasm our world expects from the young executive, I was successful at none.

36. It can be inferred the "discipline in vogue" mentioned in line 12 most nearly refers to

    (A) Socratic honesty
    (B) radical inquiry
    (C) emotional coldness
    (D) aristocratic yearning
    (E) poetic sensitivity

37. The group of "fellow odd men" mentioned in line 13 are described as being

    (A) bookish and sincere
    (B) ambitious and philosophical
    (C) unconventional and enlightened
    (D) ostentatious and shallow
    (E) worldly and knowing

38. According to the passage, the narrator and his friends revolted against all of the following EXCEPT

    (A) postwar attire
    (B) career ambition
    (C) parents
    (D) academia
    (E) the military

39. The author uses the phrase "[L]ess enlightened people" (lines 21–22) to convey a sense of

    (A) disapproval
    (B) irony
    (C) sympathy
    (D) remorse
    (E) nostalgia

40. According to the passage, French existentialist novels are meant to be read in which of the following ways?

    (A) as instructional texts
    (B) as fantasies
    (C) as allegories
    (D) as tragedies
    (E) as heroic epics

41. The narrator claims to have acquired all of the following while at Oxford EXCEPT

    (A) a costly lifestyle
    (B) a cynical worldview
    (C) a capacity for self-awareness
    (D) a sense of being gifted
    (E) a foundation for success

42. In line 32, *affected* most nearly means

    (A) influenced
    (B) concerned
    (C) pretentious
    (D) changed
    (E) infectious

43. It can be inferred from the passage that the narrator's bitterness toward the army

    (A) was not founded in deeply felt beliefs
    (B) surprised even his friends in Les Hommes Révoltés
    (C) would not have been expressed if his father were not dead
    (D) revealed a deep and abiding cynicism
    (E) led him to realize that he was not a poet

44. The passage does NOT suggest that which of the following is true about the narrator's father?

   (A) He and his son were not close.

   (B) He enjoyed entertaining others.

   (C) He held favorable attitudes toward the military.

   (D) He was a misanthrope by nature.

   (E) He had a strong effect on his son's beliefs.

45. In line 65, *transpierceable* most nearly means

   (A) easy to penetrate

   (B) easy to attempt

   (C) easy to understand

   (D) easy to achieve

   (E) easy to dismiss

46. According to the passage, the narrator and his father shared which of the following traits?

   (A) prodigality

   (B) cynicism

   (C) unconventionality

   (D) bonhomie

   (E) self-doubt

47. This passage serves mainly to

   (A) describe a dominant postwar sensibility

   (B) depict a difficult period of immaturity

   (C) condemn an emotionally callow youth

   (D) portray a bohemian element at Oxford

   (E) explain one person's failure to find a livelihood

Questions 48–60 are based on the following passages.

The following passages present two views of the genius of Leonardo da Vinci. Passage 1 emphasizes Leonardo's fundamentally artistic sensibility. Passage 2 offers a defense of his technological achievements.

Passage 1

What a marvelous and celestial creature was Leonardo da Vinci. As a scientist and engineer, his gifts were unparalleled. But his accomplishment in these capacities was hindered by the fact that he was,
(5) before all else, an artist. As one conversant with the perfection of art, and knowing the futility of trying to bring such perfection to the realm of practical application, Leonardo tended toward variability and inconstancy in his endeavors. His practice of moving
(10) compulsively from one project to the next, never bringing any of them to completion, stood in the way of his making any truly useful technical advances.

When Leonardo was asked to create a memorial for one of his patrons, he designed a bronze horse of
(15) such vast proportions that it proved utterly impractical—even impossible—to produce. Some historians maintain that Leonardo never had any intention of finishing this work in the first place. But it is more likely that he simply became so intoxicated by
(20) his grand artistic conception that he lost sight of the fact that the monument actually had to be cast. Similarly, when Leonardo was commissioned to paint the *Last Supper*, he left the head of Christ unfinished, feeling incapable of investing it with a
(25) sufficiently divine demeanor. Yet, as a work of art rather than science or engineering, it is still worthy of our greatest veneration, for Leonardo succeeded brilliantly in capturing the acute anxiety of the Apostles at the most dramatic moment of the
(30) Passion narrative.

Such mental restlessness, however, proved more problematic when applied to scientific matters. When he turned his mind to the natural world, Leonardo would begin by inquiring into the prop-
(35) erties of herbs and end up observing the motions of the heavens. In his technical studies and scientific experiments, he would generate an endless stream of models and drawings, designing complex

and unbuildable machines to raise great weights,
(40) bore through mountains, or even empty harbors.

It's this enormous intellectual fertility that has
suggested to many that Leonardo can and should be
regarded as one of the originators of modern
science. But Leonardo was not himself a true scien-
(45) tist. "Science" is not the hundred-odd principles or
*pensieri** that have been pulled out of his Codici.
"Science is comprehensive and methodical thought."
Granted, Leonardo always became fascinated by the
intricacies of specific technical challenges. He pos-
(50) sessed the artist's interest in detail, which explains
his compulsion with observation and problem-
solving. But such things alone do not constitute
science, which requires the working out of a
systematic body of knowledge—something
(55) Leonardo displayed little interest in doing.

pensieri: thoughts (Italian)

Passage 2

As varied as Leonardo's interests were, analysis
of his writings points to technology as his main
concern. There is hardly a field of applied
mechanics that Leonardo's searching mind did not
(60) touch upon in his notebooks. Yet some of his
biographers have actually expressed regret that
such a man, endowed with divine artistic genius,
would "waste" precious years of his life on such a
"lowly" pursuit as engineering.
(65) To appreciate Leonardo's contribution to technology, one need only examine his analysis of the
main problem of technology—the harnessing of
energy to perform useful work. In Leonardo's
time, the main burden of human industry still
(70) rested on the muscles of humans and animals. But
little attention was given to analyzing this primitive muscle power so that it could be brought to
bear most effectively on the required tasks. Against
this background, Leonardo's approach to work
(75) was revolutionary. When he searched for the most
efficient ways of using human muscle power, the
force of every limb was analyzed and measured.

Consider Leonardo's painstaking approach to the
construction of canals. After extensive analysis of
(80) the requirements for building a particular canal by

hand, he concluded that the only reasonable solution was to mechanize the whole operation. Then
he considered and ultimately discarded numerous
schemes to clear excavated material by wheeled
(85) vehicles. It was not that Leonardo underestimated
wheeled vehicles. But he realized that a cart is useful only on level ground; on steep terrain the material's weight would nullify the effort of the animal.

Having systematically rejected several solutions in
(90) this way, Leonardo began to examine the feasibility
of excavation techniques incorporating a system of
cranes. Power was again his main concern. To acti-
vate a crane, the only transportable motor available
at the time would have been a treadmill, a machine
(95) that converts muscle power into rotary motion. This
is not to suggest that Leonardo invented the external
treadmill. However, it was Leonardo who first used
the principle of the treadmill rationally and in
accordance with sound engineering principles.
(100) Because Leonardo's insights were sometimes so
far beyond the standards of his time, their importance to the development of modern engineering is
often underestimated. Many scholars, in fact, still
regard his work merely as the isolated accomplish-
(105) ments of a remarkably prophetic dreamer, refusing
to concede that Leonardo was one of our earliest
and most significant engineers.

48. The author of Passage 1 suggests that
Leonardo failed to bring many of his
engineering projects to completion because

(A) he knew that he could not achieve the
perfection that he found in his art

(B) his designs were limited by the energy
sources that were then available for such
projects

(C) he felt incapable of imparting a sufficiently divine demeanor to such
endeavors

(D) he preferred devoting his genius to works
of art rather than science

(E) he became engrossed in the intricacies of
specific technical challenges

49. According to the author of Passage 1, Leonardo's ability to make meaningful contributions to science was hindered by all of the following EXCEPT

    (A) an artistic sensibility

    (B) an intellectual restlessness

    (C) a propensity to come up with impractical solutions

    (D) a compulsion to observe situations and solve problems

    (E) an unsystematic method of inquiry

50. The author of Passage 1 mentions Leonardo's work on the *Last Supper* in order to

    (A) point out that he left many works of art unfinished

    (B) argue that his failure to finish projects was forgivable in the realm of art

    (C) observe his humility when approaching representations of the divine

    (D) contrast his approach to artistic projects with his approach to scientific projects

    (E) reveal his intimate understanding of the perfection of art

51. The author's tone in describing Leonardo's mental processes when "he turned his mind to the natural world" in Passage 1 (line 33) is

    (A) indifferent

    (B) awed

    (C) critical

    (D) disillusioned

    (E) ironic

52. In line 42 of Passage 1, *suggested* most nearly means

    (A) recommended

    (B) mentioned

    (C) indicated

    (D) insinuated

    (E) resembled

53. It can be inferred that the author of Passage 1 believes that Leonardo's *pensieri*

    (A) represent an incomplete attempt to advance modern science

    (B) epitomize his tendency to drift randomly from topic to topic

    (C) lack empirical data to back up their conclusions

    (D) signify the crowning achievement of his Codici

    (E) fail to present a systematic body of thought

54. The author of Passage 2 mentions some of Leonardo's biographers (lines 61–64) in order to

    (A) call into question Leonardo's artistic genius

    (B) acknowledge a downside to Leonardo's engineering pursuits

    (C) illustrate the lack of appreciation for Leonardo's engineering contributions

    (D) underscore the prodigal nature of Leonardo's gifts

    (E) demonstrate a bias against the engineering profession among biographers

55. According to the author of Passage 2, Leonardo ultimately abandoned plans to use wheeled vehicles in the construction of canals because

    (A) the excavated material had to be cleared mechanically

    (B) the vehicles were prone to breaking down on steep terrain

    (C) muscle power would prove inadequate to the task at hand

    (D) animals would be unable to pull the vehicles at the worksite

    (E) wheeled vehicles were less impressive than treadmills

56. The author of Passage 2 would agree with all of the following statements EXCEPT

    (A) Leonardo's engineering accomplishments remain undervalued by many scholars

    (B) Leonardo's inquiries led to the invention of the external treadmill

    (C) Leonardo's writings show him to be more interested in technology than in art

    (D) Leonardo was the first person to apply sound engineering principles to the harnessing of muscle power

    (E) Leonardo's engineering achievements were at least as notable as his artistic achievements

57. In line 104, *isolated* most nearly means

    (A) disconnected

    (B) inaccessible

    (C) remote

    (D) lonely

    (E) unique

58. The author of Passage 1 would probably regard the painstaking analysis of canal-building described in Passage 2 as an example of Leonardo's

    (A) revolutionary approach to work

    (B) ability to complete ambitious engineering projects

    (C) artistic fascination with details

    (D) predisposition to lose interest in specific problems

    (E) penchant for designing unbuildable machines

59. The authors of Passage 1 and Passage 2 would probably agree with which of the following statements?

    (A) Leonardo cannot properly be considered a scientist.

    (B) Leonardo's intellectual restlessness hampered his ability to complete projects.

    (C) Leonardo made significant contributions to the field of applied mechanics.

    (D) Leonardo possessed a great natural genius for engineering.

    (E) Leonardo's greatest accomplishments were in the realm of art.

60. The author of Passage 2 would most likely dispute the author of Passage 1's assessment of Leonardo's scientific contributions by pointing out that

    (A) Leonardo's inquiries spanned practically every field of applied mechanics

    (B) Leonardo considered and ultimately discarded many designs in his attempt to mechanize the building of canals

    (C) many biographers fail to grasp Leonardo's accomplishments in the field of engineering

    (D) many of Leonardo's insights were too advanced to be realized in his era

    (E) Leonardo's approach to the construction of canals demonstrated sound scientific methodology

EXPLANATIONS FOR PRACTICE SET 1

BRITISH SATIRE

1. D

The author says Pope's works are good examples of Horatian satire. So what does that tell us? Horace's works are described as elegant, deftly mocking satires. That matches (D) quite well. (A) and (E) apply to Swift, not Pope. (B) is out of the scope of the passage, since the author doesn't discuss the popularity of Pope. (C) is far too extreme and is too negative—although the author says that some writers modeled their satires on Horace, he doesn't say that they were completely devoid of originality, or "slavishly imitative."

2. E

Swift used his work to make satirical attacks. In fact, *make* is a pretty good prediction for this sentence. (E) comes the closest; he *presented* devastating attacks in his work. (A), (B), and (C) are all examples of the more common meaning for *mounted*, but they don't fit here. (D) distorts the meaning of the sentence; Swift didn't just *support* attacks made by others, he made the attacks himself.

AMERICAN ELECTIONS

3. B

The writer is worried that not enough people are voting. One result of this is that winning an election can mean that surprisingly few people actually voted for you. A majority of voters doesn't at all represent a majority of the total population. This might be surprising to many people, and the author uses quotation marks around the word *majority* in order to emphasize this distinction between a majority of voters and a majority of *potential* voters. (B) captures this well. (A) is something that the author might

agree with, but it doesn't follow directly from the quotation marks. (C) and (E) are too extreme—although the author is disappointed that so few people are voting, this doesn't mean that the process is illegitimate, or that it should be changed. (D) is true, but misses the point of the example: that such a majority represents a disappointingly small percentage of potential voters.

4. C

Don't waste time making a prediction on such an open-ended question; jump right into the answer choices. Only (C) holds up—the author says that people don't seem interested in preserving the American democratic system, and low voter turnout is evidence of this. So it must be true that the author considers voting evidence of interest in preserving the system. Although the author is worried about recall elections, he doesn't actually advocate prohibiting them (A), and even if he did, this still wouldn't address the voter turnout issue. (B) is too extreme—the author only says that this is true in closely contested elections, and doesn't imply that this is true in "most" elections. (D) is the opposite of the authors claim—he says that few would deny the advantages of the system. (E) is also an opposite choice, since the author says that governors can be ousted by "a well-organized but small minority of voters."

CAMBIUM IN TREES

5. A

Here, *pivotal* means very important, or *essential* (A). (B) and (D) are related to the another common meaning of *pivot*. (C) and (E) are not strong enough—*pivotal* means not just noteworthy or important but essential, something you can't do without.

6. E

The author says that some process is reflected in the derivation of the word *xylem*. What process? Backtrack to find out—the xylem cells become the heartwood of the tree. So the author cites the derivation of the word *xylem* in order to emphasize the role of xylem in forming wood (E). (A) is outside the scope of the passage, since the author never discusses the influences of classical languages. It's true that the heartwood supports the tree, but this is not discussed in the passage, and this role of support is not emphasized by the derivation of the word *xylem* (B). (C) references another role of xylem, but this function of circulation doesn't have a direct connection to the Greek word for wood. (D) references a valid distinction, but the author isn't discussing this distinction at the end of the paragraph where the etymology discussion occurs.

COMEDY OF MANNERS

7. A

(A) makes sense. The author says that the Restoration plays were similar to the works of Shakespeare and his contemporaries in that both were popular, but they differed in that the Restoration plays focused on "the foibles of society, rather than the fortunes of kings and heroes," (lines 13–14). So the author must think that the plays of Shakespeare focused on kings and heroes, as (A) indicates. (B) is distortion, since only the British playwrights are referred to as Restoration dramatists. (C) is out of the scope of the passage, since the author never discusses why the plays were popular. (D) mixes up some details from the passage, since it is the plays that are described as witty and cynical, not the royal and middle class subjects of those plays. (E) is too extreme, because we don't know what the author thinks about other periods of English drama.

8. B

It seems that the plays of the Restoration playwrights and Molière had similar subjects and themes. When the author writes that the British playwrights "took their cue from Molière," (lines 8–9) you know that they were influenced by Molière in their work, or their artistic aims, as (B) states. Rule out (A), since the author never describes the success of Molière. (C) and (E) are too extreme; the British were inspired by Molière, but that doesn't mean that they couldn't do anything without him (C), or that each specific work was modeled on a work by Molière (E). (D) is too literal, since you don't know that the British actually studied with Molière.

REDSHIFT

9. E

The concept of redshift is a little counterintuitive, so the author cites a familiar example to help the reader to understand. When a siren passes, it seems to get lower in pitch, just as a light source moving away from an observer seems to have a lower frequency due to redshift. This parallel is nicely summed up by (E). (A) and (B) are out, since the author is speaking of the siren as a sound, not a light source (A) or as electromagnetic radiation (B). (C) is tempting, but doesn't quite fit. The siren is an example of the sound source itself, not the distance between that source and an observer. (D) is a little too paranoid. The author isn't advising readers not to trust their senses. She's simply stating that some frequencies change depending on the relation of the source and the observer.

10. B

The author describes the implications of redshift as profound, since it supports the theory that the universe is expanding. In other words, it provides a useful clue about the nature of the universe (B).

The author describes the reason behind redshift, so we can't consider it little understood (A). The example of the siren rules out (C). (D) is the very opposite of the author's point; redshift is proof, not disproof, of this assertion. The example of the siren is used to help explain redshift, but this doesn't mean that redshift can explain the siren (E). In fact, the author specifically defines redshift as a change in light frequencies, not sound frequencies.

Mr. Nioche

11. B

The author describes Mr. Nioche's appearance at some length in order to tell us something about his personality and life. We read that he has "had losses" (line 9) but still tries to keep up appearances. So he's brushing his coat "desperately" (line 7) in order to try, somewhat unsuccessfully, to retain his prosperous appearance (B). Although the author does say that Mr. Nioche attempted to ignore confrontation (A), this isn't implied by the state of his coat. (C) misses the point that Mr. Nioche's attempts to retain his prosperous image aren't entirely successful—his coat is ill-made and his gloves have been repaired. At the same time, Mr. Nioche doesn't seem to be so poor that he can be described as "a victim of desperate poverty" (E). (D) is far too negative; there's no support that the author feels Mr. Nioche's concerns are ridiculous. In fact, the author seems to feel a little sorry for him.

12. A

Mr. Nioche has "had losses" (line 9) and had been ruined by adversity. So, he must have once been successful (A). (B) is the opposite of Mr. Nioche's response to adversity—he became meeker, not bolder. (C) is a distortion of the mention of the barber's mannequin early in the passage—there's no indication that Mr. Nioche was a barber. Mr. Nioche still seems very concerned with his appearance, so

(D) is definitely out. (E) is somewhat tempting, but read carefully. Mr. Nioche was probably a snappy dresser, but there's no indication that he was a particularly handsome man.

Weather Forecasting

13. C

The plants change according to the moisture in the air. Since they are described as "primitive hygrometers," it seems likely that a hygrometer measures the humidity of the air (C). There's no mention of the plants changing according to wind speed (A) or temperature (B). (D) and (E) are distortions; the plants can help to *predict* rainfall (D) or perhaps ocean conditions (E), but they actually *measure* humidity.

14. B

The author states that Richards wanted to makes tons of measurements. This was a "sound method" (line 24), but it couldn't really be put into practice until the arrival of supercomputers. So the problem was not with the method but with the available technology. In other words, the method was valid (B). (A) is related to a common meaning of sound that doesn't work in this sentence. Although the author might agree that the method is excellent (C), this doesn't follow from the word *sound*. There's also nothing to indicate that the method was normal (D)—in fact, it seems that it was quite an innovation. Also, the method was not at all practical (E) before the arrival of supercomputers.

15. A

Author 1 writes about the clever, low-tech solutions that people have been using for a long time to help predict weather. So he would likely regard the attempts referred to in Passage 2 as resourceful and helpful (A). (B) and (E) don't fit, because there's nothing in Passage 1 to indicate that the author would regard early weather forecasting measure as unsuccessful (B) or superstitious (E). In Passage 1, the methods are described as developing over time, so the term groundbreaking (C) doesn't fit. (D) might be tempting, but author 1 never discusses the completeness of the methods, so (D) is out of the scope of the passage.

16. E

Richardson's philosophy of weather prediction included measuring many factors (including humidity) in many different places. Since the seaweed and pine cones measured only humidity and in only one location, Richardson would likely say that they provided too little data to be successful (E). Notice, however, that since the primitive hygrometers did measure the important characteristic of humidity, they can't be said to be without scientific basis (A) or measures of irrelevant factors (B). (C) expresses the opinion of the author of Passage 1, but we have no idea how Richardson would feel about the topic. (D) misses the point that the hygrometers measure only one of several important factors. After all, even a perfect single hygrometer would provide too little data for Richardson's approach.

TEACHING WRITING

17. D

These "structures of writing" (lines 11–12) are something that basic writers are supposed to master. Backtrack from the phrase to find out what these structures are and how they fit into the passage. The author says that writing teachers should demonstrate the "logical flow of thought in a skilled writer's mind" (lines 5–6). Students can then become familiar with these stages of composition. So these "stages of composition" are the "structures of writing" that basic writers need to master (D). Author 1 is discussing the process of writing, not the

structure of a finished composition (A). Although the passage discusses instruction methods (B) and investigations into these methods (E), these are skills for teachers and researchers, not basic writers. Different social communities are discussed in Passage 2, not Passage 1.

18. C

Author 2 says that unskilled writers may already be good at communicating in other social settings, and that writing instruction should help students adapt these skills. So writing instruction needs to acknowledge the existence of other modes of communication (C). The author believes that poor writers may already be skilled at communicating with families, peers, and friends (A). (B) sums up the main idea of Passage 1, not Passage 2. (D) is a tricky distortion. Passage 2 is about building new writing skills, not new communities. (E) is the opposite of the last sentence in Passage 2, which warns against asking writing students to "learn an entirely new, entirely artificial method of thought and communication."

19. E

Both writers support special instruction for basic writers, so (E) fits. That's about all they agree on, however. (A) and (D) fit with Passage 2, though author 1 never discusses social settings (A), and you could even argue that he seems to think a somewhat artificial mode of thought is a good idea (D). (B) and (C) are supported by author 1, but author 2 argues against (B) and never addresses (C).

20. D

The final sentence of Passage 2 seems to argue pretty directly against the method of instruction proposed by Passage 1. Author 2 criticizes "artificial" methods of thought that don't make use of existing communications skills, and the method endorsed by author 1 seems to be a great example of this "artificial" type of instruction that teaches writing "from scratch." This fits (D) well. Interestingly, although author 2 criticizes this type of method, she never actually says that it won't work (A). It could just be inefficient or unpleasant, but still somewhat effective, for example. (B) is the thesis of author 1, not author 2. (C) is the opposite of our prediction, since author 2 would feel that these "classroom exercises" are not the best method of instruction for basic writers. (E) is a distortion of author 2's point. Communications skills from other social settings should be used to teach writing. This is the reverse of writing skills helping people to communicate in these other social settings.

EXPLANATIONS FOR PRACTICE SET 2

MCCARTHYISM AND POPULISM

The topic of this passage is McCarthyism, and specifically whether it drew support from the Populist movement. The author's main point is that although some would argue that McCarthyism had a following among those who supported Populism, later research does not support this thesis. Paragraph 1 presents the idea that McCarthyism represents an offshoot of Populism. Paragraph 2 describes the theories of Lipset and Feuer, who claim that McCarthyism drew its support from Populism's base in the agrarian Midwest and extended it to industrial workers. Paragraph 3 describes the case against this theory; according to Rogin, counties in Wisconsin that voted for Progressives did not vote for McCarthy. Paragraph 4 details Rogin's case against the ideas presented in the second paragraph—statistics show that industrialized workers did not in fact vote for McCarthy. The passage concludes by supporting the case against a linkage of McCarthyism with Populism.

21. D

This question covers the broad outline of the passage, so treat it as a Big Picture question and look to your purpose and main idea. Choice (D) best describes the author's attitude toward McCarthyism and Populism—although they were superficially similar, they were essentially dissimilar. Answer (A) contradicts the passage; it actually states the case against the author's views. Answer (B) is too harsh. The first paragraph does draw some parallels between both movements. Answer (C) is partly right, but partly wrong. Populism was, partially at least, a response to the conditions of farmers, but nowhere is it suggested that McCarthyism was a response to industrial conditions. The passage suggests quite the contrary: as described in the last paragraph, Rogin showed that McCarthyism had little support

from workers employed in industry. Answer (E) is out, as it's never suggested that McCarthyism has a progressive side. Only Populism is described (in the first sentence) as having both of these, a progressive and a darker side.

22. D

The substance of Rogin's criticism of Lipset, Feuer, and Shils is explained in the last two paragraphs. The second sentence of the third paragraph says what Rogin did: he "critically examined their assertions by the simple method of testing them against the evidence." This really tells you all you need to know to pick the right choice, (D). If you missed this, both of these last two paragraphs are spent describing how Rogin showed that grass roots voting patterns in both rural Wisconsin counties and more industrial Wisconsin counties failed to support the claims made by Lipset, Feuer, and Shils about who really did and didn't support McCarthy. What Rogin and the author are clearly suggesting is that Lipset, Feuer, and Shils failed to do their homework properly. (A) doesn't work, because Rogin never really quarrels with any descriptions of McCarthy. The quarrel is with the misrepresentation of lower-class voters and the real nature of Populism. Answer (B) doesn't work, since the passage never describes Rogin as disagreeing with the idea that McCarthyism is linked to anti-intellectualism. (C) is wrong since it seems that Lipset, Feuer, and Shils seemingly placed too little emphasis on the dual nature of Populism. They failed to perceive the continuity of the progressive aspects of Populism among voters in Wisconsin. And answer (E) is contradicted: Rogin was able to submit the conclusions of the three writers to a test—a devastating one—by taking a close look at the voting patterns in Wisconsin counties.

23. A

The stem is asking why Rogin studied the class character of Wisconsin voting patterns. Primarily, he did this to check to see if the voting patterns supported or contradicted the arguments of Lipset and Feuer. They argued that lower-class farmers and industrial workers provided crucial voter support for both Populism and McCarthyism, and Rogin performed his study of voting patterns in order to challenge their conclusions, by showing that lower-class farmers and workers in fact did not give their votes to McCarthy. Statement I reflects this. Statement II is wrong since Rogin was out to disprove the alleged links between Populism and McCarthyism, not explain them. Statement III is way beyond the scope of the passage.

24. A

In the last half of the second paragraph, the passage indicates that Lipset argued that lower-class support of McCarthy included urban industrial workers. The last paragraph describes the study in which Rogin found that voters in counties with high industrial employment tended to vote against McCarthy. Rogin used this study to support his counterassertion that McCarthy in fact did not enjoy extensive support among the lower-classes. Thus, an assumption made by both men is that voters among industrial workers can be classified as lower-class voters. This makes (B) a nonfactor as Rogin's overall thesis is to argue that lower-class voters voted more progressively than Lipset, Feuer, and Shils admit. (C) clearly isn't an assumption of Rogin's, who suggests something quite different: McCarthy lacked extensive support among lower classes. (D) is beyond the scope of the passage. There's not enough information to conclude that either scholar assumed this. (E) has no support, since neither Lipset nor Rogin is described in this passage as arguing that Midwestern voters are representative of more general political patterns among American voters.

25. B

This is a Detail question, and since it begins with "according to the passage," it will be a paraphrase of something that appears within it. Correct choice (B)

paraphrases the first sentence of the third paragraph and the concluding sentence of the passage. Rogin's overall charge against Lipset, Feuer, and Shils is that they not only reach faulty conclusions but are politically biased against the lower classes from the very beginning. It's this latter charge that's summed up in (B). Answer (A) goes too far. Rogin never charges deliberate falsification of evidence by the three men. (C) is out. Never does Rogin imply that the men's viewpoints will support attacks on civil liberties. (D) puts things backwards. It's Rogin who makes scrupulous use of statistical analysis. This is what Lipset, Feuer, and Shils failed to do. Finally, answer (E) is out since Rogin never suggests that the writings of Lipset, Feuer, and Shils were essentially anti-intellectual. Rogin might say that they are intellectually or professionally incompetent, since he believes their research methods lack credibility, but this choice distorts this idea.

26. E

For this Big Picture question, go to your purpose and main idea. The author's main purpose is to describe the criticism of the views on McCarthyism expressed in the second paragraph. The author states that these conclusions were not based on real evidence, and suggests that they were shaped by preconceived prejudices. These are flaws in historical methodology, (E). (A) uses the wrong verb. The author is not comparing the views; rather, he is supporting one particular view, that of Rogin. (B) goes for a detail: Rogin's research methods, and (C) distorts the author's point of view that the two movements were fundamentally dissimilar. (D) is out because, although the author would agree with it, it does not address the main point of the passage.

AC TRANSFORMER

This passage describes the origin and use of the AC transformer. In paragraphs 1 and 2, the author introduces the transformer and tells the reader about some of its far-reaching applications. Paragraph III introduces the reader to the first discoveries that led to the invention of a practical transformer. The fourth paragraph returns to the present day to explain how these early discoveries came to be the modern power grid. Paragraphs V and VI give a short history of the discovery of electromagnetic induction.

27. D

The first question is a Detail question, asking you to consider information directly from the passage. Easy enough. The passage says that Faraday "discovered the basic action of the transformer" in 1831 (lines 24–25). But note that it was not until 50 years later that a practical transformer was developed (lines 26–30). This means that the first practical transformer was developed in 1881.

28. B

Our first inference question of the bunch. Go to paragraph IV to research the answer. The paragraph lists several advances in the transformer in lines 35–39. This list is followed by the statement that the "advances reflect the marriage of theoretical inquiry and engineering that first elucidated and then exploited the phenomena governing transformer action" (lines 39–42). This makes (B) the best answer. (A) is unrelated to the question being asked, and its wording is too extreme in any case. (C) and (E), whereas possibly true, are not necessarily implied in the passage. And answer (D) is unsubstantiated.

29. C

A simple one. The answer to this Detail question is directly stated in the passage. "At the time, Oersted's discovery was considered remarkable, since electricity and magnetism were thought to be separate and unrelated forces" (lines 47–50). (C) is a nice paraphrase of this sentence. (A) is probably

true, but it has nothing to do with why Oersted's discovery was considered remarkable. (B) cannot be true because Faraday did his work much later than Oersted, and based his own work on that of Oersted. Answer (D) cannot be the correct choice because it directly contradicts the information in the passage, and (E) is a distortion: Faraday demonstrated how a magnetic field could generate current.

30. D

Here's a Vocabulary-in-Context question for you to solve. Based on the sentence in which it is found, and on the sentences just before and after it, *assumed* can best be interpreted as *taken*, or answer (D). Try to see it as a game of fill-in. Which of the choices would best replace the word in question given its context, i.e., "_____ a key role"? Choices (A), (B), (C), and (E) simply don't make sense given the gist of the paragraph.

31. A

In this EXCEPT/NOT type question, you, as an Advanced test taker, must remember that you are looking for the answer that is NOT correct. Referring directly to the passage for the answer, (A) can be found; it's a paraphrase of lines 28–29, which state that the first practical transformer "contain[ed] all the essential elements of the modern instrument." Likewise, (B) and (C) can both be located in the passage, in the discussion of the improvements in the transformer over the years (lines 35–39), and (E) is confirmed in lines 38–39: "efficiency typically exceeds 99 percent." The passage also confirms that (D) is NOT true: transformers today are said to be able to "handle…15 times the voltage" (lines 35–36) of earlier transformers, so (A) is the correct answer.

32. E

Another Detail question to dig up the answer to. Let's head back to the paragraph about the discovery by Oersted and look at lines 44–47. He "had shown in 1820 that an electric current flowing through a conducting material creates a magnetic field around the conductor," which is what (E) states. (A) contradicts direct information in the passage. (B) describes Faraday's later experiment, not that of Oersted, and (C) is too extreme, not to mention that it is not supported by information in the passage. (D), finally, is true of transformers, but is not stated as a direct result of Oersted's work.

33. A

Ah, the Detail questions keep coming! Here, the first paragraph provides the information about the transformer that we need. A transformer, it says, "can convert electricity with a low current and a high voltage into electricity with a high current and low voltage" (lines 2–5). The passage goes on to state that this "conversion is important because electric power is transmitted most efficiently at high voltages" (lines 6–8). This information supports (A) as the best answer. Answer (C) contradicts the passage, which says that without transformers, the distance between generators and consumers would have to be minimized, and (B), (D), and (E), true or not, are not addressed by the passage and therefore can be eliminated.

34. E

Now you're asked to take a step back and draw an inference, but as you know, on the SAT many so-called inferences are simply paraphrases of information found in the passage. The answer to this question can be found in the first sentence of the last paragraph. "Faraday demonstrated that in order for a magnetic field to induce a current in a conductor, the field must be changing" (lines 53–55). (E) is clearly the best answer. Of the wrong answers, (B), (C), and (D) are not true statements, as Oersted had nothing to do with the direct application of his findings and Faraday did not invent the practical transformer. Only (A) is left, and it is also

a misstatement; it's true about Oersted, not Faraday. Therefore, (E) is our best choice.

35. C

The answer to this Detail question lies in the last sentence of the first paragraph. Here, we are provided with keys to this question. "Were it not for transformers, the distance separating generators from consumers would have to be minimized" (lines 9–11). In other words, without transformers, generators would need to be built near consumers. Thus, (C) is our best answer choice. (A), whereas conceivable, is not addressed by the passage. (B) and (E) are both too speculative to be correct. There is no proof from what you've read to know for sure. (D), meanwhile, is an inference that seems to have no bearing on the information you've just read, so it's clearly not correct.

MAGDALEN COLLEGE

This narrative passage is an insightful look at one young man's struggles with growing up and his immature reaction to the outside world. Paragraph 1 quickly tells the reader about the narrator's background. Paragraph 2 speaks of the narrator's chosen life of misplaced radicalism and his camaraderie with other like-minded, would-be "existentialists." In Paragraph 3, the narrator begins to make statements of remorse and confronts his cynical and vacuous behavior. Paragraph 4 details the young man's rough exodus from school and into the real world.

36. B

So you start here with a classic Detail question asking you to go back and dig up a contextual meaning from a specific line or two. No problem. The phrase in question, "discipline in vogue" (line 12), refers, in the author's unsentimental and sarcastic tone, to his youthful and angry radical tendencies, described in the next paragraph. Thus, answer (B) is the best inference to make. While he may have also been emotionally chilly, (C) is not referenced by these words. Answers (A), (D), and (E) are all mentioned later in the piece, but not in conjunction with the phrase you have been asked about.

37. D

Back-to-back line-reference questions make life a little easier, as you know what to look for and where to look for it. The "fellow odd men" and the author, as mentioned in line 13, fancy themselves as existentialist anti-heroes. But the narrator's tone throughout this descriptive passage is far from flattering. So any of the answers that seem to imply his description is positive can be dismissed. Answers (A), (B), and (E), however true in theory, are not the intended description of the narrator and his "fellow odd men." And however unconventional they may have seemed, by the author's own admission, they were enlightened only in their own opinion, eliminating (C). Only (D) gives us a harsh, and accurate, summary description of the narrator's "ostentatious and shallow" group at Oxford.

38. D

Time to test your skills on an EXCEPT/NOT type of question. Always remember that these require you to find the correct answer choice, which, technically speaking, is the one incorrect response: the test maker understands that Advanced test takers need a good challenge. In this case, the question asks you to decide which of the five choices the narrator and his compatriots did NOT revolt against. As radicals, they made it their business to oppose all those things they saw as ordinary or expected. In lines 17–18, the narrator speaks of how they protested "those shabby duffle-coated last years of the forties." Thus, answer (A) is out. It's clear from the speaker's discussion of his boredom with "making a living" (lines 36–37) that career plans were not high on his list of priorities, so (B) is a no go as well. Finding his

revolutionary sentiments toward his father in this piece is easy enough, so clearly (C) is not the choice. One can infer from his bitter discussion with friends about the army (lines 44–45) that their attitude toward the military was one of disdain, so cancel answer (E). Only (D), academia, is something that the young wannabe intellectuals didn't protest.

39. B

Go back and check out lines 21–22 for the phrase in this line-reference question. "Less enlightened people" here isn't meant to be taken literally. It's clear from the narrator's tone that his feelings about himself and his friends in retrospect are certainly not positive. Saying that this phrase conveys a sense of disapproval, choice (A), is misleading because the phrase is intended sarcastically. Similarly, the speaker is certainly not sympathetic or nostalgic for his former self, so (C) and (E) can also be eliminated. Finally, while he may be remorseful about his actions and attitudes at the time, the narrator is not addressing that emotion in this phrase. The narrator means the phrase as a reflection of the poor attitudes he and his comrades showed—in contrast to "less enlightened people"—in those days. The phrase is a good example of irony, or (B).

40. C

Be careful with Detail questions like these. One of the young narrator's radical pastimes is trying to live the life of a character in the French existentialist novels, stories in which metaphor and symbolism play a major role. Certainly, therefore, answer (A) is incorrect, as he expressly states that the boys were mistaken in trying to take the books literally. While the books are metaphorically driven, they are not fantasy (B); nor are they classic works of tragedy (D) or heroism (E). The passage does state in lines 23–28 that the stories were not intended realistically, but rather metaphorically—i.e., they were meant to be read as allegories (C).

41. E

Here's another EXCEPT question, so let's research the passage and see what we can eliminate. In this passage, the narrator makes many claims about what he learned or did not learn in terms of knowledge and experience. He notes in line 32 that he had acquired "expensive habits" (A), and in lines 33–34 he says that he acquired a "first-class illusion: that I was a poet," which gets rid of (D), a sense of being gifted. In addition, he expresses in line 38 that he had a "cynicism" (B). In the discussion of Socratic honesty (line 42), it's noted that the narrator did acquire one useful thing: a capacity for self-awareness (C). The only one of the choices that is not found in the passage is any sense that he acquired a "foundation for success." In fact, the final paragraph implies that the idea of success was nearly impossible given his attitude. Since this is a question that asks for the one that doesn't belong, the correct choice is (E).

42. C

Finally, a Vocabulary-in-Context question! Okay, so whether or not you share our enthusiasm for vocabulary, here's a good example of one type of question you're bound to see in the CR section of the SAT. In line 32, the narrator says he acquired "affected" manners. It's clear from the passage that the narrator's attitude was shallow and his motivation self-serving; therefore the idea of his being (B), *concerned* or (D), *changed*, is questionable. Here, the speaker is referring to his effete mannerisms. Answers (A), *influenced*, and (E), *infectious*, don't apply to this specific quote. Only (C), *pretentious*, fits the bill. And it fits quite well, by all accounts.

43. A

This Inference question asks you to consider a very specific part of the passage in which the narrator refers to his heated discussion of the army (lines 44–45). You can see that he says he was "outrageously bitter." But look closer and you'll see that he admits a few lines later he "was not a cynic by nature; only by revolt," hinting that he has since realized that his beliefs were as much a response to his surroundings and his rebellion against his father as any sort of deep and profound convictions. So bearing these statements in mind, one can see that (A) makes the most sense. Answer (B) is unlikely, because his friends appeared to be cut from much the same cloth. (C), whereas conceivable, was not discussed in the passage and therefore is too speculative to be a correct answer here. (D) is directly refuted by the statement that his cynicism was not "by nature," and (E) is totally unrelated to the question.

44. D

Another EXCEPT/NOT question for you. We can infer a lot about the father of the narrator regarding his personality and his relationship with his angry son both before and after his death. From the opening paragraph, it is abundantly clear that the narrator, whether because of his age or despite it, had a strained relationship with his family. It's mentioned that he "hardly saw" his family, and later that he was revolting against "what I hated" (lines 50–51). From these statements, it's safe to say that the father and son were not close emotionally and that they had vastly different views on the world. Thus, you can dismiss (A) and (C) as incorrect answers, if only because the narrator speaks directly to the contrary. As for (B), see line 58 where the narrator notes that his father "liked to be popular" and spent a great deal of time and money entertaining his friends and supposed comrades. Finally, there is no doubt from the narrator's discussion of the contentious relationship between himself and his father (both when alive and deceased) that the father had a strong effect on his son's belief system. Because the question is asking you to find the one answer that doesn't belong, the only answer remaining is (D).

Nowhere in the passage is it discussed that the father is a misanthrope. If anything, he sounded like a fairly jovial sort.

45. E

Here's another Vocabulary-in-Context question. Read carefully the final lines of the passage to find the best possible meaning for the word *transpierceable*. When you see the word *pierce* as part of the larger word, your first instinct might be to guess that it refers to a penetrating act. But look at the context again: if something is considered "transpierceable at a glance" (line 65), it's safe to say that the implication is of a sudden or fleeting moment. Thus, easy to understand (C) and easy to penetrate (A) are not really what you're looking for. (D) is easy to eliminate if you read the final lines of the passage as well. The last words are "successful at none"; this hardly conveys a sense that any success came easily to the narrator. Of the other choices remaining, only (E) makes sense; *transpierceable* here refers to a series of choices that were easy for the flippant and naïve young narrator to dismiss.

46. A

Here's a great example of a typical Big Picture question. The test makers ask you to glean from the various parts of the text what traits are shared by the two main characters. Examining all the evidence in this case isn't enough. What happens if you aren't sure whether you understand the meaning of all the answer choices given? No worries. Start by eliminating the answers that you do know. From the text, which by now you must know nearly by heart, you can safely say that the father and the narrator shared little in the way of obvious outward personality traits. If the father had bonhomie, or good cheer, the son had extreme cynicism, and never the two shall meet. Thus, answers (B) and (D) pretty much cancel each other out. As to whether

the young man and his father shared a sense of the unconventional, one can infer from the passage that the father found refuge in the sort of ordinary existence that his son sought to eschew. So it's fairly safe to say that (C) isn't a shared trait either. Finally, there is no mention made of the father's sense of self-doubt, and since the question asks you to consider the answers in light of the passage you've read, you can eliminate (E). Thus, your best choice seems to lie in answer (A), *prodigality*, meaning reckless extravagance. The father's lack of "Financial Prudence" (lines 54–55) and the son's "expensive habits" (line 32) both fit this definition.

47. B

Now here's a classic Big Picture question. The final question in this section asks you to consider the overall purpose of the passage. A tough task for many, but not for Advanced test takers! Take a step back and consider the tone, content, and meaning, also taking into account the work you've done analyzing the passage in the questions preceding this one. While the passage certainly heads in any of several directions, note that the question asks you to name which purpose the passage seems to "mainly" serve. So answer choices such as a "postwar sensibility" (A) or a "bohemian element" (D), while aspects of the passage, do not really satisfy the needs of the question. Similarly, (E) seems too narrow a focus, as the passage's discussion of the narrator's difficulties in finding work come in only toward the end. That leaves you with two choices. Of the two, (C) comes off as too harsh and extreme. There is little in the way of true condemnation here. Only (B) really approaches all aspects of the passage, especially given the hardships that the young man faces once he is distanced from his family. The narrator is asking the reader to understand his youthful indiscretions as just that, youthful.

LEONARDO

Passage 1

The author here examines the difference between Leonardo da Vinci's brilliance as an artist and his deficiencies as a serious scientist. Paragraph 1 begins by examining the author's perception that Leonardo's artistic sensibilities led him to expect a perfection that he could not bring to science or engineering and that this led to an inconsistency in focus. Paragraph 2 provides examples of Leonardo's penchant for the impractical solution and how he understood the difference between his art and his engineering. Paragraph 3 details Leonardo's fertile if unfocused attention to detail, while Paragraph 4 summarizes and concludes with a statement that it was Leonardo's unsystematic approach to science that made him an artist with scientific interests rather than a true scientist.

Passage 2

This passage focuses on Leonardo da Vinci's prowess as an engineer and mechanical wizard. Paragraph 1 quickly rebuffs the idea that some biographers seem to have that Leonardo wasted his talent dabbling in science. Paragraph 2 conveys the author's feeling that Leonardo's greatest accomplishment may have been his realizations about power and muscle. Paragraphs 3 and 4 offer detailed examples of Leonardo's unique approach to problem solving and engineering. Paragraph 5 summarizes the author's view that Leonardo's engineering feats are misunderstood precisely because they are so revolutionary.

48. A

This first question asks you to consider the author's intent in regards to Leonardo's engineering projects in Passage 1. The best way to attack this question is to return to the paragraphs that discuss Leonardo and engineering. The test makers will, in the

Paired passages sets, try to get you to confuse the two passages. Answer (B) is a good example of this, as the subject of energy sources is addressed in Passage 2, not Passage 1. (C), regarding "divine demeanor," is a reference to a specific and unrelated part of Passage 1 and can therefore be dismissed as a possible answer. There is no proof given in either passage that (D) is a viable answer. While Leonardo certainly felt compelled to pursue his art, and while both authors acknowledge his preeminence among his peers in the fields of science and engineering, there is no discussion that he preferred doing his art. Similarly, (E) may seem feasible. But looking at lines 5–8 of the first paragraph, we see that the author notes that Leonardo perhaps did not bring the same perfectionism to his engineering tasks because he, "as one conversant with the perfection of art, and knowing the futility of trying to bring such perfection to the realm of practical application," did not feel the need to devote himself in the same way to completion, and therefore, to perfection. You can see that answer (A) nicely sums this up for you.

49. D

Here's the first EXCEPT/NOT question in this set of questions. To find the correct answer here, look back at the specifics of Passage 1, most notably any section in which the author discusses Leonardo's failures in scientific inquiry. In Paragraph 1, lines 4–5, he states that Leonardo was "hindered by the fact that he was ... an artist," answer (A). In line 31, the author says it was Leonardo's "mental restlessness" that proved "problematic," summing up answer (B). The bronze statue example given in Paragraph 2 is a solid example of the author's sentiments regarding Leonardo's penchant for impractical solutions, (C). Answer (E) can be seen in the very end of the passage, where Leonardo is noted for his unwillingness to use a "systematic body of knowledge," something this author feels true scientific discovery requires. So you're left with only answer (D), which the author discusses in lines 51–52; "a compulsion with observation and problem-solving" is not a hindrance to a scientist. Thus, given that you're looking for the one that does NOT belong, (D) is here the correct response.

50. B

A good chance to test your mettle on a Detail question. Go back to the section of Passage 1 regarding Leonardo and the *Last Supper*, namely the second half of Paragraph 2. At this point, the author has already discussed Leonardo's failure to see his scientific tasks through to their conclusion. Here, the point is that Leonardo's inability to finish the head of Jesus in the painting was forgivable because the rest of the piece was "still worthy" (line 26) of praise as a work of art. Answer (A) is from the wrong part of the passage. Whether Leonardo did or did not leave other works of art unfinished isn't the issue. Discussion of Leonardo's feelings on the divinity of his artistic subjects, answer (C), is discussed in the passage, but here it isn't the reason that the author chooses to bring up the subject of the *Last Supper*. Beware details that may be applicable but are not necessarily linked to the question at hand. (D) is a nebulous answer that is certainly at play but cannot be found in the discussion here in Paragraph 2, and (E) isn't a major part of this discussion at all, either. Only choice (B) correctly answers the question.

51. C

This *tone* question offers you an interesting mix of detail and inference. On the one hand, you are given a specific line to analyze. On the other, you are asked to infer the author's *tone*. Taken in context, you can figure out that the author doesn't mean the phrase in question, "he turned his mind to the natural world" (line 33), in an ironic way. Nor is his tone throughout the piece in any way indifferent, awed, or disillusioned. Clearly, he or she has a definite goal in writing this line and the passage

in general. Looking back at what you've read and answered about this passage, what can you say about the author's intent and tone? It's easy to see that the author is fairly critical of Leonardo's effectiveness as a scientist, observer of nature, and engineer. Thus, (C) seems the likeliest interpretation.

52. C

Ah, a Vocabulary-in-Context question to decipher. Don't you just love these? You probably know what the word *suggested* means already, even in its various forms. So looking closely at the way it's used here, you should be able to quickly figure this one out. Lines 41–44 say that it's Leonardo's intellectual genius that "has suggested to many that [he] can and should be regarded as one of the originators of modern science." You could try to predict a replacement word, or you could perform a simple fill-in-the-blank with the prospective answers. Neither answer (A), *recommended*, nor (B), *mentioned*, work. The same goes for (D), *insinuated*. None of these really captures the fact that many *do* consider Leonardo as one of the forefathers of modern science. (E), *resembled*, simply makes no sense in this context. Here, the author means the word *suggested* to mean *indicated*, (C).

53. E

Inference time! You are asked to infer the author's impressions of Leonardo's principles of science, the *pensieri* he included in his Codici. The writer implies that Leonardo's words have been "pulled out" of his writing. So he doesn't believe Leonardo meant to use the *pensieri* as proof of his scientific faculties. Only others have done this. Answer (A) implies that Leonardo had some doing in creating his reputation as a scientist. Answer (B) is a recapitulation of an argument that permeates this essay, but one which in this case does not apply to the Codici. Both (C) and (D) represent ideas that the passage does not discuss. The only mention of the Codici is in reference to Leonardo's scientific knowledge, and there is no discussion of the contents of the *pensieri*. The only thing that you do know about the author's feelings on the *pensieri* is that he or she believes they are falsely held up as proof of Leonardo's scientific acumen. It is the author's view that Leonardo did not display a systematic approach to science. Answer (E) neatly sums up this argument.

54. C

The first question related to Passage 2 asks you to consider the author's intentions in mentioning outside sources. Read over the passage's opening paragraph again. Clues to the author's intent are everywhere. There is no implication that the author questions Leonardo's artistic prowess, answer (A). Nor is there any validity to the claim in (B) that the author wishes to acknowledge Leonardo had a problem with his engineering feats. On the contrary, it is the author's aim to show that it is a too widely held belief that Leonardo's engineering contributions were second to his artistic ones. While Leonardo may have had prodigal talents, this answer makes no sense in regards to this particular passage. (E) is simply too harsh in its wording, as the author has no particular beef with the biographers, and certainly not enough to accuse them of bias. Answer (C) is the most accurate, especially if you take into account the writer's use of the words *waste* and *lowly* to describe, sarcastically, the biographer's perceptions.

55. D

This Detail question requires you to take a look at Paragraph 3 of Passage 2. Leonardo's ability to design machinery was not for pure fancy, this author seems to imply. It was utilitarian. On steep terrain, the weight and bulk of the earth that needed to be excavated and transported would "nullify the effort of the animal" that was trying to haul it away. (D) is the correct answer and is easily found in reexamining the text. Answer (A) is too simplistic,

because the excavated material had only to be moved mechanically to increase productivity. While answers (B) and (C) may have been true to some extent, they are not here mentioned by the author as reasons for why Leonardo abandoned the use of wheeled carts. Answer (E) can be dismissed entirely as it has no bearing on the passage you've just read.

56. B

This EXCEPT/NOT question wants you to find the one statement that the author of Passage 2 would not agree with. Quickly check for some direct statements in the passage that give you proof of what the author *does* think about these statements. He states in lines 103–104 that "many scholars" still believe that Leonardo's scientific exploits were "isolated" incidents of achievement. Answer (A) is, therefore, easily dismissed. In lines 94–96, the author notes that Leonardo did not invent the external treadmill. This statement certainly seems to directly refute answer (B). Quickly looking at the remaining answer choices, answer (C) is proven true by the opening few lines of the passage while (D) and (E) are nearly word-for-word statements found in the text; (D) in line 75 when his work with sound engineering principles is called "revolutionary," and (E) in the final line of the passage. Since you want to find what the author does *not* agree with, (B) is the best and only answer.

57. A

To solve this Vocabulary-in-Context question, let's head back to the final paragraph, where the word in question rests. From the sentence from which *isolated* is taken, you can tell that the author is using it in reference not to his or her own opinion, but to show that there are "many scholars" that believe that Leonardo's scientific accomplishments were not connected to the greater development of modern engineering, but rather were the *isolated* musings of an artistic genius. You might even have predicted that a good replacement word would mean "not connected"—as in the correct answer choice *disconnected* (A). In any case, you should be able to weed out a few which don't fit this tone and intent. Answer (B), *inaccessible*, and answer (E), *unique*, don't really fit with this close reading. Meanwhile, (C), *remote*, is off-kilter; despite whatever feelings the "scholars" have about why Leonardo did what he did, they don't seem to feel his work was *remote*, or for that matter, *lonely* (D). Therefore, choice (A) is your only choice.

58. E

Ah, finally a chance to test your abilities of interpretation across the two passages. Bet you couldn't wait for that one! You'll ace it if you take a really quick look at the paragraph in question and then think back to all the analysis you did in answering all the questions about Passage 1. The paragraph in question refers to Leonardo's problem solving in excavating the canals, a problem he solved by creating a design for a mechanical solution. But the author of Passage 1 pointed toward Leonardo's penchant for creating complex designs to solve what could be seen as much simpler problems. The author's fairly critical tone regarding Leonardo's engineering feats would probably make the first answer choice wrong. No way would Passage 1's author agree with (A) or (B), if only because it was the author's contention that Leonardo's designs maximized effort and that he rarely completed such projects. Similarly, answer (C) has a fairly positive slant, and thus can be disregarded in favor of a more critical response. Of the remaining two choices, (D) can't be corroborated, given the amount of time Leonardo spent on this particular project. Answer (E) is most consistent in tone and focus to Passage 1, and is therefore correct.

59. D

This Big Picture inference question also pits Passage 1's author against the author of Passage 2. This time,

the goal is to figure consensus. Take a look at each answer and think about what each author had to say and, more importantly, how he or she said it. Answer (A), for example, fits the focus of Passage 1, but most definitely not Passage 2. Same thing with answer (B). (C), on the other hand, accords with what author 2 has to say (see lines 73–75), but runs contrary to author 1's central thesis. (E) again fits author 1's thesis, but not that of author 2. Only (D) really cuts across both authors' seemingly disparate arguments. Author 1 concedes Leonardo's natural genius as an engineer in his second sentence ("As a scientist and engineer, his gifts were unparalleled"), and author 2 states the same in the concluding sentence ("…Leonardo was one of our earliest and most significant engineers").

60. E

Given the tone and content of Passage 2—which by now you are no doubt very comfortable with—you should be able to make a strong case for Leonardo's scientific achievements and address any objections from the author of Passage 1. (A) regards applied mechanics, a field into which Passage 1's author does not delve specifically. (B) does not adequately refute Passage 1's basic tenet, which is that Leonardo spread himself too thin when solving engineering problems. Answers (C) and (D), even if directly stated in Passage 2, don't really counter Passage 1's assessment of Leonardo's work. Only (E) deals directly with author 1's claim that Leonardo da Vinci did not possess sound methodology when executing scientific and engineering work. To the author of Passage 2, Leonardo's work on the canal problem is a shining example of his sound approach to engineering.

CHAPTER 6: THE SENTENCE COMPLETION CHALLENGE

- Practice the Four-Step Method for Sentence Completions.

- Learn the four categories of Sentence Completion questions.

- Find out what makes hard Sentence Completions hard.

If you're reading this book, most Sentence Completion questions are probably easy for you. In fact, you may not even have to think about how to fill in the blank; the answer is just there, staring you in the face, and all of the other choices seem absurd. That's great news, and it means that you'll have no problem getting a good score. But wait . . . you want a great score, right? Flying through the easy short verbal questions is important, but it's not going to get you a 2400. In order to ace the hard questions, you'll need to backtrack a little bit and figure out what's going on in your brain when you answer the easy ones. Knowing which strategies work for you on the easy questions is the quickest path to nailing the tough ones.

Let's slow things down for a minute and think about how you find the answer to an easy Sentence Completion.

BLATANTLY EASY SENTENCE COMPLETION

Despite getting a good night's sleep, Dennis was extremely _____ at work the next day.

Okay, so you read that sentence, then automatically filled in the blank. Right now you're flipping to the Grid-Ins section of the book, your intelligence gravely insulted. Come back! This really won't take long.

INSIDE YOUR BRAIN

"Despite *(Ding ding ding! That's a clue that something contradictory is about to happen.)* getting a good night's sleep *(lucky son-of-a-gun—wish I got a good night's sleep),* Dennis was extremely . . . *(What? tired? lethargic? perky? No, not perky, because of the word* despite. *Tired sounds good.)* at work the next day."

If your thought process was anything like this, you're on your way to that 2400. In a few split seconds, you read the sentence for clues (Step 1) and predicted an answer (Step 2).

> An Advanced test taker makes a prediction for the blank based on clues in the sentence.

On the SAT, every Sentence Completion must contain clues that lead directly to the correct answer. Finding those clues will get you points. Once you've spotted the clues in the sentence, the next step is to predict what word would fit in the blank. As you saw in the sentence above, your mind usually does this automatically. Our minds don't like to see incomplete sentences, so we rush to stick words into blanks—it's human nature. With practice, you'll learn to trust your predictions and make the right choices.

However, unlike those Grid-Ins that you're so eager to get to, Sentence Completions have answer choices for you to deal with. Let's finish this question.

BLATANTLY EASY SENTENCE COMPLETION

Despite getting a good night's sleep, Dennis was extremely _____ at work the next day.

(A) energetic
(B) fatigued
(C) motivated
(D) quixotic
(E) fractured

INSIDE YOUR BRAIN

"*Okay, which word means* tired? Fatigued *is good. Nothing else means* tired. Despite getting a good night's sleep, Dennis was extremely fatigued at work the next day. *Works for me. Choice (B) it is.*"

You just completed Steps 3 and 4: you scanned the answer choices for a match and read your selected answer choice back into the sentence.

This may seem elementary, but if you use these steps on every Sentence Completion, every time, you'll avoid careless errors on the easy questions, and you'll have a solid foundation for tackling the tough ones.

Step 1: Read the sentence for clues.

Step 2: Predict an answer.

Step 3: Scan the answer choices for a match.

Step 4: Read your selected answer choice back into the sentence.

WHAT MAKES HARD SENTENCE COMPLETION QUESTIONS HARD?

Just what is it that makes a tough question tough? There are four major categories of hard Sentence Completions. In this section, we'll introduce you to each potential problem area and talk you through four tough questions.

LONG SENTENCES

Some tough Sentence Completions will have you wondering whether you've accidentally turned the page and plunged into the Critical Reading section. These monsters look more like short passages than long sentences, and those gaping holes in the middle don't help.

Let's look at a long, tough Sentence Completion and see how we can break it down.

1. The Wankel Rotary Engine was an engineering marvel that substantially reduced automobile emissions, but because it was less fuel-efficient than the standard piston-cylinder engine, it was _____ in the early 1970s when _____ pollution gave way to panic over fuel shortages.

    (A) needed . . disillusionment with
    (B) conceived . . awareness of
    (C) modified . . opinion on
    (D) abandoned . . preoccupation with
    (E) discarded . . interest in

Whew. Between the capital letters, the hyphenated words, and the sheer length of the darned thing, this sentence is quite a mouthful. You'll certainly run into long sentences like this one toward the end of your Sentence Completions.

> An Advanced test taker tackles the easier blank first on two-blank Sentence Completions.

Your first task, as with easy questions, is to read the sentence, looking for clues. Let's go phrase by phrase.

The Wankel Rotary Engine was an engineering marvel that substantially reduced automobile emissions . . .

Try putting this into your own words.

IN YOUR BRAIN

"The engine was a marvel that reduced pollution."

And now the next section:

… but because it was less fuel-efficient than the standard piston-cylinder engine …

Here, you're given a crucial clue: *but because. But* tells you that the second part of the sentence will contrast with the first, and *because* tells you that an explanation is coming. In this section, we learn that the engine was less fuel-efficient than the standard engine. Put together, we know so far that the engine reduced pollution, but it wasn't fuel-efficient.

… it was _____ in the early 1970s when _____ pollution gave way to panic over fuel shortages.

Now we've got two blanks staring at us. Something happened in the early '70s when something about pollution gave way to fuel shortage panic.

A good prephrasing would be: the engine was *rejected or changed* in the 1970s, when *concern with* pollution gave way to panic over fuel shortages.

Now we can turn to the choices.

    (A) needed . . disillusionment with
    (B) conceived . . awareness of
    (C) modified . . opinion on
    (D) abandoned . . preoccupation with
    (E) discarded . . interest in

The first blank may seem the easier of the two to tackle, so we'll start there. Choices (C), (D), and (E) all look good. Moving to the second blank, (C) doesn't look so great. *Opinion on*, the second phrase in (C), is probably wrong, since *opinion* doesn't carry the strong feeling that would induce "panic." In (D), if a *preoccupation with* pollution gave way to panic over fuel shortages, it would explain why the engine was no longer valued. This looks like the best answer, but let's check (E) to be sure. The second word in (E) doesn't fit well in the context. A mere loss of *interest in* pollution wouldn't explain why this marvelous engine was abandoned. (D) is our best choice.

HARD VOCABULARY

You may come across one or two Sentence Completions that are Greek to you. Either the sentence or the choices will contain words that are completely unfamiliar to you, and you'll wonder how you can possibly complete a sentence that you don't even understand.

STRATEGY TIP

For any two-blank sentence, you should do the easier blank first. You can eliminate wrong choices, leaving less work for you to do with the harder blank.

STRATEGY HIGHLIGHT: LONG SENTENCES

That was a long, sticky sentence, but we handled it the same way that we handled the blatantly easy sentence, by reading the sentence, looking for clues, prephrasing, and finding the right answer. We also supplemented the basic approach with paraphrasing, a technique that we'll discuss in more detail in the next chapter.were too specific or outside the scope of the passage.

Here's an example that's chock-full of tough words:

> While the price of _____ has often been a high one, never before, it seems, has the press been so intent on _____ the lives of celebrities.

    (A) turpitude . . expunging

    (B) notoriety . . surveying

    (C) infamy . . determining

    (D) idiosyncrasy . . espousing

    (E) testimonial . . purging

This is the type of sentence that might look like a nice relief at the end of a long Sentence Completion section. It's short, it's clear, and the longest word is *celebrities*, a word everyone knows. But then you sneak a look at the choices and . . . wham! It must be a hard question after all, because you have no idea what half the words in the choices mean.

What should you do? Forget that you even looked at the choices, and proceed as you would for an easy question.

An Advanced test taker uses prephrasing to help with tough answer choices.

The "lives of celebrities" are the topic here, and the first word that probably leaps to mind for the first blank is *fame*. "The price of fame?" you may be thinking. "What a cliché. If I used that phrase in an essay, my English teacher would kick me out of class." That's probably true, but on SAT Sentence Completions, clichés can be trustworthy tools to help you make predictions.

Moving to the second blank, we can guess that it will be something like "writing about" or "exposing" the lives of celebrities. After all, that's what the press does.

So we get the sentence, we've got a strong prephrase, and it's time to tackle the choices.

(A) *Turpitude*? Does the phrase "moral turpitude" sounds familiar? You may get a serious negative feeling about this word, since it doesn't sound too pleasant. Not sure? How about the second word, *expunging*? You know that the prefix *ex* means "out"; this word probably doesn't mean anything like our prediction "writing about." Let's move on.

(B) *Notoriety*. If you don't know this word, think of *notorious*. Yup, that has something to do with fame. It's a keeper for now.

STRATEGY HIGHLIGHT: HARD VOCABULARY

Being able to understand a sentence and make good predictions will help you when you find tough vocabulary in the answer choices. In the explanation for this question, we talked a little bit about using Word Charge to help you with difficult vocabulary. We'll talk more about this strategy in the next chapter.beyond the scope of the passage.

(C) *Infamy*. The word has *fame* right in it, so we may be on the right track.

(D) *Idiosyncrasy*. Even if you don't know exactly how to define this word, you may know that it has a general meaning of being odd or offbeat. It doesn't click with *fame*.

(E) *Testimonial*. You might think of a "testimonial dinner" as something that a famous person might have, but *testimonial* doesn't mean fame.

> An Advanced test taker tries to get a fix on unfamiliar words by looking for familiar word roots and prefixes, or thinking about where he could have possibly heard the word before.

We're down to (B) and (C). *Surveying* sounds good and matches our prediction of "writing about." As for (C), does the press *determine* the lives of celebrities? No, that can't be right. (B) is correct.

SUBTLE STRUCTURAL CLUES

As you learned in the introduction to this chapter, clues are your friends. They are the fingerprints, the scraps of cloth left behind in the getaway car, that will help you solve the Mystery of the Empty Blank. However, some tough sentence completions will have subtle or ambiguous clues that may baffle you or even lead you down the path to an incorrect deduction.

Take a look at this example:

> Influenced by the years he spent growing up in a household filled with strife, the author often sought out acquaintances who demonstrated _____ for argument and showed a veritable _____ consensus.
>
> (A) a penchant . . reverence for
> (B) an animosity . . veneration of
> (C) a distaste . . disrelish for
> (D) an aptitude . . zeal for
> (E) a disdain . . contempt of

There are no ifs, ands, or buts in this sentence. (Okay, there's one *and*.) No clear, helpful structural clues jump out at us. On top of it all, there are a few tough words to deal with in the sentence.

First, let's see what we can do to make the sentence clearer. The author grew up in a household filled with strife, or conflict. This influenced him to seek friends who felt some way about *argument* and did something with *consensus*. You might guess that growing up in a strife-filled house would make him desire peaceful friends, but on the other hand, he might want friends who reminded him of his childhood.

The best clue you have in this sentence is that little word *and*. The *and* tells you that the two blanks will have opposite word charges. Why? Because *argument* and *consensus* are opposites, and the author's friends would either demonstrate a liking of argument and a dislike of consensus, or a dislike of argument and a liking of consensus.

That's as far as we can go with the sentence, so let's attack the answer choices.

In (A), we find two positive words. A *penchant* is a liking for something. (B) has *animosity*, a negative word, coupled with *veneration*, a positive word. So far, so good. Let's check the other choices. (C) is easy to eliminate, since these two *dis-* words are both negative. In (D), *aptitude* and *zeal* are both positive, and in (E), *disdain* and *contempt* are both negative. (B) is the only one that fits our prediction, and it's correct.

> An Advanced test taker knows how to recognize and use subtle structural clues to decode tough sentences.

UNPREDICTABLE TWO-BLANKERS

So far, we've looked at three tough two-blank sentences. In general, however, two-blank sentences aren't harder than one-blankers. In fact, many two-blank sentences fall into the easy category, because you have twice as many opportunities to zero in on the correct answer.

Two-blank sentences can seem tough, however, when you can't make a good prediction for either of the blanks. When this happens, as we saw in the previous example, you need to examine the relationship between the blanks.

STRATEGY HIGHLIGHT: SUBTLE STRUCTURAL CLUES

As we worked through this tough Sentence Completion, we discovered that even the most subtle structural clues can help to decode a sentence. We paraphrased in order to make the sentence clearer. We also used word charge to help with the answer choices. You'll learn more about both of these strategies in the next chapter.

Here's an example:

Considering the _____ era in which the novel was written, its tone and theme are remarkably _____ .

(A) enlightened . . disenchanted

(B) scholarly . . undramatic

(C) superstitious . . medieval

(D) permissive . . puritanical

(E) undistinguished . . commonplace

Sometimes Sentence Completions can feel like MadLibs™. In this sentence, it seems that you could just fill in (adjective)/(adjective) and the sentence would take on any meaning you wanted. Prephrasing won't do us much good here, so what can we do?

Following our standard method, let's look for clues. Two words are especially important here: *considering* at the beginning of the sentence and *remarkably* before the second blank. Thinking about how these words are typically used, we can determine that the two blank words will be opposites of each other.

With that in mind, we can go to the choices. (A) and (B) won't work because there's no specific relationship, opposite or otherwise, between *enlightened* and *disenchanted*, nor between *scholarly* and *undramatic*. (C) and (E) are out because in both of them, the words are closely related, not opposites of one another. (D) looks good: *permissive* and *puritanical* are direct opposites, making (D) our answer.

An Advanced test taker tries to determine the relationship between the blanks—i.e., whether the missing words are closely related or more like opposites—when it's impossible to make a good prediction for either blank.

CHAPTER 7: STRATEGIES FOR TOUGH SENTENCE COMPLETIONS

- Focus on the strategies of using the clues, paraphrasing, word charge, and working backward.

- Practice the strategies on the tough questions.

- Tackle long sentences, hard vocabulary, subtle sentence structure, and two-blank Sentence Completions.

Sure, the tough Sentence Completions that we looked at in the last chapter didn't seem so bad when we went through them step-by-step. But unfortunately, we won't be there with you on test day, so you're going to need some strategies to take with you. The following strategies tend to work very well for high-scoring students on hard questions. Learn them well, and they will be there to bail you out on the very hardest Sentence Completions.

In this chapter, you'll see more examples of our four categories of hard questions. Watch out for them, and read the explanations carefully.

USING THE CLUES: ADVANCED DETECTIVE WORK

As a top scorer, you probably use clues without thinking very much about it. Like Sherlock Holmes, you walk into your room and know that your little brother has been there by the trail of cookie crumbs leading to the computer.

We mentioned clues in the previous chapter, but now it's time to learn how to really put structural clues to work for you on the toughest questions. As you learned in the last chapter, clues on tough SAT Sentence Completions can be subtle, but they're often the best tools you've got for cracking the case.

Here's an example of a medium-difficulty Sentence Completion. Find the clues, and solve the case.

> An Advanced test taker recognizes that harder questions tend to have subtle clues that require careful reading.

1. Because she has often been regarded as an author of entertaining light fiction, critics were struck by the _____ of her latest novel.

   (A) somberness
   (B) jocularity
   (C) popularity
   (D) brevity
   (E) implausibility

Why Is It Hard? Subtle structural clues

Key Strategy: Using the clues

Here's a classic example of tricky clues on a not-so-hard question. You're sweeping along, filling in bubbles at a record pace. You see the obvious clue *because*. You read the rest of the clause, "she has often been regarded as an author of entertaining light fiction." You skip to the choices, pick (B), *jocularity*, the first choice that seems to go with "entertaining light fiction," and you move on. And you get the question wrong.

Yes, *because* is an important clue, but the fact that critics were "struck" by the tone of the author's latest novel indicates that the missing word contrasts with the phrase, "entertaining light fiction." A good prediction for the missing word would be *seriousness*. Only (A), *somberness*, matches that prediction.

Let's try a tougher one.

2. An ancient and mythopoeic neurological disorder, epilepsy is _____ in part by the sensation of intense and altered consciousness doctors call an "aura," which _____ the epileptic seconds before his seizure.

   (A) neutralized . . overcomes
   (B) characterized . . grips
   (C) obviated . . afflicts
   (D) enhanced . . debilitates
   (E) diagnosed . . proselytizes

Why Is It Hard? Subtle structural clues, tough vocabulary

Key Strategy: Using the clues

Okay, first of all, stop scanning your brain-dictionary for *mythopoeic*. It means "giving rise to myths," but its meaning isn't very important. In fact, you can ignore the entire first clause and focus on the blanks.

Doctors have connected this "aura" with epilepsy in some way. By taking apart this clause, we see that the word in the first blank must show this connection: epilepsy is discovered or diagnosed or accompanied by the aura. Looking at the second blank, we see that the aura has some effect on the epileptic before the seizure.

There are no stop, go, or yield signs in this sentence, yet we managed to squeeze some clues out of the dense text. Now try your prediction against the choices.

As always, you should start with the easier blank. The second blank is probably the easier place to start, but all the choices look good except for choice (E), *proselytizes*. Moving to the first blank, only (B), *characterized*, fits our prediction and is correct.

PARAPHRASING

Paraphrasing is one of the most important tools you can use to attack tough Sentence Completions. Putting difficult text into your own words probably comes easy to you. In fact, you probably do it without even realizing it. Still, practicing your paraphrasing skills now will help your speed and accuracy on test day.

> An Advanced test taker practices paraphrasing skills to help decode difficult text.

Read through the sentences below and come up with a paraphrase of your own.

> In addition to the large monetary resources allocated to the project, _____ manpower assets were made available to its director.

> Cinema's focus on the cruelty and decadence of rulers such as Nero and Caligula has led to the popular image of a Roman Emperor as being the very personification of _____ .

Here's what we came up with:

> *In addition to a lot of money, a lot of men were made available to the project.*

> *Cinema focuses on really bad rulers, so people think that the typical Roman emperor was really bad.*

Pretty easy? Let's put this strategy into practice answering a question.

3. The Victorian novel, notable for its detailed examination of the psychology of its characters, reached its _____ with the works of George Eliot, which are unmatched in their ability to delineate characters who harmonize devotion to everyday duties with the full development of inner lives.

   (A) dissolution
   (B) advent
   (C) conclusion
   (D) apex
   (E) intention

Why Is It Hard? Long sentence, tough vocabulary

Key Strategy: Paraphrasing

Paraphrasing this bloated sentence is mostly a matter of getting rid of excess verbiage. The meat of the sentence could be written as follows:

> *The Victorian novel reached its _____ with the works of George Eliot, which are unmatched in their ability to delineate characters.*

Once you've pruned the sentence, it becomes clear that the missing word means something like "height" or "pinnacle." (D), *apex*, matches this prediction beautifully.

WORD CHARGE

If you're a top scorer, you probably read all the time: newspapers, magazines, novels, nonfiction books. Odds are that you can't come up with a dictionary definition for every single word that you read on a page. However, as a good reader, you've taught yourself how to get the gist of what you're reading. You instinctively make inferences about whether a word is positive or negative based on your knowledge of roots, prefixes, and suffixes, and the context in which you've seen the word.

This skill will serve you well on tough Sentence Completions. Often, all you really need to get the correct answer is this sense of the positive or negative "charge" of a word.

Let's take a look at a few examples:
Circle the word *positive* or *negative* under each sentence to indicate the word charge of the blank.

1. His face was _____ , his features pulled downward by the weight of heavy thoughts.

   Positive   Negative

2. Though the morbid legends attached to the tower gave it a _____ aspect at first, the impression is soon softened by the sight of children playing inside.

      Positive   Negative

3. The politician's speech was _____, exaggerating the latest crime statistics in order to incite angry reactions from frustrated voters.

      Positive   Negative

How did you do? In each of these cases, we would look for a negatively charged answer choice and eliminate any neutral or positively charged answers.

In sentence 1, "pulled downward" and "heavy thoughts" indicate that a negatively charged word would appear in the blank.

In sentence 2, "morbid" and the contrast with "children playing inside" indicate that a negatively charged word would appear in the blank.

In sentence 3, "exaggerating the latest crime statistics" to "incite angry reactions" is not a positive thing for a politician to do. You would anticipate a negative word to fill this blank.

> An Advanced test taker uses her sense of a word's "charge" when the word's definition is not clear.

Let's see how Word Charge can help you cope with tough Sentence Completions.

4. Before she took dance classes, Julia was _____ on the dance floor; now she executes difficult maneuvers with _____ that impresses even experienced partners.

    (A) ecstatic . . an aplomb
    (B) awkward . . a naivete
    (C) incompetent . . an ungainliness
    (D) timorous . . a polish
    (E) assured . . an agility

Why Is It Hard? Tough vocabulary

Key Strategy: Word charge

In this sentence, it's clear that Julia's performance on the dance floor was greatly improved by dance classes, so much so that now she "impresses even experienced partners." Thus, we can expect that the first blank will be a negative word and the second blank will be a positive word.

If you start with the first blank, you can eliminate (A), *ecstatic*, and (E), *assured*, because these words are too positive to contrast with her later performance. If you then go to the second blank, you can eliminate (B), *a naivete*, and (C), *an ungainliness*, because you're looking for a positive phrase. Thus, by the process of elimination the answer has to be (D). If you read this selection back into the sentence, it does indeed make sense.

WORKING BACKWARD

As a good test taker, you probably use the process of elimination as a matter of course. If you can't predict the answer to a question, your gut instinct is to move to the choices and get rid of the ones that won't work. In this section, we can help you enhance your elimination skills and give you practice so you can cross off wrong choices quickly and accurately.

Working backward allows you to synthesize everything that you know about Sentence Completions and put that knowledge to work for you on the toughest questions.

> An Advanced test taker knows how to eliminate wrong choices on tough questions.

Try working backward on this question.

5. Anarchists contend that government is by definition the repression of natural human desire, and their _____ rivals concur; it is over the _____ of this definition that the two groups battle.

    (A) sympathetic . . phraseology
    (B) perennial . . semantics
    (C) ideological . . implications
    (D) fascistic . . expression
    (E) fiercest . . etiology

Why Is It Hard? Tough vocabulary, unpredictable two-blanker

Key Strategy: Working backward

For the first blank, which is the easier one, we need a word to describe rivals. The second blank is tougher: we need to read for context. Since the two clauses are joined by a semicolon, the two ideas will support each other or continue a similar thought. The second clause will tell us how the two rival groups differ.

It's time to work backward. Start at the top, and try out each choice. Since the first blank describes rivals, you can eliminate (A) since rivals aren't sympathetic. The second blank helps you eliminate (B): *semantics* means "the meaning of words." If the rivals agreed on the definition, they couldn't disagree on the meaning of the words in the definition. (C) looks good: ideological rivals would disagree on the philosophy of whatever it is that they disagree about. It would make sense that these rivals would differ in opinion about something important like the implications of the definition. (C) is correct.

Part of working backward is trying every choice, just in case. In (D), the second word, *expression*, means "the way something is stated." It seems unlikely that the rivals would agree on the definition, but not on how it's stated. (E) is out because *etiology* is the study of causes, and it doesn't make sense that they would disagree about the causes of the definition. Don't be tempted by a Sentence Completion answer choice just because it contains tough, unfamiliar vocabulary if there's another answer choice that makes sense.

TOUGH SENTENCE COMPLETIONS: STRATEGY RECAP

GREAT ADVICE FOR ANY SENTENCE COMPLETION

How to attack SAT Sentence Completions strategically:

Step 1: Read the sentence for clues.

Every Sentence Completion sentence contains clues that make only one of the five answer choices correct. With practice, these clues should become more and more apparent.

Step 2: Predict an answer.

Sometimes you will be able to come up with a clear, strong prediction. Other times, you will have only a sense of the "charge" of the correct answer. Regardless, it pays off to take a shot at a prediction prior to looking at the answer choices.

Step 3: Scan the answer choices for a match.

Depending on the strength of your prediction, this step can go quickly or slowly— the better your prediction, the quicker you'll be able to locate your match.

Step 4: Read your selection back into the sentence.

To confirm your choice and avoid careless errors, read your choice back into the sentence. Trust your ear at this point. If it sounds right, pick it. If it sounds wrong, check the other choices again.

How to attack two-blank Sentence Completions:

The approach is basically the same, with some slight modifications.

Step 1: Read the sentence for clues.

Step 2: Decide which blank is easier to predict.

Step 3: Predict an answer.

Step 4: Scan the answer choices and eliminate those that don't match the prediction.

Step 5: Read the remaining answer choices back into the sentence. Keep the one that works with both blanks.

Note: We added the extra step of deciding which blank is easier to work with. By focusing on one blank at a time and eliminating answer choices based on that blank, your job becomes much easier.

What makes tough Sentence Completions tough, and what to do about it:

1. Long Sentence

- Paraphrase the sentence.
- Ignore the filler.
- Use the clues.

2. Tough Vocabulary

- Use word charge and word roots.
- Look for clues.
- Work backward.

3. Subtle Structural Clues

- Read closely.
- Paraphrase the sentence.
- Use the clues.

4. Unpredictable Two-Blanker

- Focus on the relationship between the blanks.
- Use word charge.
- Work backward.

Now that you're armed with all the strategies you need to crack the really hard Sentence Completions, try your hand at the practice set in the next chapter to hone your skills.

CHAPTER 8: SENTENCE COMPLETION PRACTICE SET AND EXPLANATIONS

Directions: Each sentence below has one or two blanks, each blank indicating that something has been omitted. Beneath the sentence are five words or sets of words labeled (A) through (E). Choose the word or set of words that, when inserted in the sentence, best fits the meaning of the sentence as a whole.

Example:

Today's small, portable computers contrast markedly with the earliest electronic computers, which were ____.

(A) effective
(B) invented
(C) useful
(D) destructive
(E) enormous   Ⓐ Ⓑ Ⓒ Ⓓ ●

1. The critic was happy to report that the artist had finally attained a maturity of style utterly ____ his early amateurish pieces.

   (A) descriptive of
   (B) superseded by
   (C) absent from
   (D) celebrated in
   (E) featured in

2. Unlike the ____ pieces she composed in her youth, her later works were jarring and ____.

   (A) immature . . illicit ✓
   (B) placid . . immense
   (C) melodious . . discordant
   (D) saccharine . . prosaic ✓
   (E) dissonant . . cacophonous ✓

3. After the animal behaviorist Karl Lorenz established that many facets of animal behavior are ____, psychologists sought to build on his research by defining the influence that hereditary factors have on the development of the human personality.

   (A) unconstrained
   (B) innate ✓
   (C) destructive
   (D) meritorious
   (E) accomplished

4. Though a hummingbird weighs less than one ounce, all species of hummingbird are _____ eaters, maintaining very high body temperatures and _____ many times their weight in food each day.

    (A) voracious . . consuming
    (B) fastidious . . discarding
    (C) hasty . . locating
    (D) prolific . . producing
    (E) delicate . . storing

5. The _____ demise of the protagonist in the final scene of the movie _____ all possibility of a sequel.

    (A) catastrophic . . beguiled
    (B) lamentable . . obviated
    (C) beneficent . . raised
    (D) ironic . . exacerbated
    (E) temporary . . precluded

6. The majority of the city's police officers have nothing but _____ things to say about their new chief, a novel situation for that chronically disgruntled organization.

    (A) tepid
    (B) querulous
    (C) truculent
    (D) stentorian
    (E) laudatory

7. Usually the press secretary's replies are terse, if not downright _____, but this afternoon his responses to our questions were remarkably comprehensive, almost _____.

    (A) rude . . concise
    (B) curt . . verbose
    (C) long-winded . . effusive
    (D) enigmatic . . taciturn
    (E) lucid . . helpful

8. To the _____ of those who in bygone years tiptoed their way past poinsettia displays for fear of causing leaves to fall, breeders have developed more _____ versions of the flower.

    (A) consternation . . amorphous
    (B) dismay . . fragrant
    (C) surprise . . alluring
    (D) disappointment . . diversified
    (E) relief . . durable

9. Artists of the pop art movement emphasized contemporary social values—the vulgar, the flashy, the transitory—in a _____ from the traditional _____ with which art had been treated.

    (A) departure . . reverence
    (B) severance . . whimsy
    (C) reemergence . . respect
    (D) break . . tolerance
    (E) loss . . equality

10. Though scientific discoveries are often disproved shortly after they've been accepted as fact, scientists still seem to leap to hasty conclusions, _____ that the _____ nature of what can be called "fact" has not eroded their confidence.

    (A) proving . . undeniable
    (B) demonstrating . . transitory
    (C) showing . . predictable
    (D) denying . . distinctive
    (E) admitting . . volatile

11. Any large-scale study of another culture will likely result in stereotype by composite in the sense that it will ____ the highly variable characteristics of individuals into a more generalized norm.

    (A) adumbrate
    (B) extrapolate
    (C) qualify
    (D) abbreviate
    (E) consolidate

12. High ratings for a television show offer little indication as to its quality, as audiences have become so accustomed to ____ and so ____ to television that they will watch practically whatever is on, regardless of its merit.

    (A) inadequacy . . averse
    (B) mediocrity . . inured
    (C) drama . . endeared
    (D) entertainment . . habituated
    (E) inferiority . . opposed

13. The inflated tone with which some art historians narrate exhibitions would make one think that to attain a legitimate appreciation of art, one is required not only to devote years to its study, but also to possess the ability to offer ____ interpretations of artistic pieces.

    (A) subversive
    (B) grandiloquent
    (C) intractable
    (D) clairvoyant
    (E) immutable

14. Paradoxically, Collinsworth's remonstrations against the banality of most detective novels attest to his ____ the genre.

    (A) comprehension of
    (B) antipathy toward
    (C) ignorance of
    (D) devotion to
    (E) derision of

15. It would be ____ to try to ____ a relationship between mathematics and music, since it is already widely accepted that music is based in mathematical relationships between sounds.

    (A) apropos . . extrapolate
    (B) superfluous . . establish
    (C) intemperate . . posit
    (D) redundant . . refute
    (E) inappropriate . . fathom

16. In order to achieve her goals, a diplomat must not be too ready to ____; success in negotiation depends on the ability to ____ certain positions while maintaining a firm stance on the goals considered most essential.

    (A) compromise . . abide by
    (B) challenge . . appease
    (C) yield . . resist
    (D) persevere . . surrender
    (E) conciliate . . concede

17. Some English scholars believe that students tend to have greater difficulty understanding Shakespeare than they do other authors because his works become _____ on the printed page; it is in their performance that their meaning _____.

    (A) opaque . . emerges
    (B) obtuse . . dispels
    (C) muddled . . tapers
    (D) evident . . emanates
    (E) overwrought . . ensues

18. To some scholars, Freud's fame for popularizing the scientific study of the mind is at least partially undeserved, for he built directly upon the work of psychologists such as Charcot and Janet without _____ their contributions to his theories.

    (A) enlisting
    (B) acknowledging
    (C) disparaging
    (D) differentiating
    (E) exploring

19. The resident, in an attempt to prove his stamina, never _____ to assist in the most detailed and lengthy procedures at the end of a 36-hour shift, in spite of the _____ potential for error from subsisting on such a minimal amount of sleep.

    (A) scrupled . . elevated
    (B) failed . . diminished
    (C) presumed . . heightened
    (D) declined . . immutable
    (E) deigned . . negligible

EXPLANATIONS

1. C

You can begin by paraphrasing this sentence: The critic was happy that the artist's new work was more mature than his earlier work. A contrast is being drawn between the early, amateurish pieces and the new, mature style. We need a choice that demonstrates this contrast. Choices (A), (D), and (E) all imply that the maturity of style was part of the early pieces, which we know to be incorrect. (B), *superseded by*, doesn't make sense. Choice (C), *absent from*, works perfectly.

2. C

It's easier to predict the second blank, because the missing word has to be similar in meaning to *jarring*. Working backward, you can eliminate (A), (B), and (D). If you didn't know the meaning of *discordant*, you could have guessed that *dis-*, a negative prefix, makes this a negative word. *Cacophonous* is another negative word, so (C) and (E) are in the running.

Turning to the first blank, you'll notice the clue *unlike*, which indicates that the musician's earlier works contrasted with her later works. You can predict that the first blank will mean something like "pleasant sounding." (C)'s *melodious* matches this prediction, and is correct.

3. B

Clues don't always jump right out at you, but sometimes one word can make all the difference. *Hereditary*, or inherited, is a direct parallel with the word in the blank, and only (B), *innate*, has the same meaning.

4. A

It's all about eating habits in this question. Don't be put off by the length of the sentence or the few tough words in the answer choices. Begin by using the clue word *though*: it tells you that the hummingbird's tiny weight is at a contrast to its eating habits. You can start with the first blank and eliminate (B), (C), and (E). A fastidious, hasty, or delicate eater wouldn't be at contrast to a low weight. *Voracious* (A) and *prolific* (D) both work fairly well, so let's go to the second blank. (A) works, since *consuming* means eating, and (D) is out since we don't know anything about hummingbirds producing their food.

5. B

It's difficult to make good predictions for these blanks. However, we can get an idea of the gist of the sentence and the word charge that the blanks should have. Start with the second blank. The protagonist, or main character, dies in the last scene of the movie (*demise* means "death"). That means that a sequel would be impossible, so our second blank word must be negative. Looking back to the first blank, we can guess that the protagonist's demise was probably a negative thing.

Let's look at the choices, starting with the first blank. Only (A) and (B) have very negative words, *catastrophic* and *lamentable*. But if you turn to the second blank, *beguiled* in (A) means "tricked," which doesn't work in this context. (B), *obviated*, or removed, works, and it's the answer.

6. E

The second part of the sentence refers to the police as a "disgruntled organization," which sounds very negative. However, there's one word that changes everything: *novel*. This little clue tells us that the blank word must be positive. (E), *laudatory*, means praiseworthy, and it's correct. If the answer choices were unfamiliar to you, you could have used word charge to help eliminate negative words.

7. B

At first glance, this seems like a tough sentence. Give it a good read, however, and you'll see that there are two excellent clues staring right at you. The first blank is an extreme version of *terse*, or short, and the second blank is an extreme of *comprehensive*. Looking down the choices, you'll see that only (A), *rude,* and (B), *curt,* work for the first blank. *Concise* (A) is the opposite of *comprehensive*, and was probably put there to trick you. (B), *verbose,* or wordy, is correct.

8. E

The word choice and structure of this sentence make it seem very formal and stuffy. However, it's quite easy to decode if you start with a simple paraphrase. People who used to be very careful around poinsettias feel a certain way now that breeders have changed the plants in some way. Since the plants were fragile in the past, we can assume that they are now more hardy. Only (E), *durable*, fits the bill for the second blank, and it makes sense that the plant shoppers would feel relief that the plants don't fall apart when they walk by anymore.

9. A

The key to this question is the sense of contrast between the vulgar values of the pop art movement and the traditional something with which art used to be treated. Start with the second blank, and you can eliminate (B), *whimsy*, right off. It means "fancifulness," and it doesn't fit the sentence. (E), *equality,* just doesn't make sense, so get rid of it. There's nothing in the sentence about the pop movement being intolerant, so eliminate (D), *tolerance,* because it doesn't provide the necessary contrast. Now look at the first blank. (C) doesn't work because *reemergence* is the opposite of what you're looking for, which is a word that indicates a contrast. Only (A), *departure*, works in the first blank, and *reverence* is perfect for the second.

10. B

Paraphrasing this long sentence will help you cut to its essentials. Here, we learn that even though

discoveries are disproved quickly, scientists still jump to conclusions. What does that indicate about the scientists? It must not bother them that what is supposed to be "fact" is indeed likely to change. After all, they continue leaping to hasty conclusions even though it is common that their discoveries are disproved.

It may be hard to prephrase this one, so let's work backward. (A) can be eliminated because the second word, *undeniable*, is inconsistent with the notion that the facts are changing and that what we know about them now may not be accepted later. (B) looks good, so let's hold on to it for now. (C) is out because *predictable* is the opposite of what the sentence is saying about scientific knowledge. (D) is illogical in the context. The scientists are still jumping to conclusions, so their confidence must not have been eroded. (E) is incorrect because it's not logical to say that the scientists are admitting that they are wrong to jump to conclusions. (B) fits best, and is correct.

11. E

We would call this a definition sentence. The phrase "stereotype by composite" is being defined in the second half of the sentence. Your clue to this fact is the phrase "in the sense that." "Stereotype by composite" implies the creation of an image that doesn't quite accurately represent any given individual, but rather draws on the most common characteristics, so the missing word is probably something like *combine*.

(A), *adumbrate* (to give a sketchy outline of), is not the same thing as to combine. Don't be tempted by an answer choice just because it's a tough vocabulary word. (B), *extrapolate*, means to estimate on the basis of known facts, and taking information *outside* the given culture will not help in creating a picture *within* it. (C), *qualify*, means "modify or limit," and this sentence is not about limiting, but rather, combining. You are now left with two options, and maybe you don't know that *consolidate* means "to combine or unite," the correct answer, while to *abbreviate* is to shorten. You can guess, though, knowing that the prefix *con-* means "with" or "together." You would imagine that a verb based on bringing things together would probably fit the bill, and it clearly does.

12. B

You have two straight-ahead structural clues in this sentence, *as* and *and*. It's a safe bet that the missing words will further the concept that high ratings do not tell you how high a television show's quality is. People have probably become accustomed to *low quality television*, so the answer for the first blank should convey that concept. The second blank is best approached by examining the end of the sentence. If people will watch "practically whatever is on," they are not discriminating, and hence, are *used* to television. The second word should connote this idea.

Regarding the first blank, people could be accustomed to *inadequacy, mediocrity,* or *inferiority,* but *drama* and *entertainment* don't convey the sense of diminished quality, so (C) and (D) can be eliminated. Regarding the second blank, people who will watch "practically whatever is on" are unlikely to be (A), *averse* (hostile toward), or (E), *opposed,* to television. (B), however, works for both blanks. Even if you didn't know that *inured* means "accustomed to," you could have gotten to the correct answer by process of elimination.

13. B

Your content clue in this sentence is "inflated tone," so you can cut through all filler in the sentence and look for a word that describes an ability that would result in an "inflated tone," such as *bombastic. Grandiloquent,* (B), matches our prediction. If you don't know the definition, you could break the word apart: *grand* = big, *loq* = talk.

Of the wrong answer choices, *subversive* means "corrupting," *intractable* means "unyielding," *clairvoyant* means "psychic," and *immutable* means "unchanging," none of which matches our prediction.

14. D

Your clue word in this sentence is *paradoxically,* which means "seemingly in contradiction." Thus, Collinsworth objected to the fact that most detective novels were trite or commonplace not because he disliked such novels in general, but because he *liked* them.

Going to the answer choices, *comprehension of* is too neutral; *antipathy toward* is too negative (*antipathy* is severe dislike); *ignorance of* is at best neutral; likewise *derision of* is the wrong charge (*derision* means scorn or ridicule). So all of these choices can be eliminated for being of the wrong charge. *Devotion to* works well, as it shows that Collinsworth had a real dedication to the detective genre.

15. B

The structural clue *since* lets you know that the sentence will continue in one direction throughout. The two words need a specific relationship, and this is the best way to approach the answer choices. Since the relationship between music and math is "widely accepted," it will either be *logical* to *exploit* a relationship between them, *unnecessary* to *posit* one, or *useless* to *discredit* one. The best way to approach the answer choices is to work backward and ask yourself if each pair makes sense, given that the relationship between math and music is already accepted.

Is it *apropos* (appropriate and opportune) to *extrapolate* (infer from known information) a relationship? No, that has already been done, and the relationship established, so (A) is out. Is it *superfluous* (more than is needed) to *establish* a relationship?

Yes, that is true, since the relationship has already been established. (B) looks good, but let's check out the other answer choices. Would it be *intemperate* (excessive) to *posit* (assume the existence of) a relationship? No, it would in fact be quite fitting. Would it be *redundant* to *refute* such a relationship? That makes no sense, since the relationship is beyond refute. Would it be *inappropriate* to *fathom* (comprehend) a relationship? No, it would be highly appropriate, since the relationship is widely known. (B) is correct.

16. E

The semicolon is a clue that the second part of the sentence will describe what a diplomat must not be too ready to do. The other structure clue is the word *while*, which indicates that a diplomat must maintain two different postures, so if she holds a firm stance on essential goals, she must also be able to *give in* at other times. Thus, a good prediction for the second blank is *yield*. So let's begin eliminating based on the second blank: only (D), *surrender,* and (E), *concede,* match our prediction.

Now check out the first word. A diplomat must not be too ready to *persevere* (D)? That doesn't accord with the last part of the sentence, which states that she must maintain a firm stance, so (D) is out. How about (E)? A diplomat must not be too ready to *conciliate* (meaning "placate," as in *conciliatory*)? That does make sense with the rest of the sentence, so (E) is correct.

17. A

You have two structure clues in this sentence, the word *because* and the use of a semicolon. Each indicates that the sentence will continue in one direction throughout. If students have *difficulty* understanding Shakespeare in English classes, you can assume that his works become *harder to understand* on the printed page, which is how students would be experiencing

them. Meanwhile, in performance their meaning would *come forth*. So even though the sentence continues in one direction, the two words will contrast with each other, one meaning *harder to see* and the other meaning *easier to see*.

Regarding the first blank: neither *evident* nor *overwrought* means *difficult to understand*, so rule out (D) and (E). Regarding the second blank: neither *dispels* nor *tapers* contrasts with the first word in each set, making (B) and (C) incorrect. Try reading (A) into the sentence. To be *opaque* is to be difficult to understand, while *emerges* means "comes forth," so (A) is correct.

18. B

The word *for* is acting as a structural clue in this sentence. The missing word will continue the notion that, to some extent, Freud's fame is *undeserved*. The second half of the sentence addresses *why* his fame may be undeserved. He built directly on the work of other people without doing something to do with their *contributions to his theories*. A safe guess would be that he did not *credit* their contributions.

Enlisting (engaging the support of) is the opposite of what he did—Freud used their theories extensively, so eliminate (A). (B), *acknowledging,* means crediting or admitting, so that would work here. But let's be sure. (C), *disparaging* (belittling), is negative in tone, which does not work in this sentence. (D), *differentiating,* clearly does not work, as it means to discriminate or see as different. Finally, (E), *exploring* (searching, investigating systematically), makes no sense either, as he must have explored their work to use it. The correct answer is thus (B).

19. A

The words "in spite of" are clues in this sentence. In addition, the negatives in this sentence flip the meaning in important ways. The first half of the sentence discusses the resident's actions at work, while the second half reminds us that performing difficult procedures on little sleep can *do something* to one's potential for error. It seems obvious that the second word will be something like *increased*. So let's begin eliminating there. Only (A), *elevated*, and (C), *heightened*, match our prediction for the second blank.

Given the contrast, and the fact that the resident was attempting to prove his stamina, we can expect that he continued to offer his help in difficult procedures, even if doing so could result in a greater chance of making mistakes. Given the negative *never*, if he always offered his help, he never *hesitated* to offer his help. Now let's check out the answer choices. Your two remaining options are *scrupled* and *presumed*. Even if you didn't know that *scrupled* means to show reluctance on grounds of conscience, you should *know* that *presumed* doesn't make sense here, and so the correct answer is (A).

| Part Three |

WRITING

CHAPTER 9: STRATEGIES FOR THE WRITING SECTION ESSAY

- Understand the skills tested on the SAT Essay.

- Learn what makes the Essay hard, and how to handle it.

- Practice the Kaplan Method for the SAT Essay.

This Essay section will seem like a breeze to some of you. After all, you're accustomed to writing in class, on tests, for homework. What's the big deal?

For you high achievers, accustomed to scoring well on essays written under pressure and time constraints, there may be a temptation to skip this chapter. Our advice is: don't. If you're aiming for a perfect score on the Essay, be forewarned that such scores are not given out easily. You have to touch a number of bases to ace this part of the Writing section. Let's start with the facts.

HOW THE SAT ESSAY IS SCORED

Colleges want an assessment of your written communication skills, and that's why this essay is important. Your essay will be graded on a scale of 1 to 6, Level 6 being the best.

Graders will be looking for an overall sense of your essay, not assigning separate scores for specific elements like grammar or content. They realize you're writing under time pressure and expect you to make a certain number of mistakes. Two readers read each essay and score them independently; then those scores are added together. If there's a difference of more than two points, your essay will be read by a third reader.

The content of your essay is not relevant; readers are not checking your facts and figures, nor will they judge you on your opinions. What they want is to see how well you can communicate a point of view. They want to know how you write and think.

Statistically speaking, there will be few Level 6 Essays. If each grader gives your essay a 4 or 5, that will place you at the upper range of those taking the exam. However, in this section, we'll aim for the 6. We'll show you how to make an ordinary, acceptable essay into a top scorer.

WHAT SKILLS ARE TESTED?

The Educational Testing Service (ETS), which writes the SAT, lists the following as the skills tested in the Essay:

- Keeping on topic
- Supporting ideas well
- Presenting ideas cohesively
- Writing clearly

The first of these involves knowing the prompt, the second means tying all your ideas together. The third is the only one addressing your writing skills directly, and it's limited to clarity. The Essay is not principally a test of your grammar and punctuation—colleges want a chance to see your reasoning skills.

> An Advanced Essay writer stays on topic and organized.

The skill that ETS didn't mention is speed. The skills they list would be relevant if you were writing an essay over the course of several weeks. On the SAT, you have to do all this in 25 minutes. This CANNOT be done using the process you learned for essay writing in the past. There is no time to write and rewrite, no choice of topic, no opportunity to do research.

DO YOU NEED TO PREPARE FOR THE ESSAY?

Like the Critical Reading section, this one tends to be underestimated by SAT test takers, especially by those who think they are good writers. Most think they can just apply their everyday writing skills—a dangerous assumption.

As we've already said, the SAT Essay is not like other writing experiences. It's a first draft that will be graded. Not only must it be complete and well organized, but it must also be easy for a grader to see that it is complete and well organized (and the grader may spend as little as a minute on an essay). And to be awarded a 6, your essay must show superior writing and an interesting item the test maker calls "insight." (Don't get rattled; we'll demystify that term for you and take a look at what makes writing "insightful" in just a bit.)

The rubric used by the SAT graders for scoring a 6 Essay is the following:

- Effectively and insightfully addresses the writing task
- Is well organized and fully developed, using clearly appropriate examples to support ideas
- Displays constant facility in the use of language, demonstrating variety in sentence structure and a range of vocabulary

That's a lot to do in 25 minutes, so preparation and practice are a good idea.

By the way, practicing the SAT Essay also strengthens your Critical Reading skills. (Naturally! In the Essay you're putting together an argument. In Critical Reading, you're usually taking arguments apart.)

ESTABLISH AND ADHERE TO A PRACTICE SCHEDULE

Don't try to cut corners. Learn the Kaplan Method and practice writing at least one essay a week. The best preparation for the Essay is to internalize methods and strategies; no last-minute cramming will be effective. If you intend to maximize your score, you must establish and adhere to a practice schedule. Start practicing essay writing using the Kaplan Method, right away, and do it methodically throughout your study period.

> The SAT Advanced Essay writer internalizes essay writing methods through practice . . . practice . . . and more practice.

WRITING ESSAYS

There is no substitute for practicing writing essays. Always time yourself to internalize the necessary pacing. Never start to write until you have a complete plan, and then adhere to your plan. Always reserve two minutes to look over the essay and make needed corrections. We'll go into this technique later in this chapter when we review and use the Kaplan Method for Essay Writing.

OUTSIDE READING

The outside reading you do for Critical Reading will also help develop your writing skills for the Essay. Adopt persuasive language that you find in articles you read. After reading them, flex your own persuasive capacities by asking yourself:

- What is the author's point, and how is it supported?
- What groups or people would disagree, and why?

STRATEGY TIP

Literary or historical topics won't necessarily do better than personal experience. Choose examples that you can write about with confidence; don't try to impress the readers.

Information Banks

Don't wait until test day to think about what subjects you can draw on for your examples. The prompt will require support from your life experience, literature, history, or other subjects, so prepare yourself by refreshing your memory about your favorite subjects—collecting examples that can be used for a variety of topics.

Don't hesitate to use your examples broadly. If the topic is about history, it doesn't mean you have to use historical examples. It's better to write about things that you are comfortable with and know a lot about. A high school classmate, parent, or art teacher can be an example of a "hero" or "leader"—but be sure to make it clear how he or she is relevant to the topic.

An SAT Advanced Essay writer has an information bank of examples to use for lively and engaging essays from readings, studies, observations, and experiences.

Use Your SAT Vocabulary

Apply a few of the vocabulary words you are developing for Sentence Completions and for diction questions in the Writing section. Using them in your practice essays will help you to learn them for those other sections. However, on test day, never use a word you aren't sure of: you can earn a top score using a simple vocabulary, and a misused word can destroy the clarity of your essay.

THE KAPLAN METHOD FOR THE ESSAY

> **Step 1:** Know the prompt.
>
> **Step 2:** Plan.
>
> **Step 3:** Write.
>
> **Step 4:** Proofread.

If you plan using the Kaplan Method and adhere to your plan when you write, your essay will be solidly organized. Between now and test day, you can't drastically change your overall writing skills—and you probably don't need to. If your plan is good, all you need to do in the writing and proofreading steps is draw on your strengths and avoid your weaknesses. Get to know what those are as you practice.

MAXIMIZING YOUR SCORE

Read the Directions: Before test day, you should become familiar with the "general" instructions. These will look something like this:

Directions: Consider carefully the following statement and the assignment below it.

Assignment: What is your view of the statement above? Plan and write an essay in which you develop your point of view on this issue. Support your position with reasoning and examples taken from your reading, studies, experience, or observation.

Many scores are lower than they could be simply because these standard directions are ignored: the writer does not present a point of view or does not provide support for it. Understanding the prompt doesn't mean there is a right or wrong answer—you have to decide what you will choose as your position, and then back your ideas up with examples.

Plan and write an essay that explains your ideas as persuasively as possible. Keep in mind that the support you provide—both reasons and examples—will help make your view convincing to the reader.

Write What Counts: To maximize your score, focus on writing what the scorers will look for—and NOTHING ELSE. Kaplan has found this approach useful in its many years of experience with hundreds of sample essay statements on a wide range of tests. Let's look at what the test maker tells you about how the Essays are scored.

To score Level 4, you must:

- Address the topic
- Support ideas with examples
- Show logical thought and organization
- Avoid major errors in word use that lead to unclear writing

Organization and clarity are key to success on the Essay. If the reader can't follow your train of thought, you can't earn an upper-range score. If your writing is unclear due to errors in grammar, misspellings, and incorrectly used vocabulary, the very best ideas won't shine through in your writing.

To score Level 5, all you have to add to a score of 4 is:

- Address the topic in depth (offer examples and details)

STRATEGY TIP

Writing essays may not be your favorite pastime, but you can still succeed on the SAT Essay. If well written, just staying on topic can earn you a 6. If your writing is weak, focus on building a well-supported argument; if you have that, weaknesses and errors in writing will be less important.

Essay graders love specific examples, which help clarify your thinking. Make them as concrete as possible, with names, dates, and descriptions.

To score Level 6, all you have to add to a score of 5 is:

- Show variety in syntax and a range of vocabulary
- Show insight

STRATEGY TIP

If you do choose personal experience, choose self-improvement, positive acts, or creative work. Remember that colleges may use these essays as additional personal statements.

Varying your sentence structure, sometimes using simple sentences and other times using compound and complex structures, and adding a few well-used SAT words will also boost your score. And don't be put off by that word *insight*. As we said before, you don't have to be an award-winning novelist to bring this quality of insight to your essay. *Insight* is just another word for depth, something that can be produced with relevant examples and details that support your point of view.

For depth, start creating your information bank of examples now. Remember, insight doesn't necessarily mean coming up with scathingly original or provocative themes. It means being able to apply to the prompt skillfully something you know about—from your reading, from your personal life, from your interests. So look to your reading and life experiences for ideas before you come to the test.

An SAT Advanced Essay writer knows that insight equals relevant and well-developed examples and details.

Structure Your Essay: Give your essay a clear introduction, a distinct middle section, and a strong conclusion. With that in mind, we suggest:

- Use an effective **hook** to bring the reader in
- Regular **transitions** provide the glue that holds your ideas together
- End with a **bang** to make your essay memorable

A "hook" means avoiding an essay that opens (as thousands of other essays will): "The quotation is right because…" A "bang" means a closing that ties the three paragraphs together. Good choices for either of these can be a clear, succinct statement of your "thesis" in the Essay or a vivid example that's right on point.

Since Kaplan's Method will ensure solid organization, the difference between a 4 and a 5 comes down to "depth." The difference between a 5 and a 6 is the way your use of language ties your ideas together, plus that greater level of depth that you can achieve with your details and examples.

APPLYING THE KAPLAN METHOD

Now let's apply the Kaplan Method to the following practice Essay statement:

Directions: Consider carefully the following statement and the assignment below it.

> A democrat need not believe that the majority will always reach a wise decision. He should however believe in the necessity of accepting the decision of the majority, be it wise or unwise, until such a time that the majority reaches another decision.
>
> —Bertrand Russell

Assignment: What is your view of the idea that a democrat must accept the decision of the majority, whatever it may be? In an essay, support your position by discussing an example (or examples) from literature, science and technology, the arts, current events, or your own experience or observation.

STEP 1: KNOW THE PROMPT (ONE-HALF MINUTE OR LESS)

HOW TO DECIPHER THE PROMPT

Follow Directions: First, be sure you see precisely what the prompt asks. You can't earn a 6 on an essay that does not specifically respond to the prompt. Note that the assignment is NOT to write something vaguely inspired by the quotation given. The assignment is "What is your view of the idea that a democrat must accept the decision of the majority?"

Next, aside from being sure you are following the general instructions as we discussed earlier, highlight words in the prompt and the assignment. You don't need "the one right definition" for any word in the statement. But you can add depth and "insight" by making clear to the graders how you are using the words in your essay. Terms that might be defined or explored in this statement include *democrat* and *decision*.

You may also see a prompt with two quotations like this:

Directions: Think carefully about the issue presented in the following quotations and the assignment below.

> 1. A little inaccuracy sometimes saves a ton of explanation.
>
> —Saki

> 2. No one trivial lie undermines the liar's integrity. But the problem for liars is that they tend to see most of their lies in this benevolent light and thus vastly underestimate the risks they run.
>
> —Sisela Bok

> **Assignment:** Do people need to lie sometimes, or is lying always harmful? Plan and write an essay in which you develop your point of view on this issue. Support your position with reasoning and examples taken from your reading, studies, experience, or observations.

Don't be alarmed by a two-quote prompt. There's no difference in your approach. The two-quote prompt will usually feature diverging points of view on a given topic. You'll use the same Kaplan strategy of deciphering the prompt and mentally defining key terms. And there's the added benefit of having two points of view on the subject already outlined in the quote that you can agree or disagree with.

STEP 2: PLAN (2 MINUTES OR LESS)

HOW TO PLAN

Subject Matter: Avoid highly emotional topics, because they tend to reduce your coherence; graders won't care what you think, only how you think. Avoid potentially offensive topics or extreme positions that are hard to defend.

Controlled Brainstorming: In your high school classes, many of you learned to "brainstorm"— perhaps using a "clustering" approach to organizing your ideas. These are excellent strategies if you have the luxury of days or weeks to write your essay. They lead to unbalanced, disorganized essays if you have to write in 25 minutes. Kaplan's planning system is designed to produce balanced and integrated essays in the 25 minutes allotted on the SAT.

Let's look at a plan for our first prompt. The answer we've chosen is this:

> *A democrat should oppose majority rule if its decision is dangerous to the minority.*

Next, working with our proposed response, comb your memory or your imagination for an example. We'll use:

> Example: Opposition to slavery/Jim Crow
>
> Relevance: True democrats opposed the majority to protect minority rights.

Fill in the details mentally. Jot down any notes you need to ensure that you use the details you've developed. Here's our sample plan. Yours may be as long as this:

> Para 1: A democrat should oppose majority rule if it is dangerous to the minority.
>
> Para 2: Abolitionist movement
>
> Para 3: Rosa Parks and civil disobedience in contemporary society
>
> Para 4: Democracy can't grow to protect minority interests unless majority rule is sometimes challenged.

Or it may look more like this:

> What about minority?
>
> Abolition-J Brown/Civ. Dis.

Examples: Rosa Park, MLK

Need to challenge majority to grow.

As long as you get your ideas down and into your essay in a logical order, you'll be helping yourself meet one of the main requirements of a 6 essay: organization and cohesion.

Planning Drill: It's very important to get a handle on outlining an essay as early in your test preparation as possible. Try the following drill before you dive into writing an essay.

Outline an essay on each of the following topics, allowing yourself no more than two minutes each:

- Only the strong survive.

- Trouble is opportunity in work clothes.

- The pen is mightier than the sword.

- Make hay while the sun shines.

- All's well that ends well.

For example:

Only the strong survive.

Your plan may be as long as this:

What do you mean by strong? Strength, and the meaning of strength. Introduction: Some of the most physically weak and meek people I know have a quality that makes them stronger than anyone I know: gentleness.

Example: Aunt Marge, all 98 pounds of her. Tell the story about how she stood up to the bully.
Example: Compare Aunt Marge to Gandhi.
Conclude: Cliché ideas about strength need to be changed. Gentle is strong.

Or it may be as short as:

Intro: Gentle is strong.

Para 2: Aunt Marge and the bully

Para 3: Gandhi and the British Empire

Conclusion: Look who survived. Who's really strong?

A good plan:

1. Responds to the prompt

2. Has an introduction

3. Has strong examples, usually one per paragraph

4. Has a strong conclusion

STEP 3: WRITE (19 MINUTES)

HOW TO WRITE

Appearances Count: In purely physical terms, your essay will make a better impression if you fill a significant portion of the space provided and if it is clearly divided into three to five reasonably equal paragraphs. Use one paragraph for your introduction, one for each example or line of reasoning, and one for your conclusion so your essay will be easy for readers to follow.

Write neatly: graders can't help but feel negative about your essay if it's hard to decipher—and negative feelings affect holistic scoring. If your handwriting is a problem, print.

Writing: Write mentally before you write on paper. Each paragraph should be organized around a topic sentence that you should finish in your mind before you start to write:

- The statement means…

- One example of when the statement is wrong is…

- Another example…

- Another example…

- Therefore, we can conclude…

You don't have to write it this way in the Essay—in fact, it's better to come up with your own opening and concluding words—but completing these sentences in your mind ensures that you keep in mind what organizes each paragraph.

Given the short time you have for the Essay, it's vital to the clarity of your writing that you use the ideas and organization you established in your plan. Resist any urge to introduce new ideas—no matter how good you think they are—or to digress from the central focus or organization of each paragraph.

> An SAT Advanced essay writer plans her essay and sticks to her plan.

A few common weaknesses to keep in mind:
- Avoid using "I" excessively.
- Avoid clichés, slang, and redundancy.
- Vary sentence length and structure.

Essay Length: In addition to the time constraints, the Essay must be written on only two sides of a page of lined paper—a total of 46 lines. So if you write 10 words per line, your essay can only be a maximum of 460 words. Many writers average about 8 per line, or 368 words.

While many poor essays can be quite long, there will be few 6 Essays under 300 words, so take this into consideration as you practice, especially if your handwriting happens to be large. Practice writing on 46 lines to internalize this spacing.

STEP 4: PROOFREAD (2 MINUTES)

HOW TO PROOFREAD

Always leave yourself two minutes to review your work. The time spent will definitely pay off. Very few of us can avoid the occasional confused sentence or omitted word when writing under pressure. Quickly review your essay for errors that affect clarity.

You don't have time to look for every minor error or to revise substantially. Learn the types of mistakes you tend to make and look for them. Some of the most common mistakes in students' essays are those found in the Writing section multiple-choice questions.

COMMON WRITING ERRORS

- Omitted words
- Sentence fragments
- Subject-verb agreement errors
- Misplaced modifiers
- Pronoun agreement errors
- Misused words—especially homophones like *their* for *there* or *they're*
- Spelling errors

Don't hesitate to make corrections on your essay—these are timed first drafts, not term papers. But keep it clear: use a single line through deletions and an asterisk to mark where text should be inserted.

> **STRATEGY TIP**
>
> The test booklet has 46 lines for the Essay. If your handwriting is large, it may be a challenge getting your ideas down. You won't get any additional sheets, so practice printing, writing smaller, whatever works.

YOU BE THE GRADER

Let's look at a sample essay. We've included the plan used by its author. When you've read it, decide what holistic grade you would give it.

Directions: Consider carefully the following statement and the assignment below it.

> Cleanliness and order are not matters of instinct; they are matters of education, and like most great things, you must cultivate a taste for them.
>
> —Benjamin Disraeli

Assignment: What is your view of the idea that cleanliness and order require education and cultivation? In an essay, support your position by discussing an example (or examples) from literature, science and technology, the arts, current events, or your own experience or observation.

PLAN:

Intro: Is cleanliness a habit? What about genes?

Par 2: Musical ability, math. "Clean gene"

Par 3: My kid brother

Conc: Genetic engineering

Today, we know that a lot of habits aren't just the result of education. Genes go a long way in influnecing what people can do. And today, we are learning more and more about just how big that influence is.

Many abilities are the result of genes, like being good at music. Is there exists a "clean gene"? Maybe families with clean and orderly homes got that gene, and pass it on to their children. We may think that it is the parents that make kids room's clean. We may think it's parents nagging: "go clean your room or you're grounded." But some people may really and truly have a gene that helps them clean and organize. Others are born sloppy.

If education were the main thing, a family like mine couldn't exist. Everyone in my family was trained to be neat and clean. My sister and I turned out pretty much orderly and neat but my younger brother's room always looks like a tornadoe hit it. Now my sister and I have brown eyes and my brother's eyes are blue. Maybe he didn't get the "clean gene," just like he didn't get brown eyes.

Genetic science is telling is that it may be too soon to call being clean something you educate. It may be inherited. But who knows? In the future, genetic engineering could make people neat.

Score: _____

What score did you give this essay? A 3? Less? Actually, the above Essay, which has accomplished the basic requirements of an above-average score, would rate a 4. It's not the 6 we're aiming for, however. Let's look at why it doesn't rate the higher score.

WHAT MAKES IT WEAK?

This 4 Essay adequately addresses the writing task and is organized around its theme. In spite of a few spelling errors, it does demonstrate some facility in the use of language, although the command is inconsistent: note the clichés *really and truly*, and *more and more*. The vocabulary and word choice (*parents got that gene*) aren't anything special. Sentence structure could be varied more, and the introductory and concluding paragraphs could be longer. Still, the essay does provide examples to develop its main idea and addresses the task enough to get an upper-range score.

HOW TO TURN A 4 INTO A 6

However, since we're not aiming for a 4, let's see what getting a 6 entails. The good news is that with just a few additions and subtractions, the same plan that produced this adequate essay can be the basis for a top scorer.

We'll show you what we mean. We'll take the same topic and the same basic essay and essay plan, and create a 6.

PLAN:

Intro: Is cleanliness a habit? Nature-nurture

Par 2: Musical ability, math. "Clean gene"

Par 3: My kid brother

Conc: Genetic engineering

Although Disraeli lived in the age that discovered evolution and natural selection, he didn't live to see the nature-nurture controversy in the late 20th century. Today, we know that a lot of habits aren't just the result of education. Genetic predisposition goes a long way in influencing how people behave, science has shown us. And today, we are learning more about just how great that influence is.

Today we are discovering that many abilities, like talent at math or musical skills, are partially the result of genetic programming. We've only begun to explore what genes may or may not be responsible for in a person's development. Who knows if there isn't a "clean gene"? Maybe families with clean and orderly homes inherited that gene, and pass it on to their children. We may think that it is the training that makes for a kid's clean room. We may think its parents nagging: "go clean your room or you're grounded." But it's quite possible that some people have an innate ability to clean and organize. Others may simply have the "sloppy" gene.

If education were the main thing responsible for cleanliness and order, a family like mine couldn't exist. Everyone in my family was raised to be neat and clean. My sister and I turned out pretty much orderly and neat; however, my younger brothers room always looks like a tornado hit it. Now my sister and I have brown eyes and my brother's eyes are blue. It may be that he didn't get the "clean gene," just as he didn't get brown eyes.

Genetic science is telling us that it may be premature to call any habit a matter of education alone. Cleanliness and orderliness may be inherited traits, like the color of a flower. No amount of cultivation can change the color of a flower once it blooms. But who knows? In the future, genetic engineering might be able to make people neat. Science may accomplish what generations of Moms couldn't.

WHAT MAKES IT STRONG?

This is an essay by a confident writer and reads pretty well for a first draft. It demonstrates clear and consistent writing competence. Unlike our first 4 Essay, the vocabulary (*nature-nurture, innate, premature, genetic predisposition, inherited* instead of *got*) is relevant and well used. Ideas are better developed, and the awkward clichés are gone. As in our 4 Essay, there are weaknesses: the third paragraph still seems a bit rushed, and our writer missed a few errors in proofing. However, the writing style showcases the ideas and the way the writer thinks. Syntax is good, complex sentences vary with simple statements, and grammatical errors are at a minimum. The opening is strong and the conclusion does what a conclusion should do: it ties everything together. There's the added bonus at the end of the flower example, plus the tagline about Moms for a bit of humor and ending with a "bang."

So what did we do to our 4 to turn it into a 6?

- We added *depth* by adding examples.

- We varied sentence structure and added some well-placed and correctly used SAT words; we improved word choice (diction) by dropping some clichés and writing more clearly. That is, we *demonstrated facility of language*.

- We added "insight" by providing more detail, taking what we had learned in high-school bio about the nature-nurture controversy and applying it here in a more developed way than our 4 writer did (our use of *cultivation* in reference to the flower in Paragraph 4 reflects the prompt elegantly).

- We took the 4 writer's good idea and with examples, vocabulary, and clear writing, made it an interesting thesis to read. We added "insight" simply by taking our original idea and offering up more examples and details to support our argument, giving it the depth needed to get a high score.

STRATEGY TIP

The length of an essay is no assurance of its quality. However, it's hard to develop an argument in depth, something the graders look for, in fewer than 300 words. Don't ramble, digress, or write off topic just to make your essay longer. Practice writing organized essays with well-developed examples, and you'll find yourself writing more naturally.

- While length alone doesn't make a 6, we've added a hundred words to our original essay (332 words, up from 227). Those hundred words provide more room for detail and examples and more opportunities to show off superior vocabulary and sentence structure, the "superior language" the test maker is looking for in a 6 Essay.

Remember that your graders will be reading you holistically. They will not be grading you by assigning points to particular aspects of your writing like grammar or diction. They'll be looking at your essay as a whole. However, as you practice essay writing, you can build an otherwise humdrum essay into a 6 by working on specific elements, with the net effect of giving your essay that 6 glow.

> **STRATEGY TIP**
>
> A 6 Essay can have a single well-developed example; two or more can make strong essays, but won't guarantee a 5 or 6. However, many undeveloped examples can make weak—and low-scoring—essays.

BUILDING A 6

Here's another 4–6 pair. Before reading the 6 Essay, think of what you can do to the 4, the adequate essay, to make it shine as a 6.

> **Directions:** Consider carefully the following statement and the assignment below it.
>
> > Creativity is allowing yourself to make mistakes. Art is knowing which ones to keep.
> >
> > —Scott Adams
>
> **Assignment:** What is your view of the idea that mistakes are necessary for creativity? Support your position by discussing an example (or examples) from literature, science and technology, the arts, current events, or your own experience or observation.

4 ESSAY

PLAN

Intro: Art comes from hard work, not mistakes.

Par 1: Beethoven's early period—he is creative not trial and error.

Par 2: Later works/careful approach to work

Conclusion: Thinking art is a mistake is a mistake.

The statement says that creativity is the result of mistakes. Mistakes are infortuitous, unexpected and not always happy events, but like most art, they are usually original. But are they art? Usually art is something done on purpose and intentionally. Beethoven, a classical musician, was once considered a revolutionary and his music was considered out-of-bounds. But are originality and creativity the same as a mistake? Does the artistic process need mistakes?

Beethoven's originality was due to egregious study and work, and was not based on random mistakes. Beethoven worked constantly on his work, changing it over and over again until he was satisfied. Beethoven first made a name for himself as a pianist rather than as a composer. His dramatic improvisations and virtuoso technique made an impression in society, but not before he had carefully studied Haydn, Mozart, C.P.E. Bach and Clementi. The early work was original and highly creative, but it was based on work and practice, not trial and error, even when it was spontaneous.

In the Eroica, Symphony # 3, Beethoven introduced many creative elements that were not understood by audiences at first. These artistic creations, although called mistakes by some, were not random. In this middle period more than ever, he would work constantly on a musical idea, writing it over and over again before he called it finished. Till the end of his life, he worked this way, burdened by his deafness and many other problems.

Mistakes tend to just happen, but great art takes work and sometimes a lot of pain and suffering as Beethoven's case shows. Creativity is usually the result of training and work, not mistakes which anyone could make. Mistaking creativity for a mistake can be a mistake.

Okay, we'll give it a 4 because it does what a 4 Essay is supposed to do: addresses the prompt in a reasonably organized way with some lapses in form and style. We may be tempted to give it a 3 for the pompous language and incorrect use of *egregious* and the nonexistent *infortuitous*. The weak introduction and the short conclusion also don't help: the cutesy last line is just designed to irritate a grader. However, once you get past the introduction, there are ideas here, an example is chosen and developed, and these are presented well enough to make the grade to the bottom half of the upper scores.

WHAT MAKES IT WEAK?

We, on the other hand, want a 6, so let's see what we can do with the material we have to earn the top score. Let's do some editing and adding. Remember, you won't have time to do this kind of edit on test day, so to create an effective plan and essay when it counts, practice, practice, practice writing essays so that it becomes second nature to you by then.

What Makes It Weak? Clichés and pompous language

Key Strategy: Clear writing

Let's start with the cliché at the beginning, and get rid of *The statement says*, an opening that will make a reader's eyes glaze over (they've seen it only hundreds of times), and lose the last pompous line of the introductory paragraph, not to mention *infortuitous*.

> Mistakes are unexpected and not always happy events, but like art, they can be original. But are mistakes art? Usually art is something done on purpose and intentionally. Beethoven, a classical musician, was once considered a revolutionary and his music was considered out-of-bounds, which could be considered a mistake. But is originality and creativity the same as a mistake?

What Makes It Weak? Redundancy; unclear writing

Key Strategies: Edit the excess; add a clear topic sentence

Let's edit a bit more. *On purpose and intentionally* is redundant, and *could be considered a mistake* doesn't add much to the discussion. Let's cut and paste, and add a direct sentence about what we're planning to write about here.

> Mistakes are unexpected and not always happy events. Like art, they can be original. However, art is something done intentionally. Beethoven, a classical musician, was once considered a revolutionary and his music, original and creative, was considered out-of-bounds. But was his originality and creativity the result of mistakes? Beethoven's case seems to demonstrate that they are the result of study, practice, and careful planning.

Good. Let's see what we can do to our second paragraph. Let's lose the first sentence, since we said it in our introduction, and do a little clipping and rearranging, adding a little interesting vocabulary. (*Over and over* will go.) Let's also add some depth to our idea by elaborating a little on the nature of Beethoven's improvisations.

> Beethoven worked constantly on his compositions, changing them relentlessly until he was satisfied. Beethoven first made a name for himself as a pianist rather than as a composer. His dramatic improvisations and virtuoso technique made a powerful impression in society. These performances seemed freewheeling, and were spur-of-the moment with many original themes, but Beethoven did not come to these performances unprepared. Before becoming known as a master improvisor, Beethoven carefully studied Haydn, Mozart, C.P.E. Bach and Clementi. The early work was original and highly creative, but it was based on practice and planning, not trial and error, even when it was spontaneous.

What Makes It Weak? Weak vocabulary

Key Strategy: Use SAT words

Okay, let's tackle the last two paragraphs. We'll improve the vocabulary by upgrading *changing* to *transforming* and *shows* to *illustrates*. We can even try using *fortuitous* correctly, just for fun. Then we'll need to add something to the conclusion to beef it up, and to restate that corny last line.

> In the Eroica, Symphony # 3, Beethoven introduced many creative elements that were not understood by audiences at first. These artistic creations, called mistakes by some, were not random. In this middle period, he would work constantly on a musical idea, transforming it hundreds of times before he called it finished. Till the end of his life, he worked this way. Even though he was burdened by his deafness and many other problems, Beethoven continued composing, always changing and reworking his music, looking for perfection in his art.

> As most of us well know, mistakes tend to just happen, but great art takes work. Creativity is usually the result of training and practice, not a lucky break or fortuitous mistake. Anyone can make a mistake; not everyone can write a symphony.

Let's take a look at what we've done:

> Mistakes are unexpected and not always happy events. Like art, they can be original. However, art is something done intentionally. Beethoven, a classical musician, was once considered a revolutionary and his music, original and creative, was considered out-of-bounds. But was his originality and creativity the result of mistakes? Beethoven's case seems to demonstrate that they are the result of study, practice, and careful planning.

> Beethoven worked constantly on his compositions, changing them relentlessly until he was satisfied. Beethoven first made a name for himself as a pianist rather than as a composer. His dramatic improvisations and virtuoso technique made a powerful impression in society. These performances seemed freewheeling, and were spur-of-the moment with many original themes, but Beethoven did not come to these performances unprepared. Before becoming known as a master improvisor, Beethoven carefully studied Haydn, Mozart, C.P.E. Bach and Clementi. The early work was original and highly creative, but it was based on practice and planning, not trial and error, even when it was spontaneous.

> In the Eroica, Symphony # 3, Beethoven introduced many creative elements that were not understood by audiences at first. These artistic creations, called mistakes by some, were not random. In this middle period, he would work constantly on a musical idea, transforming it hundreds of times before he called it finished. Till the end of his life, he worked this way. Even though he was burdened by his deafness and many other problems, Beethoven continued composing, always changing and reworking his music, looking for perfection in his art.

As most of us well know, mistakes tend to just happen, but great art takes work. Creativity is usually the result of training and practice, not a lucky break or fortuitous mistake. Anyone can make a mistake; not everyone can write a symphony.

> An SAT Advanced writer strives for clarity and control.

PRACTICE AND SELF-EVALUATION

There is simply no substitute for writing SAT Essays under testlike conditions. Between now and test day, practice writing as many essays as possible. And practice at the same time of day that you will be writing on test day. The next chapter will give you essay prompts you can work on.

Be hard on yourself. Don't allow yourself any extra minutes to complete an essay; and don't look at essay topics in advance. And practice writing on no more than 46 lines on two pages.

After each practice essay, score yourself based on the guidelines provided here. As part of your self-evaluation, determine which types of examples are most useful to you and what types of errors you make most.

Then analyze how well you followed the Kaplan Method in constructing your essay, and what you might focus on to improve on the next. Do you have a tendency to rush your plan, or do you find that you haven't left two minutes to proofread? Practice to make your pacing reliable.

GET A SECOND OPINION

Ask someone else to read and critique your practice essays. If you know someone else who's taking the SAT, you might agree to assist each other in this way. Knowing whether another person can follow your reasoning is the single most important learning aid you can have for the essay.

A SPECIAL NOTE FOR STUDENTS FOR WHOM ENGLISH IS A SECOND LANGUAGE

The SAT Essay section can be a special challenge for the international student or ESL student here in the United States. The SAT Essay is different from the TOEFL Essay because the prompt can be more complex and may use language that is harder to understand. On the SAT, you will usually be taking a position on the prompt, something that sometimes but not always happens on the TOEFL. However, you will still be planning your Essay using all the tools in this chapter and writing according to your plan. Practice deciphering the prompts in the next chapter, and practice, practice, practice writing essays. Make a special point of spending time proofreading your essays when you finish them, and editing anything that would make your writing unclear. There's a strong connection between your English reading skills and your writing skills, so keep reading as well. Don't forget to looks for topics for your Essay information bank as you do.

ESSAY WRITING: STRATEGY RECAP

Here's a recap of the steps you need to take to score a 6.

DECIPHER THE PROMPT

Even though you will be writing under extreme time constraints (25 minutes to write an intro with a great hook, sentences that express your logical and persuasive ideas in the paragraphs that follow, and a strong conclusion), the first thing, of course, is to read the essay prompt. Then reread the essay prompt. Determine what you are being asked to do and how you are being asked to accomplish it.

Deciphering the steps of the prompt is your most important task. Even the very best written essay will not score well if you don't fulfill the expectations of the prompt.

PLAN AHEAD

Give yourself a hand by outlining and planning ahead. Your test booklet will have plenty of room for you to jot down ideas and organize your thoughts.

KAPLAN'S METHOD FOR THE ESSAY

Step 1: Know the prompt.

Step 2: Plan.

Step 3: Write.

Step 4: Proofread.

STRIVE FOR "SUPERIOR CONTROL OF LANGUAGE"

Language control is important; your writing should be grammatical, concise, direct, and persuasive.

Choose your words carefully. Use SAT vocabulary, but do not flaunt large or erudite vocabulary unless you know it's correct. If you are trying to impress the reader, you may *obfuscate* more than *elucidate* what you are *articulating*. You get the idea.

Be sure your sentences are constructed so that your ideas are clear and understandable. Vary your sentence structure.

DON'T SWEAT THE SMALL STUFF

Do not obsess over every little thing. If you cannot remember how to spell a word, do your best and just keep going. Even the top scoring essays are not without flaws. Essay readers understand that you are writing first-draft essays. If your essay is littered with misspellings and grammar mistakes, however, the reader may conclude that you have a serious communication problem and score your essay accordingly. More importantly, you may get a low score simply because your writing is unclear due to errors and the reader cannot understand what you are trying to say.

In the next chapter, you'll try your hand at some essay practice under timed conditions. We've provided two sample 6 Essays with reader analysis, plus ten prompts for you to work with on your own. Work with these practice exercises, and you'll be on your way to the perfect score.

CHAPTER 10: ESSAY WRITING PRACTICE SET

In this chapter, you will find 14 writing prompts for Essay writing practice. Two of the prompts are followed by benchmark essays graded 6, and a reader analysis discussing why these essays earned that grade. Twelve additional prompts are provided for practice on your own.

Write your essays under testlike conditions: take 25 minutes for each essay, work without interruptions, and follow the Kaplan Method. Good luck!

ESSAY PROMPT I

Directions: The essay gives you an opportunity to show how effectively you can develop and express ideas. You should, therefore, take care to develop your point of view, present your ideas logically and clearly, and use language precisely.

Your essay must be written on the lines provided on the following pages—you will receive no other paper on which to write. You will have enough space if you write on every line, avoid wide margins, and keep your handwriting to a reasonable size. Remember that people who are not familiar with your handwriting will read what you write. Try to write or print so that what you are writing is legible to those readers.

You have twenty-five minutes to write an essay on the topic assigned below. DO NOT WRITE ON ANOTHER TOPIC. AN OFF-TOPIC ESSAY WILL RECEIVE A SCORE OF ZERO.

Think carefully about the issue presented in the following excerpt and the assignment below.

> People are difficult to govern because they have too much knowledge.
>
> —Lao-tzu

Assignment: What is your view of the statement above? Plan and write an essay in which you develop your point of view on this issue. Support your position with reasoning and examples taken from your reading, studies, experience, or observations.

WRITE YOUR ESSAY HERE

WRITE YOUR ESSAY HERE

SAMPLE ESSAY I

Government is always difficult, but whether it is the people who cause that difficulty depends on the people and the type of government. For an absolute monarchy or a dictatorship, that is, a government by the divine right of kings or by communism, its best that people don't look too closely at the way a government works, there is no way to change any injustices that may exist or to introduce progressive ideas. In a democracy, on the other hand, informed participation is essential. Otherwise, a democracy—government of, for, and by the people—ends up not too different from a feudal state.

The ideas and trade of the Renaissance moved monarchies away from absolute monarchies to the creation of congresses and parliaments, eg the English parliament. A new class of merchants and artisans was born. The members of this new middle class considered themselves individuals and demanded not only art and recreation, but education. With greater participation of more citizens, government became more complex, and a steady stream of information was needed to it running.

In the ideal democracy a citizen participates in government on a local, state (or province, eg), and national level. To be a real citizen requires information and knowledge of the issues, whether its to build a new playground in the park or vote in a presidential election. Democracy, the ideal kind, can't work if people are uninformed and do not take the time to learn about the issues.

Unfortunately, most democracies are not ideal. People prefer sitcoms and mindless web surfing to reading newspapers or studying history. Most U.S. voters don't know the name of the Vice President, much less what he stands for. Voter turnout is at an all-time low. People complain that getting involved doesn't make much difference and that they are too overwhelmed with information to make sense of it. "Big shots will make the decisions anyway," they complain. Too little knowledge makes democracy impossible, so they are probably right.

READER GRADE FOR SAMPLE ESSAY I = 6

READER ANALYSIS OF SAMPLE ESSAY I

The writer has ideas and showcases them. The essay is lively and engaging and shows a solid grasp throughout of the issue raised by the prompt. The vocabulary is apt and the sentence structure and word choice are all well above par, earning the writer the highest score.

While the otherwise strong opening is marred by the run-on sentence beginning "For an absolute monarchy," the writer has a lot to present and lays it out well in the introductory paragraph. The second paragraph is a bit overextended as the writer tries to give a history of government from the Renaissance; however, the writing is excellent, with varied and interesting sentence structure. The "eg" usage is only slightly annoying, and the *it's-its* problem is noticeable, but doesn't interfere with the clarity of the writing.

The discussion of participatory democracy and the idea that people prefer being ruled to self-government is presented well. The standard complaint that U.S. citizens aren't involved enough in government is made interesting and developed by examples, and the conclusion is strong and compelling. While specific issues or political events could have been mentioned, the author's own observations and reflections, plus the comments on electoral turnout and voter apathy, keep the essay grounded and supported.

ESSAY PROMPT II

Directions: Think carefully about the issue presented in the following quotations and the assignment below it.

> 1. Upon books the collective education of the race depends; they are the sole instruments of registering, perpetuating and transmitting thought.
>
> —Harry S. Truman

> 2. It is not that you read a book, pass an examination, and finish with education. The whole of life, from the moment you are born to the moment you die, is a process of learning.
>
> —Jiddu Krishnamurti

Assignment: Are books the most important part of education, or are other modes of learning more important? Plan and write an essay in which you develop your point of view on this issue. Support your position with reasoning and examples taken from your reading, studies, experience, or observations.

WRITE YOUR ESSAY HERE

WRITE YOUR ESSAY HERE

SAMPLE ESSAY II

In an age when the so-called Western Canon, or the classic books of Western civilization, has fallen on hard times, the importance of books has waned. However, there is no more important way of learning. Nowadays many different other types of "knowing" are used and many people say they are superior to reading. Yet civilization and real enlightenmen are completely contained and transmitted through books.

Oral accounts have their place and importance for cultural history; the proponents of New Age philosophy may claim that illiteracy is ok (as long as you know your mantra); and illiterate "mind control" is practiced everywhere, but even gurus must have books. The written word is what makes slave narratives available to us today; Native American narratives are preserved by being written down. And we understand experience, that great teacher, by reading, and studying classic works.

Some people may abandon books on their way to enlightenment, but no one ever starts self-improvement without doing some serious reading. In our culture, the Western Canon, has given generations of readers insight into the problems of life. There is no substitute for this experience of reading for learning and growth, even though many colleges misguidedly give credit for "life" experience. Life experience is shaped by books: look at our laws, for example.

Classics of Western civilization are ignored or called irrelevant, and with other books, they languish on the shelf. However, we could save ourselves much anguish by truly learning the lessons they portray. In the Iliad, for, example, we read text that was spoken around 800 B.C.E. An oral tradition of ancient Greece is preserved through a book; without books, this classic about the horrors of war would have been lost. Even television has writers, although you might not know it. TV shows can offer a watered-down version of the life experience found in books; the TV news may not be as good as reading a newspaper, but still informs us somewhat.

Illiteracy is appalling in the United States; this dovetails with a movement toward "other ways of knowing, that is to say, avoiding reading", Books are simply not as important as they once were. This movement needs to be reversed if our civilization is to survive.

READER GRADE FOR SAMPLE ESSAY II = 6

READER ANALYSIS OF SAMPLE ESSAY II

The writer is strong and jumps out of the page with a clear point of view. The opening is unequivocal: books contain and transmit civilization. The writer goes on to explore other ways of learning in an original fashion, mentioning oral histories, bardic traditions, and slave narratives that are available only through books. The writer possesses a highly developed vocabulary and apt word choice. Sentence structure is good, and the essay is lively and entertaining.

In general, this writer's strength keeps the Essay organized, linking together disparate ideas and keeping him or her away from digression. The topic is logically brought back to books, even though the discussion is wide-ranging and broad. The writer stays in control throughout.

The fifth paragraph stays on topic and maintains organization but is weaker than the first three paragraphs. This concluding paragraph is short, possibly suggesting rushed writing, and the idea about illiteracy is not developed and isn't fully relevant to the discussion; even though illiteracy is mentioned previously *in passim*, it seems added on at the end as an afterthought.

PRACTICE ESSAY PROMPTS

Here are 12 practice prompts for your essay writing practice. Practice reading and learning the directions so they'll be familiar on test day, and be sure to write under timed conditions.

---

1. **Directions:** Think carefully about the issue presented in the following quotations and the assignment below.

> 1. If the facts don't fit the theory, change the facts.
>
> —Albert Einstein

> 2. Facts do not cease to exist because they are ignored.
>
> —Aldous Huxley

Assignment: Should facts sometimes be ignored? Plan and write an essay in which you develop your point of view on this issue. Support your position with reasoning and examples taken from your reading, studies, experience, or observations.

2. **Directions:** Consider carefully the following statement and the assignment below it.

> The weirder you're going to behave, the more normal you should look. It works in reverse, too. When I see a kid with three or four rings in his nose, I know there is absolutely nothing extraordinary about that person.
>
> —P. J. O'Rourke

Assignment: What is your view of the statement above? In an essay, support your position by discussing an example (or examples) from literature, science and technology, the arts, current events, or your own experience or observation.

3. **Directions:** Consider carefully the following statement and the assignment below it.

> Clever people seem not to feel the natural pleasure of bewilderments, and are always answering questions when the chief relish of life is to go on asking them.
>
> —Frank Moore Colby

Assignment: What is your view of the statement above? In an essay, support your position by discussing an example (or examples) from literature, science and technology, the arts, current events, or your own experience or observation.

4. **Directions:** Think carefully about the issue presented in the following quotations and the assignment below it.

> Everybody wants to be somebody. Nobody wants to grow.
>
> —Johann Wolfgang von Goethe

Assignment: What do you think of the point of view that people resist growth? Plan and write an essay in which you develop your point of view on this issue. Support your position with reasoning and examples taken from your reading, studies, experience, or observations.

5. **Directions:** Consider carefully the following statement and the assignment below it.

> People only see what they are prepared to see.
>
> —Ralph Waldo Emerson

Assignment: What is your view of the statement above? In an essay, support your position by discussing an example (or examples) from literature, science and technology, the arts, current events, or your own experience or observation.

6. **Directions:** Consider carefully the following statement and the assignment below it.

> I think there are only three things America will be known for 2,000 years from now when they study this civilization: the Constitution, jazz music, and baseball.
>
> —Gerald Early

Assignment: What is your view of the statement above? In an essay, support your position by discussing an example (or examples) from literature, science and technology, the arts, current events, or your own experience or observations.

7. **Directions:** Think carefully about the issue presented in the following quotations and the assignment below.

> 1. Happiness is that state of consciousness which proceeds from the achievement of one's values.
>
> —Ayn Rand

> 2. The pursuit of happiness is a most ridiculous phrase; if you pursue happiness you'll never find it.
>
> —C. P. Snow

Assignment: Can happiness be pursued and found, or does happiness appear when it is not sought? Plan and write an essay in which you develop your point of view on this issue. Support your position with reasoning and examples taken from your reading, studies, experience, or observations.

8. **Directions:** Consider carefully the following statement and the assignment below it.

> There is nothing like returning to a place that remains unchanged to find the ways in which you yourself have altered.
>
> —Nelson Mandela

Assignment: What is your view of the statement above? In an essay, support your position by discussing an example (or examples) from literature, science and technology, the arts, current events, or your own experience or observation.

9. **Directions:** Consider carefully the following statement and the assignment below it.

> True wisdom consists in not departing from nature and in molding our conduct according to her laws and model.
>
> —Seneca

Assignment: What is your view of the statement above? In an essay, support your position by discussing an example (or examples) from literature, science and technology, the arts, current events, or your own experience or observation.

10. **Directions:** Think carefully about the issue presented in the following quotations and the assignment below.

> 1. Advertisements contain the only truths to be relied on in a newspaper.
>
> —Mark Twain

> 2. What is the difference between unethical and ethical advertising? Unethical advertising uses falsehoods to deceive the public; ethical advertising uses truth to deceive the public.
>
> —Vilhjalmur Stefansson

Assignment: Is advertising always deceptive, or can advertising be honest? Plan and write an essay in which you develop your point of view on this issue. Support your position with reasoning and examples taken from your reading, studies, experience, or observations.

11. **Directions:** Consider carefully the following statement and the assignment below it.

> Repetition is the only form of permanence that nature can achieve.
>
> —George Santayana

Assignment: What is your view of the statement above? In an essay, support your position by discussing an example (or examples) from literature, science and technology, the arts, current events, or your own experience or observation.

12. **Directions:** Consider carefully the following statement and the assignment below it.

> Perhaps the most valuable result of all education is the ability to make yourself do the thing you have to do, when it ought to be done, whether you like it or not.
>
> —Thomas H. Huxley

Assignment: What is your view of the statement above? In an essay, support your position by discussing an example (or examples) from literature, science and technology, the arts, current events, or your own experience or observation.

CHAPTER 11: THE WRITING QUESTIONS CHALLENGE

- Understand how Writing questions are built.

- Train your "ear."

- Practice applying the Kaplan Methods.

The skills tested in Writing multiple-choice questions—the abilities to recognize faults in usage and structure and to use language with sensitivity to meaning—are editorial skills, and they will be vital to you in preparing papers and writing tests in college, as well as in any writing you do in your professional life. We all make mistakes; systematically finding and correcting them can make the difference between a weak writer and a strong one.

In addition, a good grasp of standard English is indispensable to comedy, which often uses ambiguities to set up jokes:

Herald: I come with great news: the Prince wants your daughter for his wife.
Mill Owner: Well, his wife can't have her.

While not grammatically incorrect, this exchange shows the importance of reading your work "listening" for the relationship between its ideas, rather than only for errors—especially if you want to be funny.

If you plan to get 2400, you probably often read or hear sentences that don't "sound" right, which is the principal skill you need to score well on the Writing questions. You don't have to know the names of the parts of speech or how to diagram sentences, as long as you have the ability to recognize what is right or wrong.

Our purpose in these chapters is to help you to methodically sharpen your "ear" by focusing on the error types that occur in the Writing section so that you can apply that skill confidently on test day.

But most of us, however strong our writing skills, occasionally find that what is correct in standard written English "sounds" wrong, and what is incorrect "sounds" right. As you use this book to practice for the SAT, your "ear" will become more dependable, and you will also come to know when you can't trust it—in which case, a methodical approach to the question will lead you to the answer.

HOW WRITING QUESTIONS ARE BUILT

To earn a top score, you should think about how the questions are written, as well as the points of grammar, usage, and style that will be tested. Let's just focus on the question formats first, without trying to answer the questions (we'll do them later in the chapter).

THE DIRECTIONS

The directions in the Writing section are particularly cumbersome—making it all the more important that you practice the questions enough to make it unnecessary to read directions on test day. We won't spend any time on them now. Read them carefully before doing the practice sets, and learn them by doing as many practice questions as possible.

THE QUESTIONS

Questions in the Writing section are probably not in the formats you are used to for grammar and writing tests. That can work against you on test day, unless you practice enough to make them familiar.

You'll find about 49 questions in the section, including about 18 Identifying Sentence Errors questions, 25 Improving Sentences questions, and 6 Improving Paragraphs questions. Each of us feels more comfortable with some elements of usage than with others, so the level of difficulty does not increase within the Writing section (unlike the Math sections). Let's consider each type in a little detail.

IDENTIFYING SENTENCE ERROR QUESTIONS

1. Despite of getting a good night's sleep, Dennis was
        A   B

   extremely fatigued at work the next day. No error
          C   D   E

These require only that you recognize an error within a sentence, without correcting it. Each sentence contains four underlined segments, one (and only one) of which may need correction. The correction may involve the addition or removal of a number of words, but no reorganization of the sentence can be required. Choice (E) is always "No error."

IMPROVING SENTENCES

2. Alarmed and dismayed by the prospect of another test, Dennis <u>having been sleeping badly</u> last night.

   (A) having been sleeping badly
   (B) having been sleeping bad
   (C) slept badly
   (D) sleeping badly
   (E) sleeps badly

These sentences have a single underlined segment that may require correction—but that segment can range between one word and the entire sentence. There may be as many as four errors to be corrected within the underlined segment. Choice (A) always repeats the original (meaning it's correct as written), so don't waste time reading choice (A) on test day.

IMPROVING PARAGRAPHS

3. In context, which is the best version of the underlined portion of sentence 2 (reproduced below)?

   <u>At first the length of the pages</u>—there were more than 1,500 in all—intimidated me.

   (A) (As it is now)
   (B) At first the amount of the pages
   (C) At first the number of pages
   (D) Firstly, the length of the pages
   (E) Firstly, the thickness of the book

These are based on a passage that is written to imitate a first draft and contains errors that will be addressed in the questions. The passages can be formal or very informal. Each sentence is numbered. These questions only occasionally have a "no error" choice (A) (As it is now).

Improving Paragraphs questions can cover the grammar, usage, and diction errors found in Identifying Sentence Errors and Improving Sentences questions, and add several question types rarely found in the other formats.

Additional Improving Paragraphs Question Types (in order of decreasing frequency)	
Issue Tested	How Tested
Relationship between Ideas	"Which of the following sentences is best inserted at the beginning of the second paragraph, before sentence 5?"
	"Sentence 5 would make the most sense if placed after"
	"To best connect sentence 3 to the rest of the first paragraph, which is the best word or phrase to insert at the beginning of sentence 3?"
	"Which of the following is the best way to combine sentences 2, 3, and 4 (reproduced below)?"
Style Problems (wordiness, wrong tone, unnecessary passive)	"Of the following, which is the best version of sentence 8?"
	"Which of the following is the best version of the underlined portion of sentence 10 (reproduced below)?"
Reading Comprehension (apply your Critical Reading skills)	"The sentence that best states the main idea of the passage is"
	"Including a paragraph on which of the following would most strengthen the writer's argument?"
	"The function of sentence 10 is to"

An Improving Paragraphs passage has a readily recognizable overall purpose. Except for the errors tested by the questions, each sentence and paragraph has a clear logical relationship to the other sentences and paragraphs. When you read them, remember what you learned in Sentence Completions about noting the structural clues that help you see these relationships, though their types and role are slightly different here.

What Is Signaled	Sample Clues
Similarity	and, also, furthermore
Contrast	but, however, despite, on the other hand
Causation	because, for, given
Illustration	for example, like
Opinion	"I think…," "They should…"
Relative time	for many years, before that, until he was ten
Emphasis	most, never, especially

THE WRONG ANSWER CHOICES

In all SAT questions, the wrong answer choices can significantly affect the difficulty of a question.

In Identifying Sentence Error questions, all wrong answer choices raise issues of the types covered in the section, but are correct as written.

In Improving Sentences and Improving Paragraphs, wrong answers can fall into one or more of the following categories.

Wrong Answer Choices	
No correction	Restate or rearrange the words in the original without addressing the error.
New error	Introduce additional errors of the types tested in the section.
Wrong relationship	Misrepresent the relationship between ideas or the overall ideas in the passage, distorting the meaning.
Style problem	Grammatically correct, but bad style (wordy, unnecessary passive, wrong tone).
Out of scope (Improving Paragraphs only)	Introduce ideas not relevant to the author's purpose in the passage.

TRAIN YOUR "EAR"

To improve your score, become very aware, between now and test day, of the number of speakers, writers, and others in your life who aren't offering you examples of standard written English: your family and friends, for example, who would laugh or wince if you said (correctly):

> "It is I."
>
> "To whom should I send it?"

Musicians offer:

> "Just want to know about from where I come from." (John Mellencamp)

Successful advertisers (who may not want thoughtful, analytical consumers) contribute gems like:

> "Send your kids back to school a better reader." {the kids have become one reader?}
>
> "I noticed I didn't enjoy things like I used to…" {*like* modifies nouns; it should be "*as* I used to"}
>
> "Try all seven flavors in the distinctive, re-closable bottle." {all seven in one bottle?}

Unless you note them—and make them work *for* you (instead of against you)—that flood of colloquial and nonstandard usage works to desensitize the "ear" you want to be able to rely on.

> An Advanced test taker actively trains the "ear" for sentence errors and knows how much—and for what types of errors—it can be trusted on test day.

When you can't rely on your "ear," instead of trying to remember a seemingly endless, disorganized list of frequent errors, think of the errors you'll see on test day as falling into three main categories against which you can test each sentence segment:

1. Is it the wrong word?

2. Is it the wrong word form?

3. Is it the wrong word arrangement?

The first two are most common in Identifying Sentence Errors and Improving Sentences questions, while the third group is most common in Improving Sentences and Improving Paragraphs questions.

An Advanced test taker knows the common errors tested in the Writing section.

Types of Errors	
Category:	**Includes Errors Involving:**
Wrong Word	diction
	relative pronouns (*who/which/that*)
	idiom (prepositions, double negatives)
	adjective/adverb confusion
	comparative/superlative
	irregular verbs
Category:	**Includes Errors Involving:**
Wrong Word Form	subject-verb agreement
	pronoun case and agreement
	noun agreement
	parallelism
	logical comparisons
	verb tense
Wrong Word Arrangement	fragments and run-ons
	subordination
	misplaced modifiers
	transition words
	style problems

With the exception of the semicolon sometimes used to correct a run-on sentence, the SAT does not test punctuation, capitalization, or spelling.

PRACTICE APPLYING THE KAPLAN METHODS

Now let's go over those questions again and answer them. As you grow increasingly familiar with what you can expect in each question type, you should also practice handling each question methodically.

> An Advanced test taker knows that a methodical approach can ensure success.

THE METHOD FOR IDENTIFYING SENTENCE ERRORS QUESTIONS

Step 1: Read the sentence "listening" for the error.

Step 2: Identify the error, if you didn't "hear" it.

Step 3: Check the other choices to confirm your answer, if necessary.

BLATANTLY EASY IDENTIFYING SENTENCE ERRORS QUESTIONS

1. Despite of getting a good night's sleep, Dennis was
       A   B
   extremely fatigued at work the next day. No error
            C   D   E

INSIDE YOUR BRAIN:

Despite of *sounds wrong; I've heard of* in spite of *but* despite *doesn't need any preposition.*

Step 1: Don't waste time reading past *despite of* if you know—beyond a doubt—that it's wrong. Stop as soon as you see a clear, unequivocal error—which may happen often in Identifying Sentence Errors questions. Pick up extra minutes on these questions to use on more difficult questions.

> An Advanced test taker manages time wisely, saving time on the easy questions.

Step 2: But don't rush if you have even the slightest doubt about what your "ear" is telling you. In that case, read the entire sentence; there is just no reason not to confirm that the rest sounds right, and some of the tougher sentences may be oddly (but correctly) structured with a logic that isn't apparent until you finish reading it.

Look at each underlined segment, considering the error types that are possible. In this example, if *Despite of* didn't catch your "ear," you should consider *getting*—is it the right word?—in the right form. Yes, it is idiomatically correct with *despite* and makes sense. What about *extremely fatigued*? An adverb modifying an adjective that modifies *Dennis*—no trouble there. So is there a problem in *at work*—no, again, a correct idiom. So however unsure you may be of what the problem is in (A), it must be there. For each underlined word or phrase, there are only a few possible errors to consider—just test each methodically.

In addition to getting you to the answer in each question, this methodical approach further develops your "ear"—an underlined segment that you work through carefully now will simply "sound" right the next time you face it.

THE METHOD FOR IMPROVING SENTENCES QUESTIONS

In these questions, you have to correct the problem as well as find it, so Improving Sentences require an additional step:

> **Step 1:** Read the sentence "listening" for the error.
>
> **Step 2:** Identify the error or errors.
>
> **Step 3:** Predict a correction.
>
> **Step 4:** Check the choices for a match that doesn't introduce a new error.

BLATANTLY EASY IMPROVING SENTENCES QUESTIONS

Let's look at this Sentence Correction question stem:

2. Alarmed and dismayed by the prospect of another test, Dennis <u>having been sleeping badly</u> last night.

INSIDE YOUR BRAIN:

The phrase having been sleeping *isn't right, so there's no need to read choice (A). I need a past tense verb for something that happened "last night"—what are my choices?*

An Advanced test taker predicts a correction before checking the answer choices.

2. Alarmed and dismayed by the prospect of another test, Dennis <u>having been sleeping badly</u> last night.

   (A) having been sleeping badly
   (B) having been sleeping bad
   (C) slept badly
   (D) sleeping badly
   (E) sleeps badly

After you identify the flaw in an Improving Sentences question, analyze the problem to predict the correct choice. Just knowing that the original is wrong only eliminates choice (A). In this case, analysis tells you to look for an active verb to replace the modifying form "having been sleeping"—as choice (C) does correctly here. The only other active verb, (E), is in the wrong tense.

> An Advanced test taker reads choices carefully, to avoid substituting a new error for the original one.

THE METHOD FOR IMPROVING PARAGRAPHS QUESTIONS

Because the overall context is as important as the content of any particular sentence in an Improving Paragraphs question, the Method also needs another step.

   Step 1: Read the passage quickly for the overall idea and tone.

   Step 2: Read the question.

   Step 3: Consider the context to identify the error or errors.

   Step 4: Predict the correction.

   Step 5: Check the choices for a match that doesn't introduce a new error.

BLATANTLY EASY IMPROVING PARAGRAPHS QUESTION

Read the passage quickly for the main idea and tone before trying the questions. You will probably note some errors as you read, but don't worry about finding them. They'll be identified in the questions.

Some people recommend skipping the passage and starting to answer the questions right away. This will usually slow you down, in Kaplan's experience. Although a few questions can be answered without any reference to the rest of the passage, most can't; and stopping to read the passage after you've started answering questions will probably show you that at least one question you THOUGHT you could answer with no reference to anything else in the passage actually IS affected by what you read—so you have to do it again. Use your Reading Comprehension skills to quickly glean an overview of the author's overall purpose and the point of each paragraph.

Question 3 is based on the following passage.

(**1**) I recently read the famous novel *War and Peace* by Tolstoy. (**2**) At first the length of the pages—there were more than 1,500 in all—intimidated me. (**3**) But the narrative and characters were so gripping that I hardly noticed how fast I was reading. (**4**) Many people say that *War and Peace* is the greatest novel ever written. (**5**) Particularly it is said that it has the best descriptions of military battles of any book ever.

(**6**) The fascinating characters and the action and suspense made *War and Peace* an easy read with strongly developed plot lines. (**7**) They interconnected, married, remarried, fought duels, and died suddenly. (**8**) Tolstoy wrote a great story. (**9**) He didn't just tell a story. (**10**) He described an era in history and explained it in a new way. (**11**) For example, instead of saying that the great battles of 1812 and 1813 between Russia and France were due to the genius of France's Napoleon and Russia's Alexander I, Tolstoy showed that the battles had broader causes. (**12**) The leaders were just pawns with no real control. (**13**) Each battle occured because of so many preceding factors, and so two people could not easily control them. (**14**) With this and many other arguments, Tolstoy refuted previous historical analysis.

3. In context, which is the best version of the underlined portion of sentence 2 (reproduced below)?

   At first the length of the pages—there were more than 1,500 in all—intimidated me.

   (A) (As it is now)
   (B) At first the amount of the pages
   (C) At first the number of pages
   (D) Firstly, the length of the pages
   (E) Firstly, the thickness of the book

INSIDE YOUR BRAIN

My "ear" doesn't tell me there's anything wrong with the underlined segment itself. What is the relationship between the underlined portion and the rest of the sentence?

The first part of this sentence refers to the length of the pages, the second part, added in support of the first, refers to the number of pages. These two have to make sense together, so the author must have meant: "At first the number of pages—there were more than 1,500 in all—intimidated me." (B) uses the word *amount*, which is no better than *length* in this case. (D) and (E) awkwardly change *at first* to *firstly*—and (D) doesn't address the original problem, while *thickness* in (E) is another illogical word.

> An Advanced test taker manages time wisely, avoiding bogging down on the hard questions.

If you have no idea about how to handle a question, skip it and come back when you have finished the others for the section. Each question is worth the same number of points, so don't lose easy points by struggling with a hard question.

CHAPTER 12: STRATEGIES FOR TOUGH WRITING QUESTIONS

- Know what makes some Writing questions tough, and how to handle them.
- Learn the secrets of eliminating wrong answer choices.
- Know your own weaknesses and how to correct for them.

WHAT MAKES A WRITING QUESTION TOUGH?

IDENTIFYING SENTENCE ERRORS QUESTIONS

Although Identifying Sentence Errors questions are often considered the easiest within the Writing section, in fact some of the hardest questions—that is, the ones most students get wrong—will be among them. Questions may be made tough by one or more of the following: complex sentence structure, commonly misused words or expressions, and errors that appear too early in the question.

1. The many health hazards involved in cigarette smoking

   <u>have been proven</u> <u>and measured</u> for many decades, <u>but</u> only
       A   B   C

   recently <u>has</u> the life endangering effects of secondary smoke
           D

   become known. <u>No error</u>
              E

Why Is It Hard? Complex sentence

Key Strategy: Know when to slow down.

In this long sentence, we have (correctly) varied verb tenses, a (correctly handled) relationship established between the two parts of the sentence, and finally, reversed word order in the second clause.

Whenever you notice that the subject and verb have been widely separated or their order reversed, check to see whether they agree. Here, the reversed word order makes it more difficult to notice, but the subject (*effects*) and verb (*has*) aren't in agreement. "Have been proven" is logical with "for many decades" and "has…become" is the right form for the more recent discovery. The *but* correctly establishes the contrasting relationship between these thoughts.

> An Advanced test taker always reads the tougher sentences through, inserting the correct choice to confirm it.

2. Between Sam and I, there has always been a
          A
   great deal of uncertainty about which of us should
          B   C
   play the lead in the play because we both doubt our
                                    D
   acting skills. No error
                    E

Why Is It Hard? Commonly misused expression

Key Strategy: Train your "ear" and know your weaknesses.

> An Advanced test taker doesn't conclude that the correct choice is (E) just because he didn't "hear" an error.

Pronoun case is so constantly used incorrectly in everyday conversation and writing that it's impossible for many of us to "hear" these errors. The phrase *Sam and I* is not the subject of the sentence; both *Sam* and *I* are the objects of the preposition *between* so *I* should be *me*. If you evaluate them carefully in your practice, by test day you'll "hear" them, too.

3. Although she had attempted to repair
      A   B
   the damage done to the gym, Mary was given
              C
   detention for an indecisive period. No error
                       D   E

Why Is It Hard? Commonly confused word

Key Strategy: Don't rely on your "ear" for diction.

Don't read so quickly that you miss the word *indecisive* here; the writer meant *undetermined*. *Indecisive* means unable to make a decision—it can describe only a person, not a "period."

Some other words of the type commonly confused in SAT questions are:

This word:	Confused with:	This word:	Confused with:
raise	rise	under	underneath
imaginary	imaginative	undecided	indecisive
afflict	inflict	respectively	respectfully
inferred	referred	ambivalent	ambiguous
credibility	credulity	detract	distract
eminent	imminent	formally	formerly
incredulous	incredible	ingenious	ingenuous
intent	intense	sophistic	sophisticated
lay	lie	innovative	innovation

Any words that share several letters, or are based on similar roots, may be confused if you rush—and strong readers are more likely than weak ones to see part of a word and assume the rest.

Note, too, that you don't necessarily have to know the meaning of both words to know which is correct. Even if you can't define *sophistic*, you can see that it isn't *sophisticated*.

4. Since the Titanic sank, <u>both treasure hunters</u> as well
                                          A
    as theoretical engineers have <u>been intrigued</u> by the
                                          B
    possibility of raising it <u>from</u> the ocean floor. <u>No error</u>
                              C   D   E

Why Is It Hard? Early error

Key Strategy: Think back as well as forward.

The error here is a simple one: idiomatically, the word *both* has to be followed by *and* rather than by *as well as*. But a high percentage of SAT students get this type of question wrong *simply* because when they read the first underlined segment, they don't yet have the information needed to spot the problem. If *as well as* were underlined instead, most students would catch it.

IMPROVING SENTENCES QUESTIONS

The same problems that make Identifying Sentence Errors questions hard will occur in Improving Sentences questions. In addition, the variations in wrong answer choices may add complexity.

5. The civil rights marchers, identifying what they <u>have regarded to be an unfair interpreting of the law as</u> proposed by the mayor, are calling for its clarification.

   (A) have regarded to be an unfair interpreting of the law as

   (B) regarded as an unfair interpretation for the law as

   (C) regard being an unfair interpretation of the law

   (D) are regarding as an unfair interpretation for the law

   (E) regard as an unfair interpretation of the law

Why Is It Hard? Unfamiliar idiom

Key Strategy: Learn the idioms commonly tested.

Completely unfamiliar idioms can't be figured out—you just have to know them. If an idiomatic usage that you come across in practice isn't one you are very familiar with, be sure to read all versions of it before making a choice.

The sentence in question 5 contains errors in verb tense, idiom (*regard as*), and diction (*interpretation* not *interpreting*); the choices correct one error or another, but only (E) gets them all.

> An SAT Advanced test taker writes down and memorizes any idiom she gets wrong in practice. A limited number of idioms are regularly tested on the SAT.

6. <u>The conservationist saw the eagle's nest on the crags above the sea using a refracting telescope.</u>

   (A) The conservationist saw the eagle's nest on the crags above the sea using a refracting telescope

   (B) The conservationist above the sea using a refracting telescope on the crags saw the eagle's nest

   (C) Using a refracting telescope, the conservationist saw the eagle's nest on the crags above the sea

   (D) The conservationist above the sea using a refracting telescope saw the eagle's nest on the crags

   (E) Using a refracting telescope, the conservationist on the crags saw the eagle's nest above the sea

This sentence isn't terribly complicated, but the answer choices move the text around many different ways, making it difficult to keep its ideas clear in your mind. Your "ear" won't help you here, either. None of these choices are grammatically incorrect—you have to determine the logic of the sentence to determine their correct order.

Why Is It Hard? Too many variables

Key Strategy: Predict.

In Improving Sentences or Paragraph Corrections, tough questions may have grammatically correct elements that can be rearranged in a number of ways, with varying meanings. Treat these sentences as logic problems; determine which ideas belong together before testing the choices. If you just rush into the choices, they can make a good reader dizzy.

What can we say about the intended meaning before looking at the answer choices for question 6? The only things in the sentence that can reasonably be "above the sea" are the crags, and the eagle's nest is probably on top of it (although the conservationist might be); the conservationist, not the eagle, used the telescope. Now you should be ready to sort through the choices.

> An Advanced test taker eliminates wrong answer choices that distort the meaning of the sentence.

If you had to read through them looking for the right choice, you should note that in (A) the nest uses the telescope, in (B) and (D) the conservationist is somehow above the sea, and in (E) the nest floats above the sea. Because these can't be the intended meaning, they can be eliminated as soon as you read those words.

7. It is estimated that within five years the majority of Americans will buy <u>their clothes from a shop in a highway mall</u>, rather than from stores in towns or cities.

    (A) their clothes from a shop in a highway mall
    (B) its clothes in a shop of highway malls
    (C) their clothes in shops of a highway mall
    (D) their clothes from shops in highway malls
    (E) its clothes from a shop in a highway mall

Why Is It Hard? Complex wrong answers

Key Strategy: Slow down.

There are several errors to correct in the original and several additional errors to avoid in the answer choices. *Their* refers correctly to the subject (*majority* acting as individuals). But unless you really mean they will all buy in the same shop in a single mall, both of those nouns must be plural. The prepositions are idiomatically correct in the original sentence.

> An Advanced test taker eliminates answer choices that have internal errors.

In this case, choices (A), (B), and (C) are wrong even without reference to the rest of the sentence: "a shop" can't be in "highway malls," and "a shop of highway malls" or "shops of a highway mall" isn't idiomatic or sensible. Only (D) brings together all the correct elements. Choice (E) has the wrong pronoun, *its*, as a replacement for *Americans*.

8. Having an extremely cold and dry climate, NASA chose the Dry Valley of Antarctica as the optimal terrestrial test site to design landing plans for Mars exploration.

   (A) Having an extremely cold and dry climate, NASA chose the Dry Valley of Antarctica

   (B) NASA who chose the Dry Valley of Antarctica for its extremely cold and dry climate saw it

   (C) The Dry Valley of Antarctica's extremely cold and dry climate led to its choice by NASA

   (D) Because its climate is extremely cold and dry, NASA chose the Dry Valley of Antarctica

   (E) Based on its extremely cold and dry climate, the Dry Valley of Antarctica was chosen by NASA

> An Advanced test taker skips questions that slow him down, coming back to them after answering the other questions in the set.

Why Is It Hard? Atypical correction

Key Strategy: Don't fixate on one approach.

Most often, the misplaced modifier problem presented in this question would be fixed by changing the subject of the sentence so that the modifier makes sense: "Having an extremely cold and dry climate, the Dry Valley of Antarctica…" In this case, the test makers chose less common approaches to the correction, and 90 percent of students got this type of question wrong.

Treat this as a logic question: determine the relationship between the parts of the sentence before trying to identify the right words. In this case, (D) is the clear, concise, and grammatically correct solution. (E) is a close second, but it contains a needless passive and is wordier than (D). (B) is clumsy and wordy, and it loses the causal relationship between the climate and the astronomers' choice. (C) is clumsy and convoluted, and it introduces the ambiguous pronoun *it*.

9. The best runner on the <u>team, Susan's fastest time</u> for the one-mile race was 3.27 minutes.

   (A) team, Susan's fastest time
   (B) team is Susan, whose fastest time
   (C) team is Susan, with a fastest time
   (D) team, Susan having a fastest time
   (E) team, the fastest time for Susan

Why Is It Hard? Subtle error

Key Strategy: Slow down

Very rarely, a question will hinge on a subtle distinction that even the grammarians can miss. Take your time and be very careful. Look closely at your subject and verb, at modifiers, at pronouns, and verb tenses before opting for choice (A).

In question 9, you might mistake *Susan's* for the subject of the sentence if you read quickly, but a possessive can't be the subject. It's actually her "time"—making the introductory modifying phrase "The best runner…" inappropriate. (B) is the neatest solution—and again, it's an atypical correction, with the modifying phrase converted into the main clause.

10. <u>The Amazon, the world's second longest river after the Nile, is fed by hundreds of tributaries, many of which are over 1,000 miles long.</u>

   (A) The Amazon, the world's second longest river after the Nile, is fed by hundreds of tributaries, many of which are over 1,000 miles long.
   (B) The Amazon, after the Nile the second longer river in the world, fed by hundreds of tributaries, many of which are over 1,000 miles long.
   (C) Being fed by hundreds of tributaries, many of which are over 1,000 miles long, the world's second longer river after the Nile.
   (D) After the Nile, the Amazon is the longer river in the world and fed by hundreds of tributaries, many of which are over 1,000 miles long.
   (E) The Amazon is fed by hundreds of tributaries, many of which are over 1,000 miles long, being the world's second longest river after the Nile.

Why Is It Hard? Hypercorrection

Key Strategy: Remind yourself that about one sentence in five is correct.

If you are determined to find errors, you probably will. It's a statistically proven fact that many test takers can't resist the urge to find fault with the original version. For that reason, questions for which "correct as written" is the right answer have the highest average difficulty level. Overcome the natural tendency to hypercorrect.

Here we have a long sentence, all of it underlined, and multiple meanings are possible by rearranging its components. But it's also correct as written. The Amazon and its tributaries are correctly modified by the phrase and clause that follow them, respectively. The superlative *longest* is correctly used, because the comparison is to all the other rivers in the world—not just the Nile, although it's the only one mentioned. The present tense *is fed* is reasonable, and the right relative pronoun is used (*which*). The passive is appropriate in this case—making the sentence active would mean making the tributaries the subject, when it's clear the writer meant to focus on the Amazon.

> An Advanced test taker follows the Kaplan Method in order to keep focused and save time.

IMPROVING PARAGRAPHS QUESTIONS

Improving Paragraphs are inherently more difficult than single sentence questions, because there are more factors to be considered. Even if the error is contained within a single sentence, the relationship between that sentence and the rest of the passage will generally be relevant to determining the correction.

Let's look at some harder questions for the passage you've already seen:

> An Advanced test taker knows how to recognize and use subtle clues to decode the tougher paragraphs.

Questions 11–15 are based on the following passage.

(**1**) I recently read the famous novel *War and Peace* by Tolstoy. (**2**) At first the length of the pages—there were more than 1,500 in all—intimidated me. (**3**) But the narrative and characters were so gripping that I hardly noticed how fast I was reading. (**4**) Many people say that *War and Peace* is the greatest novel ever written. (**5**) Particularly it is said that it has the best descriptions of military battles of any book ever.

(**6**) The fascinating characters and the action and suspense made *War and Peace* an easy read with strongly developed plot lines. (**7**) They interconnected, married, remarried, fought duels, and died suddenly. (**8**) Tolstoy wrote a great story. (**9**) He didn't just tell a story. (**10**) He described an era in history and explained it in a new way. (**11**) For example, instead of saying that the great battles of 1812 and 1813 between Russia and France were due to the genius of France's Napoleon and Russia's Alexander I, Tolstoy showed that the battles had broader causes. (**12**) The leaders were just pawns with no real control. (**13**) Each battle occurs because of so many preceding factors, and so two people cannot easily control it. (**14**) With this and many other arguments, Tolstoy refuted previous historical analysis.

11. In context, which is the best way to revise and combine the underlined portions of sentences 4 and 5 (reproduced below)?

    Many people say that *War and Peace* is the greatest novel ever written. Particularly it is said that it has the best descriptions of military battles of any book ever.

    (A) is the greatest novel ever written, particularly it is said that it has the best descriptions of military battles of any book ever

    (B) is the greatest novel ever written and has the best descriptions of military battles of any book ever

    (C) has the best descriptions of military battles of any book and is the greatest novel ever written

    (D) has the best descriptions of military battles of any book although it is the greatest novel ever written

    (E) is a book with the best descriptions of military battles with the greatest novel ever written

Why Is It Hard? Special SAT rules

Key Strategy: Know the test.

In everyday usage, and even in most formal writing, sentences are acceptable that are NOT acceptable on the SAT because the SAT is extremely strict about style issues: wordiness, redundancy, irrelevance, and unnecessary passives.

The question asks you to clarify the relationship between the ideas in two sentences. Each sentence states that *War and Peace* is the best: the best novel and the best at describing military battles. The two sentences complement each other and can be combined. (B), (C), and (E) combine the two like ideas, but only (C) does so without redundancies or other grammar or style problems. (A) is a run-on with a comma splice. (B) is redundant (*any book ever*) and wordy. In (D), the contrasting word *although* creates the wrong relationship between the parts of the sentence. (E) is awkward and nonsensical, and makes "the greatest novel ever" seem less important than the best battle scenes.

12. Which of the following best replaces the word *They* in sentence 7?

(A) The action and suspense
(B) The characters
(C) The Napoleonic Wars
(D) The fascinations
(E) The plot lines

Why Is It Hard? Grammatically correct, but ambiguous

Key Strategy: Read for sense as well as errors.

They might refer to the characters, the action and suspense, or the plot lines. We must clarify this. (B) gets it right; logically, the characters interconnected, married, remarried, fought duels, and died suddenly. (A) The action and suspense could have interconnected, but could not have done the rest. (C) uses a subject from later in the paragraph. (D) nonsensically changes the adjective *fascinating* into a noun. (E) picks the wrong noun.

13. In context, which is the best version of the underlined portions of sentences 8 and 9 (reproduced below)?

Tolstoy wrote a great story. He didn't just tell a story.

(A) (As it is now)
(B) Tolstoy wrote a great story but he didn't tell a story.
(C) Although Tolstoy wrote a great story, he didn't tell a story.
(D) In addition to writing a great story, Tolstoy didn't just tell a story.
(E) Tolstoy told a great story, but his book is more than just a story.

Why Is It Hard? Grammatically correct, but illogical

Key Strategy: Read for sense as well as errors.

As written, the two short sentences almost seem to contradict each other. For good SAT style, some transition word should establish their logical connection. Look to the surrounding sentences for context. The idea is that *War and Peace* is a great story, but it is more than just a story. Sentence 7 shows how the story is interesting (therefore great). Sentence 10 states that the book also describes history in a new way. Only (E) gets at that meaning. (B) and (C) don't capture the meaning and are more contradictory than the original. (D) tries to correct the problem in two different ways that don't fit together.

An Advanced test taker has the author's main idea and purpose in mind before attacking the questions.

14. In context, which of the following revisions is necessary in sentence 13?

    (A) Replace *battle* with *battles*.

    (B) Replace *factors* with *factor*.

    (C) Replace *occurs* with *occurred* and *cannot* with *could not*.

    (D) Replace *two people cannot easily control* with *two people cannot have controlled*.

    (E) Replace *because of so many* with *due to the many*.

Why Is It Hard? The question narrows your focus.

Key Strategy: Always consider context.

If, as many students do, you approach this question by simply plugging each choice into the relevant sentence, you may miss the problem. This part of the paragraph is generally in the past tense, but sentence 13 is in the present tense. (C) addresses the error and correctly uses the past tense to describe the events that occurred in 1812 and 1813. (A), (B), and (E) don't address the problem. (A) and (B) introduce new grammatical errors. (D) changes the tense of the wrong verb.

> An Advanced test taker selects the best choice offered, even if she can imagine another, better answer.

15. Which of the following would be the most suitable sentence to insert immediately after sentence 13?

    (A) Tolstoy's fresh outlook on the Napoleonic Wars makes *War and Peace* an important historical reference.

    (B) Tolstoy's fresh outlook on the Napoleonic Wars makes *War and Peace* an important historical reference as well as a great novel.

    (C) Therefore, events are random.

    (D) Therefore, the leaders should be removed from history books.

    (E) I enjoyed the book thoroughly.

Why Is It Hard? Adding new information

Key Strategy: Know the context.

The question requires you to add full sentences not included in the original. Approach these questions with a good grasp of the overall passage and careful analysis of each surrounding sentence.

When asked what could logically follow the last sentence of a passage, we have to consider the author's main idea and what might contribute to it. The passage talks about *War and Peace* as a great novel and as a historical explanation. (B) sums that up. (A) omits the fact that *War and Peace* is a great novel. (C) could be concluded from sentence 12, but it misses the passage's main idea. (D) is an extreme statement that doesn't follow logically from what came before. (E) might be a conclusion to the first paragraph, but it doesn't reflect the argument made in Paragraph 2.

ELIMINATION STRATEGIES

Even if you find a question too difficult to be sure of the answer, you can still earn points if you can eliminate some wrong answer choices.

What's more, many questions are difficult *primarily* because of the wrong answer choices—choices that offer rare usages, difficult vocabulary, and complicated constructions. Even if the error itself is a rare and complex one, if the other choices offer familiar grammar, usage, and diction, you may not find the question challenging.

> An Advanced test taker eliminates all choices that are clearly wrong before guessing.

You have seen each of these principals as we discussed specific questions. Here's a recap:

Principal 1: Eliminate choices that distort the intended meaning of the sentence.

Principal 2: Eliminate choices that contain *internal* errors.

Principal 3: Just because an answer choice uses a form that is often incorrect, don't assume it's a wrong choice. If it contains no grammar errors or awkwardness, and the other choices do, it's correct.

Principal 4: Shorter answers are right more often than long answers. If you're left with two possibilities, go with the shorter one and the odds will be in your favor.

Principal 5: If you think it might be redundant, verbose, or irrelevant, it probably is.

SELF-EVALUATION

Students hoping only to improve their scores can simply take as many practice tests as possible. If you want to score a 2400, you have to do more. Constant self-evaluation is key.

First, consider the following overview questions:

Kaplan Methods: Are you consistently applying the methods, so that you work systematically and train your "ear"?

Time Management and Order of Attack: Are you skipping difficult questions and coming back to them, rather than letting them hold you up?

Next, focus on your own particular strengths and weaknesses. After Practice Tests, instead of reviewing the explanations thoroughly, many students stop at seeing why one answer is correct. This is a costly mistake if you want to maximize your score. Learn all you can about your own strengths and weaknesses, and use that information to manage your test taking.

Why did you choose the wrong answer?

Why did you reject the right answer?

Did you misread the question or answer choice?

Did you rush yourself?

Or is it a grammar or usage issue you have to practice more?

Some students make certain mistakes consistently; others find that they simply make more mistakes at certain points in the exam. You can reduce, and even eliminate, the problem if you recognize it. Note, for example, whether you tend to make more errors at the end of a section. There are four common reasons this might be so:

Fatigue: If you just wear out, you have to build your stamina.

Rushing: Some of us speed up when the end is in sight. That's good in a horse race, but not on the SAT; be as methodical with the last questions as with the first.

Running out of time: Pacing is vital; if you have trouble finishing, you probably have to stop spending too much time on difficult questions.

Not trusting your ear: As you work on practice questions, note which ones you are guessing on and which you are certain of. When you score them, note whether you were right about being certain, and whether you guess well. Learn when you can trust your ear and when you have to slow down and work methodically.

CHAPTER 13: WRITING PRACTICE SETS AND EXPLANATIONS

Directions: The following sentences test your ability to recognize grammar and usage errors. Each sentence contains either a single error or no error at all. No sentence contains more than one error. The error, if there is one, is underlined and lettered. If the sentence contains an error, select the one underlined part that must be changed to make the sentence correct. If the sentence is correct, select choice E. In choosing answers, follow the requirements of standard written English.

Example:

Whenever one is driving late at night,
    A

you must take extra precautions against
B   C

falling asleep at the wheel. No error
            D   E

Ⓐ Ⓑ Ⓒ Ⓓ Ⓔ

1. The ballet dancers in the performance clearly
          A   B
expected to hear loudly clapping during their
        C   D
bows. No error
      E

2. Viewers of the opening night gala performance,

who attended flouting their finest evening attire,
  A   B
included as many as a dozen stars whose movies
        C   D
are popular with American audiences. No error
                            E

3. In the park, Tom delighted in observing the
                        A
softball players' well-developed skills, which he
                              B
told us were much higher than softball players in
           C   D
his home town. No error
          E

4. An intermission was required after the second act,
               A
because the elaborate set could not be dissembled
   B   C
in a few minutes, even with the full crew and some
     D
of the performers working on it. No error
                      E

5. Tolstoy's grasp of detail <u>enabled him</u> to create
                             A
novels that <u>arose from</u> and <u>reflected</u> the
            B   C
complexity of events that Russians <u>have endured</u>.
                                   D

<u>No error</u>
E

6. Many who have visited Ireland claim

<u>to have heard</u> Banshees howling, <u>but</u> most people
     A   B
agree that such creatures are <u>actually</u> <u>imaginative</u>.
                              C   D

<u>No error</u>
E

7. This month, the Five and Dime Store <u>lowered</u>
                                        A
prices as a way <u>at attracting</u> a larger number
                B
of customers during the <u>back to school</u> season.
   C   D
<u>No error</u>
E

8. Originally a <u>rally on</u> the <u>right to</u> free speech, the
               A   B
gathering <u>succeeded in exerting</u> great influence
          C
on lawmakers <u>of its</u> time. <u>No error</u>
             D   E

9. The sportscaster <u>reviewing</u> yesterday's boring
                    A
game at Yankee stadium <u>concluded</u> that the
                       B
quality of the pitching <u>was generally</u> fine but
                        C
indistinct. <u>No error</u>
D   E

10. Tornadoes are <u>such an intent</u> threat to human life
                  A
that it <u>has become</u> imperative <u>to find new ways</u> of
        B   C
predicting the speed and direction of <u>their</u>
                                       D

movements. <u>No error</u>
           E

11. If he <u>had waited</u> <u>longer</u>, he might have succeeded
          A   B
in catching a glimpse of the <u>magnificently</u>
   C   D
colorful sunset. <u>No error</u>
                 E

12. The soldier, after his successful <u>infiltration</u> into
                                      A
enemy territory, <u>went about</u> <u>heavy camouflaged</u>
                 B   C
and was reachable by <u>only a handful</u> of his
                     D
comrades. <u>No error</u>
          E

13. Health problems caused by cigarette smoking

<u>have been examined</u> for years, <u>but</u> only recently
     A   B
<u>has</u> the hazards of cellular damage <u>become</u> fully
C   D
understood. <u>No error</u>
            E

14. In the mid-twentieth century, costuming <u>for</u>
                                            A
story ballets and short dances <u>were</u> greatly
                               B
improved <u>by</u> the <u>designs of</u> the New York City
         C   D
Ballet's Karinska. <u>No error</u>
                   E

15. The basketball league <u>imposes</u> severe <u>fines on</u>
                         A   B
players who, when <u>they are</u> <u>involved in</u> outside
                  C   D
disputes, violate league policy. <u>No error</u>
                                 E

16. Many people <u>cannot scarcely</u> <u>recognize</u> the
                A   B
grammatical errors in sentences, <u>even when</u> the
                                  C
sentences <u>are</u> written down on paper. <u>No error</u>
          D   E

17. Vans and station wagons are actually very

similar cars <u>in some respects</u>, <u>but</u> vans <u>have</u>
           A   B   C

<u>the most power</u> and acceleration. <u>No error</u>
      D   E

18. According to Smith, Monet, <u>arguably</u> the
                             A

nineteenth century's <u>best-known</u> Impressionist
                       B

painter, <u>brought</u> to his art an original symbolism
         C

<u>in which</u> to express a new view of nature.
   D

<u>No error</u>
  E

19. With the aid of an enormous truck, the

<u>electric company</u> employee <u>rose</u> the new electric
        A   B

pole <u>on the</u> street corner <u>across from</u> the school.
      C   D

<u>No error</u>
  E

20. Among history's tyrannies, that of the Nazis <u>are</u>
                                          A

<u>far more infamous</u> to <u>us</u> today than <u>any other</u>.
      B   C   D

<u>No error</u>
  E

EXPLANATIONS

IDENTIFYING SENTENCE ERRORS QUESTIONS

1. D

You'll see some very easy questions in the Writing section, but don't let your guard down. They may be followed immediately by the most difficult question in the section. If you don't "hear" the error, look at each underlined segment and consider which common errors are possible. The problem in this sentence is that an adverb *loudly* is used to modify the noun *clapping*. To correct it, we should use the adjective *loud* instead. The preposition *in* in (A) and the adverb *clearly* in (B) are correctly used. The infinitive *to hear* is idiomatically correct with the verb *expected* in (C).

2. B

You should know the word *flaunt* (meaning "showing off")—which is apparently intended here. But *flout* (meaning "scoff at") is written instead, and is definitely wrong. The expression *who attended* in (A) is correctly in the past tense; *as many as* in (C) is good, idiomatic English; and *whose* in (D) is a correct relative pronoun referring to the stars.

3. D

Tom improperly compares the park's softball players' skills with his hometown softball players (rather than with the softball players' skills). The verb in "delighted in observing" is in the proper tense. The expression "which he" is correct standard written English, and "much higher" in (C) is appropriate because only two items are compared, and *much* is an adverb modifying the adjective.

4. C

The word intended is *disassembled* (which means "taken apart"), not *dissembled* (which means "disguise, or feign"). Careful reading will prevent

this kind of error. (A) is in the correct past tense and idiom. (B) is an appropriate transition word. (D) is a correct use of *few*.

5. E

Don't forget that (E) is correct just as many times as the other answer choices are. There is no error. All of the verbs listed are idiomatically correct and in the appropriate tense.

6. D

Don't read so quickly that you overlook a word that is very similar to, but not quite, the word intended. The idea here is that, although some claim to have heard Banshees, most of us know they are *imaginary*—not *imaginative*. In (A), the phrase "claim to have heard" is idiomatic in standard written English. In (B), *but* provides a logical link contrasting the two major parts of the sentence. In (C), *actually* is, correctly, an adverb modifying *are*. Hint: Don't let it throw you if a term like *Banshees* is unfamiliar. Simply identify it as a plural noun and go from there.

7. B

The sentence contains many prepositions so look to see if they are used appropriately. "At attracting" is idiomatically incorrect. The correct phrase is "as a way to attract." *Lowered* is appropriate, because it refers to something that happened in the past. "Of customers" uses the appropriate preposition. "Back to school season" is an appropriate idiomatic expression.

8. A

"Rally on" is not good, idiomatic English. The verb *rally* takes the preposition *for* in this situation (or, for the opposite meaning, you could substitute "rally against"). The noun *right* takes the correct preposition *to* in (B). In (C), "succeeded in exerting" is correctly in the past tense. The phrase "of its time" is standard written English.

9. D

The pitching may have been *undistinguished*, but the sportscaster couldn't have reviewed it if it were *indistinct*. (A) is idiomatically correct, modifying *sportscaster*. In (C), the verb *was* agrees with the subject *quality* and is an appropriate tense; and the adverb *generally* is correctly used to modify the adjective *fine*.

10. A

A threat can be *intense* (meaning "extreme") but not *intent* (meaning "engrossed"). The verb *has become* in (B) is in the correct tense. The word *necessary* properly takes the preposition *to* in (C). In (D), the plural pronoun *their* correctly refers to the plural *tornadoes*.

11. E

Don't forget that the sentence can be correct as written. The verb *had waited* (A) is in the correct tense because that action happened before "he might have succeeded in catching a glimpse." *Longer* (B) is correct standard English: this usage compares the time he did wait and the time he might have waited—two items. In (C), the verb *succeeded* properly takes the preposition *in*. *Magnificently* (D) correctly modifies the adjective *colorful*.

12. C

The word *heavy* is an adjective, which can modify only nouns or pronouns, but here it modifies the participle *camouflaged*. We need an adverb, so (C) should read "heavily camouflaged." *Infiltration* is a correct noun. "Went about" and "only a handful" are standard written English.

13. C

Sometimes an error becomes clearer if you reverse the word order. Is it correct to say "the cellular damages has become fully realized"? The singular verb *has* does not agree with its subject, the plural *cellular damages*. It should read "recently have the hazards of cellular damage" "Have been examined" (A) is in the correct tense because the action happened before the past-tense action of the second part of the sentence. The word *but* in (B) correctly introduces the contrasting relationship between the two independent clauses of the sentence. (D) uses the correct past participle *become*. You can also reverse this to say "the cellular damages have become fully understood."

14. B

The phrase "story ballets and short dances" lies in between the subject and verb, making it more difficult to see the agreement problem. The subject of the sentence is the singular noun *costuming*, and so the verb *were* (B) should be changed to the singular *was*. In (A), (C), and (D), the prepositions *for, by,* and *of* are all idiomatically correct.

15. E

(A) is correctly singular (to agree with *league*) and in the present tense. In (B), the preposition *on* is idiomatically correct with *imposes*. (C) is the right pronoun (*they* referring to the *players*), is unambiguous because there are no other plural nouns in the sentence, and agrees with its correctly present-tense verb. (D) is the correct form to modify *they*, and *in* is idiomatically correct.

16. A

Simple double negatives are easy to spot, but watch out for words that are implicitly negative (such as *rarely*). The word *scarcely* is implicitly negative, so it is inappropriate to use another negative with it. The verb *recognize* (B) is correctly in present tense. "Even when" (C) is correctly used. *Are* in (D) is the correct plural verb.

17. D

Many of us don't "hear" this kind of error—it's an issue you just have to check for whenever a comparative or superlative is underlined. Only two cars are being compared, so in standard written English, the superlative form ("the most power") is incorrect. The correct form is the comparative "more power." "In some respects" (A) is correct idiomatically. The conjunction *but* correctly sets up the contrast. The verb *have* correctly continues the present tense of the first part of the sentence.

18. E

Remember, the sentence can be correct as written. The adverb *arguably* (A) correctly modifies *best-known*. The adjective *known* (B) correctly modifies the noun *painter*. *Brought* (C) is the correct tense of the irregular verb, and correct idiomatically. *In* (D) is the correct preposition.

19. B

Good diction means learning to be sensitive to subtle distinctions between similar words. The correct word is *raised* (which means "put up" or "lifted" and usually has a direct object, as here the employee *raised* the pole). *Rose* (B) is the past tense of *rise* (which means "stand up" or "go up"), which doesn't fit. The adjectives *electric company* correctly describe the employee. The prepositions *on* and *from* are correctly used in (C) and (D).

20. A

Some SAT questions are based on sentences that, even when corrected, are awkward. Don't let them throw you; just methodically apply what you know. This sentence speaks of a particular government in the context of many historical governments, so look for subject/verb agreement. Although *Nazis* (plural) is closest to the verb *are*, the subject *that* (which refers to a tyranny) is singular. So "are far more infamous" should be "is far more infamous." The expressions *far more* and *any other* are good, idiomatic English. Finally, *us* is the correct form with the preposition *to*.

Directions: The following sentences test correctness and effectiveness of expression. Part of each sentence or the entire sentence is underlined; beneath each sentence are five ways of phrasing the underlined material. Choice A repeats the original phrasing; the other four choices are different. If you think the original phrasing produces a better sentence than any of the alternatives, select choice A; if not, select one of the other choices.

In making your selection, follow the requirements of standard written English; that is, pay attention to grammar, choice of words, sentence construction, and punctuation. Your selection should result in the most effective sentence—clear and precise, without awkwardness or ambiguity.

Example:

Every apple in the baskets are ripe and labeled according to the date it was picked.

(A) are ripe and labeled according to the date it was picked

(B) is ripe and labeled according to the date it was picked

(C) are ripe and labeled according to the date they were picked

(D) is ripe and labeled according to the date they were picked

(E) are ripe and labeled as to the date it was picked

Ⓐ ● Ⓒ Ⓓ Ⓔ

1. Many of the concepts used in forming the United States' Republic were modifications of governmental structures developed by the ancient Greeks, particularly that of the senate.

    (A) Republic were modifications of governmental structures developed by the ancient Greeks, particularly that of the senate

    (B) Republic, there were modifications of governmental structures developed by the ancient Greeks, particularly the senate

    (C) Republic, and in particular the senate, was a modification of governmental structures developed by the ancient Greeks

    (D) Republic, and in particular the senate, were modifications of governmental structures developed by the ancient Greeks

    (E) Republic being modifications, the senate in particular, of those developed by ancient Greeks

2. Accustomed to being invisible, it was only when the subordinate left the firm that he learned how exhilarating boisterousness could be.

    (A) it was only when the subordinate left the firm that he learned how exhilarating boisterousness could be

    (B) when the subordinate left the firm he learned how exhilarating boisterousness could be

    (C) leaving the firm taught the subordinate how refreshing boisterousness could be

    (D) the subordinate did not learn how exhilarating boisterousness could be until he left the firm

    (E) exhilarating boisterousness was unknown to the subordinate until he left the firm

3. The devastating impact of <u>many diseases, often unchecked in developing nations because</u> education and information are difficult to spread.

   (A) many diseases, often unchecked in developing nations because

   (B) many diseases is often unchecked in developing nations where

   (C) many diseases is often unchecked in developing nations and

   (D) many diseases, often unchecked in developing nations when

   (E) many diseases, often unchecked in developing nations and

4. The atrocities and violence of war, <u>which are abstractly depicted in the painting *Guernica* by Pablo Picasso.</u>

   (A) The atrocities and violence of war, which are abstractly depicted in the painting *Guernica* by Pablo Picasso

   (B) War's atrocities and violence being abstractly depicted in Pablo Picasso's *Guernica*

   (C) Pablo Picasso, in his *Guernica*, abstractly depicting the atrocities and violence of war

   (D) Pablo Picasso's *Guernica* abstractly depicts the atrocities and violence of war

   (E) Pablo Picasso, whose *Guernica* abstractly depict the atrocities and violence of war

5. As freshman year continues, the balance between academics and socializing <u>become more important, challenging, and it can frighten first-year students.</u>

   (A) become more important, challenging, and it can frighten first-year students

   (B) becomes important, challenging, and frightening

   (C) when it becomes important, challenging, and frightening

   (D) becoming important, challenging, and frightening to first-year students

   (E) becomes important, challenging, and it can frighten one

6. Due to its timely subject matter, Arthur Miller's latest play is earning stellar reviews.

   (A) Due to its timely subject matter

   (B) The subject matter is timely

   (C) Due to the subject matter's timeliness

   (D) The subject matter of it being timely

   (E) The subject matter having been timely

7. <u>Ronaldo is a world-class soccer player, he is famous for scoring goals in the World Cup, and he</u> will play for Brazil in the next international match.

   (A) Ronaldo is a world-class soccer player, he is famous for scoring goals in the World Cup, and he

   (B) Ronaldo is a world-class soccer player who is famous for scoring goals in the World Cup and

   (C) Ronaldo, a world-class soccer player whose goal scoring in the World Cup being famous,

   (D) Ronaldo, a world-class soccer player famous for his goal scoring in the World Cup,

   (E) Ronaldo, a world-class soccer player, the goal scoring in the World Cup of which is famous

8. Lying on Ireland's southwest shore, <u>the history of Kinsale is a prime example of</u> fierce fighting between the Irish and the English.

   (A) the history of Kinsale is a prime example of

   (B) the history of Kinsale is primarily an example of

   (C) the history of Kinsale comes from

   (D) Kinsale's history comes from

   (E) Kinsale is a prime historical example of

9. Learning two languages is common among French students, the majority <u>of them need</u> proficiency in English to embark on business careers.

   (A) of them need
   (B) of them are needing
   (C) which need
   (D) of whom need
   (E) need

10. Realizing that his brother had not eaten all day, <u>ingredients were bought by Tom to cook</u> a large dinner.

    (A) ingredients were bought by Tom to cook
    (B) ingredients to cook were bought by Tom
    (C) cooking with ingredients was done by Tom
    (D) Tom bought ingredients to cook
    (E) Tom had bought ingredients to cook

11. Mia's neighbor <u>Julio, the president of the neighborhood council, lobbying</u> for a lower speed limit and better lighting in the alleys.

    (A) Julio, the president of the neighborhood council, lobbying
    (B) Julio the president of the neighborhood council, and who lobbied
    (C) Julio was serving as the president of the neighborhood council, and he lobbies
    (D) Julio served as the president of the neighborhood council, lobbying
    (E) Julio was the president of the neighborhood council, he served to lobby

12. The choir's spirited voices and dancing <u>bring the congregation joy.</u>

    (A) bring the congregation joy
    (B) brought the congregation to a more joyful feeling
    (C) brings joy to the people who are congregated
    (D) bring the congregation joy in their listening
    (E) brings the congregation joy in listening to it

13. <u>Being as he is a skilled chess player</u>, Conor surprises his opponents with his thoughtful, daring moves.

    (A) Being as he is a skilled chess player
    (B) With being a skilled chess player
    (C) A skilled chess player
    (D) Although he is a skilled chess player
    (E) Playing chess skilledly

14. <u>Although the best-selling author never having appeared at a book signing, he thought of them</u> as unnecessary publicity stunts.

    (A) Although the best-selling author never having appeared at a book signing, he thought of them
    (B) The best-selling author never appeared at a book signing, he thought of them
    (C) Never having appeared at a book signing, they were thought of by the best-selling author
    (D) The best-selling author never appeared at book signings; however, thinking of them
    (E) The best-selling author never appeared at a book signing because he thought of them

15. The earthquake lasted for just over a <u>minute</u> <u>and was a 4.2 on the Richter scale, which</u> <u>strength made it seem</u> as if it lasted even longer.

    (A) minute and was a 4.2 on the Richter scale, which strength made it seem

    (B) minute, and because of being a 4.2 on the Richter scale, it made it seem

    (C) minute and it had the strength of a 4.2 on the Richter scale in order to make it seem

    (D) minute, and its being a 4.2 on the Richter scale made it seem

    (E) minute, and, by being a 4.2 on the Richter scale, making it seem

16. Many workplaces are opening on-site childcare <u>centers, which provide many benefits</u> <u>for both working parents and</u> their employers.

    (A) centers, which provide many benefits for both working parents and

    (B) centers, which provides many benefits for both working parents and

    (C) centers, which provide many benefits for both working parents plus

    (D) centers; this provides many benefits both for working parents and

    (E) centers, this provides many benefits for both working parents and

17. <u>Since there has begun a widespread growth in</u> <u>its population,</u> field mice are becoming one of the most common household pests in the American Southwest.

    (A) Since there has begun a widespread growth in its population

    (B) Since having begun to grow widespread

    (C) After a widespread growth in its population began

    (D) Since a widespread growth in their population began

    (E) Before there began to be a widespread population growth

18. Showing even the most reluctant readers how enjoyable stories can be, <u>the effect of</u> <u>Ms. Doyle's summer library program is to get</u> <u>students hooked on books.</u>

    (A) the effect of Ms. Doyle's summer library program is to get students hooked on books

    (B) Ms. Doyle gets students hooked on books with her summer library program

    (C) the effect of the summer library program, run by Ms. Doyle, is that it gets students hooked on books

    (D) Ms. Doyle has had the effect of getting students hooked on books with her summer library program

    (E) the summer library program, run by Ms. Doyle, has effect in getting students hooked on books

19. <u>The dress rehearsal having been completed by</u> <u>them,</u> the director and actors went out for a well-deserved dinner.

    (A) The dress rehearsal having been completed by them

    (B) The dress rehearsal being completed by them

    (C) After the dress rehearsal, when they completed it

    (D) When they had completed the dress rehearsal

    (E) When having completed the dress rehearsal

20. Brought up by intellectual parents, <u>Marin had</u> <u>learned to read simple books</u> more than a year before she started kindergarten.

    (A) Marin had learned to read simple books

    (B) Marin had read simple books and this she learned

    (C) Marin having learned to read simple books

    (D) Marin had read simple books, she learned

    (E) Marin had read simple books; learning was

21. At some community centers in our area, extra tutoring is available to assist struggling students who might otherwise graduate from high school without necessary skills.

(A) who might otherwise graduate from high school without necessary skills

(B) who otherwise, without necessary skills, might graduate from high school

(C) and they will otherwise graduate from high school without necessary skills

(D) for whom graduation would otherwise occur without necessary skills

(E) whereby those students who might otherwise graduate from high school without necessary skills do not

22. Paolo would like to work for the newspaper, but the irregular hours are unable to be accommodated by him.

(A) Paolo would like to work for the newspaper, but the irregular hours are unable to be accommodated by him.

(B) Paolo would like to work for the newspaper, but he is unable to accommodate the irregular hours.

(C) Paolo would like to work for the newspaper, but he is unable to do so because he is unable to accommodate the irregular hours.

(D) Working for the newspaper is the thing that Paolo would like to do, but he is unable to accommodate their irregular hours.

(E) Working for the newspaper is appealing to Paolo, but he was unable to accommodate the hours, which were irregular.

23. The city of Minneapolis, Minnesota, is several hours from any other major metropolitan area, and boasting a vibrant and thriving arts community.

(A) is several hours from any other major metropolitan area, and boasting

(B) although it is several hours from any other major metropolitan area, boasts

(C) being several hours from any other major metropolitan area makes it

(D) which is several hours from any other major metropolitan area, although it supports

(E) whose distance of several hours from any other major metropolitan area makes it

24. Like many beginning musicians, the reading of sheet music was a difficulty for Asha when she first started playing.

(A) the reading of sheet music was a difficulty for Asha

(B) the reading of sheet music being a difficulty for Asha

(C) Asha had difficulty reading sheet music

(D) Asha, who had difficulty with reading sheet music

(E) there was sheet music to be read, which poses a difficulty for Asha

EXPLANATIONS

IMPROVING SENTENCES QUESTIONS

1. D

There is modification involved, so look to see if the modifier is close to what it modifies. The information at the end of the sentence, "the senate," should be closer to the word it modifies, *concepts*. Even though you probably wouldn't make the mistake of thinking that "the senate" modifies "ancient Greeks" (which immediately precedes it), it isn't clear what it does relate to. (D) places "the senate" in the correct place, after *concepts*. (B) adds *there were* (a construction that is rarely correct on the SAT and makes the sentence unintelligible). (C) introduces an error in subject/verb agreement (concepts *were* modifications, not *was*). (E) has no verb (*were* is replaced by *being*, which is a modifier), and so is a sentence fragment.

2. D

There is an introductory phrase with an ambiguous pronoun (*it*), so look there. What does the pronoun *it* refer to? "Accustomed to being invisible" clearly relates to the *subordinate*, not *it*. So the *subordinate* should immediately follow the introductory phrase. Only (D) does this. (B), (C), and (E) all have the introductory phrase modify the wrong part of the sentence.

3. B

This sentence is a fragment; there is no verb in an independent clause. The verb *are* is in the second clause, which is made subordinate by the conjunction *because*. (B) and (C) add the word *is* in the independent clause and are complete sentences. Only (B) keeps the sentence's original meaning. (C) loses the causal relationship between the two clauses. (D) and (E) don't correct the original problem—they are still fragments.

4. D

The original sentence is a fragment. The verb *are* is in the second clause, which is subordinate. Only (D) corrects the problem and retains the sentence's original meaning. It changes *the painting* Guernica *by Pablo Picasso,* which is grammatically correct but awkward, to *Pablo Picasso's* Guernica. (B) and (E) are still sentence fragments. (C) replaces *depicts* with *depicting*, making it a modifier instead of a verb.

5. B

There are three major problems in this sentence. First, when you see a pronoun such as *it*, check whether the sentence clearly shows what the pronoun refers to. Second, check for parallelism in a series (here "important, challenging, and it can frighten…"). Third, check subject/verb agreement. The pronoun *it* has no clear antecedent and "it can frighten first-year students" is not parallel to the first two items *important* and *challenging*. Also, the plural verb *become* does not agree with the singular noun *balance*. Only (B) corrects all of those problems and removes the redundant "first-year students." (C) corrects the problems but introduces *when*, which is incorrect. (D) is a fragment, replacing *become* with *becoming*. (E) only addresses the subject/verb agreement problem.

6. A

Don't forget that approximately 20 percent of sentence improvement questions have no error. The sentence concisely establishes a cause in its first half and a logical result in its second half. (B) creates two separate sentences with no clear relationship. (C) is grammatically correct but much more awkward than the original sentence. (D) is even more awkward. (E) introduces the perfect tense without any reason.

7. D

This sentence is long and rambling—a sentence type that the SAT frowns on. Look for the relationship among the several ideas. What is subordinate? What is modifying or causal? The main action is that Ronaldo will play for Brazil in the next international match. Everything else provides information about Ronaldo. (D) puts all the information in the proper place. It introduces Ronaldo, gives some description, and then states that he will play for Brazil. (B) clarifies that the first two ideas are descriptions of Ronaldo, but does not make these descriptions subordinate to his playing for Brazil. (C) makes the first half of the sentence a dependent clause. (E) introduces *of which,* and it confuses the meaning of the sentence.

8.   E

When there is an introductory phrase, check to see if it is modified correctly. Kinsale lies on Ireland's southwest shore. The "history of Kinsale" does not. (E) rearranges the sentence to make this clear. (B) and (C) don't address the principle problem. (D) corrects the problem but is awkward and has the opening phrase modifying a possessive (*Kinsale's* instead of *Kinsale*). Keep this point in mind; it often appears on the SAT.

9.   D

Don't focus on only the few words that are underlined. The entire sentence is a run-on with a comma splice, as neither clause is subordinate to the other. How can we make the second clause subordinate? (D) does the trick. It uses the objective form *whom* to create a clause that correctly modifies *French students.* (B) is still a run-on and only substitutes *are serving* for the simple present used in the original sentence. (C) uses *which* to refer to people instead of *whom.* (E) is also still a run-on.

10.   D

Ingredients didn't realize that his brother hadn't eaten. Tom did. (D) and (E) correct that problem, but only (D) is in the correct tense. (E) uses past perfect (*had*

bought) which would be correct only if the sentence referred to some other past action that it preceded. (B) still has ingredients realizing that his brother hadn't eaten. (C) changes *ingredients* to *cooking,* which also did not realize anything.

11.   D

The form *lobbying* isn't a verb—it's a modifier (remember how frequently *-ing* words start the modifying phrases and clauses at the beginning of a sentence). (D) leaves it a modifier and adds a verb to the phrase preceding it. (B) is still a sentence fragment, though it changes *lobbying* to the past verb form *lobbied*—adding *who* converted that into a dependent clause, and the sentence needs an independent clause. (C) illogically uses two different verb tenses. (E) creates a run-on sentence.

12.   A

(B) is awkward and wordy, and needlessly changes the verb to the past tense. (C) and (E) use the singular *brings* with the plural, compound subject "voices and dancing." (D) and (E) both focus on listening to the choir, while the first part of the sentence states that it was the choir's dancing, as well as their singing, that had this effect.

13.   C

The opening phrase "Being as he is" is not idiomatic formal English. (B) is as awkward as the original. (D) erroneously implies a contrast between the statement that Conor is a skilled player and the rest of the sentence. (E) uses a nonstandard form, "skilledly"— the correct adverb form is *skillfully.*

14.   E

Each clause must contain a subject and a verb. As it is written, the sentence attempts to use the modifier "never having appeared" as a verb. It also uses the contrast word *although,* when it is clear that both parts are making the same point. (E) corrects both problems. (B) creates a run-on sentence. (C) uses a misplaced modifier and an unnecessary passive verb. (D) makes the same mistake as the original sentence, using a contrast word (*however*).

15. D

The phrase "which strength made it seem" is awkward and wordy. (B) uses the phrase "because of being," which is not idiomatic. (C) is wordy, and the misuse of "in order to" implies that the earthquake intentionally made itself seem longer. (E) results in a clause fragment at the end—the verb *makes* is intended. The phrase "by being" is not idiomatic English.

16. A

As it's written, this sentence has a subject and verb that agree ("centers…provide") and correctly utilizes the parallel construction of "both…and." (B) has a plural subject (*centers*) and a singular verb (*provides*). (C) has a subject and verb that agree, but incorrectly replaces "both…and" with "both…plus." (D) transposes *both* and *for*; in order for this to be correct, the second part of the construction would need to read "and for their employers." (E) creates a run-on sentence.

17. D

The singular pronoun *its* and plural subject *mice* don't agree, and the verb phrase "Since there has begun" is incorrect. (B) also uses an incorrect verb construction, and uses *widespread*, an adjective, where an adverb should be used. (C) doesn't do anything to address the pronoun agreement problem; additionally, the verb tense doesn't agree with the tense used in the second part of the sentence. (E) also uses an incorrect verb tense, confusing the meaning of the sentence.

18. B

The underlined part of the sentence needs to begin with the subject, Ms. Doyle or her program—not

the effect. This leaves us with choices (B), (D), or (E). (C) doesn't correct the problem and is wordy. (D) implies that it is Ms. Doyle herself, not the summer reading program, who gets students hooked on books; this distorts the meaning of the sentence. (E) also uses the phrase "has effect in," which is not idiomatic.

19. D

The use of the passive form makes this open phrase wordy and awkward. (D) establishes the relationship between the two parts of the sentence better than the original. The past perfect is correct, since this action precedes the past action in the second part of the sentence. (B) duplicates this error, simply changing the tense of the verb. (C) is even more wordy and awkward than the original. (E) adds the word *when* unnecessarily.

20. A

The sentence correctly uses the past and perfect tenses to show the order in which the actions occurred. (B) is wordy and misplaces the word *this*. (C) replaces the verb "had learned" with the modifier form, "having learned," making this a sentence fragment. (D) creates a run-on sentence. (E) distorts the meaning.

21. A

The underlined clause is correct as written: it modifies the *students* that precedes it. The phrasing in (B) confuses the meaning. (C) uses the certain *will* rather than the uncertain *might,* also distorting the meaning. (D) implies that the skills belong to the graduation, not to the students. (E) is wordy and redundant.

22. B

The sentence uses a passive verb where an active verb would be a better fit. (C) is redundant, using the phrase "is unable to" twice. (D) awkwardly reverses the word order, and the pronoun *their* has no clear antecedent. (E) is wordy and incorrectly shifts to the past tense.

23. B

The sentence means that the city has an active arts community despite being far from other metropolitan areas; the use of *and* fails to show this contrast. Also, the second clause (*and* is used to introduce independent clauses) doesn't contain a verb. (B) uses *although* to convey the element of contrast that is present in the sentence, and changes *boasting* to *boasts*. (C) uses the modifier form *being* instead of a verb. (D) is a sentence fragment because both *which* and *although* introduce dependent clauses. (E) erroneously uses *whose* to refer to a city.

24. C

The first portion of the sentence is a modifier that describes the subject (Asha), so the underlined portion of the sentence should begin with the subject. This eliminates everything but (C) and (D). (C) also uses the correct idiom: "Asha had difficulty" is better than either it "was a difficulty for Asha." Both (B) and (D) result in sentence fragments. (E) does not correct the modifier issue, and also introduces another verb tense into the sentence.

Directions: The following passage is an early draft of an essay. Some parts of the passage need to be rewritten.

Read the passage and select the best answers for the questions that follow. Some questions are about particular sentences or parts of sentences and ask you to improve sentence structure or word choice. Other questions ask you to consider organization and development. In choosing answers, follow the conventions of standard written English.

---

(1) Many U.S. citizens, including me, are against smoking, as it is harmful to smokers and to those around them. (2) They work to restrict smoking to open-air areas. (3) It's been proven that smoking can lead to many different diseases, especially cancer. (4) Many states have lawsuits against tobacco companies in the court system right now. (5) The tobacco companies should pay for all of the damage they've caused—to people and to the government.

(6) I recently heard a pro-smoking argument that made me so angry. (7) I think it's sick to make human lives statistics. (8) Some economists say that it is good for the economy to have smokers. (9) In fact it is good to have many smokers. (10) Smokers die early and therefore leave resources for the rest of us who don't die. (11) They essentially will say "celebrate the fact that smokers have short life-spans!" (12) I couldn't believe the heartlessness of the economists, even if numerically their argument works. (13) How can you decide how much a human life is worth numerically? (14) I for one would rather have much less social security when I'm 80 years old and have my mother still alive. (15) My mother who died from cancer and emphysema due to smoking.

1. Which of the following best replaces the word *They* in sentence 2?

   (A) Citizens
   (B) We
   (C) Smokers
   (D) Those around smokers
   (E) Anti-smokers

2. Which sentence would be most appropriate to follow sentence 4?

   (A) I side with the tobacco companies.
   (B) I hope that the states win.
   (C) I am sure that the courts will be fair in their decision.
   (D) Human life should not be given a number.
   (E) We, American citizens, must decide what is best.

3. Sentence 7 would make most sense if placed after

   (A) sentence 5
   (B) sentence 8
   (C) sentence 12
   (D) sentence 13
   (E) sentence 14

4. Which of the following is the best way to combine sentences 8, 9, and 10 (reproduced below) in order to convey clearly the relationship of the ideas?

    Some economists say that it is good for the economy to have smokers. In fact it is good to have many smokers. Smokers die early and therefore leave resources for the rest of us who don't die.

    (A) Some economists say that it is good for the economy to have many, strongly addicted smokers because smokers die early and leave more resources for nonsmokers.

    (B) Some economists say that it is good for the economy to have smokers and for smokers to be strongly addicted and smokers die early to leave more resources for nonsmokers.

    (C) Nonsmokers get more resources when strongly addicted smokers die early.

    (D) Strongly addicted smokers are good for the economy because they die early and leave more resources for the rest of us nonsmokers.

    (E) Economically it is good that smokers are highly addicted because they die early and leave more resources for nonsmokers.

5. In context, which is the best version of "They essentially will say" in sentence 11?

    (A) (As it is now)
    (B) The economists say to them
    (C) In this they are saying
    (D) The economists essentially say
    (E) The economists suggest that:

6. In context, which is the best version of sentences 14 and 15 (reproduced below)?

    I for one would rather have much less social security when I'm 80 years old and have my mother still alive. My mother who died from cancer and emphysema due to smoking.

    (A) My mother who died from cancer and emphysema due to smoking, I would much rather have much less social security when I'm 80 years old and have her still alive.

    (B) My mother who died from cancer and emphysema due to smoking, I would much rather have alive than more social security when I'm 80 years old.

    (C) I for one would rather have my mother, who died from cancer and emphysema due to smoking, alive than much less social security when I'm 80 years old.

    (D) I for one would rather have much less social security when I'm 80 years old and have my mother still alive; my mother who died of cancer and emphysema due to smoking.

    (E) I for one would rather have less social security when I'm 80 years old and have my mother, who died from cancer and emphysema due to smoking, still living.

EXPLANATIONS

IMPROVING PARAGRAPHS

1. A

In context, *They* could refer to the citizens, the citizens and the author, the smokers, or those around the smokers. (A) fits the bill. The citizens work to restrict smoking. (B) is tricky. The author includes herself in the group of citizens against smoking, but not necessarily with those who work to restrict smoking. (C) and (D) chose the wrong noun. (E) is also tricky as the citizens are anti-smoking, but not necessarily anti-smokers.

2. B

When asked what should follow a sentence, we need to consider the main idea of the passage so far and put it in context. In the first paragraph, the author includes herself among the citizens who are against smoking. Sentence 5 states that tobacco companies, participants in the lawsuit mentioned in sentence 4, should pay for the damage they cause. The author clearly sides with the states, and (B) is your answer. (A) is the opposite. (C) is out of scope. The article doesn't focus on the court system, it is merely an example. (D) illogically brings in a point from the second paragraph. (E) is incorrect because the courts will decide, not American citizens.

3. D

As written, sentence 7 interrupts sentences 6, 8, 9, and 10, in which the author states her anger at the argument and then describes the argument. Making human lives a statistic fits best with the idea that economists attempt to decide the numerical worth of human life. This is discussed in sentences 12 and 13, so (D) works. Sentence 7 has no place in the first paragraph, so (A) is incorrect. It disrupts the idea developed in sentences 6, 8, 9, and 10, so (B) is wrong. (C) is incorrect because it would interrupt

sentences 12 and 13, which are connected by the repetition of *numerically*. (E) is incorrect because it would interrupt the idea about the author's mother (sentences 14 and 15).

4. A

Three short sentences that repeat ideas aren't good SAT style, so we must clarify the relationships between the sentences and logically combine them. Economists say that it is good for the economy to "have smokers" and "for smokers to be strongly addicted" because smokers die early and leave resources for nonsmokers. (A) combines these ideas neatly without losing any meaning. (B) simply strings the sentences together without the causal relationship. (C), (D), and (E) all get at the main idea, but lose the fact that "some economists" say this.

5. D

Sentence 11 begins with *they*, but the only plural noun in sentence 10 to which *they* could refer (smokers) doesn't make sense. (B), (D), and (E) correctly substitute *the economists* for *they*. (D) also correctly puts *say* in the present tense, instead of the future *will say*. (B) incorrectly introduces a new ambiguous pronoun *them*. (E) weakens the meaning of the phrase from the economists saying to the economists suggesting. (C) ignores the pronoun problem.

6. E

Sentence 15, which is a fragment, describes someone in sentence 14. (E) combines sentences 14 and 15, keeping the descriptive relationship intact. (C) changes the meaning, stating that "I would rather have my mother...than much less social security." (D) adds a semicolon between an independent and a dependent clause. For this to work, each clause must be independent. (A) and (B) make *my mother* the subject and add introductory phrases which do not logically lead to the independent clause.

Part Four

SAT ADVANCED MATH—THE BASICS

SAT MATH DIRECTIONS

MULTIPLE-CHOICE QUESTIONS

Directions: Fill in the corresponding oval on the answer sheet. You may use any available space for scratchwork.

Notes:
(1) Calculator use is permitted.
(2) All numbers used are real numbers.
(3) Figures are provided for some problems. All figures are drawn to scale and lie in a plane UNLESS otherwise indicated.
(4) Unless otherwise specified, the domain of any function f is assumed to be the set of all real numbers x for which $f(x)$ is a real number.

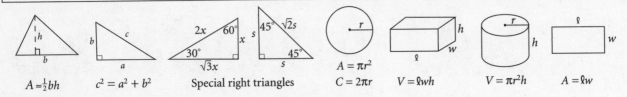

$A = \frac{1}{2}bh$ $c^2 = a^2 + b^2$ Special right triangles $A = \pi r^2$ $C = 2\pi r$ $V = \ell wh$ $V = \pi r^2 h$ $A = \ell w$

The sum of the degree measures of the angles in a triangle is 180.
The number of degrees of arc in a circle is 360.
A straight angle has a degree measure of 180.

GRID-INS

For each of the questions, solve the problem and indicate your answer by darkening the ovals in the special grid. For example:

Answer: 1.25 or $\frac{5}{4}$ or 5/4

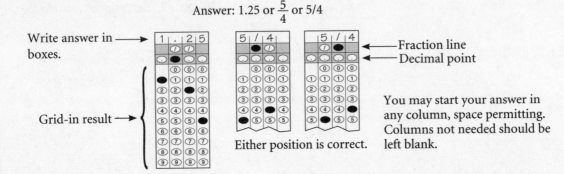

Write answer in boxes.

Grid-in result

Fraction line
Decimal point

Either position is correct.

You may start your answer in any column, space permitting. Columns not needed should be left blank.

- It is recommended, though not required, that you write your answer in the boxes at the top of the columns. However, you will receive credit only for darkening the ovals correctly.
- Grid only one answer to a question, even though some problems have more than one correct answer.
- Darken no more than one oval in a column.
- No answers are negative.
- Mixed numbers cannot be gridded. For example: the number $1\frac{1}{4}$ must be gridded as 1.25 or 5/4.

  (If $\boxed{1 \mid 1 \mid / \mid 4}$ is gridded, it will be interpreted as $\frac{11}{4}$ not $1\frac{1}{4}$.)

- Decimal Accuracy: Decimal answers must be entered as accurately as possible. For example, if you obtain an answer such as 0.1666…, you should record the result as .166 or .167. Less accurate values such as .16 or .17 are not acceptable. Acceptable ways to grid $\frac{1}{6}$ = .1666…

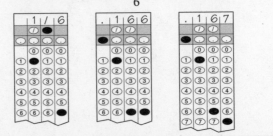

CHAPTER 14: THE SAT MATH CHALLENGE

- What to expect from SAT Math

- Where the hard SAT Math questions are found and what makes them hard

- Tricks for dealing with Grid-Ins

If you're already an above-average test taker and if you've ever taken an SAT or PSAT Math section, you probably aren't overly fearful of SAT Math. After all, the truly scary math that you've had to study in high school—like precalculus and calculus—doesn't even appear on the SAT. As a result, you don't even have to enjoy math to do fairly well on this portion of the SAT. But whether you do or don't enjoy high school math, we bet you could be doing even better.

If math is one of your favorite subjects, you probably find taking practice SAT Math sections to be fairly painless, if not downright pleasant. But then when it comes to scoring yourself and seeing how you did, you may also find that you didn't do as well as you thought. Why? Well, it could be you thought that the same skills that reward success on other math tests necessarily translate to success on the SAT. Alas, they do not. On other math tests, solving a problem the way you've been taught to in class is rewarded. On the SAT, solving problems the correct way can often get you into trouble. On other math tests, if you do the work properly but accidentally miss a step, you'll still get partial credit. On the SAT you will not.

SAT Math isn't very tough, but it can be tricky. Turning a good SAT Math score into a great SAT Math score requires learning to avoid "careless" errors—and realizing that these errors are often the result of traps built into the questions. We want to show you a different approach to test taking, one that takes advantage of, rather than falls prey to, the nature of the SAT.

> An Advanced test taker learns how to watch out for traps, and thus avoids making "careless" errors.

If, on the other hand, you're a generally good test taker but math isn't one of your favorite subjects, you can still do great on the SAT Math sections. We'll show you how to avoid doing more math than is necessary for the SAT. By following our advice and taking advantage of the standardized test format of the SAT, you too can get an excellent Math score. But to do that, first you need to understand the nature of the test.

KNOW WHAT TO EXPECT FROM SAT MATH

As you probably know, there are about 55 questions in the Math portion of the SAT. The questions are divided into two 25-minute sections and one 20-minute section.

All the SAT Math question sets are arranged to start off with easy questions and gradually increase in difficulty. On sections where the questions are segregated—some multiple-choice and then some Grid-Ins, or vice-versa—each section will start off easy and get hard separately. This means that such sections will have two easiest questions—at the beginning of each question type—and two hardest questions—at the end of each question type.

In the Math sections, it's especially important to be aware of where you are in the question set. The later you are in the set, the more traps you're likely to encounter.

> An Advanced test taker pays attention to where he is in a Math question set. If a late-appearing question seems easy, he knows to double-check the question for traps.

WHAT MAKES AN SAT MATH QUESTION HARD?

That's a good question, and there's not just one answer to it. Here are the four most common ways that SAT Math questions are deemed hard enough to end up in the latter part of the set:

1. They look easy, but contain traps for the unwary.

2. They deal with a straightforward concept, but in tricky ways that involve added steps.

3. They seem overly abstract, containing variables or unknown values instead of actual numbers.

4. They contain math concepts that many high school students don't quite "get."

To show you the difference between an easy SAT Math question and a more difficult one, we'll begin by giving you four blatantly easy SAT Math questions to do. Then we'll give you four hard questions that somewhat resemble the easy questions, but have been made tricky in one of the four ways described above.

FOUR BLATANTLY EASY SAT MATH QUESTIONS

Consider these a warm-up, and be prepared to feel embarrassed if you get them wrong.

1. One number is 3 times another number and their sum is 60. What is the lesser of the two numbers?

   (A) 12
   (B) 15
   (C) 20
   (D) 40
   (E) 45

2. Which of the following is not a prime number?

   (A) 2
   (B) 19
   (C) 37
   (D) 51
   (E) 67

3. Six years from now, Clyde will be twice as old as his cousin Bonnie will be then. If Clyde is now 16 years old, how many years old is Bonnie?

   (A) 2
   (B) 4
   (C) 5
   (D) 10
   (E) 11

4. A high school band is composed of 13 freshmen, 20 sophomores, 16 juniors, and 15 seniors. What is the probability that a band member chosen at random will be a sophomore?

   (A) $\dfrac{2}{5}$

   (B) $\dfrac{1}{3}$

   (C) $\dfrac{4}{13}$

   (D) $\dfrac{5}{16}$

   (E) $\dfrac{3}{10}$

EXPLANATIONS: BLATANTLY EASY QUESTIONS

You still want to be somewhat careful when you're answering early questions on the SAT. If you rush through them in your race to get to the tough ones, you can easily get them wrong. This is criminal on the SAT, since an early, easy question is worth exactly the same as a difficult question.

1. B

Let's translate the English into Math: $x + 3x = 60$, $4x = 60$, so $x = 15$ and the two numbers are 15 and 45. Thus, the lesser number is 15. The correct answer is (B).

2. D

We hope you are comfortable with basic mathematical definitions. 2, 19, 37, and 67 are all prime. $51 = 3 \times 17$, so it is not prime. (D) is correct.

3. C

This problem is a bit trickier than the previous two, but it's still easy enough if you read carefully. You're told that Clyde is now 16; thus, in six years he will be 22. If he will be twice as old as Bonnie will be then, that means Bonnie will be 11 years old in six years. Thus, she must be $11 - 6 = 5$ years old now, making (C) the correct answer.

4. D

To figure out the probability that a band member chosen at random will be a sophomore, you just have to apply the probability formula:

$$\text{Probability} = \frac{\#\text{ of favorable outcomes}}{\#\text{ of possible outcomes}}, \text{ or in this case:}$$

$$\text{Probability} = \frac{\#\text{ of sophomores}}{\#\text{ of band members}} = \frac{20}{13 + 20 + 16 + 15} = \frac{20}{64} = \frac{5}{16}.$$

Thus, the correct answer is (D).

An Advanced test taker handles the easy math questions quickly, but not so quickly as to possibly get them wrong.

FOUR DIFFICULT MATH QUESTIONS

Now here are some similar, but more difficult questions.

5. One number is 5 times another number and their sum is –60. What is the lesser of the two numbers?

   (A) –5
   (B) –10
   (C) –12
   (D) –48
   (E) –50

6. A positive integer n is defined as a "prime interlude" if $n-1$ and $n+1$ are both prime numbers. Which of the following is NOT a "prime interlude"?

   (A) 4
   (B) 18
   (C) 30
   (D) 72
   (E) 90

7. Six years from now, Clyde will be twice as old as his Cousin Bonnie will be then. If Clyde is now C years old, how many years old is Bonnie?

   (A) $\dfrac{C-12}{2}$
   (B) $C-12$
   (C) $\dfrac{C-6}{2}$
   (D) $C-6$
   (E) $\dfrac{C+6}{2}$

8. A class contains five juniors and five seniors. If one member of the class is assigned at random to present a paper on a certain subject, and another member of the class is randomly assigned to assist him, what is the probability that both will be juniors?

(A) $\dfrac{1}{10}$

(B) $\dfrac{1}{5}$

(C) $\dfrac{2}{9}$

(D) $\dfrac{2}{5}$

(E) $\dfrac{1}{2}$

EXPLANATIONS: DIFFICULT MATH QUESTIONS

5. E

Again, let's translate the English into math: $x + 5x = -60$, $6x = -60$, so $x = -10$, and the two numbers are -10 and -50. Thus, the lesser number is -50, making (E) correct.

This is where most students mess up. They forget that the "lesser" of two negative numbers is the negative number with the larger absolute value (since *less* means to the left of on the number line):

By the way, numbers on the SAT are usually listed in the answer choices from lowest to highest, but you're not guaranteed of this. Here, the numbers were listed from highest to lowest just to trip students up.

6. E

Once you figure out what "prime interlude" means (i.e., the integers immediately before and after your number are both prime), you're ready to tackle the answer choices:

(A) 4   3 and 5 are both prime, so eliminate.

(B) 18   17 and 19 are both prime, so eliminate.

(C) 30   29 and 31 are both prime, so eliminate.

(D) 72   71 and 73 are both prime, so eliminate.

(E) 90   89 and 91 may both seem prime, but $91 = 7 \times 13$.

7. C

Here's the "textbook approach" to solving this one. If Clyde is now C years old, then in six years he will be $C + 6$.

If Bonnie is now B years old, in six years she will be $B + 6$.

So in six years, $2(B + 6) = C + 6$, or $2B + 12 = C + 6$.

Solving for B, we get:

$$2B = C + 6 - 12 = C - 6$$

So $B = \dfrac{C - 6}{2}$, making (C) the correct answer.

If you're not 100 percent confident of your ability to solve this problem algebraically, here's a safer method for handling this question. This is actually the exact same problem as question 3 earlier, but with a variable, C, instead of the number 16 for Clyde's age. So to make this question easier and more concrete, we just need to replace Clyde's age with a number, such as 16 (or any number that makes sense).

We then get:

7. Six years from now, Clyde will be twice as old as his cousin Bonnie will be then. If Clyde is now 16 years old, how many years old is Bonnie?

(A) $\dfrac{C - 12}{2} = \dfrac{16 - 12}{2} = 2$

(B) $C - 12 = 16 - 12 = 4$

(C) $\dfrac{C - 6}{2} = \dfrac{16 - 6}{2} = 5$

(D) $C - 6 = 16 - 6 = 10$

(E) $\dfrac{C + 6}{2} = \dfrac{16 + 6}{2} = 11$

STRATEGY TIP

On questions that ask "Which of the following . . ." and require you to check out the answer choices, you can usually save time by starting with choice (E).

STRATEGY TIP

It's very easy to set up an algebra equation wrong, and if you do, the test maker will often include your mistake among the five answer choices.

> An Advanced test taker picks numbers to make abstract questions concrete.

We'll examine this technique of picking numbers in much more depth in the next chapter.

8. **C**

Finally, this is considered a tough problem simply because most students don't know how to handle "multiple event" probability questions. To find the probability of two events happening, first calculate the probability of one event, then calculate the probability of the second event occurring given that the first event occurred.

Probability that the first student picked will be a junior $= \dfrac{\# \text{ of juniors}}{\# \text{ of students}} = \dfrac{5}{10} = \dfrac{1}{2}$.

Probability that the second student picked will be a junior given that the first student picked is a junior $= \dfrac{\# \text{ of juniors remaining}}{\# \text{ of students remaining}} = \dfrac{4}{9}$.

Probability that both students will be juniors $= \dfrac{1}{2} \times \dfrac{4}{9} = \dfrac{2}{9}$. The correct answer is (C).

> An Advanced test taker knows what math could appear on the SAT and learns all the relevant formulas.

So far we've looked at only regular Math questions. Now let's take a quick look at the "weird" question type.

GRID-INS

The Grid-In questions on the SAT are designed to be more like the math questions you are used to answering in math class. In school math tests, you usually don't get five answer choices from which to choose the correct answer. Likewise, when you come to a Grid-In in the SAT test booklet, you'll see only a question and have to come up with the answer yourself.

So far, so simple. The tricky thing about Grid-Ins is that you have to fill your answer in to this funny looking grid:

FILLING IN THE GRID

Here's all you need to know about Grid-Ins. First, note that the grid cannot accommodate the following:

- Negative answers
- Answers with variables
- Answers greater than 9,999
- Answers with commas
- Mixed numbers
- Fractions with more than four digits

So if you come up with an answer that cannot be gridded, look again. For instance, if you come up with a mixed number, or a fraction that won't fit, you should be able to convert it into a decimal or a fraction that does fit.

For instance, let's say you came up with an answer of $2\frac{1}{2}$. That's a mixed number, and if you tried to grid it as is, your answer would be misinterpreted as $\frac{21}{2}$. So you could either turn your answer into the fractional equivalent $\frac{5}{2}$, or the decimal equivalent 2.5.

Now let's say you came up with an answer of $\frac{25}{27}$. You can't reduce this fraction any further, and it's too big as is to fit into the grid. You can, however, easily turn it into its decimal equivalent by pulling out your calculator. $25 \div 27 = .925925925...$

Note that when you get an answer in decimal form, you have to grid your answer as fully as possible, but you don't have to bother to round up. For instance, here either .925 or .926 would be acceptable, but .92 or .93 would not. Because of this need to fill in numbers as fully as possible, we have some general recommendations.

Always start your answer in the first column box. Do this even if your answer has only one or two figures. Technically, you can start in any column, but by following this rule you'll avoid mistakes. If you always start with the first column, your answers will always fit. Since there is no oval for 0 in the first column, grid an answer of 0 in any other column. Also, since you don't have to round up on decimal answers, why bother?

Now you can try some Grid-In problems on your own.

> **STRATEGY TIP**
>
> There may be several acceptable ways to grid in an answer, and there may be several possible correct answers to a Grid-In question. Just look for a safe, correct answer and fill in the grid carefully.

GRID-IN PRACTICE

9. The expression $\dfrac{7x+11}{5} - \dfrac{2x-2}{5}$ is how much more than x?

10. A video store sells a certain video for \$32, which is 60 percent more than it costs the store to purchase this video. During an inventory sale, employees are invited to purchase remaining videos at 25 percent off the cost to the store. If an employee purchases this video during the sale, the employee's purchase price would be what percent of the price the store originally charged for the video? (Disregard the % sign when gridding your answer.)

EXPLANATIONS: GRID-IN PRACTICE

9. $\dfrac{13}{5}$ or 2.6

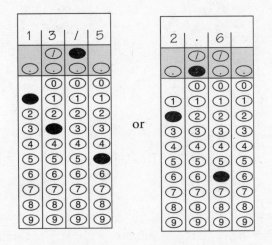

This problem may look funny at first because it's an algebra problem, and yet Grid-In answers can't have variables. Just have faith. There are two ways to answer this question, depending on how much you enjoy doing algebra.

Let's say that algebra is not your first love. In that case, you can pick a number for x to get rid of the algebra. Just make it a nice and easy number. For instance, you could pick $x = 1$. In that case:

$\dfrac{7x + 11}{5} - \dfrac{2x - 2}{5} = \dfrac{7 + 11}{5} - \dfrac{2 - 2}{5} = \dfrac{18}{5}$. Since $\dfrac{18}{5}$ is $\dfrac{13}{5}$ more than 1, the answer is $\dfrac{13}{5}$ or 2.6.

Alternatively, you could just do the algebra:

$\dfrac{7x + 11}{5} - \dfrac{2x - 2}{5} = \dfrac{7x + 11 - (2x - 2)}{5} = \dfrac{5x + 13}{5} = \dfrac{5x}{5} + \dfrac{13}{5} = x + \dfrac{13}{5}$, which is $\dfrac{13}{5}$ more than x.

An Advanced test taker knows that there's usually more than one way to the correct answer, and she chooses the approach that she finds safest and quickest.

10. 46.8 or 46.9

or

Okay, so this problem is as tough as it gets on the SAT. That's all right, you're tough too. On long, multiple-step word problems such as this one, just take it one step at a time.

First, you're told that a store sells a certain video for $32, which is 60 percent more than it costs the store. So to figure out the store's cost, translate the English into math: $32 = 1.6x$, where x is the cost to the store. $x = \dfrac{32}{1.6} = 20$, so the store's cost is $20. During a sale it's offered to employees at 25 percent off the store's cost, or $.75 \times \$20 = \$15$, so $15 is the final price to the employee.

But wait! The question asks what percent of the original price the employee pays, so pull out your calculator and divide 15 by 32. You should get .46875, or 46.875 percent, which you can grid as either 46.8 or 46.9.

> An Advanced test taker handles lengthy word problems by taking it one sentence at a time.

Now that you've had a chance to see what the SAT Math challenge is all about, our next chapter will show our favorite strategies for taking on the challenge.

CHAPTER 15: ESSENTIAL MATH STRATEGIES

- Picking numbers
- Back-solving
- Calculator strategies

In the last chapter, we looked at what the SAT 2400 Math challenge is all about, and we introduced you to some of our favorite strategies for meeting the challenge. In this chapter, we'll explore our favorite strategies in more detail. Many of these strategies will avail themselves over and over again as you work your way through the remaining math chapters. Even more important, they should prove extremely useful when you take an actual SAT.

We'll begin by taking a closer look at our old friend, Picking Numbers.

PICKING NUMBERS

As we saw in the last chapter, Picking Numbers is an extremely handy strategy for handling "abstract" problems—you know, the ones that insist on dealing with variables rather than good old numbers. Picking Numbers makes abstract problems concrete. We've already seen that Picking Numbers can be an effective strategy for dealing with certain regular math problems, and Grid-Ins.

But let's take a minute to break down the process as it relates to our most common case, the regular math problem with variables in the question and in the answer choices. Without any further ado, here's the method:

THE KAPLAN METHOD FOR PICKING NUMBERS

Step 1: Pick simple numbers to stand in for the variables.

Step 2: Answer the question using the numbers you picked.

Step 3: Try out all the answer choices using the numbers you picked, eliminating those that give you a different result.

Step 4: Try out different values if more than one answer choice works.

Don't worry. Step 4 is rarely necessary.

And since you're an aspiring 2400 hotshot and have already seen this strategy in action, we'll give you a few problems and let you try out this strategy for yourself. You can then compare your technique with ours in the explanations that follow.

STRATEGY TIP

When a problem involves a unit conversion—for instance, from minutes to hours or cents to dollars—you can Pick Numbers that do the converting for you, such as 60 for the number of minutes or 100 for the number of cents.

QUESTIONS 1–3

1. If a sausage-making machine produces 3,000 sausages in h hours, how many sausages can it produce in m minutes?

    (A) $\dfrac{m}{50h}$

    (B) $\dfrac{50h}{m}$

    (C) $\dfrac{mh}{50}$

    (D) $\dfrac{50m}{h}$

    (E) $50mh$

2. If $a > 1$, what is the value of $\dfrac{2a+6}{a^2+2a-3}$?

    (A) a

    (B) $a + 3$

    (C) $\dfrac{2}{a-1}$

    (D) $\dfrac{2a}{a-3}$

    (E) $\dfrac{a-1}{2}$

3. If $r = 3s$, $s = 5t$, $t = 2u$, and $u \neq 0$, what is the value of $\frac{rst}{u^3}$?

   (A) 30

   (B) 60

   (C) 150

   (D) 300

   (E) 600

STRATEGY TIP

When Picking Numbers for several related variables, start with the variable that all the other variables build upon.

EXPLANATIONS: QUESTIONS 1–3

1. D

You may feel like solving this problem algebraically, but Picking Numbers here is just as quick, and a whole lot safer. The key is to Pick Numbers that do the unit converting for you. For instance, here the rate is given as 3,000 sausages in h hours, but the question asks you how many sausages can be made in m minutes. So let's begin by picking 60 for m. And now make h an easy number, such as $h = 2$. Now the question asks: if 3,000 sausages can be made in 2 hours, how many sausages can be made in 60 minutes? The answer is quite obviously 1,500. Now go to the answer choices to find 1,500.

(A) $\dfrac{m}{50h} = \dfrac{60}{50 \times 2}$, which is way too small.

(B) $\dfrac{50h}{m} = \dfrac{50 \times 2}{60}$, which is still too small.

(C) $\dfrac{mh}{50} = \dfrac{60 \times 2}{50}$, which is also too small.

(D) $\dfrac{50m}{h} = \dfrac{50 \times 60}{2} = 1,500$. That's the ticket!

(E) $50mh = 50 \times 60 \times 2 = 6,000$, which is too big.

2. C

Again, you may be itching to do this one using algebra, but let's try our approach. The question tells you that $a > 1$, so you could begin by picking 2 for a here.

Thus, $\dfrac{2a + 6}{a^2 + 2a - 3} - \dfrac{2(2) + 6}{2^2 + 2(2) - 3} = \dfrac{10}{5} = 2.$

So you are looking for an answer choice that equals 2 when $a = 2$.

(A) $a = 2$, so keep it.

(B) $a + 3 = 2 + 3 = 5$. Eliminate.

(C) $\dfrac{2}{a - 1} = \dfrac{2}{2 - 1} = 2$, so keep it.

(D) $\dfrac{2a}{a-3} = \dfrac{2 \times 2}{2-3} = -4$. Eliminate.

(E) $\dfrac{a-1}{2} = \dfrac{2-1}{2} = \dfrac{1}{2}$. Eliminate.

All right, we confess. We did this deliberately, just to make you go through Step 4. Now pick a different number for a, say $a = 3$. If we run that through the expression in the question stem, we get:

$$\frac{2a+6}{a^2+2a-3} - \frac{2(3)+6}{3^2+2(3)-3} = \frac{12}{12} = 1$$

So 1 is our new target number. Now if we put $a = 3$ into the remaining answer choices, there's only one choice that works:

(A) $a = 3$. No good.

(C) $\dfrac{2}{a-1} = \dfrac{2}{3-1} = 1$, so (C) is the answer. Okay, it took some effort, but it wasn't so bad.

> An Advanced test taker tries out all the answer choices when Picking Numbers and picks a second time if necessary.

3. E

The other variables all build upon u, so pick a small number for u and figure out values for r, s, and t.

For instance, if $u = 1$, and $t = 2u$, then $t = 2$; $s = 5t$, so $s = 10$; and $r = 3s$, so $r = 30$.

So $\dfrac{rst}{u^3} = \dfrac{30 \times 10 \times 2}{1 \times 1 \times 1} = 600$.

You'll notice that Picking Numbers worked in question 3, even though there were numbers, rather than variables, in the answer choices. We often employ a different strategy when there are numbers in the answer choices, which we will look at soon. But there are two other times when there won't be variables in the answer choices or even explicitly in the questions, but the questions will be perfect candidates for Picking Numbers.

We refer to those funky word problems that contain percents or fractions in the answer choices and unknown values in the questions. By Picking Numbers for the unknown values in these questions, they become much easier to answer. The key is to know what numbers to pick.

Here, take a look. Try answering the following questions on your own by Picking Numbers, and then we'll see how your method squares with ours.

QUESTIONS 4–5

4. An antique dealer usually charges 20 percent more than his purchase price for any vase sold in his store. During a clearance sale, all items are marked 10 percent off. If the dealer sells a vase during the clearance sale, his profit on the vase (sale price minus purchase price) is what percent of the purchase price of the vase?

   (A) 8%
   (B) 9%
   (C) 10%
   (D) 11%
   (E) 12%

STRATEGY TIP

On percent questions that contain unknown values, such as the price of the vase in question 4, try picking 100 for the value.

5. In a certain orchestra, each musician plays exactly one instrument. If $\frac{1}{5}$ of the musicians play brass instruments, and the number of musicians playing wind instruments is $\frac{2}{3}$ greater than the number of musicians playing brass instruments, what fraction of the musicians in the orchestra play neither brass nor wind instruments?

   (A) $\frac{1}{5}$
   (B) $\frac{2}{5}$
   (C) $\frac{7}{15}$
   (D) $\frac{8}{15}$
   (E) $\frac{2}{3}$

STRATEGY TIP

On fraction problems that contain unknown values, such as the number of musicians in the orchestra in question 5, try picking the largest denominator in the answer choices for the value.

EXPLANATIONS: QUESTIONS 4–5

4. A

Let's begin by picking $100 for the original cost of the vase. So the dealer pays $100 for the vase, but he usually charges 20 percent more, or $120 for it. During the sale the vase's price is reduced 10 percent. Ten percent of $120 is $12, so the final sale price of the vase is $108, meaning the dealer made a profit of $\frac{8}{100}$, or 8 percent of his original purchase price.

5. C

Since 15 is the largest denominator in the answer choices, let's assume there are 15 musicians in the orchestra. Since $\frac{1}{5}$ of these are brass musicians, that means there are 3 brass musicians in the orchestra. The number of wind musicians is $\frac{2}{3}$ greater than this, that is $\frac{2}{3}$ greater than 3, so there are 2 more wind musicians than brass musicians, or 5 wind musicians altogether. So, of the 15 musicians, $3 + 5 = 8$ play either wind or brass instruments. That leaves 7 people who play neither instrument. So the fraction of musicians who play neither instrument is $\frac{7}{15}$.

Now let's look at our next strategy for dealing with ugly math questions.

BACK-SOLVING

Some of the nastiest SAT Math problems have numbers in the answer choices, and the Picking Numbers technique just won't cut it. On these questions, you can try Back-solving instead. When you Back-solve, you simply plug the answer choices back into the question until you find one that works. If you do it systematically, it shouldn't take you too much time. Here's the system:

THE KAPLAN METHOD FOR BACK-SOLVING

Step 1: Start with (C).

Step 2: Eliminate choices you know are too big or too small.

Step 3: Keep going until you find the choice that works.

Let's take a look.

6. Employee X is paid $12.50 an hour for the first 36 hours he works in a week, and is paid double that rate for every hour over that. Employee Y is paid $15.00 an hour for the first 40 hours she works in a week, and is paid 1.5 times that rate for every hour over that. On a certain week, both employees worked the same number of hours and were paid the same amount. How many hours did each employee work that week?

(A) 48

(B) 50

(C) 54

(D) 60

(E) 64

Notice that the problem itself is long and nasty. The pay scales don't match, and overtime kicks in at different points and at different rates. But the question itself is clear enough. "How many hours did each employee work that week?" Since there are numbers in the answer choices, let's go ahead and Back-solve.

By the way, here's a good occasion to pull out your calculator. Let's begin with choice (C) and assume that each employee worked 54 hours. That means that Employee X earned $(36 \times 12.50) + (18 \times 25.00) = \$900$, and Employee Y earned $(40 \times 15.00) + (14 \times 22.50) = \$915$. So (C) is out. But can we eliminate anything else? Employee Y here earned more than Employee X, but the more hours each employee works, the more Employee X's earnings close in on Employee Y's, since Employee X earns a higher overtime wage. So we want a larger number, meaning (A) and (B) are out.

Now let's try (D), and assume that they each worked 60 hours. Now Employee X earns $(36 \times 12.50) + (24 \times 25.00) = \$1,050$, and Employee Y earns $(40 \times 15.00) + (20 \times 22.50) = \$1,050$.

The wages match! We found the answer, and it's (D).

Now try some Back-solving problems on your own.

QUESTIONS 7–8

7. At Central Park Zoo, the ratio of sea lions to penguins is 4 to 11. If there are 84 more penguins than sea lions, how many sea lions are there?

   (A) 24
   (B) 36
   (C) 48
   (D) 72
   (E) 121

8. What is the value of x if $\dfrac{x+1}{x-3} - \dfrac{x+2}{x-4} = 0$?

   (A) −2
   (B) −1
   (C) 0
   (D) 1
   (E) 2

> **STRATEGY TIP**
>
> If you don't know in which direction to go after you've tried and eliminated (C), pick the next easiest number to work with.

EXPLANATIONS: QUESTIONS 7–8

7. C

The correct answer should yield a ratio of sea lions to penguins of 4 to 11, so try out choice (C). If there are 48 sea lions, there are $48 + 84 = 132$ penguins, so the ratio of sea lions to penguins is $\dfrac{48}{132} = \dfrac{4}{11}$, which is just what we want. That means we're done.

8. D

As always, we'll start with (C). We're looking for an answer choice that gives us zero on the left side of the equation:

(C) $\dfrac{x+1}{x-3} - \dfrac{x+2}{x-4} = \dfrac{0+1}{0-3} - \dfrac{0+2}{0-4} = -\dfrac{1}{3} + \dfrac{1}{2} \neq 0$, so we have to keep fishing.

But in this case, it may not be easy to know which number to pick next, so pick one of the remaining numbers that's easy to work with:

(D) $\dfrac{x+1}{x-3} - \dfrac{x+2}{x-4} = \dfrac{1+1}{1-3} - \dfrac{1+2}{1-4} = -1 + 1 = 0$

Since the equation is true for (D), it must be the answer.

CALCULATOR STRATEGIES

The official SAT guide says that no problems on the test require a calculator, but they recommend bringing one. Having a good calculator and knowing how to use all the functions on it that the SAT might ask for are keys to making many questions on the test much easier.

Let's look at one:

9. If P is the product of the first seven positive integers, then P is NOT a multiple of

(A) 27
(B) 35
(C) 42
(D) 63
(E) 72

While the use of logic and knowledge of multiples and primes is certainly one way to do this problem, another way that many Advanced test takers find fast and easy is to use their calculators.

1. On your calculator, multiply $1 \times 2 \times 3 \times 4 \times 5 \times 6 \times 7$.

2. Record the result (5,040), either in the calculator memory or next to the problem.

3. Divide 5,040 by each of the answer choices. As soon as you get a result that isn't an integer, you're done! In this case, choice (A) is the only answer that P is not a multiple of.

As was mentioned earlier, Back-solving will tend to involve calculator use fairly often.

In addition to helping clean up gross arithmetic work, the calculator can make graph analysis problems a breeze. Take a look at this question.

10. At which points do the graphs of $y = 2x^2 + 1$ and $y = x + 7$ intersect?

    (A) $\left(2, -\dfrac{3}{2}\right)$ and $\left(9, \dfrac{11}{2}\right)$

    (B) $(2, 9)$ and $\left(-\dfrac{3}{2}, \dfrac{11}{2}\right)$

    (C) $(2, 9)$ and $(-3, 11)$

    (D) $(0, 1)$ and $(1, -7)$

    (E) $(1, 7)$ and $(2, 1)$

Now, if we just graph these two equations on the calculator and trace one of the plots (the linear one is probably easier), we can easily see in the trace info box the coordinates of the point where it intersects the curve. The intersection point on the right is $x = 2$. This eliminates answer choices (A) and (D). We will need to translate decimals that may not be *exactly* at the intersection to the appropriate fractions for this problem, but that's quite straightforward, as they're only $\dfrac{1}{2}$s. The left intersection point is at $x = -1\dfrac{1}{2}$. This means the answer has to be (B).

Now try some on your own.

11. If $f(x) = x^2 + 5$ and $g(x) = x + 7$, what are the values of x where $f(x) = g(x)$?

    (A) -2 and 1
    (B) -2 and 2
    (C) -1 and 1
    (D -1 and 2
    (E) 5 and 7

For this problem, don't get confused by the function notation. Just graph $y = x^2 + 5$ and $y = x + 7$ on your calculator. Look at the two intersection points, see where they are and how their x-coordinates compare with the answer choices. Only (D) fits.

12. If $f(x) = x^2 - 4$, at which value(s) of x does the graph of $y = f(x)$ cross the x-axis?

    (A) 2 only
    (B) 0 only
    (C) -2 only
    (D) 4 only
    (E) -2 and 2

Once again, making a simple graph of $y = x^2 - 4$ on your calculator makes this problem trivial. The answer is (E).

13. If $f(x) = |x^2 - 2x|$, what is the value of $f(7)$?

   (A)   0
   (B)   7
   (C) 14
   (D) 35
   (E) 49

Again, don't let the function notation throw you off. This is a pretty straightforward plug-and-chug problem. Just plug 7 in for x in the function, and calculate. (D) is the correct answer.

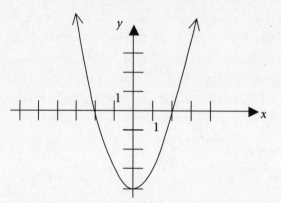

14. Which of the following equations best describes the curve shown in the graph above?

   (A) $y = x - 4$
   (B) $y = x^2 - 2$
   (C) $y = x^2 - 4$
   (D) $y = x^2 + 4$
   (E) $y = (x + 4)^2$

If you recognize the shape in the graph and remember transposition rules, great, you can move straight to the answer. If you don't, though, just graph the five answer choices, one at a time, on your calculator, and see which matches the curve shown. Remember: your calculator may distort the shape of the curve differently than the test does, depending on the scaling you use on your graphical view. To make sure, count the tics on the number line to verify that all the x- and y-intercepts are in the right places. The answer is (C).

15. Point Q is on the same line as $(0, 0)$ and $(3, 9)$. Which of the following could be point Q?

   (A) $(0, 1)$
   (B) $(1, 3)$
   (C) $(2, 4)$
   (D) $(-3, 9)$
   (E) $(-6, -2)$

To graph this, we first need to put it in $y = mx + b$ format. The coordinates of the first point make the y-intercept pretty obvious. Use the slope formula, $\dfrac{y_2 - y_1}{x_2 - x_1}$, to calculate the slope: $\dfrac{9 - 0}{3 - 0} = \dfrac{9}{3} = 3$. Then graph $y = 3x$ on you calculator and trace until you find an answer choice on the line. (A) isn't, but (B) is, so you're done.

If the y-intercept weren't so obvious, this method wouldn't be the best choice. In this case, we would find the slope of the line going through the two points of the question stem. Then, for the answer choices, we would find the slope of the line going through the point of an answer choice and one of the points of the question stem until the slope from an answer choice equaled the slope of the line going through the two points of the question stem.

ESSENTIAL MATH STRATEGIES RECAP

HOW TO ATTACK SAT MATH SECTIONS STRATEGICALLY

- Do all the questions you can handle easily first. Do the tough stuff after you've answered all of the other questions in a set.
- Look for shortcuts and Back-solving approaches to the answer. Choose the approach that works best for you.
- Make sure, especially toward the end of a question set, that you have read the question carefully and are answering the question that's been asked of you.
- Make sure you know how to do all of the following on your calculator:
  - Use parentheses correctly, especially in fractions
  - Convert exponents and roots to fractions and large numbers
  - Graph lines and curves, including those with absolute values
  - Trace graphs

REGULAR MATH STRATEGIES

- Pick Numbers
- Back-solve

HOW TO PICK NUMBERS ON REGULAR MATH QUESTIONS

Step 1: Pick simple numbers to stand in for the variables.

Step 2: Answer the question using the numbers you picked.

Step 3: Try out all the answer choices using the numbers you picked, eliminating those that give you a different result.

Step 4: Try out different values if more than one answer choice works.

HOW TO BACK-SOLVE ON REGULAR MATH QUESTIONS

Step 1: Start with (C).

Step 2: Eliminate choices you know are too big or too small.

Step 3: Keep going until you find the choice that works.

We know that you're just dying to test out all of these strategies. That's what the next chapter is all about.

CHAPTER 16: SAT MATH STRATEGIES PRACTICE SET AND EXPLANATIONS

Directions: Fill in the corresponding oval on the answer sheet. You may use any available space for scratchwork.

Notes:

(1) Calculator use is permitted.

(2) All numbers used are real numbers.

(3) Figures are provided for some problems. All figures are drawn to scale and lie in a plane UNLESS otherwise indicated.

(4) Unless otherwise specified, the domain of any function f is assumed to be the set of all real numbers x for which $f(x)$ is a real number.

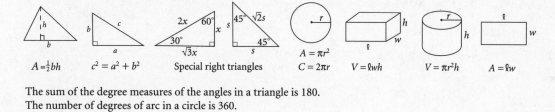

$$A = \tfrac{1}{2}bh \qquad c^2 = a^2 + b^2 \qquad \text{Special right triangles} \qquad A = \pi r^2 \qquad V = \ell wh \qquad V = \pi r^2 h \qquad A = \ell w$$
$$C = 2\pi r$$

The sum of the degree measures of the angles in a triangle is 180.
The number of degrees of arc in a circle is 360.
A straight angle has a degree measure of 180.

1. If n is an even number, which of the following must be odd?

   (A) $\dfrac{3n}{2}$

   (B) $2(n-1)$

   (C) $n(n+1)$

   (D) $\dfrac{n}{2}+1$

   (E) $2n+1$

2. If $\dfrac{3x}{4}+10=\dfrac{x}{8}+15$, then $x=$

   (A) 4

   (B) 8

   (C) 10

   (D) 12

   (E) 16

3. A water tower is filled to $\frac{3}{4}$ of its capacity. If $\frac{3}{5}$ of the water it is currently holding were to be released, what fraction of its capacity would it hold?

    (A) $\frac{1}{20}$

    (B) $\frac{3}{20}$

    (C) $\frac{1}{5}$

    (D) $\frac{1}{4}$

    (E) $\frac{3}{10}$

4. Louis is three times as old as his sister Denise, who is five years older than their cousin Celeste. If in 18 years Louis will be twice as old as Celeste will be then, how old is Denise?

    (A) 7
    (B) 8
    (C) 9
    (D) 10
    (E) 12

5. The diagram above represents a square garden. If each side of the garden is increased in length by 50 percent, by what percent is the area of the garden increased?

    (A) 50%
    (B) 100%
    (C) 125%
    (D) 150%
    (E) 225%

6. The cost to rent a boat for a fishing trip is x dollars, which is to be shared equally among the people taking the trip. If 12 people go on the trip rather than 20, how many more dollars, in terms of x, will it cost per person?

    (A) $\frac{x}{8}$

    (B) $\frac{x}{12}$

    (C) $\frac{x}{16}$

    (D) $\frac{x}{20}$

    (E) $\frac{x}{30}$

7. A car rental company charges for mileage as follows: x dollars per mile for the first n miles and $x + 1$ dollars per mile for each mile over n miles. How much will the mileage charge be in dollars for a journey of d miles where $d > n$?

    (A) $d(x + 1) - n$
    (B) $xn + d$
    (C) $xn + d(x + 1)$
    (D) $x(n + d) + d$
    (E) $(x + 1)(d - n)$

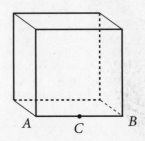

8. The surface area of the cube above is 294 square centimeters. If C is the midpoint of AB, what is the length of AC in centimeters?

    (A) 3
    (B) 3.5
    (C) 4
    (D) 4.5
    (E) 6

9. Twenty percent of the trees in an orchard are apple trees, and $\frac{1}{3}$ of the trees that are not apple trees are cherry trees. If $\frac{3}{4}$ of the trees in the orchard are fruit trees, and the only types of fruit trees in the orchard are apple trees, cherry trees, and plum trees, what fraction of the trees in the orchard are plum trees?

(A) $\frac{1}{30}$

(B) $\frac{3}{40}$

(C) $\frac{1}{12}$

(D) $\frac{17}{60}$

(E) $\frac{13}{45}$

10. At a lightbulb factory, 1 out of every 30 lightbulbs produced is defective. Ninety-two percent of the defective light bulbs are discarded at the factory, and the remaining defective lightbulbs are shipped to customers. If 1,200 defective lightbulbs were shipped to customers over the course of one year, how many lightbulbs were produced by the factory during that year?

(A) 300,000

(B) 450,000

(C) 500,000

(D) 540,000

(E) 600,000

11. If y is a positive number, which of the following is equivalent to increasing y by 40 percent and then decreasing the result by 50 percent?

(A) Decreasing y by 30%

(B) Decreasing y by 25%

(C) Decreasing y by 10%

(D) Increasing y by 10%

(E) Increasing y by 20%

12. If a speedboat travels at a rate of $\frac{x}{10}$ miles every y seconds, how many miles will the speedboat travel in z minutes?

(A) $\frac{xy}{10z}$

(B) $\frac{xz}{10y}$

(C) $\frac{xyz}{10}$

(D) $\frac{6xy}{z}$

(E) $\frac{6xz}{y}$

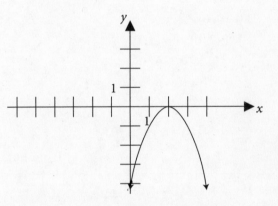

13. Which of the following equations best describes the curve shown in the graph above?

(A) $y = -x^2 + 2$

(B) $y = x^2 - 2$

(C) $y = (x + 2)^2$

(D) $y = (x - 2)^2$

(E) $y = -(x - 2)^2$

14. If $g(x) = x^2 + x - 20$, and a is the x-coordinate of the point at which the graph of $y = g(x)$ crosses the y-axis, what is the value of $g(a)$?

(A) −20

(B) −5

(C) −4

(D) 0

(E) 5

15. $\dfrac{3\sqrt{3}}{\sqrt{2}} \times \dfrac{4\sqrt{3}}{3} =$

   (A) 3

   (B) $6\sqrt{2}$

   (C) 12

   (D) $12\sqrt{2}$

   (E) 36

16. If $f(x) = x^2 - x + 4$, at which points does the graph of $y = f(x)$ cross the x-axis?

   (A) $f(x)$ does not cross the x-axis.

   (B) $(-2, 0)$

   (C) $(4, 0)$

   (D) $(0, 0)$

   (E) $(-2, 0)$ and $(2, 0)$

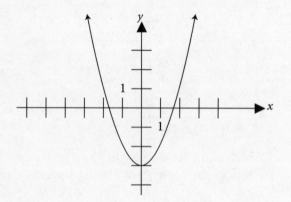

17. Which of the following equations best describes the curve above?

   (A) $y = (x - 3)^2$

   (B) $y = (x + 3)^2$

   (C) $y = x^2 - 3$

   (D) $y = x^2 - \sqrt{3}$

   (E) $y = x^2 + 3$

18. Which of the following graphs shows the graph of $f(x) = |x - 4|$?

   (A)

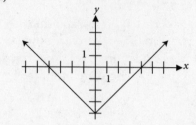

   (B)

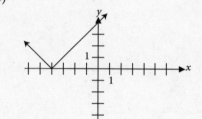

   (C)

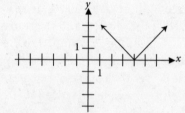

   (D)

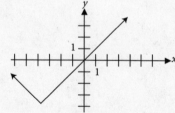

   (E)

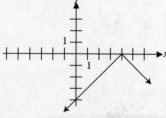

19. At an international dinner $\frac{5}{21}$ of the people attending were from South America. If the number of North Americans at the dinner was $\frac{3}{10}$ less than the number of South Americans, what fraction of people at the dinner were from neither South America nor North America?

(A) $\frac{1}{6}$

(B) $\frac{3}{7}$

(C) $\frac{10}{21}$

(D) $\frac{25}{42}$

(E) $\frac{197}{210}$

20.* A candy jar contains only grape, cherry, orange, and lemon candies. In the jar there are twice as many grape candies as cherry candies, and twice as many cherry candies as orange and lemon candies combined. If there are three times as many orange candies as lemon candies, what is the probability that a candy drawn at random from the jar will be an orange candy?

EXPLANATIONS

1. E

Try picking an even number for n to plug into the answer choices, such as 2.

(A): $\dfrac{3n}{2} = \dfrac{3 \times 2}{2} = \dfrac{6}{2} = 3$. Keep it for now.

(B): $2(n-1) = 2(2-1) = 2$. This is not odd. Discard.

(C): $n(n+1) = 2(2+1) = 6$. This is not odd. Discard.

(D): $\dfrac{n}{2} + 1 = \dfrac{2}{2} + 1 = 2$. This is not odd. Discard.

(E): $2n + 1 = 2 \times 2 + 1 = 5$. Keep it for now.

Now try picking a different even number for n, such as 4:

(A): $\dfrac{3n}{2} = \dfrac{3 \times 4}{2} = \dfrac{12}{2} = 6$. This is not odd. Discard.

(E): $2n + 1 = 2 \times 4 + 1 = 9$. This is odd. Bingo!

2. B

Let's Back-solve to answer this. Normally we would begin with (C), but since it's clear that 10 does not yield nice round numbers when plugged into $\dfrac{3x}{4}$ or $\dfrac{x}{8}$, we'll start with an easier number, such as (B), $x = 8$:

$$\frac{3 \times 8}{4} + 10 = \frac{8}{8} + 15\,?$$
$$\frac{24}{4} + 10 = 1 + 15$$
$$6 + 10 = 16$$

3. E

Here we want to pick a number for the capacity of the water tower, making sure the number works well with the fractions in the problem. Let's use the largest denominator in the answer choices and say that the water tower holds 20 gallons.

Thus, if the tower is filled to $\dfrac{3}{4}$ of its capacity, it contains 15 gallons. And if $\dfrac{3}{5}$ of that were to be released, 9 gallons would be released, leaving 6 gallons. Thus, the tower would be left holding $\dfrac{6}{20} = \dfrac{3}{10}$ of its capacity.

4. B

Here's another opportunity to Back-solve, so let's start with choice (C):

If Denise is 9, then Louis is 27 and Celeste is 4. In 18 years, Louis will be 45 and Celeste will be 22, so Louis will be *slightly more than* twice as old as Celeste.

That didn't work, so let's try (B):

If Denise is 8, then Louis is 24 and Celeste is 3. In 18 years, Louis will be 42 and Celeste will be 21, so Louis will be twice as old as Celeste will be then. That works, so (B) is the answer.

5. C

Since we are dealing with a square garden, both sides are the same, and the area = (side)^2. And because this is also a percent problem, we can make the original dimensions 10 ft by 10 ft, so the original area would be 100 sq. ft. Then if we increase each side length by 50 percent, the new dimensions would be 15 ft by 15 ft, for a new area of $15 \times 15 = 225$ sq. ft.

If you figured this much out and then picked (E), you didn't read the question carefully enough. The question asks by what percent the area of the garden is *increased*. The amount of increase is $(225 - 100) = 125$ sq. ft, which is 125 percent of 100 sq. ft, making (C) the correct answer.

6. E

Pick a number for x, making sure that the number you pick works well with the numbers in the problem. You want a number that both 12 and 20 divide into evenly, so let's try $x = 60$:

If 12 people go on the trip, the cost will be $\frac{60}{12} = 5$ dollars per person.

If 20 people go on the trip, the cost will be $\frac{60}{20} = 3$ dollars per person.

Consequently, the additional cost per person will be $5 - 3 = 2$ dollars, and 2 is the target number:

(A) $\frac{x}{8} = \frac{60}{8}$, which is not 2. Discard.

(B) $\frac{x}{12} = \frac{60}{12} = 5$. Discard.

(C) $\frac{x}{16} = \frac{60}{16}$, which is not 2. Discard.

(D) $\frac{x}{20} = \frac{60}{20} = 3$. Discard.

(E) $\frac{x}{30} = \frac{60}{30} = 2$. This is it!

7. A

Say you picked $x = 2$ and $n = 3$ and $d = 4$. Use these numbers to work out how much a journey of 4 miles costs.

The first 3 miles cost 2 dollar per mile, so the charge for the first 3 miles is 6 dollars.

The final mile costs $2 + 1 = 3$ dollars per mile, so the charge here is 3 dollars.

The total charge is $6 + 3 = 9$ dollars. This is your target number. Look for it when you substitute $x = 2$ and $n = 3$ and $d = 4$ into the answer choices.

(A) $d(x + 1) - n = 4(2 + 1) - 3 = 9$. Keep this.

(B) $xn + d = 2(3) + 4 = 10$. Eliminate.

(C) $xn + d(x + 1) = 2(3) + 4(2 + 1) = 18$. Eliminate.

(D) $x(n + d) + d = 2(3 + 4) + 4 = 18$. Eliminate.

(E) $(x + 1)(d - n) = (2 + 1)(4 - 3) = 3$. Eliminate.

Only choice (A) gives you your target number, so that's the answer.

8. B

Let's Back-solve this confusing geometry problem. Let's assume $AC = 4$: if $AC = 4$, the edge length of the cube is 8, so each face of the cube is $8^2 = 64$ square centimeters. There are 6 faces to a cube, so the entire surface area would be $64 \times 6 = 384$ square centimeters. This is too large so (C), (D), and (E) are all out.

Try $AC = 3.5$: if $AC = 3.5$, the edge length of the cube is 7, so each face of the cube is $7^2 = 49$ square centimeters. There are 6 faces to a cube, so the entire surface area would be $49 \times 6 = 294$ square inches, which is what we want, so the answer is (B).

9. D

We'll treat this as we would any fraction problem with an unknown value, and plug in the largest denominator in the answer choices for the number of trees in the orchard. So we'll assume there are 60 trees. Twenty percent, i.e., $\frac{1}{5}$ of these, or 12 of the trees, are apple trees, leaving 48 trees, of which $\frac{1}{3}$, or 16 trees, are cherry trees. $\frac{3}{4}$ of all the trees, or 45 trees, are fruit trees, and since all the fruit trees are either apple, cherry or plum, that leaves $45 - (12 + 16) = 17$ plum trees. Thus, the fraction of all the trees in the orchard that are plum trees is $\frac{17}{60}$.

10. B

Let's Back-solve this one. If you start with (C), you quickly see that 500,000 cannot be the answer because 1 in 30 lightbulbs are defective, and 500,000 is not divisible by 30. Eliminate.

Let's try (B): out of 450,000 lightbulbs, 1 in 30, or $450,000 \div 30 = 15,000$ lightbulbs are defective.

If 92 percent of these are discarded, 8 percent are shipped out: $15,000 \times 0.08 = 1,200$. So (B) is the answer.

11. A

This question begs to be solved by picking numbers. Let $y = 100$. Increasing 100 by 40 percent gives you 140. Decreasing that by 50 percent leaves you with 70. Going from 100 to 70 is the same as decreasing by 30 percent. That was too easy. Choice (A) is correct.

12. E

Here's another opportunity to pick numbers, and since the problem involves a unit conversion from seconds to minutes, we want to pick numbers that do the converting for us. For instance, we could make $x = 20$ and $y = 60$, so that the speedboat travels $\frac{20}{10}$ or 2 miles every 60 seconds, or one minute. So if we make $z = 2$ (the number of minutes), then the boat travels 2 miles a minute, so it must travel 4 miles in 2 minutes. So 4 is your target number when $x = 20$, $y = 60$, and $z = 2$. Now try out the answer choices.

(A) $\dfrac{xy}{10z} = \dfrac{20 \times 60}{10 \times 2}$, which is too large.

(B) $\dfrac{xz}{10y} = \dfrac{20 \times 2}{10 \times 60}$, which is too small.

(C) $\dfrac{xyz}{10} = \dfrac{20 \times 60 \times 2}{10}$, which is way too large.

(D) $\dfrac{6xy}{z} = \dfrac{6 \times 20 \times 60}{2}$, which is even larger.

(E) $\dfrac{6xz}{y} = \dfrac{6 \times 20 \times 2}{60} = 4$. We finally found it!

13. E

If you recognize the shape in the graph and remember transposition rules, great, you can move straight to the answer. If you don't, though, just graph the five answer choices, one at a time, on your calculator, and see which matches the curve shown.

14. A

Once again, making a simple graph of $y = x^2 + x - 20$ on your calculator makes this problem trivial. About as easy is remembering that 0 is the x-value when a graph crosses the y-axis. Plugging in 0 for x gives you the answer quickly too.

15. B

Without a calculator, this problem is somewhat annoying. But with one, it's pretty trivial—if you use your parentheses correctly. The result you get is $8.485\ldots$, which isn't obviously among the answer choices, if you remember that the answer choices are always in numerical order. (A) is 3 and (C) is 12, so only (B) is in the right possible range. If you want to double-check, calculate the value of (B) to compare.

16. A

Knowing that $y = 0$ when a function crosses the x-axis won't make things easy here, as $x^2 - x + 4 = 0$ does not solve easily. This means the calculator will definitely be a faster route to the solution. A graph shows you that (A) is the correct answer here.

17. C

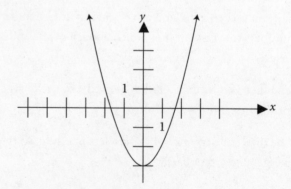

Once again, recognition or graphing are the two routes to the answer to this question. If you can't immediately identify the answer (and most people can't), graph answer choices on your calculator until you find the one that matches.

18. C

This is a slightly trickier version of the "which graph matches" question, as you have to remember how to put absolute values into your graphs. If you get stuck and can't remember, graph $y = x - 4$ and $y = -x + 4$ on the same graph. This will give you a big X on the screen. There may be two answers that match that X, one for the top half, and another for the bottom half, as is the case here for (C) and (E). To choose between them, we need to note that y values should always be positive or zero. This means (C) has to be the right answer.

19. D

You should notice immediately that the problem contains two fractions: $\dfrac{5}{21}$ and $\dfrac{3}{10}$. The least common denominator is 210, so let's say the number of people at the dinner was 210. That means there were $\dfrac{5}{21}(210) = 50$ South Americans. We also had North Americans numbering $\dfrac{3}{10}$ less than that, so there were $50 - \dfrac{3}{10}(50) = 50 - 15 = 35$ North Americans. So there were $50 + 35 = 85$ people from South America or North America, which means that $210 - 85 = 125$ people were not from either place. So $\dfrac{125}{210} = \dfrac{25}{42}$ of the people were from neither South America nor North America. The correct answer, therefore, is (D).

20. $\dfrac{3}{28}, \dfrac{6}{56}, \dfrac{9}{84}$, or .107

As you should know, every now and then you can pick numbers, even on a Grid-In. Here's a perfect example. Let's assume there's 1 lemon candy (since all the other numbers seem to build on this one). Read carefully through the question, and you'll see that that means there are 3 orange candies, 8 cherry candies, and 16 grape candies.

So the probability of picking an orange candy is:

$$\dfrac{\text{Number of orange candies}}{\text{Total number of candies}} = \dfrac{3}{1 + 3 + 8 + 16} = \dfrac{3}{28}$$

or .107.

Part Five

STRAIGHT MATH ON THE SAT

CHAPTER 17: SAT ARITHMETIC

- Number properties
- Roots and exponents

Okay, now that you've seen the basic math strategies Kaplan has to offer a top-notch test taker, it's time to see how they come into play on straight-ahead math questions. More often than not, the math tested on the SAT doesn't get too fancy. But what can get tricky at times is how the questions are put together.

But don't worry. A systematic approach to these questions is all it takes for an Advanced test taker to demonstrate the straight-ahead math knowledge they've already mastered in junior high and high school math class.

NUMBER PROPERTIES

Questions concerning number properties are some of the toughest non–word problem questions on the SAT.

But what do we mean by number properties?

"Number properties" refer to ideas such as: Is a number odd or even? Positive or negative? Greater or smaller than another number? It sounds simple enough, but these kinds of questions can get tough since we tend not to think in these terms when we do everyday math.

On number properties questions, you need to think about how numbers behave and how certain numbers behave differently than others. For instance, if a question asks about even numbers, remember that 0 is even. If a question asks about prime numbers, think about 2, since it's the smallest prime number and the only even prime number. Understanding how numbers behave is what number properties questions are all about.

Let's look at some tough number properties questions.

QUESTIONS 1–3

1. If j and k are integers, and $2j + k = 15$, which of the following must be true?

    I. j is odd.
    II. k is odd.
    III. $j + k$ is even.

  (A) None
  (B) I only
  (C) II only
  (D) III only
  (E) I, II, and III

2. If the sum of five consecutive integers is a, then the sum of the next five consecutive integers is

  (A) $a + 1$
  (B) $a + 5$
  (C) $a + 25$
  (D) $2a$
  (E) $5a$

3. If N is the product of the first five positive even integers, then N is NOT a multiple of

  (A) 30
  (B) 48
  (C) 60
  (D) 75
  (E) 120

EXPLANATIONS: QUESTIONS 1–3

1. C

Roman numeral questions can be tricky since you need to work through the statements first, and then see how they affect the answer choices. A quick scan of the statements tells you that you're dealing with properties of odd and even numbers. If you remember the properties (such as odd + even = odd, and odd × odd = odd) you could try to reason the problem out, but in our humble opinion, there's an easier approach.

You may have guessed it. It's time to Pick Numbers. The question asks which of the following MUST be true, and statement I says j is odd, so let's see if we can make j even by picking 2 for j; $2(2) + 11 = 15$. Since 2 works, statement I doesn't have to be true, and (B) and (E) are out. Now look at statement II, which says k is odd. When we picked 2, an even number, for j we got 11, an odd number, for k. So let's try an odd number for j, say 3; $2(3) + 9 = 15$. Since we tried both even and odd numbers for j and both times k came out odd, we know now that statement II must be true. Now look at the answer choices and see what you can eliminate. (A) and (D) are both out, so the answer has to be (C), without even looking at statement III.

> An Advanced test taker handles Roman numeral questions one statement at a time, eliminating answer choices as she goes along. That way, she sometimes doesn't have to evaluate all three statements.

Let's check out statement III anyway. It says $j + k$ is even. Let's look at the numbers we've already picked. We first picked $j = 2$, which leads to $k = 11$; $2 + 11 = 13$, which is odd, so statement III is out, just as we suspected.

2. C

If the sum of five consecutive integers in a set is a, then each of the next five consecutive integers will be five greater than the corresponding integer in the original set. Since there are five integers in the new set, the sum of the five integers in the new set must be $a + 5(5) = a + 25$. (C) is correct. You can easily prove this to yourself by Picking Numbers, if you have the time.

> An Advanced test taker relies on logic and reasoning to handle questions like this one, and then confirms his work by Picking Numbers if time permits.

3. D

If N is the product of the first five positive even integers, then all of its factors will be combinations of these integers, or at least their prime factors. Break down the first five positive even integers into their prime factors, and see which answer choice cannot be the product of some combination of these prime factors; 2 is prime. $4 = 2 \times 2$, $6 = 2 \times 3$, $8 = 2 \times 2 \times 2$, and $10 = 2 \times 5$. So the prime factorization of N is $2 \times (2 \times 2) \times (2 \times 3) \times (2 \times 2 \times 2) \times (2 \times 5) = 2 \times 2 \times 2 \times 2 \times 2 \times 2 \times 2 \times 2 \times 3 \times 5$. Only $75 = 3 \times 5 \times 5$ cannot be produced from these prime factors since 5 only appears once in the prime factorization of N.

> An Advanced test taker knows how to work with prime factors in order to get a better handle on questions involving multiples.

QUESTION 4

4. If $-1 < b < 0$, which must be true?

    (A) $b^2 < b < 0$

    (B) $0 < b < b^2$

    (C) $b < b^3 < b^5$

    (D) $b < b^2 < b^3$

    (E) $b < b^2 < b^4$

> An Advanced test taker knows that a negative number raised to an even exponent results in a positive number, while a negative number raised to an odd exponent results in a negative number.

EXPLANATION: QUESTION 4

4. **C**

This question tests your ability to understand how a number behaves. In this case, b is a negative fraction. This allows you to eliminate (B). Since b is negative, b raised to an even exponent is positive, and b raised to an odd exponent is negative. This allows you to quickly eliminate (A) and (D).

You're left with (C) and (E). Now it may be time to pick an easy negative fraction, say $-\dfrac{1}{2}$.

$$\left(-\frac{1}{2}\right)^2 = \frac{1}{4}; \left(-\frac{1}{2}\right)^3 = -\frac{1}{8}; \left(-\frac{1}{2}\right)^4 = \frac{1}{16}; \text{ and } \left(-\frac{1}{2}\right)^5 = -\frac{1}{32}.$$

Now, $-\dfrac{1}{2} < -\dfrac{1}{8} < -\dfrac{1}{32}$, so choice (C) is correct.

> An Advanced test taker uses logic and insight whenever possible, but is never afraid to confirm her results using concrete numbers.

ROOTS AND EXPONENTS

Along with questions about number properties, those testing roots and exponents are among the toughest straightforward arithmetic questions on the SAT. To get a top-notch score on the SAT, you'll need to get comfortable with square roots and with all rules concerning adding and multiplying exponents.

The following questions should give you a pretty good idea of your current skill level.

QUESTIONS 5–7

5. $3^5 + \dfrac{1}{3^5} =$

(A) 1

(B) 3

(C) $\dfrac{3^6 - 1}{3}$

(D) $\dfrac{3^{10} + 1}{3^5}$

(E) $\dfrac{3^{25}}{3^5 + 1}$

6. If $2^x = y$, which of the following equals $8y$ in terms of x?

(A) 2^{2+x}

(B) 2^{2x}

(C) 2^{3+x}

(D) 2^{3x}

(E) 2^{8x}

7. $\dfrac{5\sqrt{14}}{2\sqrt{2}} \times \dfrac{4\sqrt{2}}{3\sqrt{7}} =$

(A) $\dfrac{5\sqrt{2}}{12}$

(B) $\dfrac{5}{3}$

(C) $\dfrac{5\sqrt{2}}{3}$

(D) $\dfrac{10\sqrt{2}}{3}$

(E) $\dfrac{20}{3}$

EXPLANATIONS: QUESTIONS 5–7

5. D

Remember that you can add only fractions with the same denominator.

Convert 3^5 to a fraction with a denominator of 3^5. Then, the numbers can be added.

$$3^5 + \frac{1}{3^5} = \left(\frac{3^5}{1} \times \frac{3^5}{3^5} \right) + \frac{1}{3^5}$$

$$= \frac{3^{10}}{3^5} + \frac{1}{3^5} = \frac{3^{10}+1}{3^5}$$

Answer (D) it is.

> An Advanced test taker knows that when you multiply exponential expressions with the same base, you add the exponents, and when you divide exponential expressions with the same base, you subtract the exponents.

6. C

Questions like this one are susceptible to one of two approaches, and it's important that you understand yourself as a test taker and use the approach you are most comfortable with. Let's begin with the arithmetic approach.

We are told that $2^x = y$ and asked to express $8y$ in terms of x. If $2^x = y$, then $8(2^x) = 8y$. In order to rewrite $8(2^x)$, we need to rewrite 8 so that it has the same base of 2. Since $8 = 2^3$, we can rewrite the expression as:

$8(2^x) = 2^3 \times 2^x = 2^{3+x}$. (C) is correct.

The alternative approach is to Pick Numbers. When Picking Numbers, choose numbers that are easy to work with. In this case, let's say $x = 2$. If x is 2, then $y = 2^x = 2^2 = 4$. If $y = 4$, then $8y = 32$. Now we can substitute 2 for x for each answer choice, looking for the result of 32. Quickly work through the calculations:

(A) $2^{2+x} = 2^{2+2} = 2^4 = 16$. Eliminate.

(B) $2^{2x} = 2^{2\times2} = 2^4 = 16$. Eliminate.

(C) $2^{3+x} = 2^{3+2} = 2^5 = 32$. Possibly correct.

(D) $2^{3x} = 2^{3\times2} = 2^6 = 64$. Eliminate.

(E) $2^{8x} = 2^{8\times2} = 2^{16} = 65{,}536$. Way too big. Eliminate.

Once again, (C) is correct.

An Advanced test taker "rewrites" her answer to match the form used in the answer choices.

7. **D**

Get comfortable plowing through calculations like those you see below:

$$\frac{5\sqrt{14}}{2\sqrt{2}} \times \frac{4\sqrt{2}}{3\sqrt{7}} = \frac{5\sqrt{14} \times 4\sqrt{2}}{2\sqrt{2} \times 3\sqrt{7}}$$

$$= \frac{5 \times 4 \times \sqrt{14} \times \sqrt{2}}{2 \times 3 \times \sqrt{2} \times \sqrt{7}}$$

$$= \frac{10 \times \sqrt{14}}{3 \times \sqrt{7}}$$

$$= \frac{10}{3} \times \sqrt{2}$$

$$= \frac{10\sqrt{2}}{3}$$

CHAPTER 18: SAT ALGEBRA

- Straightforward algebra

- Inequalities

- Absolute value problems

- Simultaneous equations

- Radical and exponential equations

- Quadratics

- Function questions

STRAIGHTFORWARD ALGEBRA

Most often, algebra questions test your ability to translate English into math, perform basic algebraic manipulations, and solve for a single variable.

The first question in the following practice set is a good example of a straightforward algebra problem.

QUESTIONS 1–2

1. If $x = \dfrac{x + y}{z}$, which of the following must be equal to z?

   (A) $\dfrac{x}{y} + x$

   (B) $\dfrac{x}{y} + 1$

   (C) $\dfrac{y}{x} + y$

   (D) $\dfrac{y}{x} + x$

   (E) $\dfrac{y}{x} + 1$

2. $(R^c)(R^d)(R^e) = R^{-12}$. If $R > 0$, and c, d, and e are each different negative integers, what is the smallest number that c could be?

   (A) −1

   (B) −6

   (C) −9

   (D) −10

   (E) −12

EXPLANATIONS: QUESTIONS 1–2

1. E

Now you could always go ahead and Pick Numbers on a question like this one, but let's just see if your algebra is up to the challenge. We want to solve for z here, so let's begin by taking z out of the denominator by multiplying both sides by z:

$x = \dfrac{x + y}{z}$, so $zx = x + y$. Now you can divide both sides by x:

$z = \dfrac{x + y}{x}$. And now you can distribute out the denominator on the right side of the equation:

$z = \dfrac{x}{x} + \dfrac{y}{x} = 1 + \dfrac{y}{x} = \dfrac{y}{x} + 1$. So (E) is the correct answer here. By the way, did we mention that you can Pick Numbers here?

2. C

This question tests your basic understanding of exponents and algebra. When numbers with the same base are multiplied together, you add the exponents. So $(R^c)(R^d)(R^e) = R^{c + d + e} = R^{-12}$. We know now that $c + d + e = -12$. In order for c to be as small as possible, d and e must be as large as possible. The question states that c, d, and e are each different negative integers. Remember that negatives get larger as they approach zero, so the greatest values we can choose for d and e are −1 and −2. Substitute in these numbers to determine the value of c if $d = -1$ and $e = -2$.

$$c + d + e = -12$$
$$c + (-1) + (-2) = -12$$
$$c - 3 = -12$$
$$c = -9$$

(C) is correct.

An Advanced test taker never forgets that a negative number becomes greater as its absolute value becomes smaller.

INEQUALITIES

Inequalities appear quite often on the SAT. Treat them as you would regular equations, but remember to flip the sign when you multiply or divide both sides by a negative value. Also note that an inequality represents a range of values, as opposed to an equation, which represents a single value.

QUESTIONS 3–4

3. If $-2 \le x \le 2$ and $3 \le y \le 8$, which of the following represents the range of all possible values of $y - x$?

   (A) $5 \le y - x \le 6$
   (B) $1 \le y - x \le 5$
   (C) $1 \le y - x \le 6$
   (D) $5 \le y - x \le 10$
   (E) $1 \le y - x \le 10$

4. If $8 < \sqrt{(n+6)(n+1)} < 9$, then n could equal

   (A) 5
   (B) 6
   (C) 7
   (D) 8
   (E) 9

EXPLANATIONS: QUESTIONS 3–4

3. **E**

The greatest value of $y - x$ will occur when y is as large as possible and x is as small as possible. That is, $y - x \leq 8 - (-2)$, or 10. The smallest value of $y - x$ will occur when y is as small as possible and x is as large as possible. That is $y - x \geq 3 - 2$, or 1. So $1 \leq y - x \leq 10$.

> An Advanced test taker applies reasoning to determine what the least or greatest possible value of something could be.

4. **A**

When solving an inequality like this one, treat it like an equation, that is, by doing the same thing to all its parts. There are two important things to remember when dealing with inequalities: (1) multiplying or dividing an inequality by a negative number reverses the sign, and (2) you are solving for a range of values rather than a single value.

For starters, you can get rid of that nasty radical sign by squaring all the elements in the inequality $8 < \sqrt{(n + 6)(n + 1)} < 9$. The direction of the signs won't change since all the elements are greater than 0.

So $64 < (n + 6)(n + 1) < 81$. Now you could try Back-solving; the answer choice for which this relationship is true will be correct.

As always, start with choice (C): $(n + 6)(n + 1) = (7 + 6)(7 + 1) = 104$. This is greater than 81, so discard and move on to a smaller answer choice.

(B) $(n + 6)(n + 1) = (6 + 6)(6 + 1) = 84$. This is still greater than 81, so the correct answer choice must be smaller still, which only leaves (A).

> An Advanced test taker isn't afraid to combine a backdoor approach like Back-solving with a front-door approach like algebraic manipulation.

ABSOLUTE VALUE PROBLEMS

Remember that the absolute value of x could be equal to either x or $-x$, depending on whether x was positive or negative to start with. If $|a| = |b|$, then $a = b$ or $a = -b$.

QUESTIONS 5–7

5. If $|w + 4| = |w - 7|$, what is the value of w?

    (A) -2

    (B) $-\dfrac{2}{3}$

    (C) 0

    (D) $\dfrac{3}{2}$

    (E) 4

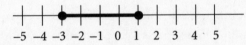

6. Which of the following inequalities best describes the indicated values on the number line above?

    (A) $|x - 3| \geq 1$

    (B) $|x + 3| \leq 1$

    (C) $|x + 1| \leq 2$

    (D) $|x + 1| \leq 3$

    (E) $|x - 1| \leq -2$

7. If $|x - 3| = |y - 4|$, and $y = 2$, what is one possible value of x?

    (A) 1

    (B) 2

    (C) 4

    (D) 6

    (E) 8

EXPLANATIONS: QUESTIONS 5–7

5. **D**

The expression inside an absolute value sign can be positive or negative. Since $|w + 4| = |w - 7|$, either $w + 4 = w - 7$ or $w + 4 = -(w + 7)$. If $w + 4 = w - 7$, then $4 = -7$, which is not true, so the other possibility must be correct.

$$w + 4 = -(w - 7)$$
$$w + 4 = -w + 7$$
$$2w = 3$$
$$w = \frac{3}{2}$$

Thus, $w = \dfrac{3}{2}$.

6. C

It may be easiest simply to check the endpoints of the highlighted section of the number line against each inequality. Alternatively, you could find the center of the segment and the distance from there to each endpoint. The absolute value of the difference between x and the center must be less than or equal to the distance from the center to either endpoint. The endpoints of the line segment are at -3 and 1. The center of the line segment is at $\dfrac{-3 + 1}{2} = \dfrac{-2}{2} = -1$. Thus, the center of the region is -1. The endpoints are each 2 units away from the center. Therefore, the distance between any selected point and -1 must be less than or equal to 2. Another way to write this is $|x - (-1)| \le 2$, which simplifies to $|x + 1| \le 2$.

7. A

First, substitute $y = 2$ into the right side of the equation and simplify. Then solve for x. After making this substitution, we will see that the right side does not result in 0. Because the right side does not result in 0, there will be two possible values for $x - 3$:

$$|x - 3| = |2 - 4|$$

$$|x - 3| = |-2|$$

$$|x - 3| = 2$$

$$x - 3 = 2 \text{ or } x - 3 = -2$$

If $x - 3 = 2$, then $x = 5$.

If $x - 3 = -2$, then $x = 1$.

So x could be 1 or 5. Choice (A), 1, is correct. The other possible value of x, 5, is not among the answer choices.

SIMULTANEOUS EQUATIONS

Sometimes the SAT requires you to deal with more than one equation in a single question. We refer to these kinds of questions as simultaneous equations. The two ways to handle simultaneous equations are *substitution* and *combination*.

See which technique works best in each of the next two questions.

QUESTIONS 8–9

8. For the positive values a, b, c, and d, $a = 2b$, $\frac{1}{2}b = c$, and $4c = 3d$. What is the value of $\frac{d}{a}$?

9. If $2x - 4y = -2$ and $3x - 2y = 3$, then $2y + x =$

(A) $\frac{3}{2}$

(B) 2

(C) $3\frac{1}{2}$

(D) 5

(E) $5\frac{1}{2}$

EXPLANATIONS: QUESTIONS 8–9

8. $\frac{1}{3}$ or .333

To find the ratio of d to a, you need to get a and d together in a single equation. You can do this by substituting for the variables b and c in order to eliminate them. Working from the information that $a = 2b$, we get $\frac{a}{2} = b$. We can substitute this into the equation $\frac{1}{2}b = c$, to get $\frac{1}{2}\left(\frac{a}{2}\right) = c$ or $\frac{a}{4} = c$. Since $4c = 3d$, we can substitute for c to get $4\left(\frac{a}{4}\right) = 3d$, or $a = 3d$. So $\frac{d}{a} = \frac{d}{3d} = \frac{1}{3}$, or .333.

Of course you could also solve this problem by Picking Numbers, but you'd have to be a bit thoughtful. You're told that for the positive values a, b, c, and d, $a = 2b$, $\frac{1}{2}b = c$, and $4c = 3d$. You could try to pick a value for a, but you're better off starting on the other end. If $4c = 3d$, then you could pick $c = 3$ and $d = 4$. Thus, $\frac{1}{2}b = 3$, so $b = 6$, and $a = 2b$, so $a = 12$. So $\frac{d}{d} = \frac{4}{12} = \frac{1}{3}$.

An Advanced test taker knows whether he's better off trusting his algebra skills or Picking Numbers, and proceeds accordingly.

9. D

Two equations, two variables. We can express one variable in terms of the other using one equation, and then plug this expression for the variable we solved for into the other equation, but there's a faster method. If we subtract the first equation from the second we get—on the left side—exactly the expression that we are asked the value of:

$$3x - 2y = 3$$
$$\underline{-(2x - 4y = -2)}$$
$$x + 2y = 5$$

Although the order of x and y is reversed from the expression in the question, the left side of the last equation contains the same expression. Choice (D) it is.

RADICAL AND EXPONENTIAL EQUATIONS

Equations with variables in radicals are getting more emphasis on the SAT. If that's the only variable, just solve for the radical, then square both sides. If there are variables inside and outside the radical, substitution, Back-solving, or other tricks make the problem easier.

Negative exponents and fractional exponents are new this year too. Remember that $x^{-y} = \dfrac{1}{(x^y)}$, and that $x^{\left(\frac{y}{z}\right)} = \sqrt[z]{x^y}$.

QUESTIONS 10–14

10. If $6\sqrt{x} + 4 = 16$, what is the value of x^2?

11. If $x - 4\sqrt{x} + 4 = 0$, what is the value of x?

    (A) -2

    (B) 0

    (C) 2

    (D) 4

    (E) 16

12. If $abcd \neq 0$, which of the following is equal to $\dfrac{6a^3 b^{-2} c^{-2}}{3ab^{-3}d} - \dfrac{abcd}{a^{-1}c^3 d^2}$?

    (A) $abcd$

    (B) $\dfrac{1}{abcd}$

    (C) $\dfrac{ab}{cd}$

    (D) $\dfrac{ab^2}{cd^2}$

    (E) $\dfrac{a^2 b}{c^2 d}$

13. If $d^{\frac{3}{2}} = 8$, what is the value of d?

    (A) 2

    (B) 4

    (C) 8

    (D) 32

    (E) 64

14. If $3x^{\frac{3}{4}} = x$ and $x > 0$, what is the value of x?

EXPLANATIONS: QUESTIONS 10–14

10. 16

Be sure not to stop working too early. You do need to find the value of x, but that is not the answer. The question asks for the value of x^2:

$$6\sqrt{x} + 4 = 16$$
$$6\sqrt{x} = 12$$
$$\sqrt{x} = 2$$
$$x = 4$$
$$x^2 = 16$$

11. D

Back-solving is probably the easiest way to solve this problem.

You can also factor the left side of the equation in terms of $\sqrt{x}$, as shown below.

$$x - 4\sqrt{x} + 4 = (\sqrt{x})^2 - 2(\sqrt{x})(2) + 2^2 = (\sqrt{x} - 2)^2 = (\sqrt{x} - 2)(\sqrt{x} - 2)$$

Then $(\sqrt{x} - 2)(\sqrt{x} - 2) = 0$.

So $\sqrt{x} - 2 = 0$.

Then $\sqrt{x} = 2$.

Squaring both sides of this equation, we have $x = 4$.

Let's note that $x - 4\sqrt{x} + 4$ was factored by using the identity $(a - b)^2 = a^2 - 2ab + b^2$. (Here, we actually went from the form $a^2 - 2ab + b^2$ to the form $(a - b)^2$.) We let $a = \sqrt{x}$ and $b = 2$ to say that $x - 4\sqrt{x} + 4 = (\sqrt{x} - 2)^2 = (\sqrt{x} - 2)(\sqrt{x} - 2)$.

12. E

Simplify, simplify, simplify. Even though this problem looks complicated, all you really have to do is use a law of exponents, which is really equivalent to canceling things out.

Remember: $x^{-y} = \dfrac{1}{x^y}$ and $\dfrac{b^x}{b^y} = b^{x-y}$.

$$\frac{6a^3b^{-2}c^{-2}}{3ab^{-3}d} - \frac{abcd}{a^{-1}c^3d^2} = \frac{2a^{3-1}b^{-2(-3)}}{c^2d} - \frac{a^{1-(-1)}b}{c^{3-1}d^{2-1}} = \frac{2a^2b}{c^2d} - \frac{a^2b}{c^2d} = \frac{a^2b}{c^2d}.$$

13. B

This problem is most easily solved with Back-solving.

But if this problem showed up as a Grid-In, instead, you'd have to do things the hard way:

Fractional exponents can be expressed as roots. For instance, $d^{\frac{3}{2}}$ could be expressed as $(\sqrt{d})^3$ or $\sqrt{d^3}$. Expressing powers with fractional exponents in this more familiar way may help you work with them more easily.

$$\sqrt{d^3} = 8$$
$$d^3 = 64$$
$$d = 4$$

14. 81

Isolate x on one side of the equation first, then deal with the exponent. Note that it is okay to divide both sides of the equation by $x^{\frac{3}{4}}$, since the question tells you that $x > 0$, which means that $x^{\frac{3}{4}} > 0$.

$$3x^{\frac{3}{4}} = x$$

$$\frac{3x^{\frac{3}{4}}}{x^{\frac{3}{4}}} = \frac{\frac{x}{3}}{x^{\frac{3}{4}}}$$

$$3 = x^{1-\frac{3}{4}}$$

$$3 = x^{\frac{1}{4}}$$

$$3^4 = x$$

$$81 = x$$

Thus, $x = 81$.

QUADRATICS

Quadratic equations appear quite often on the SAT. Quadratic expressions are what you get when you multiply two binomials, for instance, $x + 2$ and $x - 3$, to get $(x + 2)(x - 3) = x^2 - x - 6$.

Occasionally, you may see cubic equations—equations with an x^3 component in them. These will require only that you factor out an x from all components first, then treat them like normal quadratics.

Fortunately, these questions tend not to test more than your ability to FOIL and reverse FOIL an expression. Take a crack at the following examples of tricky quadratic questions.

QUESTIONS 15–19

15. If $s \neq -2$, then $\dfrac{2s^2 - 8}{s + 2} =$

   (A) $s - 4$

   (B) $s + 4$

   (C) $s^2 + 4$

   (D) $s^2 - 4$

   (E) $2s - 4$

16. If $n > 0$ and $4x^2 + kx + 25 = (2x + n)^2$ for all x, what is the value of $k + n$?

17. For all $x > 2$, $\dfrac{x^2 - 4x + 4}{x^2 - 4} =$

   (A) -1

   (B) 2

   (C) $\dfrac{x - 2}{x + 2}$

   (D) $\dfrac{x + 2}{x - 2}$

   (E) $-4x$

18. For all $x > 0$, $\dfrac{6x^3 + 8x^2}{6x^2 + 4x} =$

   (A) $\dfrac{x(3x + 4)}{3x + 2}$

   (B) $\dfrac{4x}{2}$

   (C) $\dfrac{4}{2x}$

   (D) $4x + 6$

   (E) $3x$

19. If $x \neq -1$ and $\dfrac{x^2 + 2x + 1}{x + 1} > 4$, which of the following is true?

   (A) $x > 4$

   (B) $x > 3$

   (C) $x < 2$ and $x \neq -1$

   (D) $x < 3$ and $x \neq -1$

   (E) $x < 4$ and $x \neq -1$

EXPLANATIONS: QUESTIONS 15–19

15. E

When asked to simplify an expression like this one, use the clues the test maker gives you. If you see $s + 2$ in the denominator, there's a strong chance that you will be able to factor the numerator so that an $(s + 2)$ appears there as well. Here's how to work through this one:

$$\frac{2s^2 - 8}{s + 2} = \frac{2(s^2 - 4)}{s + 2} = \frac{2(s + 2)(s - 2)}{s + 2} = 2(s - 2).$$

Distribute the 2 over the expression inside the parentheses to get $2s - 4$.

> An Advanced test taker knows the common quadratics and knows automatically that when an expression is in the form $A^2 - B^2$, she should rewrite it as $(A + B)(A - B)$, and vice versa.

Did we mention, by the way, that you could Pick Numbers here? Try picking $s = 3$ and see what happens.

16. 25

If we multiply out $(2x + n)^2$ using FOIL, we have $(2x + n)(2x + n) = (2x)(2x) + (2x)(n) + (n)(2x) + (n)(n) = 4x^2 + 2nx + 2nx + n^2 = 4x^2 + 4nx + n^2$.

So $4x^2 + kx + 25 = 4x^2 + 4nx + n^2$. Then $k = 4n$ and $25 = n^2$. Since $4n$ is positive and $n^2 = 25$, $n = 5$. Since $k = 4n$, $k = 4(5) = 20$. Thus, $k = 20$ and $n = 5$. So $k + n = 20 + 5 = 25$.

17. C

Picking Numbers works well for this problem. Alternatively, you could factor the numerator and denominator of the given expression, then simplify:

$$\frac{x^2 - 4x + 4}{x^2 - 4} = \frac{(x - 2)(x - 2)}{(x - 2)(x + 2)} = \frac{x - 2}{x + 2}$$

In the simplification of $\dfrac{x^2 - 4x + 4}{x^2 - 4}$ above, we used the identity $(a - b)^2 = a^2 - 2ab + b^2$. We let $a = x$ and $b = 2$ to say that $x^2 - 4x + 4 = (x - 2)^2$.

In the simplification of $\dfrac{x^2 - 4x + 4}{x^2 - 4}$ above, we also used the difference of squares identity $a^2 - b^2 = (a - b)(a + b)$. We let $a = x$ and $b = 2$ to say that $x^2 - 4 = (x - 2)(x + 2)$.

18. A

Factor the numerator and denominator to see what you can cancel out. Pay careful attention to parenthesis and the rules of multiplication. Picking Numbers would also work well for this problem.

$$\frac{6x^3 + 8x^2}{6x^2 + 4x} = \frac{2x^2(3x + 4)}{2x(3x + 2)} = \frac{x(3x + 4)}{3x + 2}$$

19. B

When dealing with rational equations, try to factor and simplify complicated expressions first.

Here, $\dfrac{x^2 + 2x + 1}{x + 1} = \dfrac{(x + 1)(x + 1)}{x + 1} = x + 1$.

Here, we used the identity $(a + b)^2 = a^2 + 2ab + b^2$. We let $a = x$ and $b = 1$ to say that $x^2 + 2x + 1 = (x + 1)^2$.

So $x + 1 > 4$.

Then $x > 3$.

FUNCTION QUESTIONS

Function questions have always been on the SAT; they've just been disguised as the weird symbol questions until now. It doesn't matter if the test introduces the question as $(x) = 2x + 4$ or $f(x) = 2x + 4$; it's the same concept.

If $z(m) = m^3 + 4$, what is the value of m when $z(m) = -4$?

(A) -60

(B) -8

(C) -2

(D) 2

(E) 8

Don't worry about the function notation. All this question really says is, "$m^3 + 4 = -4$. What's m?"

$$m^3 + 4 = -4$$
$$m^3 = -8$$
$$m^3 = (-2)^3$$
$$m = -2$$

QUESTIONS 20–25

The following two questions refer to the following definitions for integers c greater than 1.

$$\boxed{c}\hspace{-1.9em}\bigcirc = c^2 - 2c$$
$$\boxed{c} = c^2 + 2c$$

20. $\bigcirc\!\!\!\!3 + \boxed{2} =$

   (A) 3
   (B) 7
   (C) 11
   (D) 15
   (E) 19

21. If c is an integer greater than 1, then $\bigcirc\!\!\!\!\!\!\bigcirc\,(c+2) =$

   (A) c^2
   (B) $c^2 + 2$
   (C) $\bigcirc\!\!\!c$
   (D) $\bigcirc\!\!\!c + 2$
   (E) $\boxed{c}$

Some function questions will ask about the range or domain of the function. These are likely to involve fractions, where you need to make sure the denominator does not equal zero, or radicals, where you need to make sure the value under the radical is not negative.

22. If $f(x) = \dfrac{x^2 - 1}{x^2 + x - 6}$, then for what values of x is $f(x)$ undefined?

   (A) -3 and -1
   (B) $-3, -1,$ and 2
   (C) $-3, -1, 1,$ and 2
   (D) -3 and 2
   (E) -1 and 1

23. If $g(y) = y^4 + 17y^2 + 2$, which of the following COULD NOT be a value of $g(y)$?

(A) 1

(B) 2

(C) 2.05

(D) 4.3

(E) 6.33

Some function questions will also "nest" the functions. In these cases, work from the inside outward—first solve the innermost function, then work outward.

24. If $g(a) = a^2 - 4$ and $h(b) = \sqrt{b} + 4$, what is the value of $h(g(4))$?

(A) 4

(B) $4 + \sqrt{3}$

(C) $4 + 2\sqrt{3}$

(D) 12

(E) 32

25. Let $\boxed{x} = \dfrac{x^2 + 1}{2}$ and $\boxed{y} = \dfrac{3y}{2}$, for all integers x and y. If $m = \boxed{2}$, $\boxed{m}$ is equal to which of the following?

(A) $\dfrac{13}{8}$

(B) 3

(C) $\dfrac{15}{4}$

(D) 5

(E) $\dfrac{37}{2}$

EXPLANATIONS: QUESTIONS 20–25

20. C

Don't be intimidated by the unfamiliar symbols here. This question is really a simple algebraic computation question in disguise. Just refer to the right-hand sides of the symbolism equations. All you need to do is plug 3 in for c in $\boxed{c} = c^2 - 2c$, and 2 in for c in $\boxed{c} = c^2 + 2c$.

$\boxed{3} + \boxed{2} = 3^2 - 2(3) + 2^2 + 2(2) = 9 - 6 + 4 + 4 = 11$. (C) is correct.

An Advanced test taker is never intimidated by weird-looking symbols.

21. E

This question can be handled algebraically or by Picking Numbers. Since our focus in this chapter is on algebra, we'll lead with the algebraic solution, then quickly run through how to handle this question by Picking Numbers.

Each technique is effective. The key, as always, is to quickly decide on the approach that works best for you.

We're asked to find $\left(\overline{(c+2)}\right)$. Just as we plugged in numbers for c on the previous question, here we will substitute in the expression $(c+2)$ for c.

$$\overline{c} = c^2 - 2c, \text{ so } \overline{(c+2)} = (c+2)^2 - 2(c+2).$$

This expression can be simplified as follows:

$$(c+2)^2 - 2(c+2) = (c^2 + 4c + 4) - (2c + 4)$$
$$= c^2 + 4c + 4 - 2c - 4$$
$$= c^2 + 2c$$

$$\boxed{c} = c^2 + 2c.$$

If you prefer to Pick Numbers here, see what happens when $c = 2$. $\overline{(c+2)} = \overline{4} = 4^2 - 2(4) = 16 - 8 = 8$. Now substitute 2 in for c for each answer choice, and eliminate any choice that does not give you an outcome of 8:

(A) $c^2 = 2^2 = 4$

(B) $c^2 + 2 = 2^2 + 2 = 4 + 2 = 6$

(C) $\overline{c} = c^2 - 2c = 2^2 - 2(2) = 4 - 4 = 0$

(D) $\overline{c} + 2 = (c^2 - 2c) + 2 = 2^2 - 2(2) + 2 = 4 - 4 + 2 = 2$

(E) $\boxed{c} = c^2 + 2c = 2^2 + 2(2) = 4 + 4 = 8$

Only (E) produces the desired outcome.

Of course, you always have to try all the answer choices any time you Pick Numbers. Sometimes two or more answer choices will work for the particular value that you chose. When this happens, you must go back and pick another value to eliminate the remaining incorrect answer choices.

22. D

This function will be undefined when the denominator is equal to zero (since a number divided by zero is undefined). Set the denominator equal to zero and solve for x. You could also plug each number given in the answer choices into the function to see which ones it is undefined for:

$$x^2 + x - 6 = (x-2)(x+3) = 0$$
$$x = 2 \text{ or } -3$$

23. A

Think about what each part of the function could be. y isn't restricted at all, so it could be any real number, including fractions, negative numbers, and zero. No matter what y is, y^4 and y^2 can only be zero or positive numbers. Therefore, the smallest possible value of $g(y)$ is $0 + 0 + 2 = 2$. It could also equal any number greater than 2. Choice (A) is the only choice less than 2, so it is correct.

24. C

Whenever you see nested functions, work from the inside out. In this case, you should first substitute 4 for a in $g(a)$, then plug the result into $h(b)$, where $b = g(4)$:

$$g(4) = 4^2 - 4 = 16 - 4 = 12$$
$$h(12) = \sqrt{12} + 4 = 4 + 2\sqrt{3}$$

25. D

This symbolism problem is simpler than it looks. Replace y with 2 to find the value of m.

$$\bigcirc\!\!\!y = \frac{3y}{2} \text{ becomes}$$
$$\bigcirc\!\!\!2 = \frac{3(2)}{2} = 3$$

Thus, $m = 3$. So $\boxed{m} = \boxed{3}$. Replace x with 3 to find the value of $\boxed{3}$.

$$\boxed{x} = \frac{x^2 + 1}{2} \text{ becomes}$$
$$\bigcirc\!\!\!3 = \frac{3^2 + 1}{2} = 5.$$

This concludes the algebra chapter. Next we'll cover the last piece of straight-ahead math, geometry.

CHAPTER 19: SAT GEOMETRY

- Triangles, rectangles, and circles

- Mixed figures

- Coordinate geometry

- Solid geometry

- Function graphing

As with the other math topics, SAT geometry draws from topics covered in junior high and high school math. It's a sampling of angles, triangles, rectangles, circles, and the (x, y) coordinate plane. This is true for both the straight math problems and—as you'll soon see—the word problems.

Don't be afraid to use your trig if you know it. The SAT will include many questions that rely on the special properties of 30-60-90 triangles or 45-45-90 triangles. These questions can be answered by using trigonometric methods, as well as your basic geometry. Also, some questions on the SAT may require you to know that a line tangent to a circle is perpendicular to a radius drawn to the point of tangency. You knew that already, though.

GEOMETRIC NOTATION FOR LENGTH, SEGMENTS, LINES, RAYS, AND CONGRUENCE

You should expect SAT geometry questions to use the symbols $\leftrightarrow$, —, and $\cong$.

$\leftrightarrow$ signifies a line. $\overleftrightarrow{XY}$ is the line that passes through points X and Y.

— signifies a line segment: $\overline{XY}$ is the line segment whose endpoints are X and Y.

≅ symbolizes congruence. If two triangles are congruent, they coincide exactly when superimposed. You may want to think of two congruent figures as identical twins.

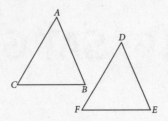

TRIANGLES, RECTANGLES, AND CIRCLES

Triangles, rectangles, and circles are the SAT "Gang of Three" when it comes to geometry. These figures are by far the most commonly tested. And as you will soon see, they are most commonly tested together.

GEOMETRY QUESTIONS 1–4

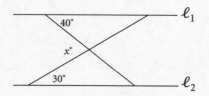

1. In the figure above, if $\ell_1 \parallel \ell_2$, what is the value of x?

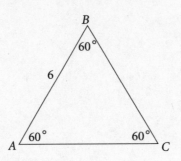

2. What is the area of $\triangle ABC$ in the figure above?

    (A) $3\sqrt{3}$
    (B) $6\sqrt{3}$
    (C) $9\sqrt{3}$
    (D) $18\sqrt{3}$
    (E) $36\sqrt{3}$

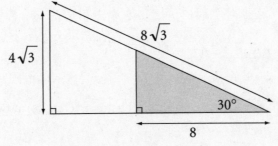

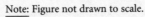

Note: Figure not drawn to scale.

3. What is the probability that a point randomly selected from the interior of the figure above will fall within the shaded region?

    (A) $\dfrac{1}{9}$

    (B) $\dfrac{1}{3}$

    (C) $\dfrac{4}{9}$

    (D) $\dfrac{1}{2}$

    (E) $\dfrac{9}{4}$

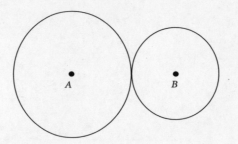

4. In the figure above, circles A and B are tangent. The circumference of circle A is 6π and the circumference of circle B is 4π. If point P lies on circle A and point Q lies on circle B, what is the greatest possible distance between points P and Q?

    (A) 5
    (B) $5\sqrt{2}$
    (C) 10
    (D) 5π
    (E) 10π

EXPLANATIONS: QUESTIONS 1–4

1. 70

Fill information into the diagram as you go along. The transversals form two pairs of alternate interior angles, as below.

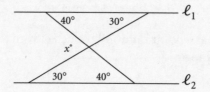

The interior angles of a triangle sum to 180°, so the angle supplementary to x is $180° - 30° - 40° = 110°$.

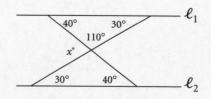

If the angle marked x is supplementary to an angle of 110°, then $x = 180 - 110 = 70$.

2. C

The formula for area of a triangle is $\frac{1}{2}bh$. You will need to find the base and height of this triangle. Since it is an equilateral triangle, all three sides will be equal, which tells you that the base is 6.

To find the height, you can sketch a line down the middle of the triangle, breaking it into two 30-60-90 triangles. You should either have the ratio of the sides of a 30-60-90 triangle memorized ($x : x\sqrt{3} : 2x$), or use trig to calculate the other two lengths.

Getting to the answer:

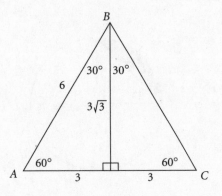

The area of the triangle is $\frac{1}{2}(6)(3\sqrt{3}) = 9\sqrt{3}$.

3. C

The probability that a point from within this figure will fall within the shaded triangle is the ratio of the area of the smaller shaded triangle to the area of the larger triangle. To find the area of a triangle, you will need the length of its base and its height. These triangles are both 30-60-90 right triangles. The sides of a 30-60-90 triangle are in the ratio $x : x\sqrt{3} : 2x$, so the base of the larger triangle must be $4\sqrt{3} \times \sqrt{3} = 12$. Its area is $\frac{1}{2}(12)(4\sqrt{3}) = 24\sqrt{3}$. Now let's consider the shaded triangle. If we call the vertical leg the height, and we let this height be h, then $\frac{h}{8} \times \frac{x}{x\sqrt{3}} \times \frac{1}{3}$ and $h = \frac{8}{\sqrt{3}}$. Let's not rewrite $\frac{8}{\sqrt{3}}$ right now. We might obtain a cancellation or some other type of simplification later. The area of the shaded triangle is $\frac{1}{2}(8)\left(\frac{8}{\sqrt{3}}\right) = \frac{32}{\sqrt{3}}$. The ratio of the area of the shaded triangle to the area of the larger triangle, which is the probability to be found, is

$$\frac{\frac{32}{\sqrt{3}}}{24\sqrt{3}} = \frac{32}{\sqrt{3}} \times \frac{1}{24\sqrt{3}} = \frac{32}{24 \times 3} = \frac{32}{72} = \frac{4}{9}.$$

Notice that we obtained the simplification that $\sqrt{3} \times \sqrt{3} = 3$ while dividing $\frac{32}{\sqrt{3}}$ by $24\sqrt{3}$, and we saved time by not rewriting $\frac{8}{\sqrt{3}}$, which is the height of the shaded triangle.

4. C

The diagram below shows that P and Q are as far apart as possible when separated by a diameter of both circles.

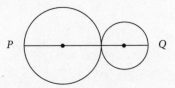

The circumference of circle A is 6π, so the diameter of A is 6 ($2\pi \times$ radius $= \pi \times$ diameter $=$ circumference). Circle B's circumference is 4π, so its diameter is 4. Therefore, the greatest possible distance between point P and point Q is $6 + 4$, or 10.

GEOMETRY QUESTIONS 5–9

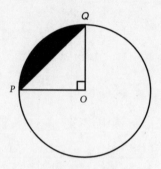

5. In circle O above, if $\triangle POQ$ is a right triangle and radius $OP = 2$, what is the area of the shaded region?

   (A) $4\pi - 2$
   (B) $4\pi - 4$
   (C) $2\pi - 2$
   (D) $2\pi - 4$
   (E) $\pi - 2$

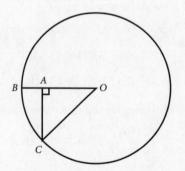

Note: Figure not drawn to scale.

6. If the area of the circle with center O on the previous page is 100π and $\overline{AC}$ has a length of 6, what is the length of $\overline{AB}$?

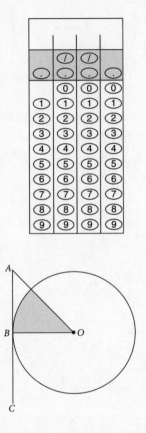

7. In the figure above, $\overline{AC}$ is tangent to the circle at point B and $\overline{OB} = \overline{AB}$. If a point is randomly selected from the interior of the circle, what is the probability that it falls within the shaded region?

(A) $\dfrac{1}{8}$

(B) $\dfrac{1}{6}$

(C) $\dfrac{1}{4}$

(D) $\dfrac{3}{4}$

(E) $\dfrac{7}{8}$

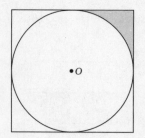

8. A circle is inscribed in a square as shown above. What is the probability that a randomly selected point from inside the square will fall within the shaded region?

    (A) $\dfrac{1}{32}$

    (B) $\dfrac{1}{16}$

    (C) $\dfrac{4-\pi}{64}$

    (D) $\dfrac{4-\pi}{16}$

    (E) $\dfrac{\pi}{18}$

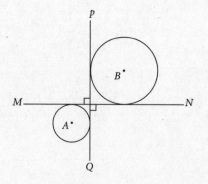

9. In the figure above, the area of circle A is 4π and the area of circle B is 16π. $\overline{MN}$ and $\overline{PQ}$ are each tangent to both circles. What is the length of $\overline{AB}$?

    (A) 6

    (B) $6\sqrt{2}$

    (C) $6\sqrt{3}$

    (D) 12

    (E) $12\sqrt{2}$

EXPLANATIONS: QUESTIONS 5–9

5. E

The area of the shaded region is the area of sector OPQ minus the area of ΔPOQ. Since $\angle POQ$ is 90°, sector OPQ is a quarter-circle. The circle's radius, $\overline{OP}$, is 2, so the area of the circle is $\pi(2^2) = 4\pi$. Therefore, the quarter-circle's area is π.

ΔPOQ's area is $\frac{1}{2}(b \times h) = \frac{1}{2}(2 \times 2) = 2$. So the area of the shaded region is $\pi - 2$. (E) is correct.

6. 2

Since we know the area of the circle, we can find the length of radii $\overline{OB}$ and $\overline{OC}$. We can't find $\overline{AB}$ directly, but if we can find the length of $\overline{OA}$, then $\overline{AB}$ is just the difference between $\overline{OB}$ and $\overline{OA}$.

The circle's area, πr^2, is 100π, so its radius is $\sqrt{100}$ or 10. So $\overline{OC}$ is 10 and, as we've been told, $\overline{AC}$ is 6. ΔAOC is a right triangle, so we can use the Pythagorean theorem to find $\overline{OA}$. Ideally, you should recognize that ΔAOC is a 3-4-5 right triangle; $\overline{OC}$ is twice 5, AC is twice 3, so $\overline{OA}$ must be twice 4, or 8. (If you didn't see this: $(OA)^2 + 6^2 = 10^2$, $(OA)^2 + 36 = 100$, $(OA)^2 = 64$, and $OA = 8$.) AB is the difference between the radius OB and segment OA, so its length is $10 - 8$, or 2.

> An Advanced test taker "sees" lengths and regions that need to be measured as parts of larger lengths and areas with already known measurements.

7. A

The probability of selecting a point from the shaded region is the area of the shaded region divided by the area of the circle. To find the area of the shaded sector, you should find $\angle AOB$ to figure out what fraction of the entire circle the shaded sector is. Since $\overline{AC}$ is tangent to the circle at point B, $\angle ABO$ is a right angle. $OB = AB$, so ΔABO is a 45-45-90 special right triangle, and $\angle AOB$ is a 45-degree angle. The ratio between this angle and the full 360° angle measure of the circle will be the same as the ratio between the area of the shaded sector and the area of the circle, which is also the probability that a randomly selected point from within the circle will fall within the shaded sector. So the probability of the chosen point being within the shaded region is $\frac{45}{360} = \frac{1}{8}$.

8. D

Many geometry problems are easier to think about if you assign numbers to unspecified lengths. In this case, try assuming that the radius of the circle is 1. Then the diameter, which is also the length of one side of the square, is 2.

Area of square: $2^2 = 4$

Area of circle: $\pi(1)^2 = \pi$

Total area outside the circle and inside the square: $4 - \pi$

Shaded area: $\dfrac{\text{Area of shaded region}}{\text{Area of square}} = \dfrac{\frac{4-\pi}{4}}{4} = \dfrac{4-\pi}{4\times 4} = \dfrac{4-\pi}{16}$

9. B

For this problem, like many higher-difficulty geometry problems, you'll need to draw in some extra lines. Remember the relationship between a circle's radius and its area, and the fact that a line tangent to a circle is perpendicular to the radius drawn to the point of tangency. Using these facts, you can construct a right triangle in which the hypotenuse is $\overline{AB}$ and the other two sides are of known length. You can then find the length of $\overline{AB}$.

Radius of larger circle:

$$16\pi = \pi r^2$$
$$16 = r^2$$
$$4 = r$$

Radius of smaller circle:

$$4\pi = \pi r^2$$
$$4 = r^2$$
$$2 = r$$

Sketch in radii of the circles:

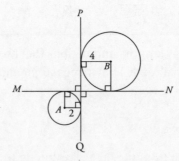

Extend the horizontal radius drawn from point A to the right, and extend the vertical radius drawn from point B downward so that the two extensions meet at point C.

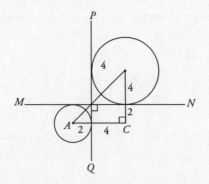

You can tell that right triangle ABC is a 45-45-90 triangle since the two known legs $\overline{AC}$ and $\overline{BC}$ are equal. The ratio of the lengths of the sides in a 45-45-90 triangle is $x : x : x\sqrt{2}$, so the hypotenuse, $\overline{AB}$, must be $6\sqrt{2}$ units long.

GEOMETRY QUESTIONS 10–11

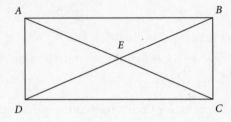

10. In the figure above, *ABCD* is a rectangle. If the area of △*AEB* is 8, what is the area of △*ACD*?

    (A) 8
    (B) 12
    (C) 16
    (D) 24
    (E) 32

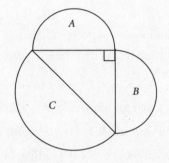

11. In the figure above, if semicircles *A* and *B* each have area 4π, what is the area of semicircle *C*?

    (A) 4π
    (B) 4π√2
    (C) 6π
    (D) 8π
    (E) 16

EXPLANATIONS: QUESTIONS 10–11

10. C

$\triangle CDE$ has the same area as $\triangle AEB$; they're congruent triangles. But we want the area of $\triangle ACD$, which means that we need to know $\triangle ADE$'s area as well. So we want to find a relationship between $\triangle ADE$'s area and $\triangle CDE$'s area.

Let's make $\overline{AD}$ the base of $\triangle ADE$. Its height, a line drawn perpendicularly from E (the rectangle's midpoint, where its diagonals meet) to $\overline{AD}$ is just one-half the length of side $\overline{DC}$. So the area of $\triangle ADE$ is $\frac{1}{2} \times AD \times \frac{DC}{2} = \frac{1}{4} \times AD \times DC$.

Applying similar reasoning, let $\overline{DC}$ be the base of $\triangle CDE$. Its height is then a line drawn perpendicularly from E to DC, which is one-half the length of side $\overline{AD}$. So $\triangle CDE$'s area is: $\frac{1}{2} \times DC \times \frac{AD}{2} = \frac{1}{4} \times DC \times AD$.

The two triangles are equal in area; each has an area of 8. Therefore, the area of $\triangle ACD$ is $8 + 8 = 16$. (C) is correct.

11. D

The areas of semicircles A and B are equal, so their diameters are equal. Therefore, $\triangle ABC$ is an isosceles right triangle, and the ratio of each leg to the hypotenuse (the diameter of semicircle C) is $1:1:\sqrt{2}$.

Method I: Move step-by-step from the area given for semicircles A and B to the radius of semicircle C, and find its area with that. The area of a small semicircle is $\frac{1}{2} \times \pi r^2 = 4\pi$; $\pi r^2 = 8\pi$; $r^2 = 8$; $r = \sqrt{8}$. Each leg of the triangle is a diameter, so its length is twice the radius, or $2\sqrt{8}$. Therefore, the hypotenuse of the triangle, h, is found with the Pythagorean theorem:

$$(2\sqrt{8})^2 + (2\sqrt{8})^2 = h^2$$
$$32 + 32 = h^2$$
$$64 = h^2$$
$$8 = h$$

which is also the diameter of semicircle C. The radius is half of 8, or 4. The area of semicircle C is $\frac{1}{2} \times \pi(4^2) = 8\pi$.

Method II: Use the ratios more directly. Since the diameters of circles A, B, and C are in the ratio $1:1:\sqrt{2}$, the ratio of their areas will be $1^2:1^2:(\sqrt{2})^2$ or $1:1:2$. C must have twice the area of A, or 8π.

An Advanced test taker uses the diagrams to record, and then derive, important information.

GEOMETRY QUESTIONS 12–13

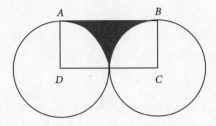

12. In the figure above, $ABCD$ is a rectangle and $\overline{DA}$ and $\overline{CB}$ are radii of the circles shown. If $\overline{AB} = 4$, what is the perimeter of the shaded region?

    (A) $2\pi + 4$

    (B) $4\pi + 4$

    (C) $4\pi + 8$

    (D) $8\pi + 8$

    (E) $8\pi + 16$

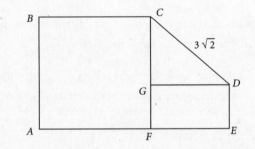

13. In the figure above, the area of square $ABCF$ is 25, and $\triangle CDG$ is an isosceles right triangle. What is the area of rectangle $DEFG$?

    (A) 15

    (B) 12

    (C) 9

    (D) $6\sqrt{2}$

    (E) 6

EXPLANATIONS: GEOMETRY QUESTIONS 12–13

12. A

The perimeter of the shaded region is the length of $\overline{AB}$, plus the length of the two arcs that are part of the perimeter of the shaded region. We already know $\overline{AB} = 4$, so we have only to find the length of the two arcs.

Since $ABCD$ is a rectangle, $\overline{DA} = \overline{CB}$, and the two circles have equal radii. $\overline{DC}$ consists of a radius of the circle on the left and a radius of the circle on the right, so $\overline{DC} = 2r$. But $\overline{DC} = \overline{AB} = 4$. Therefore, $2r = 4$, $r = 2$. The sectors are both quarter-circles (the central angle is a right angle). The arc length of a quarter-circle is $\frac{1}{4}$ of the circumference of the whole circle, or $\frac{1}{4} \times 2\pi r$. So the perimeter of each quarter-circle is $\frac{1}{4} \times 2 \times \pi \times 2 = \pi$. The perimeter of the shaded region is $4 + 2 \times \pi$, or $4 + 2\pi$. That makes (A) the winner.

13. E

You have to find the area of rectangle $DEFG$ that is embedded in a diagram with two other shapes. The area of rectangle $DEFG$ = length × width = $\overline{GD} \times \overline{GF}$.

Remember in multiple figure problems that the solution usually lies in the features that the shapes share. The length of $\overline{GF}$ is equal to $\overline{CF} - \overline{CG}$, so we need to find $\overline{CF}$ and $\overline{CG}$ in order to find $\overline{GF}$.

We're also told that triangle CDG is an isosceles right triangle. You can use the Pythagorean theorem or the known ratio of the sides of a right isosceles triangle to find the length of leg $\overline{GD}$, which is what we'll call the length of rectangle $DEFG$. Also, $\overline{GD} = \overline{CG}$, and $\overline{CG}$ is one of the two lengths you need to find in order to find the width, $\overline{GF}$.

We're told that the area of the square $ABCF$ is 25. The area of a square is the length of one side squared. So each side is equal to $\sqrt{25} = 5$. $\overline{CF}$, then, equals 5.

The leg length to leg length to hypotenuse length ratio of an isosceles right triangle is $1{:}1{:}\sqrt{2}$. We know that here the hypotenuse is $3\sqrt{2}$. So the legs $\overline{CG}$ and $\overline{GD}$ each have a length of 3. Now let's go back and try to figure out what $\overline{GF}$ equals. $\overline{GF} = \overline{CF} - \overline{CG}$. So $\overline{GF} = 5 - 3$ or 2.

Now we know that the width, $\overline{GF}$, of rectangle $DEFG$ is 2. The length, $\overline{GD}$, is 3. So the area is 3×2 or 6, (E).

COORDINATE GEOMETRY

Coordinate geometry deals with two-dimensional planes. The planes are defined by an *x*-axis (which runs horizontally) and a *y*-axis (which runs vertically).

A location on the plane is expressed in (*x*, *y*) coordinates.

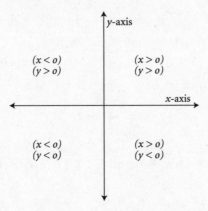

Now try a few questions. Bear in mind that you can always draw a quick coordinate plane if it helps you (and the question doesn't provide one).

COORDINATE GEOMETRY QUESTIONS 14–23

14. In the *xy*-plane, at what point does the graph of the equation $x + 3y = 9$ cross the *y*-axis?

(A) $(-3, 0)$

(B) $(0, -3)$

(C) $(0, 3)$

(D) $(0, 9)$

(E) $(9, 0)$

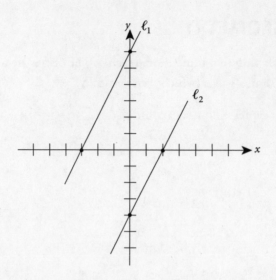

15. The equation of ℓ_1 is $y = 2x + 6$. ℓ_2 is parallel to ℓ_1. Which of the following is the equation of ℓ_2?

(A) $y = -4x + 2$

(B) $y = -2x + 4$

(C) $y = 2x - 4$

(D) $y = 2x + 4$

(E) $y = 4x + 2$

Questions 16–17 refer to the following figure:

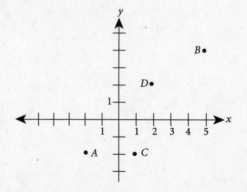

16. In the figure above, what is the length of $\overline{AB}$?

(A) $\sqrt{13}$

(B) 5

(C) $2\sqrt{13}$

(D) $\sqrt{85}$

(E) 25

17. In the previous figure, what is the length of $\overline{CD}$?

(A) $\sqrt{13}$

(B) $\sqrt{17}$

(C) $\sqrt{19}$

(D) $2\sqrt{13}$

(E) $2\sqrt{17}$

Questions 18–19 refer to the following figure:

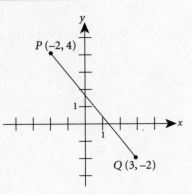

18. What is the midpoint of $\overline{PQ}$?

(A) $\left(-\dfrac{1}{2}, 2\right)$

(B) $\left(0, \dfrac{3}{2}\right)$

(C) $\left(\dfrac{3}{4}, \dfrac{3}{4}\right)$

(D) $\left(\dfrac{1}{2}, 1\right)$

(E) $\left(1, \dfrac{1}{2}\right)$

19. What is the distance between P and Q?

(A) $\sqrt{5}$

(B) 3

(C) 5

(D) 7

(E) $\sqrt{61}$

20. Which of the following lines are parallel to the line $y = 4x - 6$?

I. $y = x - 6$
II. $y = 6x - 4$
III. $y = 4x + 6$

(A) I only
(B) II only
(C) III only
(D) I and II only
(E) II and III only

21. Line l passes through the points $(-5, 2)$ and $(10, 12)$. What is the equation of line l?

(A) $y = -\dfrac{2}{3}x - \dfrac{16}{3}$

(B) $y = \dfrac{2}{3}x - \dfrac{16}{3}$

(C) $y = \dfrac{2}{3}x + \dfrac{16}{3}$

(D) $y = \dfrac{3}{2}x - \dfrac{16}{3}$

(E) $y = \dfrac{3}{2}x + \dfrac{16}{3}$

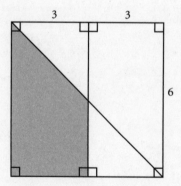

22. If a point is selected at random from the figure above, what is the probability that it will fall within the shaded region?

(A) 0.125
(B) 0.177
(C) 0.225
(D) 0.375
(E) 0.875

23. Three points $P(-6, 3)$, $Q(8, 5)$, and $R(-3, 1)$ lie in the coordinate plane. What is the distance between R and the midpoint of $\overline{PQ}$?

    (A) 13

    (B) 5

    (C) $\dfrac{\sqrt{13} + \sqrt{137}}{2}$

    (D) $\sqrt{137}$

    (E) 25

EXPLANATIONS: GEOMETRY QUESTIONS 14–23

14. C

Since every point on the y-axis has an x-coordinate of 0, when a line crosses the y-axis, its x-coordinate is 0 (that already eliminates (A) and (E)). We can substitute $x = 0$ into the equation to find the y-coordinate of the line when it crosses the y-axis. $x + 3y = 9$, $0 + 3y = 9$, $3y = 9$, $y = 3$. So the line crosses the y-axis at $(0, 3)$, making (C) correct.

> An Advanced test taker sometimes uses scratch paper to sketch the coordinate plane when it isn't provided, in order to visualize what's going on.

15. C

Since parallel lines on the coordinate plane have the same slope, the correct answer must have the same slope as $y = 2x + 6$.

The answer choices are in $y = mx + b$ form, where m is the slope and b is the y-intercept. Find the slope and the y-intercept of ℓ_2.

$y = 2x + 6$ is in the $y = mx + b$ form, so the slope is the coefficient of the x term, or 2. This means we can eliminate (A), (B), and (E)—none of them has slope +2. Since line ℓ_2 crosses the y-axis at the point $(0, -4)$, the y-intercept is -4, and the equation of the line must be $y = 2x - 4$.

16. D

The coordinates of point A are $(-2, -2)$ and the coordinates of point B are $(4, 5)$. The distance d between two points (x_1, y_1) and (x_2, y_2) can be found by using the formula $d = \sqrt{(x_2 - x_1)^2 + (y_2 - y_1)^2}$. As long as you work carefully and remember your order of operations, the formula is easy to work with.

The distance between point $A(-2, -2)$ and point $B(4, 5)$ is

$$\sqrt{(4 - (2))^2 + (5 - (2))^2} = \sqrt{6^2 + 7^2} = \sqrt{36 + 49} = \sqrt{85}$$

17. B

The distance d between two points (x_1, y_1) and (x_2, y_2) can be found by using the formula $d = \sqrt{(x_2 - x_1)^2 + (y_2 - y_1)^2}$. As long as you work carefully and remember your order of operations, the formula is easy to work with. The distance between point $C(1, -2)$ and point $D(2, 2)$ is $\sqrt{(2 - (2))^2} = \sqrt{1^2 + 4^2} = \sqrt{1 + 16} = \sqrt{17}$.

18. D

Let the coordinates of the endpoints of a line segment be (x_1, y_1) and (x_2, y_2). The coordinates of the midpoint of this line segment are $\dfrac{x_1 + x_2}{2}, \dfrac{y_1 + y_2}{2}$.

The midpoint of the line segment with endpoints $(-2, 4)$ and $(3, -2)$ is the point $\left(\dfrac{-2 + 3}{2}, \dfrac{4 + (-2)}{2} \right)$, which is the point $\left(\dfrac{1}{2}, 1 \right)$.

19. E

The distance d between two points (x_1, y_1) and (x_2, y_2) can be found by using the formula $d = \sqrt{(x_2 - x_1)^2 + (y_2 - y_1)^2}$.

The distance between the points $(-2, 4)$ and $(3, -2)$ is
$\sqrt{(3 - (-2))^2 + (-2 - 4)^2} = \sqrt{5^2 + (-6)^2} = \sqrt{25 + 36} = \sqrt{612}$

20. C

Two lines are parallel if their slopes are the same. When a line is written in the form $y = mx + b$, m equals the slope of the line. Look for the options that have the same slope as that given in the problem. Only III has the same slope as the line given in the question stem, so choice (C) is correct.

21. C

The slope-intercept form of the equation of a line is $y = mx + b$, where m is the slope and b is the y-intercept. You can use the slope formula, $m = \dfrac{y_2 - y_2}{x_2 - x_2}$, to find m, then plug one of the given points into the equation $y = mx + b$ to find b.

$$m = \frac{12 - 2}{10 - (-5)} = \frac{10}{15} = \frac{2}{3}$$

$$2 = \frac{2}{3}(-5) + b$$

$$2 = -\frac{10}{3} + b$$

$$\frac{16}{3} = b$$

$$y = \frac{2}{3}x + \frac{16}{3}$$

22. D

The large figure is a square, since all four angles are right angles and a pair of consecutive sides have the same length. Therefore, the vertical line segment that divides the large square into two identical rectangles and the diagonal of the large square create two small 45-45-90 triangles with legs of length 3. You can find the area of one of these small right triangles, then subtract that from half the area of the square to find the area of the shaded region. Divide this by the area of the square to find the probability that a randomly selected point will fall within the shaded area. The area of each small isosceles triangle is $\frac{1}{2}(3)(3) = \frac{9}{2}$, since the two legs of a 45-45-90 triangle are the same length. The area of the square is $6(6) = 36$. The probability that a point will fall within the shaded region is

$$\frac{\frac{36}{2} - \frac{9}{2}}{36} = \frac{36 - 9}{2(36)} = \frac{27}{72} = \frac{3}{8} = 0.375.$$

23. B

First, find the midpoint of $\overline{PQ}$ by using the midpoint formula, $\left(\frac{x_1 + x_2}{2}, \frac{y_1 + y_2}{2}\right)$.

Then, use the distance formula, $d = \sqrt{(x_2 - x_1)^2 + (y_2 - y_1)^2}$, to find the distance between that point and point R.

$$\left(\frac{-6 + 8}{2}, \frac{3 + 5}{2}\right) = \left(\frac{2}{2}, \frac{8}{2}\right) = (1, 4).$$ The midpoint is $(1, 4)$.

The distance between $R(-3, 1)$ and the midpoint $(1, 4)$ is

$$\sqrt{(1 - (3))^2 + (4 - 1)^2} = \sqrt{4^2 + 3^2} = \sqrt{16 + 9} = \sqrt{25} = 5.$$

Finally, a little taste of the geometry of solids.

GEOMETRY QUESTION 24

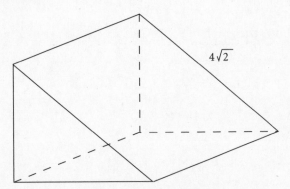

4√2

24. If the solid above is half of a cube, then the volume of the solid is

(A) 16

(B) 32

(C) 42

(D) 64

(E) 64√2

EXPLANATION: QUESTION 24

24. B

This requires some intuition. The solid is half of a cube; you can imagine an identical solid lying on the top of this one to form the complete cube. Then it becomes clear that the line segment with length $4\sqrt{2}$ is the diagonal of a square face. The diagonal is the hypotenuse of a right isosceles triangle with the two edges of the cube as legs; you can find the length of an edge by using the sides ratio for such triangles. In right isosceles triangles, the hypotenuse is $\sqrt{2}$ times either of the legs. Since the hypotenuse has length $4\sqrt{2}$, the legs (which are also the edges of the cube) have length 4. So the cube's volume is $4^3 = 64$. But be careful, that's not the answer to the question! The volume of the solid in the diagram is half the cube's volume, or 32.

FUNCTION GRAPHING

The SAT tests the ability to interpret graphs. This will include straightforward interpretation, as well as range and domain questions. Also tested will be your understanding of transformations.

Questions 25–27 relate to the following diagram:

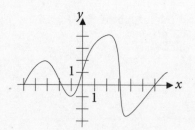

25. The figure above shows the graph of $f(x)$. What are the values of x such that $-5 \leq x \leq 6$ and $f(x) = 2$?

(A) −5 and 3

(B) −3, 0.5, and 3

(C) −3 and 2

(D) 0.5 and 6

(E) 4

26. Which of the following graphs shows $f(x) + 1$?

(A)

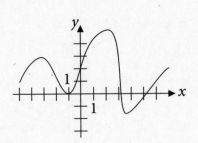

(B)

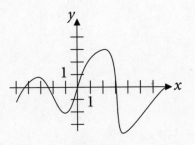

(C)

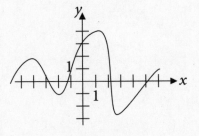

(D)

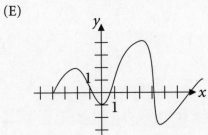

(E)

27. Which of the following graphs shows $f(x+1)$?

(A)

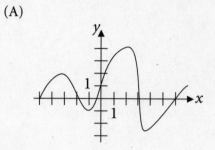

(B)

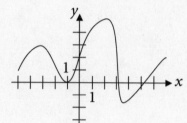

(C)

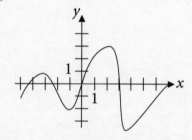

(D)

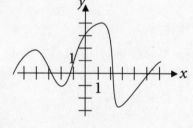

(E)

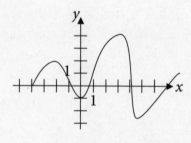

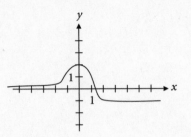

28. The graph above shows the function $f(x)$. What is the range of $f(x)$?

(A) All real numbers

(B) All numbers less than or equal to 2

(C) All numbers greater than or equal to −1

(D) All numbers greater than or equal to 0 and less than or equal to 2

(E) All numbers greater than or equal to −1 and less than or equal to 2

EXPLANATIONS: QUESTIONS 25–28

25. B

Locate the points on the graph where $f(x)$ (the y-value) is equal to 2. Look down at the x-axis to find the value of x at each of those points:

$f(x) = 2$ at $(-3, 2)$, $(0.5, 2)$, and $(3, 2)$.

26. B

The graph of $f(x) + 1$ will be the graph of $f(x)$ shifted up one unit. You may want to check a few points to be sure. Graph (B) appears to be the graph of $f(x)$ shifted up one unit.

27. D

The graph of $f(x + 1)$ will appear to have been shifted one unit to the left. If you're not sure what that would look like, try comparing a few points. $f(1 + 1)$ should be equal to $f(2)$. Graph (D) appears to have been shifted one unit to the left.

28. E

The range of a function is all the values that function can equal. The value of the function at a particular point is shown by where it is on the y-axis. The highest value this function reaches is 2, and the lowest value is −1.

CHAPTER 20: STRAIGHT MATH PRACTICE SET AND EXPLANATIONS

Directions: Fill in the corresponding oval on the answer sheet. You may use any available space for scratchwork.

Notes:

(1) Calculator use is permitted.

(2) All numbers used are real numbers.

(3) Figures are provided for some problems. All figures are drawn to scale and lie in a plane UNLESS otherwise indicated.

(4) Unless otherwise specified, the domain of any function f is assumed to be the set of all real numbers x for which $f(x)$ is a real number.

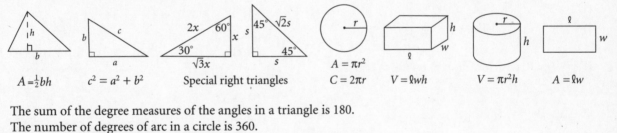

$$A = \tfrac{1}{2}bh \qquad c^2 = a^2 + b^2 \qquad \text{Special right triangles} \qquad \begin{array}{c} A = \pi r^2 \\ C = 2\pi r \end{array} \qquad V = \ell wh \qquad V = \pi r^2 h \qquad A = \ell w$$

The sum of the degree measures of the angles in a triangle is 180.
The number of degrees of arc in a circle is 360.
A straight angle has a degree measure of 180.

1. If x is the sum of n odd integers, which of the following must be true?

   (A) x is odd.

   (B) x is even.

   (C) $x \neq 0$.

   (D) If x is even, n is even.

   (E) If x is odd, x is even.

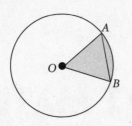

2. If $\overline{OA} = \overline{AB} = 6$ in the figure above, what is the area of the shaded region?

(A) 36π

(B) 12π

(C) 6π

(D) $9\sqrt{3}$

(E) 18

3. For all $x > 0$ and all $y > 0$ such that $x \neq y$,

$$\frac{\dfrac{x}{y} - \dfrac{y}{x}}{\dfrac{1}{x} - \dfrac{1}{y}} =$$

(A) $y(x + y)$

(B) $y(-x - y)$

(C) $-x + y$

(D) $x + y$

(E) $-x - y$

4. If $x^2 - 9 < 0$, which of the following is true?

(A) $x < -3$

(B) $x > 3$

(C) $x > 9$

(D) $x < -3$ or $x > 3$

(E) $-3 < x < 3$

5. If 4 is one of the solutions of $x^2 + cx - 24 = 0$, what is the value of c?

(A) -6

(B) -2

(C) 2

(D) 4

(E) 6

6. If the lengths of all three sides of a triangle are integers, and the length of one side is 7, what is the least possible perimeter of the triangle?

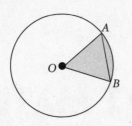

7. If $9^{2x-1} = 3^{3x+3}$, then $x =$

(A) -4

(B) $-\dfrac{7}{4}$

(C) $-\dfrac{10}{7}$

(D) 2

(E) 5

8. If $f(x) = x^3 - x^2 - x$, what is the value of $f(-3)$?

(A) -39

(B) -33

(C) -21

(D) -15

(E) 0

9. If a certain line in the coordinate plane contains points $(3, 8)$ and $(5, 2)$, which of the following represents the equation for that line?

(A) $y = -\dfrac{1}{3}x - 9$

(B) $y = 3x - 1$

(C) $y = 3x - 13$

(D) $y = -3x + 17$

(E) $y = -3x + 2$

10. If $|a+3|=1$ and $|b-2|=4$, what is one possible value of $|a+b|$?

   (A) −6

   (B) −4

   (C) 0

   (D) 3

   (E) 6

11. If $x \neq 0$, $x \neq 4$, and $\dfrac{x^3 - 2x^2 - 8x}{x^2 - 4x} = 0$, what is the value of x?

   (A) −4

   (B) −2

   (C) 2

   (D) 3

   (E) 8

12. If $s(t) = t^t - \sqrt{t} + 1$ for all positive values of t, which of the following is the value of $s(4)$?

   (A) 1

   (B) 15

   (C) 31

   (D) 156

   (E) 255

13. If $g(y) = y^{\frac{4}{3}} - y^{\frac{1}{3}}$, what is the value of $g(8)$?

   (A) 3

   (B) 6

   (C) $8\sqrt[3]{4}$

   (D) 14

   (E) 16

14. If $f(a) = \dfrac{a^2 + a^{-1} - 4}{(1 - a^{-3})^2} = 0$, what is the value of $f(2)$?

   (A) $\dfrac{32}{49}$

   (B) $\dfrac{128}{49}$

   (C) $\dfrac{49}{32}$

   (D) $\dfrac{63}{128}$

   (E) $\dfrac{128}{63}$

15. If $f(y) = \dfrac{1}{\sqrt{y} - 7}$, at which of the following values of y is $f(y)$ undefined?

   (A) 49

   (B) 7

   (C) $\sqrt{7}$

   (D) 1

   (E) 0

16. If $h(t) = 7t^4 + 3t^2$, and t is a real number, which of the following is NOT a possible value of $h(t)$?

   (A) −10

   (B) 0

   (C) 0.23

   (D) $4\sqrt{2}$

   (E) 6

17. If $g(a) = a^2 - 4$ and $h(b) = 2^b + 4$, what is the value of $h(g(2))$?

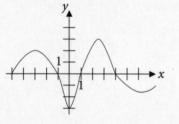

18. The figure above shows the graph of the function $f(x)$. Which of the following figures shows the graph of the function $f(x) + 1$?

(A)

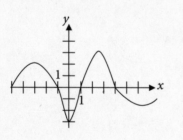

(B)

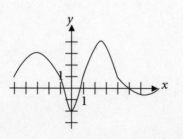

(C)

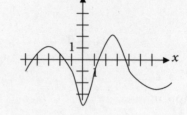

(D)

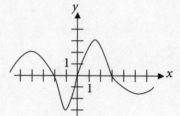

(E)

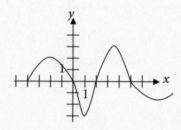

(D)

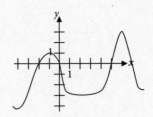

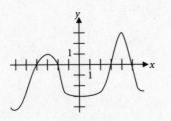

19. The graph above shows $f(x)$. Which of the following is the graph of $f(x-2)$?

(A)

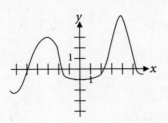

(E)

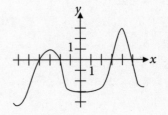

(B)

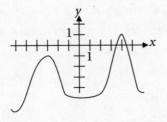

(C)

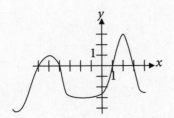

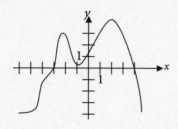

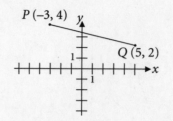

20. The figure above shows the graph of $f(x)$. For which values of x is $f(x) \geq 0$?

(A) $x \leq -3$ and $x \geq 4$

(B) $x \leq 4$

(C) $x \geq -3$

(D) $x \leq 3.5$

(E) $-3 \leq x \leq 4$

21. Which of the following lines are perpendicular to the line that goes through the points $(-1, 4)$ and $(3, -8)$?

   I. $y = -\dfrac{1}{3}x - 7$

   II. $y = \dfrac{1}{3}x + 10$

   III. $y = 3x + 5$

(A) I only

(B) II only

(C) III only

(D) I and II only

(E) II and III only

22. Which of the following describes a line that intersects $\overline{PQ}$ at its midpoint and is perpendicular to $\overline{PQ}$?

(A) $y = 4x - 3$

(B) $y = 4x - 1$

(C) $y = \dfrac{1}{4}x + 1$

(D) $y = -\dfrac{1}{4}x - 1$

(E) $y = -4x + 3$

23. $\overline{PQ}$ extends from $(-4, -8)$ to $(2, 10)$. Which of the following equations describes a line that intersects $\overline{PQ}$ at its midpoint and is perpendicular to $\overline{PQ}$?

(A) $y = \dfrac{1}{3}x - \dfrac{1}{3}$

(B) $y = -\dfrac{1}{3}x + \dfrac{2}{3}$

(C) $y = \dfrac{1}{3}x + \dfrac{2}{3}$

(D) $y = 3x - \dfrac{1}{3}$

(E) $y = 3x + \dfrac{2}{3}$

24. The points $(-1, -1)$, $(-1, 5)$, $(5, 5)$, and $(5, -1)$ form a square. What is the length of a diagonal of this square?

(A) 6

(B) $6\sqrt{2}$

(C) 12

(D) 24

(E) 36

EXPLANATIONS

1. D

You want to try out a few possibilities since n could be even or odd.

For instance, n could be 3 and all the odd integers could equal 1 for a sum of $x = 3$. Eliminate (B) and (E).

Or n could be 2 and all the odd integers could equal 1 for a sum of $x = 2$. Eliminate (A).

Or x could be the sum of -1 and 1; thus $x = 0$ and choice (C) is out as well.

2. C

Notice two sides of the triangle are radii. This means they must be the same length, so $\overline{OB} = \overline{OA} = \overline{AB} = 6$, which means the triangle is equilateral. Since all three angles of an equilateral triangle are 60 degrees, the shaded region must take up 60 degrees of the 360 degrees in the circle; in other words, $\frac{1}{6}$ of the circle $\left(\frac{60}{360} = \frac{1}{6} \right)$.

We know that the area of the entire circle is πr^2 or 36π. We want only $\frac{1}{6}$ of that though, which is 6π. So the area of the shaded region is 6π.

3. E

Now here's an ugly problem. Both the numerator and the denominator involve the subtraction of fractions. In both cases, you can use xy as a common denominator:

$$\frac{\dfrac{x}{y} - \dfrac{y}{x}}{\dfrac{1}{x} - \dfrac{1}{y}} = \frac{\dfrac{x^2}{xy} - \dfrac{y^2}{xy}}{\dfrac{y}{xy} - \dfrac{x}{xy}}$$

$$= \frac{\dfrac{x^2 - y^2}{xy}}{\dfrac{y - x}{xy}}$$

$$= \frac{x^2 - y^2}{y - x}$$

The numerator is in the factorable "difference-of-squares" form:

$$\frac{x^2 - y^2}{y - x} = \frac{(x - y)(x + y)}{y - x}$$

Because $x - y = -1(y - x)$, you can cancel them out, leaving a factor of -1:

$$\frac{(x - y)(x + y)}{y - x} = -1(x + y) = -x - y$$

4. E

Rearrange $x^2 - 9 < 0$ to get $x^2 < 9$. We're looking for all the values of x that would fit this inequality. We need to consider both positive and negative values of x. Remember that $3^2 = 9$ and also that $(-3)^2 = 9$. If x is positive, and $x^2 < 9$, we can simply say that $x < 3$. But what if x is negative? x can take on only values whose square is less than 9. In other words, x cannot be less than or equal to -3. (Think of smaller numbers like -4 or -5; their squares are greater than 9.) So if x is negative, $x > -3$. x can also be 0. Therefore, $-3 < x < 3$. If you had trouble solving algebraically, you could have tried each answer choice:

(A) Say $x = -4$. $(-4)^2 - 9 = 16 - 9 = 7$. No good.

(B) Say $x = 4$; $4^2 - 9 = 16 - 9 = 7$. No good.

(C) Since 4 was too big, anything greater than 9 is too big. No good.

(D) Combination of (A) and (B), which were both wrong. No good.

Clearly, (E) must be correct.

5. C

Let's substitute 4 for x into the equation $x^2 + cx - 24 = 0$, and then solve the resulting equation for c:

$$4^2 + c(4) - 24 = 0$$
$$16 + 4c - 24 = 0$$
$$4c - 8 = 0$$
$$4c = 8$$
$$c = 2$$

6. 15

You are told that the two unknown side lengths are integers, and if the length of the known side is 7, you should know the sum of the two unknown lengths has to be greater than 7, because the Triangle Inequality Theorem states that the length of any side of a triangle must be less than the sum of the other two sides. So the least amount the two unknown sides could add up to is 8, which would make the perimeter $7 + 8 = 15$.

7. E

Rewrite the left side of the equation so that both sides have the same base:

$$9^{2x-1} = 3^{3x+3}$$
$$(3^2)^{2x-1} = 3^{3x+3}$$

When you raise a power to an exponent, you multiply the exponents, so you now have:

$$3^{4x-2} = 3^{3x+3}$$

Now that the bases are the same, just set the exponents to be equal:

$$4x - 2 = 3x + 3$$
$$4x - 3x = 3 + 2$$
$$x = 5$$

8. B

This looks like a question in which you have to understand how functions work, but in fact it's just a "plug in the number and see what you get" question.

$$f(x) = x^3 - x^2 - x$$
$$f(-3) = (-3)^3 - (-3)^2 - (-3)$$
$$= -27 - 9 + 3$$
$$= -33$$

9. D

There are, as usual, a couple of ways you could approach this question. If you wanted to try a backdoor approach, you could plug in the values for the two points you're given into answer choices until you find an equation that works for both points. If you tried this approach, we would recommend that you start with (E) and work your way up, because of the SAT's tendency for (D) and (E) to be the more likely answer choices on "which of the following" questions.

But let's try answering this the old-fashioned way. The first thing you want to do is figure out the slope of the line, which is equal to $\frac{y_2 - y_1}{x_2 - x_1}$, so here, that equals $\frac{2 - 8}{5 - 3} = \frac{-6}{2} = -3$. Since the slope equals m when the linear equation is in the form $y = mx + b$, you know that this equation will be written $y = -3x + b$, so (A), (B), and (C) are all out. Now just plug in the values for one of the points in order to solve for b. If you plug in (3, 8), you get

$$8 = -3(3) + b$$
$$8 = -9 + b$$

and then $17 = b$. The equation of the line is $y = -3x + 17$, $y = -3x + 17$, so the answer is (D).

10. E

First, find all possible values of a and b. Then find all possible values of $a + b$. Then take the absolute value of each possible value of $a + b$, and see which answer choice matches one of the possibilities. Even before you calculate anything, you can rule out (A) and (B), since they are negative and $|a + b|$ must be nonnegative.

$$|a + 3| = 1$$
$$a + 3 = 1 \text{ or } a + 3 = -1$$
$$a = -2 \text{ or } a = -4$$
$$b - 2 = 4 \text{ or } b - 2 = -4$$
$$b = 6 \text{ or } b = -2$$

The possible values of a are -2 and -4.

The possible values of b are 6 and -2.

These are the possible values of $a + b$.

$$-2 + 6 = 4$$
$$-2 + (-2) = -4$$
$$-4 + 6 = 2$$
$$-4 + (-2) = -6$$

Thus, the possible values of $a + b$ are 4, -4, 2, and -6. Now $|4| = 4$, $|-4| = 4$, $|-2| = 2$, $|4| = 4$, and $|-6| = 6$. The possible values of $|a + b|$ are 2, 4, and 6. Choice (E), 6, is the only possible value of $|a + b|$ among the answer choices.

11. B

Although Back-solving will work on this sort of problem, it is often faster to factor the numerator and denominator, then simplify.

$$\frac{x^3 - 2x^2 - 8x}{x^2 - 4x} = \frac{x(x^2 - 2x - 8)}{x(x - 4)}$$
$$= \frac{(x - 4)(x + 2)}{x - 4} = x + 2$$

So $x + 2 = 0$. Then $x = -2$.

12. E

Substitute $t = 4$ into the function and simplify. Work carefully, and problems like this will be no trouble.

$$s(4) = 4^4 - \sqrt{4} + 1 = 256 - 2 + 1 = 255$$

13. D

Substitute 8 for y into the function. Be sure to follow the order of operations, and remember that $y^{\frac{4}{3}} = \sqrt[3]{y^4}$ and $y^{\frac{1}{3}} = \sqrt[3]{y}$.

$$g(8) = 8^{\frac{4}{3}} - 8^{\frac{1}{3}} = \left(\sqrt[3]{8}\right)^4 - \sqrt[3]{8} = 2^4 - 2$$
$$= 16 - 2 = 14$$

14. A

Plug 2 for a into the function and simplify. Respect the order of operations and work very carefully.

$$f(2) = \frac{2^2 + 2^{-1} - 4}{(1 - 2^{-3})^2} = \frac{4 + \frac{1}{2} - 4}{\left(1 - \frac{1}{8}\right)^2} = \frac{\frac{1}{2}}{\left(\frac{7}{8}\right)^2}$$
$$= \frac{1}{2} \times \frac{8^2}{7^2} = \frac{1}{2} \times \frac{64}{49} = \frac{32}{49}$$

If you want to do this with your calculator, instead, be very careful with parentheses.

15. A

This function is undefined when the denominator, $\sqrt{y} - 7$, equals 0:

$$\sqrt{y} - 7 = 0$$
$$\sqrt{y} = 7$$
$$y = 7^2 = 49$$

16. A

Think about what kinds of numbers can appear in the function. Remember than any real number raised to a positive even exponent will be nonnegative: $h(t)$ is a nonnegative number plus a nonnegative number. There is no way $h(t)$ can be negative. The function $h(t)$, however, can equal zero, if $t = 0$.

17. 5

Although functions can look complicated and confusing, they are really just simple substitution problems. As long as you remember all the rules and work carefully, these problems can be easy points. Remember to start from the inside of the parenthesis and work out:

$$g(2) = 2^2 - 4 = 4 - 4 = 0$$
$$h(0) = 2^0 + 4 = 1 + 4 = 5$$

18. B

The graph of $f(x) + 1$ will appear to be the graph of $f(x)$ shifted one unit up. You can check this by plugging in a few points. For instance, $f(0) = -3$. $f(0) + 1 = -3 + 1 = -2$, so you should look for the graph which crosses the y-axis at -2.

19. D

The graph of $f(x - 2)$ will appear to be the graph of $f(x)$ shifted two units to the right. You can check your answer by comparing some points on the graphs.

$$f(0) = -3$$
$$f(2 - 2) = -3$$

20. E

$f(x)$ is ≥ 0 where the graph is at or above the x-axis. Find the values of x at those points. $f(x) = 0$ when $x = -3$ and when $x = 4$. It is positive (above the x-axis) at all points in between. So $f(x) \geq 0$ when $-3 \leq x \leq 4$.

21. B

The slope m of a line that goes through the points (x_1, y_1) and (x_2, y_2) is given by the formula $m = \frac{y_2 - y_1}{x_2 - x_1}$. The slope of the line that goes through the points $(-1, 4)$ and $(3, -8)$ is $\frac{-8 - 4}{3 - (-1)} = \frac{-12}{4} = -3$. The slope of a line that is perpendicular to a line with a nonzero slope m is the negative reciprocal of the slope of the line, or $\frac{-1}{m}$. So the slope of a line that is perpendicular to the line that goes through the points $(-1, 4)$ and $(3, -8)$ is the negative reciprocal of -3, which is $\frac{-1}{-3} = \frac{1}{3}$. Now each of the options is in the slope-intercept form $y = mx + b$ where m is the slope and b is the y-intercept. Only option II has a slope of $\frac{1}{3}$. Choice (B) is correct.

22. B

First, you'll need to find the midpoint and the slope of $\overline{PQ}$. Let the coordinates of the endpoints of a line segment be (x_1, y_1) and (x_2, y_2). The coordinates of the midpoint of this line segment are $\left(\frac{x_1 + x_2}{2}, \frac{y_1 + y_2}{2} \right)$. The slope of a line perpendicular to $\overline{PQ}$ will be the negative reciprocal of the slope of $\overline{PQ}$. That is, if the nonzero slope of one line is m, the slope of a perpendicular line would be $-\frac{1}{m}$. You can use this information with the midpoint to find an equation for the perpendicular line.

Midpoint:

$$\frac{-3 + 5}{2} = \frac{2}{2} = 1$$
$$\frac{4 + 2}{2} = \frac{6}{2} = 3$$

The midpoint of $\overline{PQ}$ is (1, 3).

Slope of $\overline{PQ}$:

$$\frac{2 - 4}{5 - (-3)} = \frac{-2}{8} = \frac{-1}{4} = -\frac{1}{4}$$

So the slope of the perpendicular line is $\frac{-1}{\left(-\frac{1}{4} \right)}$, which is 4.

We can write an equation for it as $y = 4x + b$. Plug in the known point (the midpoint of $\overline{PQ}$) to find b.

$$3 = 4(1) + b$$
$$-1 = b$$

So the equation for the perpendicular line is $y = 4x - 1$.

23. B

You will need to find the midpoint of $\overline{PQ}$ and its slope. You can then use the slope to find the slope of a line perpendicular to $\overline{PQ}$, and plug in the midpoint of $\overline{PQ}$ (since it is on the perpendicular line) to find the y-intercept of the line using the equation $y = mx + b$. Let the coordinates of the endpoints of a line segment be (x_1, y_1) and (x_2, y_2). The coordinates of the midpoint of this line segment are $\left(\dfrac{x_1 + x_2}{2}, \dfrac{y_1 + y_2}{2} \right)$.

Here,

$$\frac{x_1 + x_2}{2} = \frac{-4 + 2}{2} = \frac{-2}{2} = -1$$

$$\frac{y_1 + y_2}{2} = \frac{-8 + 10}{2} = \frac{2}{2} = 1$$

Midpoint of $\overline{PQ}$: $(-1, 1)$.

The slope m of a line passing through the points (x_1, y_1) and (x_2, y_2) is given by $m = \dfrac{y_2 - y_1}{x_2 - x_1}$.

Slope of $\overline{PQ}$: $\dfrac{10 - (-8)}{2 - (-4)} = \dfrac{18}{6} = 3$.

The slope of any line perpendicular to $\overline{PQ}$ is $\dfrac{-1}{3}$, or $-\dfrac{1}{3}$.

Finding b: The equation of the line perpendicular to $\overline{PQ}$ is:

$$y = -\frac{1}{3}x + b$$

$$1 = \left(-\frac{1}{3} \right)(-1) + b$$

$$\frac{2}{3} = b$$

Equation of the perpendicular line: $y = -\dfrac{1}{3}x + \dfrac{2}{3}$.

24. B

Use the distance formula, $d = \sqrt{(x_2 - x_1)^2 + (y_2 - y_1)^2}$, to find the distance between two points which are opposite each other diagonally. To figure out which points are opposite each other diagonally, you might want to sketch the points.

A pair of points which are the endpoints of a diagonal are $(-1, -1)$ and $(5, 5)$.

The distance d between two points (x_1, y_1) and (x_2, y_2) can be found by using the formula $d = \sqrt{(x_2 - x_1)^2 + (y_2 - y_1)^2}$.

The distance between the points $(-1, -1)$ and $(5, 5)$ is $\sqrt{(5 - (-1))^2 + (5 - (-1))^2} = \sqrt{6^2 + 6^2} = \sqrt{72} = 6\sqrt{2}$.

Part Six

SAT MATH WORD PROBLEMS

CHAPTER 21: ARITHMETIC AND ALGEBRA WORD PROBLEMS

- Ratios, proportions, and variations

- Percent problems

- Rate problems

- Set terminology

- Average problems

- Algebra word problems

- Exponential sequences

The majority of word problems you'll encounter on the SAT will test either arithmetic or algebra, and very often both. Since you will frequently be solving for an unknown, you'll often have to use some algebra even on arithmetic questions. To muddy the waters even more, word problems will often concern two or more math topics or techniques.

The trick, of course, is to unpack the English to get at the specific math being tested, and then to answer the *question being asked*. Since many word problems contain more than one step, you may have to solve for more than one value. Picking the answer choice with the value that is asked for, rather than another value, is a crucial but often messed up last step.

Before we examine some of the most common arithmetic and algebra word problem questions, what follows are some overarching strategies for handling any type of word problem you might encounter on the SAT.

WORD PROBLEM STRATEGIES

Here's the general approach to any word problem:

1. Read through the whole question. Do this to get a sense of what's going on. You want to know the basic situation described, the type of information you've been given, and—most important of all—what exactly you are being asked.

2. Identify the different variables or unknowns and label them. For example, if the problem discusses Charlie's and Veronica's warts, you may wish to use c to represent Charlie's warts and v to represent Veronica's warts. Notice that we didn't use x and y. If we had, we might later forget whether x represented Charlie's warts or Veronica's.

3. Translate the problem into math. This usually entails rewriting the English sentences into equations or statements. The sentence "Veronica has four fewer warts than Charlie has would become: $v = c - 4$. Notice that the math terms are not in the same order as the English terms in the sentence. When you translate, you are translating the ideas. The idea here is "four fewer warts than Charlie." That means $c - 4$, not $4 - c$!

4. Tackle the math. Solve the equations. Use a calculator, where needed, to help crunch the numbers. Make sure you've determined the value that the question is asking you for.

5. Check your work, if you have time.

The Translation Table

It's a good idea to familiarize yourself with the mathematical meanings of some of the most common words used in word problems. Knowing these equivalencies can provide you with a specific, concrete starting point, especially when a word problem seems incomprehensible.

The table below can be a lifesaver—the sort of thing you really want to understand clearly.

English	"Mathish"
equals is, was, will be has costs adds up to is the same as	=
times of multiplied by product of twice, double, triple, half	×
per out of divided by each ratio of __ to __	÷
and plus added to sum combined total	+
minus subtracted from less than decreased by difference between	−
what how much how many a number	x, n (variable)

Remember: If you are completely baffled by a word problem, look for some of the words in the left-hand column. Then work from their math equivalent and try to construct an equation.

RATIOS, PROPORTIONS, AND VARIATIONS

The statements "x is proportional to y," "x varies directly with y," and "the ratio of x to y is a constant" are all equivalent. They all say that $\dfrac{x}{y}$ = a constant. This constant is traditionally called k. The only distinction for inverse variation relationships is that, if x is inversely proportional to y, then the fraction becomes $\dfrac{x}{(\text{reciprocal of } y)} = \dfrac{x}{\left(\dfrac{1}{y}\right)} = x \times y$.

So $x \times y = k$ for inverse variation. The most straightforward word problems test the related concepts of ratios, proportions, and variations. Look at these two:

QUESTIONS 1–2

1. At College X, the faculty-to-student ratio is 1:9. If two-thirds of the students are female and one-quarter of the faculty is female, what fraction of the combined students and faculty are female?

   (A) $\dfrac{11}{24}$

   (B) $\dfrac{5}{8}$

   (C) $\dfrac{25}{56}$

   (D) $\dfrac{11}{12}$

   (E) It cannot be determined from the information given.

2. A batch of cookies was divided among three tins: $\dfrac{2}{3}$ of all the cookies were placed in either the blue tin or the green tin, and the rest were placed in the red tin. If $\dfrac{1}{4}$ of all the cookies were placed in the blue tin, what was the ratio of cookies that were placed in the green tin to cookies that were placed in tins other than the blue tin?

   (A) $\dfrac{15}{2}$

   (B) $\dfrac{9}{4}$

   (C) $\dfrac{5}{9}$

   (D) $\dfrac{7}{5}$

   (E) $\dfrac{9}{7}$

EXPLANATIONS: QUESTIONS 1–2

1. B

Pick a number for the smallest given quantity described in the question—the number of female faculty: If there's 1 female member of the faculty, then the total number of faculty is 4 times 1, or 4. There are 9 times as many students, or 36 students. $\frac{2}{3}$ of 36 students are female, so there are 24 female students. Therefore, the total number of females is $1 + 24$, or 25, and the total number of students and faculty is $4 + 36$, or 40. That makes the fraction $\frac{25}{40}$, or $\frac{5}{8}$.

> An Advanced test taker often decides to Pick Numbers when working with word problems. This works best when the numbers picked are smart numbers.

2. C

Pay attention to what you're asked for—it can be written as follows:

$$\frac{\text{Number of cookies in green tin}}{\text{Number of cookies in green tin} + \text{Number of cookies in red tin}}$$

You are told that $\frac{1}{4}$ of the cookies are in the blue tin and, since $\frac{2}{3}$ of the cookies were placed in either the blue or the green tin, $\frac{1}{3}$ must go in the red tin. Also notice that actual numbers for the cookies are not given; you have only fractions to work with.

You already know the fractions of the cookies that go in the red tin and blue tin, so work out the fraction of cookies that go in the green tin.

The fractions of the total cookies in each tin must add up to 1, so the fraction of all the cookies in the green tin is given by the equation $\frac{1}{3} + \frac{1}{4} +$ (fraction in green tin) $= 1$. That is, fraction in green tin =

$$1 - \frac{1}{3} - \frac{1}{4} = \frac{12}{12} - \frac{4}{12} - \frac{3}{12} = \frac{5}{12}.$$

So:

$$\frac{\text{Number of cookies in green tin}}{\text{Number of cookies in green tin} + \text{Number of cookies in red tin}} =$$

$$\frac{\frac{5}{12}}{\frac{5}{12} + \frac{1}{3}} = \frac{\frac{5}{12}}{\frac{5}{12} + \frac{4}{12}} = \frac{\frac{5}{12}}{\frac{9}{12}} = \frac{5}{9}.$$

QUESTIONS 3–6

3. An assortment of candies consists of x chocolates and y buttercreams. If 2 chocolates are added and 3 buttercreams are removed, what fraction of the remaining candies, in terms of x and y, are chocolates?

   (A) $\dfrac{x+2}{y}$

   (B) $\dfrac{x}{y-1+2}$

   (C) $\dfrac{x-1}{x+y+2}$

   (D) $\dfrac{x+2}{x+y-1}$

   (E) $\dfrac{x+3}{x+y}$

4. The number of ice cream cones the Ice Cream Hut sells is directly proportional to the highest temperature recorded that day. On a day with a high of 88 degrees, the Ice Cream Hut sold 220 ice cream cones. How many cones did the Ice Cream Hut sell on a day with a high of 94 degrees?

   (A) 226

   (B) 235

   (C) 286

   (D) 308

   (E) 385

5. n and p are inversely proportional. If $p = 100$ when $n = 2$, what is n when $p = 2$?

   (A) 25

   (B) 50

   (C) 100

   (D) 200

   (E) 400

6. The number of butterflies in Gloria's garden varies directly with the number of flowers that are in bloom. On Monday, when 50 flowers were in bloom, 10 butterflies visited the garden. By Friday, 30 more flowers had bloomed. How many butterflies visited the garden on Friday?

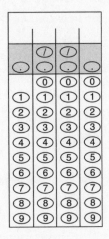

EXPLANATIONS: QUESTIONS 3–6

3. D

You are asked to find what fraction of all the candies will be chocolates after the total has been adjusted. This fraction is simply the number of chocolates over the total number of candies after the change has been made.

Find the number of chocolates and buttercreams by translating the stem. Then divide the number of chocolates by the total number of chocolates and buttercreams. Alternatively, since all the answer choices contain variables, you could try Picking Numbers.

You initially had x chocolates, but now have two more, or $x + 2$. The original number of buttercreams was y, and 3 were removed, so the number of buttercreams is $y - 3$.

So the fraction of candies that are chocolates =

$$\frac{\text{Number of chocolates}}{\text{Number of candies}} = \frac{x + 2}{x + 2 + y - 3} = \frac{x + 2}{x + y - 1}.$$

Once again, if translating this problem was difficult—many people have trouble sorting out parts and totals—you should have tried plugging in numbers. For instance, say there are initially 5 chocolates and 5 buttercreams—10 candies total. After the 2 chocolates are added and the 3 buttercreams are removed, there are 7 chocolates and 9 candies total. Plugging in 5 and 5 for x and y in the answer choices, only choice (D) works out to $\frac{7}{9}$.

4. B

To solve this problem, you should set up an equation to express the relationship between number of cones sold and high temperature. You can then use the given information to find k, then use k to find the information asked for. Say c is the number of cones sold in a day and t is the highest recorded temperature. Then the relationship between the two is $\frac{c}{t} = k$.

$$\frac{220}{88} = k$$

$$2.5 = k$$

When $t = 94$, $\frac{c}{94} = 2.5$ and $c = 235$.

Thus, 235 ice cream cones were sold.

If you were getting stuck on this question, Back-solving is another tool you could have used.

5. C

If n and p are inversely proportional, they obey the relation $pn = k$, where k is a constant. Use the given set of values to find k, then find the value of n at the second point.

$$(100)(2) = k$$

$$k = 200$$

So $pn = 200$.

If $p = 2$, $2n = 200$, and $n = \frac{200}{2} = 100$.

6. 16

If a quantity b varies directly with another quantity f, the relation between them can be expressed as $\frac{b}{f} = k$, where k is a constant. In this case, b and f represent the number of butterflies and the number of flowers in the garden. You can use the given values of b and f to find k.

$$\frac{10}{50} = k$$

$$0.2 = k$$

So $\frac{b}{f} = 0.2$.

Now let's find b when $f = 50 + 30 = 80$.

$$\frac{b}{80} = 0.2$$

$$b = 16$$

PERCENTS

Percents show up frequently in SAT word problems. And that just makes sense, really. Word problems rely on "real life" scenarios (well, *somebody's* real life, if not yours). Percents are common in everyday life—money, taxes, etc. Thus, they make excellent material for the test makers that devise word problems.

Let's look at a representative pair.

QUESTIONS 7–9

7. In 1966, the operative mortality rate in open heart surgery at a certain hospital was 8.1 per 100 cases. By 1974, the operative mortality rate had declined to 4.8 per 100 cases. If the rate declined by 20 percent from 1973 to 1974, by approximately what percent did it decline from 1966 to 1973?

   (A) 6%

   (B) 21%

   (C) 26%

   (D) 41%

   (E) 49%

8. If Ms. DeLong travels to state *A* to purchase camping equipment, she must pay the prevailing sales tax of 8 percent on what she buys. The store will ship her purchase to her home in state *B* without charging tax, but with a fixed shipping fee of $3.20. What is the least number of dollars she can spend so that having the purchase shipped will not be more expensive than paying the sales tax? (Disregard the $ sign when gridding in your answer.)

9. At a certain store, each item that normally costs $20 or less is on sale for 80 percent of its normal price, and each item that normally costs more than $20 is on sale for 75 percent of its normal price. If a customer purchases c items, each of which normally costs $15, and d items, each of which normally costs $24, what is the average (arithmetic mean) amount, in dollars, that she pays for each item?

(A) $\dfrac{c+d}{30}$

(B) $\dfrac{12}{c}+\dfrac{18}{d}$

(C) $\dfrac{12c+18d}{2}$

(D) $\dfrac{12c+18d}{c+d}$

(E) $\dfrac{30}{c+d}$

EXPLANATIONS: QUESTIONS 7–9

7.   C

To determine the percent decrease in the rate from 1966 to 1973, you need to find the rate for 1973. You know the actual rate for 1974, and since you also know the percent decrease from 1973 to 1974, you can find the 1973 rate. The rate dropped 20% from 1973 to 1974, so the 1974 rate represents $100\% - 20\% = 80\%$ of the 1973 rate. Let the 1973 rate be represented by x, and plug it into the percent formula: Percent $\times$ Whole = Part, so $0.8x = 4.8$, $x = \dfrac{4.8}{0.8} = 6$. So the rate decreased by $8.1 - 6 = 2.1$ from 1966 to 1973.

Percent decrease $= \dfrac{\text{Part decrease}}{\text{Whole}} \times 100\%$, or in this case, $\dfrac{2.1}{8.1} \times 100\%$. It's time to pull out your calculator. $2.1 \div 8.1 = .\overline{259}$. Convert this decimal into a percent by multiplying by 100% and you get $25.\overline{925}\%$. (C) comes closest, and it's the correct answer.

8.   40

The sales tax on her purchase must equal the fixed shipping fee of $3.20. Let $x =$ the purchase amount, in dollars. We must find the smallest number of dollars that can be spent so that the cost of having the purchase shipped will not be more expensive than paying the sales tax. In other words, we must find the smallest number of dollars that can be spent so that the cost of having the purchase shipped will be less than or equal to the sales tax. So $3.20 \leq 0.08x$. Then $\dfrac{3.20}{0.08} \leq x$. Now $\dfrac{3.20}{0.08} = \dfrac{3.20 \times 100}{0.08 \times 100} = \dfrac{320}{8} = 40$. So $40 \leq x$. That is $x \geq 40$. The smallest possible values of x is 40. Grid in 40 as the correct answer.

9. D

This is a complicated word problem; translate it one step at a time. Items that are less than or equal to $20 are discounted by 80%, items that are over $20 are discounted by 75%. The customer purchases c items costing $15 and d items costing $24, that is, c items discounted by 80% and d items discounted by 75%. The average price then is

$$\frac{\text{Total discounted cost of articles purchased}}{\text{Number of articles purchased}}$$

Find the average of the discounted prices of all the articles.

80% of $15 = $12; total amount spent on these c items: $12c$
75% of $24 = $18; the total amount spent on these d items: $18d$

$$\text{Average} = \frac{\text{Total discounted cost of articles purchased}}{\text{Number of articles purchased}}$$

$$= \frac{12c + 18d}{c + d}, \text{ or (D)}.$$

As you are probably starting to realize, one of the keys to not fouling up a word problem is to read carefully. Often, similar terms will be employed and you must keep them straight.

If these next questions spin your head around like a gyroscope, consider employing a strategy like Back-solving or Picking Numbers.

QUESTIONS 10–12

10. At car dealership X, the total profit from sales increased by 10 percent over the previous year, while the number of cars sold decreased by 10 percent over the previous year. Approximately what was the average percent increase in profit per car over the previous year?

   (A) 18%
   (B) 20%
   (C) 22%
   (D) 23%
   (E) 25%

11. A magazine's survey of its subscribers finds that 20 percent are male. If 70 percent of the subscribers are married, and 10 percent of these are male, what percent of the male subscribers are not married? (Disregard % sign when gridding your answer.)

12. An empty metal box weighs 10 percent of its total weight when filled with varnish. If the weight of a partly filled box is one-half that of a completely filled box, what fraction of the box is filled?

    (A) $\dfrac{3}{5}$

    (B) $\dfrac{5}{9}$

    (C) $\dfrac{1}{2}$

    (D) $\dfrac{4}{9}$

    (E) $\dfrac{2}{5}$

EXPLANATIONS: QUESTIONS 10–12

10. C

Pick Numbers for the original number of cars sold and the original profit per car. If the car dealership sold 10 cars at a $10 profit per car, it originally made $100 profit total. The next year it sold 10% fewer cars, or 9 cars. The profit, however, increased by 10%, so the profit equaled $100 + (10% of $100) = $110. The profit per car increased from $10 to $\dfrac{\$110}{9}$. If you pull out your calculator, you'll see that $\dfrac{\$110}{9} \approx \$12.22$, so the amount of increase is $12.22 − $10.00 = $2.22. The percent increase in profit per car is the amount of increase divided by the original profit per car: $\dfrac{\$2.22}{10.00}$, or approximately 22%.

> An Advanced test taker is able to quickly choose an alternative strategy when the situation demands it.

11. 65

Pick a number to represent magazine subscribers. Pick 100 because it's easy to find percents of 100. 70% of the magazine subscribers are married, so there are 70 married subscribers. 10% of the married subscribers are male, so there are $10\% \times 70 = 7$ married male subscribers. 20% of all the subscribers are male, so 20 of them are males. If 7 of the 20 males are married, $20 - 7 = 13$ of them are not married. So the percent of male subscribers who are not married is given by $\frac{\text{Part}}{\text{Whole}} \times 100\%$, which is $\frac{13}{20} \times 100\% = 65\%$. Fill in the grid with 65.

12. D

Pick Numbers. Since you are dealing with percents, pick 100, so say the box weighs 100 pounds when full. In this case, the weight of the metal box is 10 percent, or $\frac{1}{10}$, of 100 pounds, which is 10 pounds. That leaves 90 pounds of varnish to fill the box. The weight of the partly filled box is half of 100 pounds, or 50 pounds. Since the box itself weighs 10 pounds, 40 pounds of varnish are in the partly filled box. Since the box has the capacity to hold 90 pounds of varnish, the box is $\frac{4}{9}$ full.

RATES AND AVERAGES

The paradigmatic SAT word problem is probably the "rates" word problem. A rate is just a ratio involving units. It expresses the units of one item per units of another. So we can solve for a rate like so:

$$\text{Rate} = \frac{\text{Units of } A}{\text{Unit of } B}$$

The rate that you'll most often encounter on the SAT is speed. Speed is specifically the ratio of distance to time. Here's the formula:

$$\text{Rate} = \frac{\text{Distance}}{\text{Time}}$$

This can also be written as either of the following:

$$\text{Time} = \frac{\text{Distance}}{\text{Rate}}$$

$$\text{Distance} = \text{Rate} \times \text{Time}$$

All three equations say the same thing. And if we have any two of the three components (Rate, Time, and Distance), we can solve for the third.

Let's take a look at some of the tougher rate problems the SAT may throw at you. Here are two problems with the characteristic SAT twist: you have to work with more than just one speed. Give them a try.

Questions 13–14

13. A riverboat leaves Mildura and travels upstream to Renmark at an average speed of 6 miles per hour. It returns by the same route at an average speed of 9 miles per hour. What is its average speed for the round trip, in miles per hour?

    (A) 7.0
    (B) 7.2
    (C) 7.5
    (D) 7.8
    (E) 8.2

A couple of word problems on the SAT will invariably deal with averages, and they may also include the related concepts of median and mode. Mostly, these questions simply test your ability to use the average formula and/or understand the difference between mean, median, and mode.

Let's take a look and see if you're sufficiently above average when it comes to handling average problems.

14. The average (arithmetic mean) age of the members of a five-man rock group is 42. After the original drummer quits and is replaced by a 27-year-old, the average age of the rock group is now 38. What was the age of the original drummer?

EXPLANATIONS: QUESTIONS 13–14

13. B

Each leg of the trip will take a different amount of time and you must work correctly to account for this. Pick a number for the distance from Mildura to Renmark; try 18 since it is evenly divisible by both speeds. On the first leg of the trip, traveling 18 miles at 6 miles per hour will take 3 hours. On the return trip, traveling 18 miles at 9 miles per hour will take 2 hours. So the average speed for the entire trip is $\frac{18 + 18}{3 + 2} = \frac{36}{5} = 7\frac{1}{5}$, or 7.2 miles per hour. (B) wins.

> An Advanced test taker knows the formulas cold for determining Time, Rate, and Distance.

14. 47

The average formula states that $\text{Average} = \frac{\text{Sum of the terms}}{\text{Number of terms}}$. So there are three components to the formula, and just as with a rate question, whenever you have two out of three of the components, you should automatically calculate the third component. Let's apply that strategy here.

You are first told that the average age of the members of the five-man group is 42, so the sum of their ages is $42 \times 5 = 210$. After the original drummer is replaced with a 27-year-old, the new average age of the group is 38, so the sum of the ages of the new group is $38 \times 5 = 190$. After you subtract out the age of the new drummer, or 27, you have the age of the original members minus the drummer: $190 - 27 = 163$. So the age of the original drummer must be the sum of the ages of the original five members minus the sum of the ages of the other original four members: $210 - 163 = 47$.

SET TERMINOLOGY

The SAT will test your knowledge of the terminology used in talking about sets. You will need to be comfortable with finding modes, medians, and ranges for sets, as well as intersections and unions of two or more sets.

QUESTIONS 15–17

15. If Tim's test scores in math class were 92, 78, 92, 77, and 86, which of the following is greater than 85?

    I. The mode of the test scores

    II. The median of the test scores

    III. The average (arithmetic mean) of the test scores

    (A) I only

    (B) II only

    (C) I and II only

    (D) I and III only

    (E) I, II, and III

16. Set R contains the integers from -10 through -2, inclusive. Set S contains the absolute value of each number in Set R. How many numbers are in the intersection of sets R and S?

    (A) 18

    (B) 16

    (C) 6

    (D) 4

    (E) 0

17. If Set A consists of all the positive integers from 10 through 20, inclusive, and Set B consists of all the odd integers between 2 and 14, which of the following numbers is in the intersection of sets A and B?

    (A) 3

    (B) 9

    (C) 10

    (D) 11

    (E) 14

EXPLANATIONS: QUESTIONS 15–17

15. C

This question isn't that hard, but you need to know the definitions of median and mode. You are asked to determine which of the three values is greater than 85, so start with option I, the mode of the test scores. *Mode* simply means the most frequently appearing number in a set, and in this case there's only one number that appears more than once, 92, so 92 is the mode. Since 92 is greater than 85, you can eliminate any answer choice that does not contain option I, in this case (B).

Now check option II, the median of the test scores. *Median* means the number that falls in the middle after the numbers have been arranged in ascending order, so let's rearrange the test scores: 77, 78, 86, 92, 92. The number in the middle is 86, so that's the median, and 86 > 85, so option II is good as well. We can eliminate (A) and (D), but it looks like we'll also have to check out option III in this case.

The average (arithmetic mean) of the test scores is the sum of the scores divided by the number of scores, or $\dfrac{92 + 78 + 92 + 77 + 86}{5} = \dfrac{425}{5} = 85$, which is equal to, but not greater than 85, so option III is out, making (C) the answer.

> An Advanced test taker knows the definitions for all the math terms that could appear on the SAT.

16. E

The intersection of two sets consists of all the elements that are in both sets. Since all the numbers in set R are negative and all the numbers in set S are positive, no number can be in both sets.

17. D

The intersection of two sets consists of the elements found in both sets. There are only two integers that are odd integers between 2 and 14 and are also among the integers 10 through 20, inclusive: these integers are 11 and 13. Choice (D) is 11, while 13 is not among the answer choices.

EXPONENTIAL SEQUENCES

Exponential sequences, also known as geometric sequences, are sets of numbers where each term is a constant multiple of the previous term. Questions about exponential sequences will often be written to make counting difficult. This means that calculator use for this will get tough, as you try to remember while you're multiplying: "Was that the 12th term or the 13th term? nth term?" This means that being familiar with the formula for these problems will make things easier. This formula is:

(the first term) $\times$ (second term/first term)$^{(n-1)}$

…where n is the number in the sequence you want to calculate.

QUESTIONS 18–21

18. The first five terms of a geometric sequence are 3, 6, 12, 24, and 48. What is the 15th term of this sequence?

    (A) 16,384
    (B) 24,576
    (C) 32,768
    (D) 49,152
    (E) 98,304

Day:	Number of bacteria:
0	100
1	141
2	200
3	283
4	400
5	566
6	800
7	1,131

19. The table above shows the number of bacteria in a scientist's petri dish. If n is the number of bacteria and t is the number of days that have passed since the start of the experiment, which of the following equations best describes the situation?

    (A) $n = 100 \times t^2$
    (B) $n = 100 \times (2t)^2$
    (C) $n = 100 \times 2^{\frac{t}{2}}$
    (D) $n = 100 \times 2^t$
    (E) $n = 100 \times 2^{2t}$

Sometimes you'll be asked for the formula (Picking Numbers works well here) or be given the formula (where simple plugging in should work).

20. The population of Katysville in the year 1900 was 1,200. Since then, the population has doubled every 14 years. If n is the number of people living in Katysville and t is the number of years since 1900, which of the following equations represents the population of Katysville t years after 1900?

    (A) $n = 1,200(2^t)$

    (B) $n = 1,900(2^{14})$

    (C) $n = 1,200(2^{\frac{t}{14}})$

    (D) $n = 1,200(2^{14t})$

    (E) $n = 1,900\left(\dfrac{14}{t}\right)$

21. The population of Smallville was 100 in the year 1900, and since then it has doubled every four years. The population of the town can be described by the equation $n = 100(2^{\frac{t}{4}})$, where n is the population and t is the number of years that have passed since 1900. What was the population of Smallville in the year 1952?

    (A)   8,192
    (B)   10,400
    (C)   81,920
    (D) 100,481
    (E) 819,200

EXPLANATIONS: QUESTIONS 18–21

18. D

When you see a sequence, look for a pattern. In this case, every number after the first is twice the previous number. You could find the 15th term simply by doubling each term until you reached the 15th, but that could be time-consuming. The nth term of the sequence can be written as $3 \times 2^{n-1}$, where n is the position of the term (the first term is $3 \times 2^{1-1} = 3 \times 2^0 = 3 \times 1 = 3$). Using this formula will let you get the answer more quickly.

$$3 \times 2^{n-1} = 3 \times 2^{15-1} = 3 \times 2^{14} = 3 \times 16,384 = 49,152$$

19. C

Even if you're not familiar with exponential growth (the situation described in this question), you can still plug values from the table into each possible equation to see which one is most nearly correct. If you are familiar with exponential growth, the easiest way to get the equation from the given information is to notice that the number of bacteria doubles every two days. Say you tried plugging $t = 2$ into the equations. (A) and (D) would both give you $n = 400$, which isn't right. (B) and (E) would give you 1,600. Only (C) gives you $n = 200$, the right answer.

20. C

If a population starts with x members in 1900, then doubles every y years, then n, the number of members of the population t years after 1900, is given by the equation $n = x(2^{\frac{t}{y}})$. This population starts at 1,200 individuals and doubles every 14 years, so the equation should be $n = 1,200(2^{\frac{t}{14}})$. If you do not remember this equation, you can solve the problem by Picking Numbers. If t equals 14, then n must equal 2,400, since the population has doubled once in 14 years. Now substitute 14 for t into each answer choice. Any answer choice that does not equal 2,400 when $t = 14$ can be eliminated. With the method of Picking Numbers, all four incorrect answer choices must be eliminated because sometimes one or more incorrect answer choices work for the particular values that you choose.

Choice (A): $n = 1,200(2^t) = 1,200(2^{14})$, which is much greater than 2,400. Eliminate choice (A).

Choice (B): $n = 1,900(2^{14})$, which is much greater than 2,400. Eliminate choice (B).

Choice (C): $n = 1,200(2^{\frac{t}{14}}) = 1,200(2^{\frac{14}{14}}) = 1,200(2) = 2,400$. Possibly correct.

Choice (D): $n = 1,200(2^{14t}) = 1,200(2^{14(14)}) = 1,200(2^{196})$, which is much greater than 2,400. Eliminate choice (D).

Choice (E): $n = 1,900(2^{\frac{14}{t}}) = 1,900(2^{\frac{14}{14}}) = 1,900(2^1) = 1,900(2) = 3,800$. This is not 2,400. Eliminate choice (E).

Now that all four incorrect answer choices have been eliminated, we know that choice (C) must be correct.

21. E

Substitute the given value of t into the equation. Remember that t is the number of years since 1900, not just the year.

$t = 1,952 - 1,900 = 52$

$n = 100 \times 2^{\frac{52}{4}} = 100 \times 2^{13} = 100 \times 8,192 = 819,200$

ALGEBRA WORD PROBLEMS

You may be surprised to learn that straightforward algebra accounts for relatively few SAT word problems. But algebra will nonetheless appear from time to time. The good news is that when these problems do appear, they can almost always be solved by Picking Numbers or Back-solving.

If you are rusty with equations, variables, and all that good stuff, you may want to brush up a bit. Use the next four algebra word problems to measure yourself.

QUESTIONS 22–23

22. On four successive days, a farmer picks exactly twice as many apples each day as on the previous day. If in the course of the four days he picks a total of 12,000 apples, how many apples does he pick on the second of the four days?

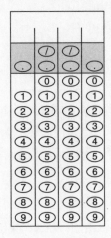

23. If $8 < x < 9$, and $x^2 = (10 - y)(10 + y)$, which of the following is a possible value for y?

   (A) −7
   (B) −6
   (C)   3
   (D)   4
   (E)   5

EXPLANATIONS: QUESTIONS 22–23

22. 1,600

Solve for the number of apples picked on the first day, then double that amount to get the number picked on the second day. Let x represent the number of apples that the farmer picks on the first day. Then on the second, third, and fourth days, the farmer picks $2x$, $4x$, and $8x$ apples, respectively. Since he picks a total of 12,000 apples, $12,000 = x + 2x + 4x + 8x$, and $12,000 = 15x$. Therefore, $x = \dfrac{12,000}{15}$, or 800 apples. But that's for the first day. On the second day, he picks twice as many: $800 \times 2 = 1,600$.

23. E

This problem is best solved by working backwards from the answer choices. If $8 < x < 9$, then $64 < x^2 < 81$. Multiplying through the expression given for x^2, you get $x^2 = 10^2 - y^2$ or $x^2 = 100 - y^2$. Each answer choice gives a possible value for y, so try plugging each of these values into the equation, starting with (E), until you get a value for x^2 such that $64 < x^2 < 81$. (You should know why you're starting with (E) for this problem by now. But if not, read the following.)

(E) $x^2 = 100 - 5^2 = 100 - 25 = 75$; $64 < 75 < 81$, so this choice is correct. Let's check the other answer choices just for the sake of the discussion.
(D) $x^2 = 100 - 4^2 = 100 - 16 = 84$. Eliminate.
(C) $x^2 = 100 - 3^2 = 100 - 9 = 91$. Eliminate.
(B) $x^2 = 100 - (-6)^2 = 100 - 36 = 64$. Eliminate.
(A) $x^2 = 100 - (-7)^2 = 100 - 49 = 51$. Eliminate.

> An Advanced test taker starts with (E) and works back to (A) whenever the question asks: *which of the following . . . ?*

QUESTIONS 24–25

24. A travel agent offers a vacation plan which costs z dollars for the first day, and $\dfrac{z}{6}$ dollars for each additional day. How much does a vacation of y days cost, in dollars, where $y > 1$?

    (A) $\dfrac{yz}{6}$

    (B) $\dfrac{yz}{3}$

    (C) $\dfrac{yz + 6z}{6}$

    (D) $\dfrac{yz + 5z}{6}$

    (E) $\dfrac{y^2 + 5yz + z^2}{3}$

25. If $y \neq 3$, $y \neq -4$, and $\dfrac{7y - 21}{y - 3} = \dfrac{y^2 - y - 20}{y + 4}$, what is the value of y?

    (A) -12

    (B) 4

    (C) 7

    (D) 10

    (E) 12

24. D

Pick Numbers for y and z that are easy to work with: since $y > 1$, try $y = 2$; to make $\dfrac{z}{6}$ an integer, try $z = 6$. In that case, the first day costs 6 dollars and the second day costs $\dfrac{6}{6}$, or 1 dollar. So the total cost for the 2 days is 7 dollars. Now see which answer choices yield 7 when $y = 2$ and $z = 6$. Remember to try all the answer choices, just in case more than one answer choice works for the numbers you picked.

(A) $\dfrac{2 \times 6}{6} = 2$. Eliminate.

(B) $\dfrac{2 \times 6}{3} = 4$. Eliminate.

(C) $\dfrac{2 \times 6 + 6 \times 3}{6} = 8$. Eliminate.

(D) $\dfrac{2 \times 6 + 5 \times 6}{6} = 7$. Possibly correct.

(E) $\dfrac{2^2 + 5 \times 2 \times 6 + 6^2}{3} = \dfrac{100}{3}$. Eliminate.

Since only (D) works, it is the correct answer.

25. E

For this particular problem, it is easiest to factor and simplify both sides of the equation before solving for y. You could also cross-multiply, and then simplify; however, you will be led to considerably more complicated expressions to simplify.

$$\frac{7y - 21}{y - 3} = \frac{y^2 - y - 20}{y + 4}$$

$$\frac{7(y - 3)}{y - 3} = \frac{(y + 4)(y - 5)}{y + 4}$$

$$7 = y - 5$$

$$12 = y$$

Thus, $y = 12$.

CHAPTER 22: GEOMETRY AND DATA INTERPRETATION WORD PROBLEMS

- Garden variety geometry word problems

- 3-D geometry word problems

- Data interpretation

- The tricky stuff

The SAT test makers occasionally test geometry in the form of word problems. This gives them the opportunity to combine the different areas of geometry, assigning you, the test taker, the task of working with circles and triangles, or triangles and rectangles, etc.

Of course, we can't review all of high school geometry here. This book focuses on the 2400-level questions that the SAT presents. Between the examples here and those in the geometry part of the Straight Math section, however, you'll get a very good idea of what geometry skills and information you need to have.

GEOMETRY WORD PROBLEMS

QUESTIONS 1–3

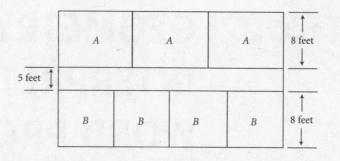

1. The figure above shows the floor plan of an office in which there are seven rectangular rooms and a rectangular hallway. The three rooms labeled *A* have dimensions 8 feet by 12 feet, and the four rooms labeled *B* have dimensions 8 feet by 9 feet. What is the total area of the entire office, in square feet (ignoring the thickness of the walls)?

2. A garden measuring 40 meters by 50 meters is to be surrounded by a flagstone walkway
    5 meters wide. If each stone is rectangular and has the dimensions 2 meters by 1 meter,
    how many stones will be needed to cover the walkway?

    (A) 250
    (B) 275
    (C) 425
    (D) 450
    (E) 500

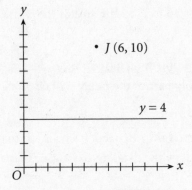

3. In the diagram above, the line $y = 4$ is the perpendicular bisector of segment JK (not
    shown). What is the distance from the origin O to point K?

    (A) 4
    (B) $2\sqrt{10}$
    (C) 8
    (D) $6\sqrt{20}$
    (E) $4\sqrt{34}$

EXPLANATIONS: QUESTIONS 1–3

1. 756

The entire office is rectangular, so its area equals its length times its width. You can use the given information to figure out these dimensions. The vertical length is fairly easy to find: it's just the vertical length of an *A*-room, plus the vertical length of a *B*-room, plus the length of the hallway, or $8 + 8 + 5 = 21$. Now, notice that the horizontal width of the entire office is made up of three *A*-rooms across the top or four *B*-rooms across the bottom. You're told that each *A*-room is 8 feet × 12 feet, and since the diagram shows the vertical length as 8 feet, the horizontal width of each *A*-room must be 12 feet. So the width of the entire office is equal to the sum of the widths of the three *A*-rooms, or $3 \times 12 = 36$ feet. So the area of the entire office is 21×36, or 756 square feet.

Notice that this geometry word problem included a nice, clean, helpful diagram. That will not always be the case. Very often, only part of the figure will be provided. Sometimes a figure will be described solely in words.

When you don't have all the illustration you need, it's your job to provide it. Put your pencil and scrap paper to work. Draw or redraw the diagram to fit your needs.

2. E

The easiest thing to do here is to draw a diagram:

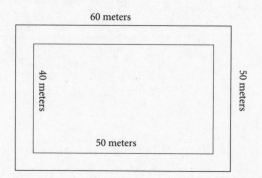

You get two rectangles: one with dimensions 40 meters by 50 meters (the lawn); one with dimensions 50 meters by 60 meters (the lawn and the walk). The area of the walk alone is the difference between the two rectangular areas, or $(50 \times 60) - (40 \times 50) = 3,000 - 2,000 = 1,000$ square meters. Since each stone has area $2 \times 1 = 2$ square meters, you would need 500 stones for the whole walk.

3. B

Don't try to keep all the information in your head—add to the diagram so you can refer to it as you solve. Horizontal line $y = 4$ is the perpendicular bisector of $\overline{JK}$, so $\overline{JK}$ must be vertical and parallel to the y-axis. Draw in segment $\overline{JK}$, dropping straight down from point J through the x-axis. Before you can find the distance from the origin to point K, you need to know the coordinates of point K. K is directly below J, so both points are the same distance from the y-axis, and their x-coordinates must be the same. So the x-coordinate of K is 6. Since the line $y = 4$ bisects $\overline{JK}$, the vertical distance from J to the line must be the same as the vertical distance from the line to K. Vertical distance is the positive difference between the y-coordinates, so the vertical distance from J to line $y = 4$ is $10 - 4$, or 6. Therefore, the positive difference between the y-coordinates of line $y = 4$ and point K is also 6, so the y-coordinate of K is $4 - 6$, making -2 the y-coordinate of point K. So the coordinates of point K are $(6, -2)$.

The distance d between the points (x_1, y_1) and (x_2, y_2) is given by the formula $d = \sqrt{(x_2 - x_1)^2 + (y_2 - y_1)^2}$. The distance from the origin $O(0, 0)$ to point $K(6, -2)$ is:

$$\sqrt{(6 - 0)^2 + (-2)^2}$$
$$= \sqrt{6^2 + (-2)^2}$$
$$= \sqrt{36 + 4} = \sqrt{40}$$
$$= \sqrt{4(10)} = \sqrt{4}\sqrt{10}$$
$$= 2\sqrt{10}$$

(B) it is.

> An Advanced test taker draws useful diagrams when the word problem doesn't provide them and adds to diagrams information that is discovered.

Just as with straightforward geometry problems on the SAT, geometry word problems often contain circles, triangles, or a combination of the two.

QUESTIONS 4–5

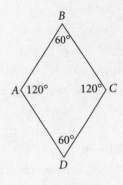

4. If *AB*, *BC*, *CD*, and *AD* are all equal to 4, what is the area of the figure above?

    (A) 8
    (B) $8\sqrt{2}$
    (C) $8\sqrt{3}$
    (D) 16
    (E) 20

5. A circular manhole is covered by a circular cover which has a diameter of 32 inches. If the manhole has a diameter of 30 inches, how much greater than the area of the manhole is the area of the cover, in square inches?

    (A) 2π
    (B) 4π
    (C) 24π
    (D) 31π
    (E) 124π

Explanations: Questions 4–5

4. C

Adding extra lines to geometry problems is often helpful. See if you can make any familiar shapes, like squares or right triangles.

Sketch two perpendicular lines from the corners of the figure. This will produce four 30-60-90 triangles.

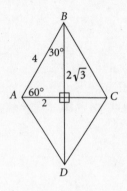

The area of one of these triangles is $\frac{1}{2}(2)(2\sqrt{3}) = 2\sqrt{3}$, so the area of the entire figure is $4(2\sqrt{3}) = 8\sqrt{3}$.

5. D

Knowing the diameter of a circle is enough to determine its area, since area $= \pi r^2$, and r, the radius, is half the diameter. The radius of the cover is $\frac{1}{2}(32) = 16$, so the cover has an area of $\pi(16)^2$, or 256π. The manhole has a radius of $\frac{1}{2}(30)$, or 15, so its area is $\pi(15)^2$, or 225π. So the area of the cover is $256\pi - 225\pi$ or 31π square inches greater than the area of the manhole. (D) it is.

The key to answering many of the most difficult SAT word problems is to see the figure differently. Often the figure presented can be broken down into smaller figures, or extended to create larger figures. By examining these "secondary" figures, you can derive the information you need to answer the question.

This is a skill best taught by example. Here are two of them.

QUESTIONS 6–7

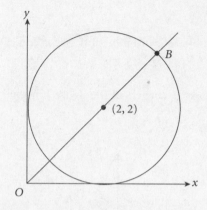

6. In the rectangular coordinate system above, the circle is tangent to both the *x*-axis and *y*-axis, and has center (2, 2). The center of the circle is on line segment $\overline{OB}$. What is the length of $\overline{OB}$?

   (A) $2\sqrt{2}$

   (B) $2 + \sqrt{2}$

   (C) 4

   (D) $2 + 2\sqrt{2}$

   (E) $4\sqrt{2}$

7. If each curved portion of the boundary of the figure above is formed from the circumferences of two semicircles, each with a radius of 2, and each of the parallel sides has length 4, what is the area of the shaded figure?

   (A) 16

   (B) 32

   (C) $16 - 8\pi$

   (D) $32 - 8\pi$

   (E) $32 - 4\pi$

EXPLANATIONS: QUESTIONS 6–7

6. D

Look for some way to break down $\overline{OB}$ into familiar segments whose lengths you are able to find. Notice that the distance from the center of the circle to B is a radius of the circle. The radius of the circle is the distance from point (2, 2) to the point where the circle touches the x-axis, or (2, 0). This distance is 2. So the radius is 2. But what about the distance from O to the center of the circle? Well, if you draw a perpendicular line from the center of the circle down to the x-axis, you form a right triangle whose hypotenuse is the distance from O to the center of the circle. The horizontal leg of this triangle extends from the origin to 2 on the x-axis, so its length is 2. The vertical leg extends from the x-axis to a height of 2 parallel to the y-axis, so its length is also 2. The triangle is an isosceles right triangle. The leg length to leg length to hypotenuse length ratio in an isosceles right triangle is $1:1:\sqrt{2}$. So the hypotenuse has a length of $2\sqrt{2}$. Therefore, the length of $\overline{OB}$ is $2 + 2\sqrt{2}$.

7. B

This looks pretty tricky at first glance, but in reality is quite simple. The shaded figure looks like a rectangle which has had two semicircles removed and two added on. In other words, whatever has been cut out of the original rectangle has been added back on. In other words, what we have here is really just the area of the rectangle. What are the dimensions of this rectangle? They've told us that the vertical dimension, which we will call the width, is 4 units. The area of a rectangle is length × width, so look for a way to find the length.

There are two circles along the length of the rectangle—the length is equal to four times the circle's radius.

If each radius is 2 and there are 4 of them along each horizontal side, then the length is 8 units. Since area = length × width, the area is 8 × 4 = 32 square units, answer (B).

> An Advanced test taker modifies the diagrams given to create "secondary" diagrams, which help him to discover information hidden in the original.

THREE-DIMENSIONAL GEOMETRY WORD PROBLEMS

QUESTIONS 8–10

You will probably see one or two word problems on the SAT involving three-dimensional geometry. There's a good chance that the problem will involve cylinders, which we think you'll agree shouldn't worry you too much. But there's also a chance that the problem will involve surface area. We'll see what you think about that.

8. How many cylindrical oil drums, with a diameter of 1.5 feet and a height of 4 feet, would be needed to hold the contents of a full cylindrical fuel tank, with a diameter of 12 feet and a height of 60 feet?

   (A) 640
   (B) 720
   (C) 840
   (D) 880
   (E) 960

9. Can A and can B are both right circular cylinders. The radius of can A is twice the radius of can B, while the height of can A is half the height of can B. If it costs \$4 to fill half of can B with a certain brand of gasoline, how much would it cost to completely fill can A with the same brand of gasoline?

   (A) \$1
   (B) \$2
   (C) \$4
   (D) \$8
   (E) \$16

10. A certain box has dimensions of n, $2n$, and $3n$, where n is an integer. Which of the following could be the surface area of the box?

   (A)   48
   (B)   64
   (C) 150
   (D) 198
   (E) 220

EXPLANATIONS: QUESTIONS 8–10

8. E

To find the number of drums needed to hold the contents of the tank, set the combined volume of all the drums equal to the volume of the tank. The combined volume of the drums is the volume per drum × the total number of drums. The volume of a cylinder is the area of the circular base × the height, and the area of the circular base is equal to π × radius squared. Since the question gives the diameter of each cylinder, you'll need to halve each diameter to find the radius, and then you can find the volume. The radius of each drum is $\frac{1.5}{2} = 0.75$ or $\frac{3}{4}$. So the volume of each drum is $\pi\left(\frac{3}{4}\right)^2 (4) = \left(\frac{9}{16}\right)(4)\pi = \frac{9\pi}{4}$. The number of drums is unknown, so use a variable such as x to represent it. So the total volume of the drums is $(x)\frac{9\pi}{4}$. The volume of the tank is $\pi(6^2)$ $(60) = (36)(60)\pi$. So $(x)\frac{9\pi}{4} = (36)(60)\pi$; $x = (36)(60)\pi\left(\frac{4}{9\pi}\right) = (4)(60)(4) = 960$. (E) is correct.

9. E

The volume of a cylinder is (area of the base) × (height).

Find out the volumes of the cylinders, and work out how the complete volume of can A compares with half the volume of can B.

Volume of can B: $\pi r^2 h$.

Volume of can A: $\pi(2r)^2 \times \frac{h}{2} = \pi 4r^2 \times \frac{h}{2} = 2\pi r^2 h$, which is twice the volume of can B.

Therefore, if it takes \$4 to fill half of can B, then it will take \$8 to completely fill can B, and it will take twice \$8, or \$16, to completely fill can A. (E) wins again.

10. D

Perhaps drawing a diagram of the box would help:

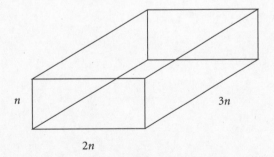

The surface area is the combined area of all the sides, or faces, of the box. There are two sides that are n by $2n$, two sides that are n by $3n$, and two sides that are $2n$ by $3n$.

Thus, the surface area of the entire box is:

$2(n \times 2n) + 2(n \times 3n) + 2(2n \times 3n) = 4n^2 + 6n^2 + 12n^2 = 22n^2$

If you had trouble visualizing this, you can memorize the surface area formula:

Surface area of a box = $2lw + 2lh + 2wh$, where l = length, w = width, and h = height.

So $22n^2$ must be an integer.

(A) 48   Not divisible by 22.   Eliminate.

(B) 64   Ditto.   Eliminate.

(C) 150   Ditto.   Eliminate.

(D) 198 = 22 × 9, 9 = 3^2, so n = 3   Choice (D) is correct.

If we were taking an actual test, we would move on to the next question. For the sake of the discussion, let's look at choice (E).

(E) 220 = 22 × 10, but 10 is not a perfect square. Eliminate.

An Advanced student uses visualization to help with surface area problems, or if that doesn't work, memorizes the surface area formula.

GEOMETRY WORD PROBLEMS (MODIFYING DIAGRAMS)

QUESTIONS 11–12

We'll finish up with two more examples of modifying a diagram. Hint: The first one is worth sketching so you have a diagram to make things clear. The second one is a suitable ending to geometry word problems.

11. If a square is formed by joining the points A $(-2, 1)$, B $(1, 5)$, C $(5, 2)$, and D $(2, -2)$, what is the area of square $ABCD$?

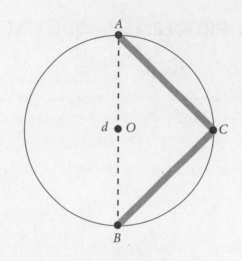

12. Points *A* and *B* are at opposite ends of a circular pond with diameter *d*. A bridge connects point *A* with point *C*, and another bridge connects point *C* with point *B*. The two bridges are of equal length. What is the ratio of the distance traveled in going from *A* to *B* when traveling along the two bridges, to the distance traveled in going from *A* to *B* when traveling along the edge of the pond?

(A) $\dfrac{2\sqrt{2}}{\pi}$

(B) $\dfrac{d\sqrt{2}}{\pi}$

(C) $\dfrac{2}{\pi}$

(D) $\dfrac{\sqrt{2}}{2\pi}$

(E) $\dfrac{2\sqrt{2}}{\pi d}$

EXPLANATIONS: QUESTIONS 11–12

11. 25

First sketch the square *ABCD*. The area of any square is equal to the length of one of its sides squared. So if we can find the length of any one side of square *ABCD*, we can find the area of the square.

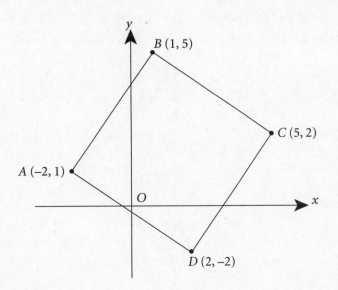

The distanced between two points (x_1, y_1) and (x_2, y_2) can be found using the formula $d = \sqrt{(x_2 - x_1)^2 + (y_2 - y_1)^2}$. So the length of side *AB* of the square is $\sqrt{(1 - (-2))^2 + (5 - 1)^2} = \sqrt{3^2 + 4^2} = \sqrt{9 + 16} = \sqrt{25} = 5$. The area of the square is then $5 \times 5 = 25$.

12. A

Approach this tough geometry problem step by step, that is, unless you're running short on time and/or geometry problems aren't your strong suit to begin with, in which case you'll want to check out our alternative approach on the next page. The best place to start on this one is to first figure out the distance from A to B around the edge of the pond, which you can see is half of the circle's circumference. Circumference is π times diameter, so the circumference of the entire circle is πd, making the distance along the edge from A to B half this or $\frac{\pi d}{2}$. Finding the distance from A to B across the bridges is a bit more involved. Draw a line from point C to the center of the circle, O.

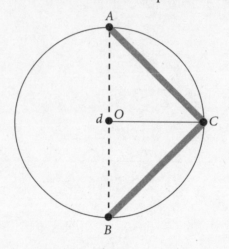

$\overline{AC}$ and $\overline{BC}$ are the same length. $\overline{OA}$, $\overline{OC}$, and $\overline{OB}$ are all radii of the circle so they are all the same length. So $\triangle AOC$ and $\triangle BOC$ are congruent isosceles right triangles. (That is, their interior angles and the length of their sides are the same.) The sides of an isosceles right triangle are in the ratio $1:1:\sqrt{2}$. Since the legs have a length of $\frac{d}{2}$, the hypotenuses, $\overline{AC}$ and $\overline{BC}$, have a length of $\frac{d\sqrt{2}}{2}$, and $\overline{AC} + \overline{BC} = \frac{d\sqrt{2}}{2} + \frac{d\sqrt{2}}{2} = d\sqrt{2}$. This is the distance from A to B when traveling along the bridges. So the ratio of the route over the bridges to the route around the edge of the pond is

$$\frac{\sqrt{2}d}{\frac{\pi d}{2}} = \frac{\sqrt{2}d}{1} \times \frac{2}{\pi d} = \frac{2\sqrt{2}}{\pi}, \text{ or (A).}$$

Alternative Approach: If you found the previous explanation confusing, there is another approach that works especially well on tough geometry word problems such as this one. We call this approach "eyeballing." The question asks for the ratio of the distance when traveling from point A to point B along the bridges, to the distance when traveling along the edge of the pond. Well, just take a look at the picture. Is the distance when traveling along the bridges shorter than when traveling along the edge of the pond? Yes, it is. Is it much shorter? No, it is not. So what sort of "eyeball" ratio would you come up with? Something just a little less than 1, we hope.

So now let's examine the answer choices, looking for an answer that's slightly less than 1 (and for the purposes of eyeballing, we can say $\sqrt{2} = 1.4$ and $\pi = 3.14$):

(A) $\dfrac{2\sqrt{2}}{\pi} = \dfrac{2.8}{3.14}$, which is slightly less than 1. Looks good!

(B) $\dfrac{2\sqrt{2}}{\pi} = \dfrac{d(1.4)}{3.24}$. But since d can be any value, such as $d = 5$, that can't be right. Eliminate.

(C) $\dfrac{2}{\pi} = \dfrac{2}{3.14} < \dfrac{2}{3}$. That seems too small. Eliminate.

(D) $\dfrac{\sqrt{2}}{2\pi} = \dfrac{1.4}{6.28}$. That is way too small. Eliminate.

(E) $\dfrac{2\sqrt{2}}{\pi d} = \dfrac{2.8}{(3.14)d}$. There's that d again, which you know can't be right. Eliminate.

Thus, by the process of elimination the answer must be (A).

An Advanced test taker is not afraid to use the strategy of "eyeballing" on tough geometry problems.

DATA INTERPRETATION

Questions on the SAT will test your ability to interpret data—that is, to read and understand charts, tables, and graphs, and pull the necessary information out of them to answer the question. In most other question types you will use every bit of information in the question to find the answer; however, in Data Interpretation questions you are tested on your ability to pull out only the relevant information and ignore the rest.

Number of Animals in Zoos		
	Zebras	Zebus
Alphaville	4	2
Betatown	0	3
Delta City	5	4

Pounds of Food Eaten Each Day		
	Hay	Clover	Fresh Grass
Zebra	8	6	6
Zebu	12	11	10

13. The charts above show how many zebras and zebus the zoos in three different towns have and how much food each animal needs each day if it is fed one of three different kinds of food. If the Delta City zoo feeds its animals fresh grass, how many pounds of fresh grass does the zoo feed its zebras and zebus each day?

Data Interpretation questions usually come in blocks, with several questions referring to the same data set. Typically, the first question in these blocks is easier than you would expect from the question number, and the last one is harder—so be a little more careful with it. Since multiple questions will refer to the same data set, take a little time to become familiar with the tables, charts, and/or graphs before looking at the questions. This familiarization time will save time on answering questions and help prevent mistakes.

Questions 14–16 refer to the following figures:

Pets Owned			
	Guinea Pigs	Rabbits	Rats
Joe	2	2	0
Dave	0	3	2
Alice	3	0	4

Cups of Food Eaten by One Animal Each Week			
	Guinea Pig	Rabbit	Rat
Vegetables	6	4	1
Pellets	2	3	1

The tables above show how many pets three people own, along with how much food each animal needs each week.

14. How many cups of vegetables does Joe need to feed his pets each week?

    (A) 8
    (B) 10
    (C) 12
    (D) 20
    (E) 22

15. How many cups of pellets does Alice need to feed her pets?

    (A) 8
    (B) 10
    (C) 12
    (D) 20
    (E) 22

16. How many more cups of vegetables does Alice need each week than Dave does?

    (A)   8
    (B)   10
    (C)   14
    (D)   22
    (E)   36

Questions 17–18 refer to the following figure:

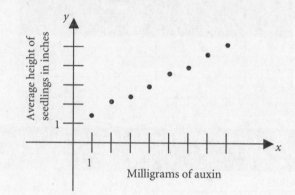

17. A scientist added various quantities of auxin to a number of plant seedlings and observed their growth. The figure above summarizes her findings. Which of the following is most likely to be the height of a seedling given 10 milligrams of auxin?

    (A)   1 inch
    (B)   2 inches
    (C)   3.5 inches
    (D)   6 inches
    (E)   10 inches

18. Which of the lines described by the following equations best fits this data?

    (A) $y = \dfrac{1}{4}x - 1$

    (B) $y = \dfrac{1}{2}x$

    (C) $y = \dfrac{1}{2}x + 1$

    (D) $y = x + \dfrac{1}{2}$

    (E) $y = 2x - 1$

EXPLANATIONS: QUESTIONS 13–18

13. 70

To solve this problem, you need one row from the top chart (how many animals of each type the Delta City zoo has) and one column from the bottom chart (how much fresh grass those animals eat each day): $5(6) + 4(10) = 30 + 40 = 70$.

14. D

Whenever you see a question that involves a table or a chart, read the question first so you know what information you're looking for. In this case, you need to find out how many of each kind of pet Joe has and how many cups of vegetables those pets need to eat each week: $2(6) + 2(4) = 12 + 8 = 20$.

15. B

This time, you need to know how many of each kind of pet Alice has and how many cups of pellets they each need: $3(2) + 4(1) = 6 + 4 = 10$.

16. A

Now you need a little more information. You'll need to know how many of each kind of pet Alice and Dave have, and the amount of vegetables eaten by each type:

$3(6) + 4(1) = 18 + 4 = 22$ (how many cups of vegetables Alice needs)
$3(4) + 2(1) = 12 + 2 = 14$ (how many cups of vegetables Dave needs)
$22 - 14 = 8$

17. D

The general trend of the graph is for the height to increase as the amount of auxin increases. These points form an almost straight line, so you could sketch in a line to see where points not already on the graph should fall. Since the height increases with the amount of auxin, you can rule out (A), (B), and (C). A height of 6 inches at 10 milligrams of auxin would fall very near or on the straight line best representing the existing points, while a height of 10 inches would be well above this line, so (D) is more likely.

18. C

You could solve this problem by selecting a few points from the graph and plugging them into the equations in the answer choices. You could also estimate the slope and y-intercept. The slope of this line must be positive but less than one, since the line slopes gently up as x increases. It looks like it should cross the y-axis somewhere near 1.

Therefore, the closest line is $y = \frac{1}{2}x + 1$. To test this, try plugging in a point; for example $(4, 3)$. $\frac{1}{2}(4) + 1 = 2 + 1 = 3$.

CHAPTER 23: ODDBALL WORD PROBLEMS

- What to do when you encounter a question type you've never seen before

- How to deal with clock questions, combination questions, "weird definition" questions, pattern problems, etc.

- How to be ready for anything

As with other SAT question types, perhaps even more so, word problems are often oddballs. Because they deal with "real world" situations, word problems can be used to test just about every math and logic skill under the sun. You wouldn't be properly prepared for the 2400-level math questions if your practice didn't include a sampling of these.

On test day, of course, you may encounter other oddballs. That's just the nature of the game. But bear in mind that just because a question seems completely new to you, it doesn't have to be difficult.

ODDBALL WORD PROBLEM SETS

QUESTIONS 1–3

1. A computer is programmed to generate two numbers according to the following scheme: the first number is to be a randomly selected integer from 0 to 99; the second number is to be an integer which is less than the square of the units' digit of the first number. Which of the following pairs of numbers could NOT have been generated by this program?

    (A) 99, 10
    (B) 60, −10
    (C) 58, 63
    (D) 13, 11
    (E) 12, 3

2. A certain clock rings two notes at quarter past the hour, four notes at half past, and six notes at three-quarters past. On the hour, it rings eight notes plus an additional number of notes equal to whatever hour it is. How many notes will the clock ring between 1:00 P.M. and 5:00 P.M., including the rings at 1:00 and 5:00?

3. Each of three after-school student clubs—the chess club, the German club, and the debating society—has exactly 8 members. If exactly 4 students are members of all 3 clubs and if each pair of these 3 clubs has 5 members in common, then how many different students are members of one or more of these clubs?

(A) 8

(B) 13

(C) 16

(D) 24

(E) 27

EXPLANATIONS: QUESTIONS 1–3

1. D

Don't waste time abstractly pondering the question stem's special instructions; turn to the answer choices and start testing the given pairs of numbers. As always, start at (D) or (E) for this question, since the SAT favors these two answer choices when the question asks "which of the following."

(E) The units' digit of 12 is 2 and $2^2 = 4$; $4 > 3$, so eliminate.

(D) The units' digit of 13 is 3, and $3^2 = 9$; $9 < 11$, so this pair does not meet the conditions, making (D) correct.

That wasn't too bad, was it? The simple technique of Back-solving allowed us to ignore all of the strangeness and focus on the task at hand.

So there are two lessons here. One, oddball word problems can be easy word problems. And two, the basic approach to oddball word problems is to focus on what is familiar—what you know—and employ the same strategies you use for common word problem types.

> An Advanced test taker doesn't panic when she encounters a strange word problem. She instead evaluates the question dispassionately, knowing that many "oddballs" are fairly easy and meant to distinguish the formulaic thinkers (who panic and screw up) from the creative thinkers (who rise to the challenge).

2. 103

Even though the problem involves only simple arithmetic, don't try to do all the work in your head. Be systematic. Notice that the rings occur in an hourly pattern. The total number of rings on the hour $= (1 + 8) + (2 + 8) + (3 + 8) + (4 + 8) + (5 + 8) = 9 + 10 + 11 + 12 + 13 = 55$. The clock rings twice at a quarter past and it does this 4 times, so the total number of rings at a quarter past $= 2(4) = 8$. Likewise, the total number of rings at half past $= 4(4) = 16$, and the total number of rings at three-quarters past $= 6(4) = 24$. Adding up, $55 + 8 + 16 + 24 = 103$.

You also could have set up a chart to organize information, like the one below. Setting up the chart will take a few extra seconds, but if arranging the information visually so you can see it all at once makes the difference between a confusing problem and an intuitively clear one, by all means, draw the chart, like this:

	:00	:15	:30	:45
1 P.M.	9	2	4	6
2 P.M.	10	2	4	6
3 P.M.	11	2	4	6
4 P.M.	12	2	4	6
5 P.M.	13			

Total $=$ 55 $+$ 8 $+$ 16 $+$ 24 $=$ 103

3. B

To keep track of all the confusing information, set up a sketch like the one below and fill in the information as you go along.

Club 1: __ __ __ __ __ __ __ __
Club 2: __ __ __ __ __ __ __ __
Club 3: __ __ __ __ __ __ __ __

Since 4 students are members of all 3 clubs, fill in a letter for each person for 4 slots on each board; it doesn't matter where. This takes care of 4 of the 5 persons that are common to each pair of clubs (1-2, 2-3, and 1-3):

Club 1:   A   B   C   D   __ __ __ __
Club 2:   A   B   C   D   __ __ __ __
Club 3:   A   B   C   D   __ __ __ __

Now you can fill in the fifth and sixth slots on each board with the fifth member common to each pair. And that means that the two positions left for each club must be occupied by students who are members of only one club.

The results look like this:

Club 1:   A   B   C   D   E   F   H   K
Club 2:   A   B   C   D   E   G   I   L
Club 3:   A   B   C   D   F   G   J   M

Since each distinct letter represents a distinct person, just count up the number of distinct letters to get the number of distinct persons in the clubs. The total number of people represented is the number of letters from A through M, inclusive, and a quick count of the letters on the chart will show that this is 13. So a total of 13 students are members of one or more clubs, making (B) correct.

QUESTIONS 4–5

As if there weren't enough real math in the world, the test makers sometimes make up their own definitions that are used to create math questions. Don't let it throw you. The question will always provide the information you need.

Questions 4–5 refer to the following definition.

The "connection" between any two positive integers a and b is the ratio of the smallest common multiple of a and b to the product of a and b. For instance, the smallest common multiple of 8 and 12 is 24, and the product of 8 and 12 is 96, so the connection between 8 and 12 is $\frac{24}{96} = \frac{1}{4}$.

4.   What is the connection between 12 and 21?

(A) $\frac{1}{9}$

(B) $\frac{1}{7}$

(C) $\frac{1}{3}$

(D) $\frac{4}{7}$

(E) $\frac{1}{1}$

5. The positive integer y is less than 20 and the connection between y and 6 is equal to $\frac{1}{1}$. How many possible values of y are there?

(A) 7
(B) 8
(C) 9
(D) 10
(E) 11

EXPLANATIONS: QUESTIONS 4–5

4. C

When a problem includes a special term or symbol, just follow the instructions that define it. There are two parts to a "connection": the smallest common multiple and the product. To get the smallest common multiple of 12 and 21, break each number down into its prime factors and multiply them together, counting common factors only once: $12 = 2 \times 2 \times 3$, and $21 = 3 \times 7$, giving you $2 \times 2 \times 3 \times 7$ for the least common multiple. The product of 12 and 21 is $(2 \times 2 \times 3) \times (3 \times 7)$. Therefore, the "connection" is $\dfrac{2 \times 2 \times 3 \times 7}{2 \times 2 \times 3 \times 3 \times 7}$ which reduces to $\dfrac{1}{3}$. Notice how easy it is to reduce the fraction when both the numerator and denominator are broken down into factors.

5. A

If the connection between y and 6 is $\frac{1}{1}$, then the smallest common multiple of y and 6 must equal the product $6y$. The lowest common multiple of two numbers equals the product of the two numbers only when there are no common factors (other than 1). Since y is a positive integer less than 20, check all the integers from 1 to 19 to see which ones have no factors greater than 1 in common with 6: 1, 5, 7, 11, 13, 17, and 19. So there are 7 possible values for y.

And how about a final pair, before leaving Oddball Word Problems for good?

QUESTIONS 6–7

9	8	6	3

6. The figure above shows an example of a 4-digit identification code used by a certain bank for its customers. If the digits in the code must appear in descending numerical order, and no digit can be used more than once, what is the difference between the largest and the smallest possible codes?

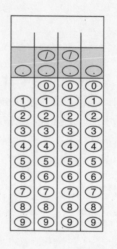

7. A machine is made up of two components, A and B. Each component either works or fails. The failure or nonfailure of one component is independent of the failure or nonfailure of the other component. The machine works if at least one of the components works. If the probability that each component works is $\frac{2}{3}$, what is the probability that the machine works?

(A) $\frac{4}{9}$

(B) $\frac{1}{2}$

(C) $\frac{2}{3}$

(D) $\frac{5}{6}$

(E) $\frac{8}{9}$

EXPLANATIONS: QUESTIONS 6–7

6. **6,666**

You need the difference between the largest and smallest possible codes. A digit cannot be repeated, and the digits must appear in descending numerical order. The largest such number will have the largest digit, 9, in the thousands' place, followed by the next largest digits, 8, 7, and 6 in the next three places, so 9,876 is the largest possible number. For the smallest, start with the smallest digit, 0, and put it in the ones' place. Work up from there—you end up with 3,210 as the smallest possible code. The difference between the largest and smallest codes is $9,876 - 3,210 = 6,666$, the correct answer on this one.

7. E

The fastest way to do this is to find the probability that neither component works, and subtract that from 1. Since the probability of a component working is $\frac{2}{3}$, the probability of a component not working is $1 - \frac{2}{3} = \frac{1}{3}$. Therefore, the probability that neither component works is $\frac{1}{3} \times \frac{1}{3} = \frac{1}{9}$, and the probability that the machine works is $1 - \frac{1}{9} = \frac{8}{9}$.

CHAPTER 24: SAT WORD PROBLEMS PRACTICE SET AND EXPLANATIONS

Directions: Fill in the corresponding oval on the answer sheet. You may use any available space for scratchwork.

Notes:

(1) Calculator use is permitted.

(2) All numbers used are real numbers.

(3) Figures are provided for some problems. All figures are drawn to scale and lie in a plane UNLESS otherwise indicated.

(4) Unless otherwise specified, the domain of any function f is assumed to be the set of all real numbers x for which $f(x)$ is a real number.

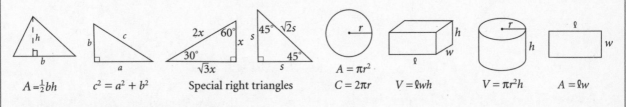

$A = \frac{1}{2}bh$ $c^2 = a^2 + b^2$ Special right triangles $A = \pi r^2$
$C = 2\pi r$ $V = \ell wh$ $V = \pi r^2 h$ $A = \ell w$

The sum of the degree measures of the angles in a triangle is 180.
The number of degrees of arc in a circle is 360.
A straight angle has a degree measure of 180.

1. Dr. Hasenpfeffer's physics midterm has 60 questions. He scores the test as follows: for each correct answer, he gives 2 points; for each wrong answer, he subtracts $\frac{2}{3}$ of a point; for unanswered questions, he neither gives nor subtracts points. If Denise scored a 68 and did not answer 2 of the questions, how many questions did she answer correctly?

   (A) 34
   (B) 36
   (C) 38
   (D) 40
   (E) 42

2. In a bag of candy, there are twice as many nut chewies as marshmallow delights. The nut chewies are either pecan or cashew and there are $\frac{1}{3}$ as many cashew chewies as there are peanut chewies. If Julie selects one piece of candy at random, what are the odds that she picks a cashew chewy?

   (A) $\frac{1}{6}$
   (B) $\frac{1}{3}$
   (C) $\frac{1}{2}$
   (D) $\frac{2}{3}$
   (E) $\frac{2}{5}$

3. Five runners run in a race. The runners who come in first, second, and third place will win gold, silver, and bronze medals respectively. How many possible outcomes for gold, silver, and bronze medal winners are there?

   (A) 5
   (B) 10
   (C) 15
   (D) 30
   (E) 60

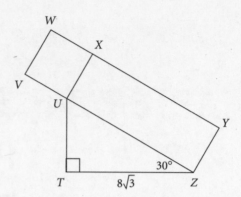

4. In the figure above, the perimeter of square $UVWX$ is 24. What is the area of rectangle $UXYZ$?

   (A) 48
   (B) $48\sqrt{3}$
   (C) 96
   (D) $72\sqrt{3}$
   (E) 192

5. In a certain club, the average (arithmetic mean) age of the male members is 35, and the average age of the female members is 25. If 20 percent of the members are male, what is the average age of all the club members?

   (A) 26
   (B) 27
   (C) 28
   (D) 29
   (E) 30

6. In a group of 50 students, 28 speak English and 37 speak Spanish. If five members of the group speak neither language, how many speak both English and Spanish?

   (A) 16
   (B) 17
   (C) 18
   (D) 19
   (E) 20

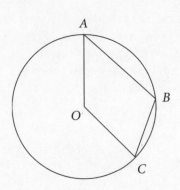

7. In the figure above, points A, B, and C lie on the circumference of the circle centered at O. If ∠OAB measures 50° and ∠BCO measures 60°, what is the measure of ∠AOC?

   (A) 110°
   (B) 120°
   (C) 130°
   (D) 140°
   (E) 150°

8. From 1980 through 1990, the population of City Q increased by 20 percent. From 1990 through 2000, the population increased by 30 percent. What was the combined percent increase for the period 1980–2000?

   (A) 25%
   (B) 26%
   (C) 36%
   (D) 50%
   (E) 56%

9. The line that passes through the points (1, 1) and (2, 16) in the standard (x, y) coordinate plane is parallel to the line that passes through the points (−10, −5) and (a, 25). What is the value of a?

   (A) −8
   (B)   3
   (C)   5
   (D) 15
   (E) 20

10. Maura drives to work, a distance of 30 miles, in 40 minutes. She takes the same route to return home. If her average speed on the trip home is half as fast as her average speed on the trip to work, what is her average speed, in miles per hour, for the entire round trip?

    (A) 22.5
    (B) 30
    (C) 35
    (D) 40
    (E) 45

Year	Income
1995	$20,000
1996	$25,000
1997	$30,000
1998	$33,000
1999	$36,000
2000	$44,000

11. The table above displays Jamie's income for each of the years 1995–2000. Which of the years 1996–2000 shows the greatest percent increase over the previous year?

    (A) 1996
    (B) 1997
    (C) 1998
    (D) 1999
    (E) 2000

12. The formula for converting a Fahrenheit temperature reading to Celsius is $C = \dfrac{5}{9}(F - 32)$, where C is the reading in degrees Celsius and F is the reading in degrees Fahrenheit. Which of the following is the Fahrenheit equivalent to a reading of 95° Celsius?

    (A)   35° F
    (B)   53° F
    (C)   63° F
    (D) 203° F
    (E) 207° F

13. A bowler plays five games and scores 140, 130, 165, 140, and 195 on those games. Which of the following is true of these scores?

   I. The median is higher than the mode.
   II. The average (arithmetic mean) is higher than the median.
   III. The average (arithmetic mean) is higher than 150.

(A) None

(B) III only

(C) I and II only

(D) II and III only

(E) I, II, and III only

14. The formula for the lateral surface area, S, of a right circular cone is $S = \pi r \sqrt{r^2 + h^2}$, where r is the radius of the base and h is the altitude. What is the lateral surface area, in square feet, of a right circular cone with a base radius of 3 feet and an altitude of 4 feet?

(A) $3\pi\sqrt{5}$

(B) $3\pi\sqrt{7}$

(C) 15π

(D) 21π

(E) $\dfrac{75\pi}{2}$

15. Two airplanes are 300 miles apart and flying directly toward each other. One is flying at 200 miles per hour, and the other at 160 miles per hour. How many minutes will it take for the two planes to meet?

16. John is trying to remember a three-digit identification number. He knows that one of the last two digits in the number 138 is wrong, but he's not sure which. He also knows that all the digits in the identification number are distinct. If he were to start trying all the combinations that fit these conditions, what is the probability he would get the right combination on the first try?

17. Alex wishes to plant three different fruit trees in his front yard. He has five different types of fruit trees he can choose from: cherry, plum, apple, peach, and pear. How many different combinations of fruit trees are possible?

18. The length of each side of square A is increased by 100 percent to make square B. If the length of each side of square B is increased by 50 percent to make square C, by what percent is the area of square C greater than the sum of the areas of squares A and B? (Disregard % sign when gridding your answer.)

19. Carla is having a dinner party and is inviting 5 guests, 3 boys and 2 girls. Carla knows that she needs to sit at the head of the table, but hasn't decided on fixed seats for anyone else. If she decides not to sit any of her guests next to someone else of the same gender, how many different seating arrangements are possible?

20. If the median value in a set of five *different* positive integers is 12 and the average (arithmetic mean) is 13, what is the greatest possible value of one of the integers in the set?

21. The population of Fridaville was 6,250 in the year 2000, and since then it has doubled every three years. The population of the town can be described by the equation $n = 6,250 \times (2^{\frac{t}{3}})$, where n is the population and t is the number of years that have passed since 2000. What will the population of Fridaville be in the year 2015?

(A) 20,000

(B) 50,000

(C) 200,000

(D) 2,048,000

(E) 204,800,000

22. The population of Davis City was 450 in the year 1900, and since then it has doubled every six years. The population of the town can be described by the equation $n = 450(2^{\frac{t}{6}})$, where n is the population and t is the number of years that have passed since 1900. In what year did the population of Davis City reach 28,800?

EXPLANATIONS

1. D

The long way to solve this problem is to pick variables for correct and incorrect answers, form two equations, and solve for the number of correct answers. It's quicker to Back-solve this one. Denise answered 58 of 60 questions. Start with (C). If she answered 38 correctly, she answered 20 incorrectly. $2(38) - \frac{2}{3}(20) = 62\frac{2}{3}$. This is less than 68, so Denise must have answered more questions correctly. Try (D). If she answered 40 correctly, she answered 18 incorrectly. $2(40) - \frac{2}{3}(18) = 68$.

2. A

This is a probability question, and we want to use the basic probability formula. Since no actual number of any type of item is given, let's pick a number for our smallest value and work backwards. We are told that there are two types of candy, nut chewies and marshmallow delights. There are twice as many nut chewies as marshmallow delights. From here, the category of nut chewies is narrowed down further. The nut chewies can be either peanut or cashew and there are $\frac{1}{3}$ as many cashew chewies as peanut chewies. Cashew chewies seem like the smallest number so far, so let's assign a value to them. If we say that there is 1 cashew chewy, there are $\frac{1}{3}$ as many cashew chewies as peanut chewies, so there must be 3 peanut chewies. So together, there are 4 nut chewies. We know that there are twice as many nut chewies as marshmallow delights, and so there must be only 2 marshmallow delights. Now that we have our numbers straight, we can plug them into the probability formula:

$$\text{Probability} = \frac{\text{\# of desired outcomes}}{\text{\# of possible outcomes}}$$

Since we are trying to find the probability of selecting a cashew chewy, the number of cashew chewies is the number of desired outcomes and the

total number of pieces of candy is the number of possible outcomes:

$$\frac{\text{\# of desired outcomes}}{\text{\# of possible outcomes}} = \frac{1}{6}$$

(A) is the correct answer.

3. E

Any of the 5 runners could come in first place, leaving 4 runners who could come in second place, leaving 3 runners who could come in third place, for a total of $5 \times 4 \times 3 = 60$ possible outcomes for gold, silver, and bronze medal winners.

4. C

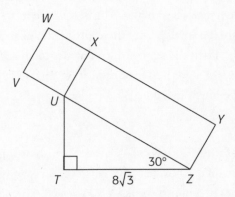

We want to find the area of rectangle $UXYZ$. The area of any rectangle is length times width. Let's call UZ the length of rectangle $UXYZ$ and let's call UX the width. So let's find the length UZ. In right triangle UZT, UZ is the hypotenuse. One angle of the right triangle is 90° and another is 30°, so the third angle has a measure of 180°−90°−30°, or 60°, making this a 30-60-90 triangle. In a 30-60-90 triangle, the sides have lengths that are in the ratio $1:\sqrt{3}:2$. In this right triangle, leg $\overline{TZ}$, which is opposite the 60° angle has length $8\sqrt{3}$. The leg of a 30-60-90 right triangle that is opposite the 60° angle corresponds to the middle term in the $1:\sqrt{3}:2$ ratio. So the short leg of right triangle TUZ is equal to 8, and the hypotenuse UZ is equal to 16. Now let's find the width UX of rectangle $UXYZ$. The perimeter of square $UVWX$ is 24. The perimeter of any square is

4 times the length of any side. Since the perimeter of square *UVWX* is 24, the width *UX* has length $\frac{24}{4}$ or 6. So the length *UZ* of rectangle *UXYZ* is 16 and the width *UX* of this rectangle is 6; the area of rectangle *UXYZ* = length × width, which is 16 × 6, or 96. (C) is correct.

5. B

The overall average is not simply the average of the average ages for male members and female members. Because there are a lot more women than men, women carry more weight, and the overall average will be a lot closer to 25 than 35. This problem's easiest to deal with if you pick particular numbers for the females and males. The best numbers to pick are the smallest: say there are 4 females and 1 male. Then the ages of the 4 females total 4 times 25, or 100, and the age of the 1 male totals 35. The average, then, is (100 + 35) divided by 5, or 27.

6. E

Out of the 50 students, 45 speak Spanish or English. If you add the number of English speakers and the number of Spanish speakers, you get 28 + 37 = 65. But there are only 45 students who speak Spanish or English, so 65 − 45 = 20 of them are being counted twice because those 20 speak both languages.

7. D

The key to solving this problem is to draw in $\overline{OB}$ and fill in the angle measures for the angles you are given:

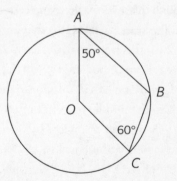

Because $\overline{OA}$, $\overline{OB}$, and $\overline{OC}$ are all radii of the same circle, $\triangle AOB$ and $\triangle BOC$ are both isosceles triangles, and therefore both have equal base angles:

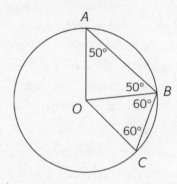

Using the fact that the three interior angles of a triangle add up to 180°, you can figure out that the vertex angles *AOB* and *BOC* measure 80° and 60°, respectively, as shown:

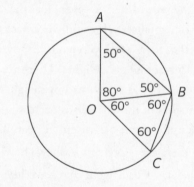

$\angle AOC$ measures 80° + 60° = 140°.

8. E

You know by now to be careful with combined percent increases. If you just add 20 percent and 30 percent to get 50 percent, you fall into the test maker's trap. The best way to do a problem like this one is to pick a number for the original whole and just see what happens. And, as usual, the best number to pick here is 100.

If the 1980 population was 100, then a 20 percent increase would put the 1990 population at 120.

Now, to figure the 30 percent increase, multiply 120 by 130 percent:

$$x = 1.3(120)$$
$$x = 156$$

Since the population went from 100 to 156, that's a 56 percent increase.

9. A

Parallel lines have the same slope. Use the first pair of points to figure out the slope:

$$\text{Slope} = \frac{y_2 - y_1}{x_2 - x_1} = \frac{16 - 1}{2 - 1} = 15$$

Then use the slope to figure out the missing coordinate in the second pair of points:

$$\text{slope} = \frac{y_2 - y_1}{x_2 - x_1}$$
$$15 = \frac{25 - (-5)}{a - (-10)}$$
$$15 = \frac{30}{a + 10}$$
$$15a + 150 = 30$$
$$15a = -120$$
$$a = -8$$

10. B

Maura drives to work in 40 minutes, but returns home at half that speed. Common sense, or else the distance formula $R \times T = D$, should tell you that if she travels home at half the speed, it will take her twice as long, or 80 minutes, to return home. So the entire round trip will take $40 + 80 = 120$ minutes, or 2 hours, and the entire distance she travels is 60 miles. Thus, her average speed for the entire trip, in miles per hour, is $\frac{60 \text{ miles}}{2 \text{ hours}}$, or 30 miles per hour.

11. A

The greatest dollar increase came in 1999–2000, but that's not necessarily the greatest percent increase. The $5,000 increase for 1995–96 is an increase of $\frac{1}{4}$, or 25 percent. The $5,000 increase the following year is an increase of just $\frac{1}{5}$, or 20 percent. You don't even have to give much thought to the $3,000 increases of the next 2 years—but what about the $8,000 increase in 1999–2000? $8,000 out of $36,000 is less than $\frac{1}{4}$, so there's no need to calculate the percent; the 1995–96 increase wins.

12. D

This looks like a physics question, but in fact it's just a "plug in the number and see what you get" question. Be sure you plug 95 in for C (not F):

$$C = \frac{5}{9}(F - 32)$$
$$95 = \frac{5}{9}(F - 32)$$
$$\frac{9}{5} \times 95 = F - 32$$
$$171 = F - 32$$
$$F = 171 + 32 = 203$$

13. D

You should begin by rearranging the scores in ascending order: 130, 140, 140, 165, 195.

The resulting middle number, 140, is the median, and since 140 is the only recurring number, it is also the mode. Thus statement I is not true, and (C) and (E) are out.

It looks like we're going to have to calculate the average:

$$\text{Average} = \frac{\text{Sum}}{\text{\# of terms}} =$$
$$\frac{130 + 140 + 140 + 165 + 195}{5} = \frac{770}{5} = 154$$

So statements II and III are both true, and (D) is the answer.

14. C

This looks like a solid geometry question, but in fact it's another "plug in the numbers and see what you get" question.

$$S = \pi\sqrt{r^2 + h^2}$$
$$S = 3\pi\sqrt{3^2 + 4^2}$$
$$S = 3\pi\sqrt{9 + 16}$$
$$S = 3\pi\sqrt{25}$$
$$S = 3\pi \times 5$$
$$S = 15\pi$$

15. 50

The distance formula tells you that Distance = Speed × Time, or as might be more useful in this case, Time = $\dfrac{\text{Distance}}{\text{Speed}}$. It would take the same amount of time for a plane traveling 200 mph and a plane traveling 160 mph to meet as it would if one plane were standing still and the other traveling at $200 + 160 = 360$ mph. It would take a plane traveling at 360 mph $\dfrac{300}{360} = \dfrac{5}{6}$ hours = 50 minutes to travel 300 miles.

16. $\dfrac{1}{14}$ or .071

The wording on this problem is tricky, so take it one piece at a time. To find the probability that John gets the right combination on the first try, you have to find the number of possible combinations.

You know that one of the last two digits in 138 is correct and the other is incorrect. You also know that all the digits are distinct; that is, none of the digits are the same. So what possibilities are there? If 3 is correct, then 8 is wrong and the possible options are 130, 132, 134, 135, 136, 137, and 139. (Note there was no 131 and 133, since the digits must be distinct, and no 138, since you already know that

is wrong.) Similarly, if 8 is the correct digit, the possibilities are 108, 128, 148, 158, 168, 178, and 198. All told, there are 14 possibilities.

If there are 14 possibilities, the probability that he gets the right combination on the first try is 1 in 14, or 1/14 (which can also be written .071).

17. 10

Here you want to choose three different trees out of five possibilities. So go ahead and call the trees A, B, C, D, and E. Now start listing out the possibilities systematically. One trick is to list out the possibilities in alphabetical order starting with ABC, and to work your way through the possibilities:

ABC
ABD
ABE
ACD
ACE
ADE
BCD
BCE
BDE
CDE

Thus, there are a total of ten possible combinations.

18. 80

The best way to solve this problem is to pick a value for the length of a side of square A. We want our numbers to be easy to work with, so let's pick 10 for the length of each side of square A. The length of each side of square B is 100 percent greater, or twice as great as a side of square A. So the length of a side of square B is 2×10, or 20. The length of each side of square C is 50 percent greater, or $1\dfrac{1}{2}$ times as great as a side of square B. So the length of a side of square C is $1\dfrac{1}{2} \times 20$ or 30. The area of square A is 10^2, or 100. The area of square B is 20^2, or 400. The sum of the areas of squares A and B is $100 + 400$, or 500. The area of square C is 30^2, or 900. The area of square C is greater than the sum of the areas of squares A and B by $900 - 500$, or 400. By what percent is the area of square C greater than the sum of the areas of squares A and B? $\frac{400}{500} \times 100\%$, or 80%.

19. 12

This is a tricky seating arrangement question, so think about it systematically. It may also help to draw a diagram here. If Carla is seated at the head of the table, and no two people of the same gender may sit next to each other, then our seating arrangement must look something like this:

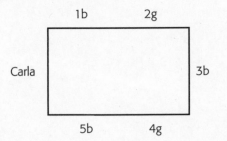

Now let's work our way around the table and figure out how many different arrangements are possible. Moving clockwise around the table, we know that seat 1 must be occupied by a boy, and there are 3 different boys who could fill this spot. Seat 2 must then be a girl. There are 2 different girls who could fill this spot. Seat 3 is another boy. Now that 1 of the boys is seated (next to Carla), only 2 boys remain for this seat. Seat 4 is a girl, and only 1 girl remains to sit here. Finally, only 1 boy remains for seat 5 next to Carla. To find the answer, multiply these possibilities. $3 \times 2 \times 2 \times 1 \times 1 = 12$.

20. 37

The median is the number in the middle after the numbers have been arranged in ascending order.

The average is the $\dfrac{\text{sum of all the terms}}{\text{\# of terms}}$

So, given the average is 13, we know that the sum of all the terms is the average times the number of terms, or $13 \times 5 = 65$.

And we know from the median that the terms arranged in ascending order are:

$$\_\_, \_\_, 12, \_\_, \_\_$$

We want to make one of the terms as *big* as possible, so that means we want to make all the other terms as *small* as possible. Since all the terms are *different* positive integers, when we minimize the other terms we get:

$$1, 2, 12, 13, \_\_$$

And since the sum of the terms is 65, that means the fifth term is 37, which is the correct answer.

21. C

Find the number of years that have passed since 2000 and plug it into the equation to find n. Work carefully, and you should have no trouble.

$$n = 6{,}250 \times (2^{\frac{15}{3}}) = 6{,}250 \times 2^5$$
$$= 6{,}250 \times 32 = 200{,}000$$

22. 1936

First, plug the given population into the equation and solve for t. Then add t to 1900 to find the year.

$$28{,}800 = 450(2^{\frac{t}{6}})$$
$$64 = 2^{\frac{t}{6}}$$
$$2^6 = 2^{\frac{t}{6}}$$
$$6 = \frac{t}{6}$$
$$36 = t$$

So the year is 1936.

Part Seven

SAT RESOURCES

100 ESSENTIAL MATH CONCEPTS

The math on the SAT covers a lot of ground—from arithmetic to algebra to geometry.

Don't let yourself be intimidated. We've highlighted the 100 most important concepts that you'll need for SAT Math and listed them in this chapter.

Use this list to remind yourself of the key areas you'll need to know. Do four concepts a day, and you'll be ready within a month. If a concept continually causes you trouble, circle it and refer back to it as you try to do the questions.

You've probably been taught most of these concepts in school already, so this list is a great way to refresh your memory.

NUMBER PROPERTIES

1. Number Categories

Integers are whole numbers; they include negative whole numbers and zero.

A **rational number** is a number that can be expressed as a **ratio of two integers. Irrational numbers** are real numbers—they have locations on the number line—but they **can't be expressed precisely as a fraction or decimal.** For the purposes of the SAT, the most important **irrational numbers** are $\sqrt{2}$, $\sqrt{3}$, and π.

2. Adding/Subtracting Signed Numbers

To **add a positive and a negative,** first ignore the signs and find the positive difference between the number parts. Then attach the sign of the original number with the larger number part. For example, to add 23 and –34, first ignore the minus sign and find the positive difference between 23 and 34— that's 11. Then attach the sign of the number with the larger number part—in this case, it's the minus sign from the –34. So, $23 + (-34) = -11$.

Make **subtraction** situations simpler by turning them into addition. For example, you can think of $-17 - (-21)$ as $-17 + (+21)$.

To **add or subtract a string of positives and negatives,** first turn everything into addition. Then combine the positives and negatives so that the string is reduced to the sum of a single positive number and a single negative number.

3. Multiplying/Dividing Signed Numbers

To multiply and/or divide positives and negatives, treat the number parts as usual and **attach a minus sign if there were originally an odd number of negatives.** For example, to multiply –2, –3, and –5,

first multiply the number parts: $2 \times 3 \times 5 = 30$. Then go back and note that there were *three*—an *odd* number—negatives, so the product is negative: $(-2) \times (-3) \times (-5) = -30$.

4. PEMDAS

When performing multiple operations, remember to perform them in the right order: **PEMDAS,** which means **Parentheses** first, then **Exponents,** then **Multiplication** and **Division** (left to right), and lastly **Addition** and **Subtraction** (left to right). In the expression $9 - 2 \times (5 - 3)^2 + 6 \div 3$, begin with the parentheses: $(5 - 3) = 2$. Then do the exponent: $2^2 = 4$. Now the expression is: $9 - 2 \times 4 + 6 \div 3$. Next do the multiplication and division to get: $9 - 8 + 2$, which equals 3. If you have difficulty remembering PEMDAS, use this sentence to recall it: **P**lease **E**xcuse **M**y **D**ear **A**unt **S**ally.

5. Counting Consecutive Integers

To count consecutive integers, **subtract the smallest from the largest and add 1.** To count the integers from 13 through 31, subtract: $31 - 13 = 18$. Then add 1: $18 + 1 = 19$.

NUMBER OPERATIONS AND CONCEPTS

6. Exponential Growth

If r is the ratio between consecutive terms, a_1 is the first term, a_n is the nth term, and S_n is the sum of the first n terms, then $a_n = a_1 r^{n-1}$ and $S_n = \dfrac{a_1 - a_1 r^n}{1 - r}$.

7. Union and Intersection of Sets

The things in a set are called elements or members. The union of Set A and Set B, sometimes expressed as $A \cup B$, is the set of elements that are in either or both of Set A and Set B. If Set $A = \{1, 2\}$ and Set $B = \{3, 4\}$, then $A \cup B = \{1, 2, 3, 4\}$. The intersection of Set A and Set B, sometimes expressed as $A \cap B$, is the set of elements common to both Set A and Set B. If Set $A = \{1, 2, 3\}$ and Set $B = \{3, 4, 5\}$, then $A \cap B = \{3\}$.

DIVISIBILITY

8. Factor/Multiple

The **factors** of integer n are the positive integers that divide into n with no remainder. The **multiples** of n are the integers that n divides into with no remainder. For example, 6 is a factor of 12, and 24 is a multiple of 12. 12 is both a factor and a multiple of itself, since $12 \times 1 = 12$ and $12 \div 1 = 12$.

9. Prime Factorization

To find the prime factorization of an integer, just keep breaking it up into factors until **all the factors are prime.** To find the prime factorization of 36, for example, you could begin by breaking it into 4×9: $36 = 4 \times 9 = 2 \times 2 \times 3 \times 3$.

10. Relative Primes

Relative primes are integers that have no common factor other than 1. To determine whether two integers are relative primes, break them both down to their prime factorizations. For example: $35 = 5 \times 7$, and $54 = 2 \times 3 \times 3 \times 3$. They have **no prime factors in common,** so 35 and 54 are relative primes.

11. Common Multiples

A common multiple is a number that is a multiple of two or more integers. You can always get a common multiple of two integers by **multiplying** them, but unless the two numbers are relative primes, the product will not be the *least* common multiple. For example, to find a common multiple for 12 and 15, you could just multiply: $12 \times 15 = 180$.

To find the **least common multiple,** check out the **multiples of the larger integer** until you find one that's **also a multiple of the smaller.** To find the LCM of 12 and 15, begin by taking the multiples of 15: 15 is not divisible by 12; 30 is not; nor is 45. But the next multiple of 15, 60, *is* divisible by 12, so it's the LCM.

12. Greatest Common Factor (GCF)

To find the greatest common factor, break down both integers into their prime factorizations and multiply **all the prime factors they have in common.** $36 = 2 \times 2 \times 3 \times 3$, and $48 = 2 \times 2 \times 2 \times 2 \times 3$. What they have in common is two 2s and one 3, so the GCF is $2 \times 2 \times 3 = 12$.

13. Even/Odd

To predict whether a sum, difference, or product will be even or odd, just **take simple numbers like 1 and 2 and see what happens.** There are rules—"odd times even is even," for example—but there's no need to memorize them. What happens with one set of numbers generally happens with all similar sets.

14. Multiples of 2 and 4

An integer is divisible by 2 (even) if the **last digit is even.** An integer is divisible by 4 if the **last two digits form a multiple of 4.** The last digit of 562 is 2, which is even, so 562 is a multiple of 2. The last two digits form 62, which is *not* divisible by 4, so 562 is not a multiple of 4. The integer 512, however, is divisible by 4 because the last two digits form 12, which is a multiple of 4.

15. Multiples of 3 and 9

An integer is divisible by 3 if the **sum of its digits is divisible by 3.** An integer is divisible by 9 if the **sum of its digits is divisible by 9.** The sum of the digits in 957 is 21, which is divisible by 3 but not by 9, so 957 is divisible by 3 but not by 9.

16. Multiples of 5 and 10

An integer is divisible by 5 if the **last digit is 5 or 0.** An integer is divisible by 10 if the **last digit is 0.** The last digit of 665 is 5, so 665 is a multiple of 5 but *not* a multiple of 10.

17. Remainders

The remainder is the **whole number left over after division.** 487 is 2 more than 485, which is a multiple of 5, so when 487 is divided by 5, the remainder will be 2.

FRACTIONS AND DECIMALS

18. Reducing Fractions

To reduce a fraction to lowest terms, **factor out and cancel** all factors the numerator and denominator have in common.

$$\frac{28}{36} = \frac{4 \times 7}{4 \times 9} = \frac{7}{9}$$

19. Adding/Subtracting Fractions

To add or subtract fractions, first find a **common denominator,** then add or subtract the numerators.

$$\frac{2}{15} + \frac{3}{10} = \frac{4}{30} + \frac{9}{30} = \frac{4+9}{30} = \frac{13}{30}$$

20. Multiplying Fractions

To multiply fractions, **multiply** the numerators and **multiply** the denominators.

$$\frac{5}{7} \times \frac{3}{4} = \frac{5 \times 3}{7 \times 4} = \frac{15}{28}$$

21. Dividing Fractions

To divide fractions, **invert** the second one and **multiply.**

$$\frac{1}{2} \div \frac{3}{5} = \frac{1}{2} \times \frac{5}{3} = \frac{1 \times 5}{2 \times 3} = \frac{5}{6}$$

22. Mixed Numbers and Improper Fractions

To convert a mixed number to an improper fraction, **multiply** the whole number part by the denominator, then **add** the numerator. The result is the new numerator (over the same denominator). To convert $7\frac{1}{3}$, first multiply 7 by 3, then add 1, to get the new numerator of 22. Put that over the same denominator, 3, to get $\frac{22}{3}$.

To convert an improper fraction to a mixed number, divide the denominator into the numerator to get a **whole number quotient with a remainder.** The quotient becomes the whole number part of the mixed number, and the remainder becomes the new numerator—with the same denominator. For example, to convert $\frac{108}{5}$, first divide 5 into 108, which yields 21 with a remainder of 3. Therefore, $\frac{108}{5} = 21\frac{3}{5}$.

23. Reciprocal

To find the reciprocal of a fraction, **switch the numerator and the denominator.** The reciprocal of $\frac{3}{7}$ is $\frac{7}{3}$. The reciprocal of 5 is $\frac{1}{5}$. The product of reciprocals is 1.

24. Comparing Fractions

One way to compare fractions is to **re-express them with a common denominator.** $\frac{3}{4} = \frac{21}{28}$, and $\frac{5}{7} = \frac{20}{28}$. $\frac{21}{28}$ is greater than $\frac{20}{28}$, so $\frac{3}{4}$ is greater than $\frac{5}{7}$. Another method is to **convert them both** to decimals. $\frac{3}{4}$ converts to .75, and $\frac{5}{7}$ converts to approximately .714.

25. Converting Fractions and Decimals

To convert a fraction to a decimal, **divide the bottom into the top.** To convert $\frac{5}{8}$, divide 8 into 5, yielding .625.

To convert a decimal to a fraction, set the decimal over 1 and **multiply the numerator and denominator by 10** raised to the number of digits to the right of the decimal point.

To convert .625 to a fraction, you would multiply $\frac{.625}{1}$ by $\frac{10^3}{10^3}$ or $\frac{1,000}{1,000}$. Then simplify:

$$\frac{625}{1,000} = \frac{5 \times 125}{8 \times 125} = \frac{5}{8}$$

26. Repeating Decimal

To find a particular digit in a repeating decimal, note the **number of digits in the cluster that repeats.** If there are 2 digits in that cluster, then every second digit is the same. If there are 3 digits in that cluster, then every third digit is the same. And so on. For example, the decimal equivalent of $\frac{1}{27}$ is .037037037…, which is best written $.\overline{037}$. There are 3 digits in the repeating cluster, so every third digit is the same: 7. To find the 50th digit, look for the multiple of 3 just less than 50—that's 48. The 48th digit is 7, and with the 49th digit the pattern repeats with 0. The 50th digit is 3.

27. Identifying the Parts and the Whole

The key to solving most fractions and percents story problems is to identify the part and the whole. Usually you'll find the **part** associated with the verb *is/are* and the **whole** associated with the word *of.* In the sentence "Half of the boys are blonds," the whole is the boys ("*of* the boys"), and the part is the blonds ("*are* blonds").

PERCENTS

28. Percent Formula

Whether you need to find the part, the whole, or the percent, use the same formula:

Part = Percent × Whole

Example:	What is 12 percent of 25?
Setup:	Part = .12 × 25
Example:	15 is 3 percent of what number?
Setup:	15 = .03 × Whole
Example:	45 is what percent of 9?
Setup:	45 = Percent × 9

29. Percent Increase and Decrease

To increase a number by a percent, **add the percent to 100 percent,** convert to a decimal, and multiply. To increase 40 by 25 percent, add 25 percent to 100 percent, convert 125 percent to 1.25, and multiply by 40. 1.25 × 40 = 50.

30. Finding the Original Whole

To find the **original whole before a percent increase or decrease,** set up an equation. Think of the result of a 15 percent increase over *x* as 1.15*x*.

Example:	After a 5 percent increase, the population was 59,346. What was the population before the increase?
Setup:	1.05*x* = 59,346

31. Combined Percent Increase and Decrease

To determine the combined effect of multiple percent increases and/or decreases, **start with 100 and see what happens.**

Example: A price went up 10 percent one year, and the new price went up 20 percent the next year. What was the combined percent increase?

Setup: First year: 100 + (10 percent of 100) = 110. Second year: 110 + (20 percent of 110) = 132. That's a combined 32 percent increase.

RATIOS, PROPORTIONS, AND RATES

32. Setting Up a Ratio

To find a ratio, put the number associated with the word *of* **on top** and the quantity associated with the word *to* **on the bottom** and reduce. The ratio of 20 oranges to 12 apples is $\frac{20}{12}$, which reduces to $\frac{5}{3}$.

33. Part-to-Part Ratios and Part-to-Whole Ratios

If the parts add up to the whole, a part-to-part ratio can be turned into two part-to-whole ratios by putting **each number in the original ratio over the sum of the numbers.** If the ratio of males to females is 1 to 2, then the males-to-people ratio is $\frac{1}{1+2} = \frac{1}{3}$, and the females-to-people ratio is $\frac{2}{1+2} = \frac{2}{3}$. In other words, $\frac{2}{3}$ of all the people are female.

34. Solving a Proportion

To solve a proportion, **cross multiply:**

$$\frac{x}{5} = \frac{3}{4}$$
$$4x = 3 \times 5$$
$$x = \frac{15}{4} = 3.75$$

35. Rate

To solve a rates problem, **use the units** to keep things straight.

Example: If snow is falling at the rate of one foot every four hours, how many inches of snow will fall in seven hours?

Setup:
$$\frac{1 \text{ foot}}{4 \text{ hours}} = \frac{x \text{ inches}}{7 \text{ hours}}$$
$$\frac{12 \text{ inches}}{4 \text{ hours}} = \frac{x \text{ inches}}{7 \text{ hours}}$$
$$4x = 12 \times 7$$
$$x = 21$$

36. Average Rate

Average rate is *not* simply the average of the rates.

$$\text{Average } A \text{ per } B = \frac{\text{Total } A}{\text{Total } B}$$
$$\text{Average Speed} = \frac{\text{Total distance}}{\text{Total time}}$$

To find the average speed for 120 miles at 40 mph and 120 miles at 60 mph, **don't just average the two speeds.** First figure out the total distance and the total time. The total distance is 120 + 120 = 240 miles. The times are two hours for the first leg and three hours for the second leg, or five hours total. The average speed, then, is $\frac{240}{5} = 48$ miles per hour.

AVERAGES

37. Average Formula

To find the average of a set of numbers, **add them up and divide by the number of numbers.**

$$\text{Average} = \frac{\text{Sum of the terms}}{\text{Number of terms}}$$

To find the average of the 5 numbers 12, 15, 23, 40, and 40, first add them: $12 + 15 + 23 + 40 + 40 = 130$. Then divide the sum by 5: $130 \div 5 = 26$.

38. Average of Evenly Spaced Numbers

To find the average of evenly spaced numbers, just **average the smallest and the largest.** The average of all the integers from 13 through 77 is the same as the average of 13 and 77:

$$\frac{13 + 77}{2} = \frac{90}{2} = 45$$

39. Using the Average to Find the Sum

$$\text{Sum} = (\text{Average}) \times (\text{Number of terms})$$

If the average of 10 numbers is 50, then they add up to 10×50, or 500.

40. Finding the Missing Number

To find a missing number when you're given the average, **use the sum.** If the average of 4 numbers is 7, then the sum of those 4 numbers is 4×7, or 28. Suppose that 3 of the numbers are 3, 5, and 8. These 3 numbers add up to 16 of that 28, which leaves 12 for the 4th number.

41. Median and Mode

The median of a set of numbers is the **value that falls in the middle of the set.** If you have 5 test scores, and they are 88, 86, 57, 94, and 73, you must first list the scores in increasing or decreasing order: 57, 73, 86, 88, 94.

The median is the middle number, or 86. If there is an even number of values in a set (6 test scores, for instance), simply take the average of the two middle numbers.

The mode of a set of numbers is the **value that appears most often.** If your test scores were 88, 57, 68, 85, 99, 93, 93, 84, and 81, the mode of the scores would be 93 because it appears more often than any other score. If there is a tie for the most common value in a set, the set has more than one mode.

POSSIBILITIES AND PROBABILITY

42. Counting the Possibilities

The fundamental counting principle: If there are **m ways** one event can happen and **n ways** a second event can happen, then there are **$m \times n$ ways** for the two events to happen. For example, with 5 shirts and 7 pairs of pants to choose from, you can have $5 \times 7 = 35$ different outfits.

43. Probability

$$\text{Probability} = \frac{\text{Favorable Outcomes}}{\text{Total Possible Outcomes}}$$

For example, if you have 12 shirts in a drawer and 9 of them are white, the probability of picking a white shirt at random is $\frac{9}{12} = \frac{3}{4}$. This probability can also be expressed as .75 or 75 percent.

POWERS AND ROOTS

44. Multiplying and Dividing Powers

To multiply powers with the same base, **add the exponents and keep the same base:**

$$x^3 \times x^4 = x^{3+4} = x^7$$

To divide powers with the same base, **subtract the exponents and keep the same base:**

$$y^{13} \div y^8 = y^{13-8} = y^5$$

45. Raising Powers to Powers

To raise a power to a power, **multiply the exponents:**

$$(x^3)^4 = x^{3 \times 4} = x^{12}$$

46. Simplifying Square Roots

To simplify a square root, **factor out the perfect squares** under the radical, unsquare them, and put the result in front.

$$\sqrt{12} = \sqrt{4 \times 3} = \sqrt{4} \times \sqrt{3} = 2\sqrt{3}$$

47. Adding and Subtracting Roots

You can add or subtract radical expressions **when the part under the radicals is the same:**

$$2\sqrt{3} + 3\sqrt{3} = 5\sqrt{3}$$

Don't try to add or subtract when the radical parts are different. There's not much you can do with an expression like:

$$3\sqrt{5} + 3\sqrt{7}$$

48. Multiplying and Dividing Roots

The product of square roots is equal to the **square root of the product:**

$$\sqrt{3} \times \sqrt{5} = \sqrt{3 \times 5} = \sqrt{15}$$

The quotient of square roots is equal to the **square root of the quotient:**

$$\frac{\sqrt{6}}{\sqrt{3}} = \sqrt{\frac{6}{3}} = \sqrt{2}$$

49. Negative Exponents and Rational Exponents

To find the value of a number raised to a negative exponent, simply rewrite the number, without the negative sign, as the bottom of a fraction with 1 as the numerator of the fraction: $3^{-2} = \frac{1}{3^2} = \frac{1}{9}$. If x is a positive number and a is a nonzero number, then $x^{\frac{1}{a}} = \sqrt[a]{x}$. So $4^{\frac{1}{2}} = \sqrt[2]{4} = 2$. If p and q are integers, then $x^{\frac{p}{q}} = \sqrt[q]{x^p}$. So $4^{\frac{3}{2}} = \sqrt[2]{4^3} = \sqrt{64} = 8$.

ABSOLUTE VALUE

50. Determining Absolute Value

The absolute value of a number is the distance of the number from zero on the number line. Because absolute value is a distance, it is always positive. The absolute value of 7 is 7; this is expressed $|7| = 7$. Similarly, the absolute value of –7 is 7: $|-7| = 7$. Every positive number is the absolute value of two numbers: itself and its negative.

ALGEBRAIC EXPRESSIONS

51. Evaluating an Expression

To evaluate an algebraic expression, **plug in** the given values for the unknowns and calculate according to **PEMDAS.** To find the value of $x^2 + 5x - 6$ when $x = -2$, plug in –2 for x: $(-2)^2 + 5(-2) - 6 = -12$.

52. Adding and Subtracting Monomials

To combine like terms, **keep the variable part unchanged while adding or subtracting the coefficients:**

$$2a + 3a = (2 + 3)a = 5a$$

53. Adding and Subtracting Polynomials

To add or subtract polynomials, **combine like terms.**

$$(3x^2 + 5x - 7) - (x^2 + 12) =$$
$$(3x^2 - x^2) + 5x + (-7 - 12) =$$
$$2x^2 + 5x - 19 =$$

54. Multiplying Monomials

To multiply monomials, **multiply the coefficients and the variables separately:**

$$2a \times 3a = (2 \times 3)(a \times a) = 6a^2$$

55. Multiplying Binomials—FOIL

To multiply binomials, use **FOIL.** To multiply $(x + 3)$ by $(x + 4)$, first multiply the **F**irst terms: $x \times x = x^2$. Next the **O**uter terms: $x \times 4 = 4x$. Then the **I**nner terms: $3 \times x = 3x$. And finally the **L**ast terms: $3 \times 4 = 12$. Then add and combine like terms:

$$x^2 + 4x + 3x + 12 = x^2 + 7x + 12$$

56. Multiplying Other Polynomials

FOIL works only when you want to multiply two binomials. If you want to multiply polynomials with more than two terms, make sure you **multiply each term in the first polynomial by each term in the second.**

$$(x^2 + 3x + 4)(x + 5) =$$
$$x^2(x + 5) + 3x(x + 5) + 4(x + 5) =$$
$$x^3 + 5x^2 + 3x^2 + 15x + 4x + 20 =$$
$$x^3 + 8x^2 + 19x + 20$$

After multiplying two polynomials together, the number of terms in your expression before simplifying should equal the number of terms in one polynomial multiplied by the number of terms in the second. In the example, you should have $3 \times 2 = 6$ terms in the product before you simplify like terms.

FACTORING ALGEBRAIC EXPRESSIONS

57. Factoring Out a Common Divisor

A factor common to all terms of a polynomial can be **factored out.** All three terms in the polynomial $3x^3 + 12x^2 - 6x$ contain a factor of $3x$. Pulling out the common factor yields $3x(x^2 + 4x - 2)$.

58. Factoring the Difference of Squares

One of the test maker's favorite factorables is the **difference of squares.**

$$a^2 - b^2 = (a - b)\ (a + b)$$

$x^2 - 9$, for example, factors to $(x - 3)(x + 3)$.

59. Factoring the Square of a Binomial

Recognize polynomials that are squares of binomials:

$$a^2 + 2ab + b^2 = (a + b)^2$$
$$a^2 - 2ab + b^2 = (a - b)^2$$

For example, $4x^2 + 12x + 9$ factors to $(2x + 3)^2$, and $n^2 - 10n + 25$ factors to $(n - 5)^2$.

60. Factoring Other Polynomials—FOIL in Reverse

To factor a quadratic expression, **think about what binomials you could use FOIL on to get that quadratic expression.** To factor $x^2 - 5x + 6$, think about what **F**irst terms will produce x^2, what **L**ast terms will produce $+6$, and what **O**uter and **I**nner terms will produce $-5x$. Some common sense—and a little trial and error—lead you to $(x - 2)(x - 3)$.

61. Simplifying an Algebraic Fraction

Simplifying an algebraic fraction is a lot like simplifying a numerical fraction. The general idea is to **find factors common to the numerator and denominator and cancel them.** Thus, simplifying an algebraic fraction begins with factoring.

For example, to simplify $\dfrac{x^2 - x - 12}{x^2 - 9}$, first factor the numerator and denominator:

$$\frac{x^2 - x - 12}{x^2 - 9} = \frac{(x - 4)(x + 3)}{(x - 3)(x + 3)}$$

Canceling $x + 3$ from the numerator and denominator leaves you with $\dfrac{x - 4}{x - 3}$.

SOLVING EQUATIONS

62. Solving a Linear Equation

To solve an equation, do whatever is necessary to both sides to **isolate the variable.** To solve the equation $5x - 12 = -2x + 9$, first get all the xs on one side by adding $2x$ to both sides: $7x - 12 = 9$. Then add 12 to both sides: $7x = 21$. Then divide both sides by 7: $x = 3$.

63. Solving "In Terms Of"

To solve an equation for one variable **in terms of** another means to **isolate the one variable on one side of the equation,** leaving an expression containing the other variable on the other side of the equation. To solve the equation $3x - 10y = -5x + 6y$ for x in terms of y, isolate x:

$$3x - 10y = -5x + 6y$$
$$3x + 5x = 6y + 10y$$
$$8x = 16y$$
$$x = 2y$$

64. Translating from English into Algebra

To translate from English into algebra, look for the key words and systematically turn phrases into algebraic expressions and sentences into equations. Be careful about order, especially when subtraction is called for.

Example: The charge for a phone call is r cents for the first 3 minutes and s cents for each minute thereafter. What is the cost, in cents, of a phone call lasting exactly t minutes? $(t > 3)$

Setup: The charge begins with r, and then something more is added, depending on the length of the call. The amount added is s times the number of minutes past 3 minutes. If the total number of minutes is t, then the number of minutes past 3 is $t - 3$. So the charge is $r + s(t - 3)$.

65. Solving a Quadratic Equation

To solve a quadratic equation, put it in the "$ax^2 + bx + c = 0$" form, **factor** the left side (if you can), and set each factor equal to 0 separately to get the two solutions. To solve $x^2 + 12 = 7x$, first rewrite it as $x^2 - 7x + 12 = 0$. Then factor the left side:

$$(x - 3)(x - 4) = 0$$
$$x - 3 = 0 \text{ or } x - 4 = 0$$
$$x = 3 \text{ or } 4$$

66. Solving a System of Equations

You can solve for two variables only if you have two distinct equations. Two forms of the same equation will not be adequate. **Combine the equations** in such a way that **one of the variables cancels out.** To solve the two equations $4x + 3y = 8$ and $x + y = 3$, multiply both sides of the second equation by –3 to get: $-3x -$ $3y = -9$. Now add the two equations; the $3y$ and the $-3y$ cancel out, leaving: $x = -1$. Plug that back into either one of the original equations and you'll find that $y = 4$.

67. Solving an Inequality

To solve an inequality, do whatever is necessary to both sides to **isolate the variable.** Just remember that when you **multiply or divide both sides by a negative number,** you must **reverse the sign.** To solve $-5x + 7 < -3$, subtract 7 from both sides to get: $-5x < -10$. Now divide both sides by -5, remembering to reverse the sign: $x > 2$.

68. Radical Equations

A radical equation contains at least one radical expression. Solve radical equations by using standard rules of algebra. If $5\sqrt{x} - 2 = 13$, then $5\sqrt{x} = 15$ and $\sqrt{x} = 3$, so $x = 9$.

FUNCTIONS

69. Function Notation and Evaluation

Standard function notation is written $f(x)$ and read "f of 4." To evaluate the function $f(x) = 2x + 3$ for $f(4)$, replace x with 4 and simplify: $f(4) = 2(4) + 3 = 11$.

70. Direct and Inverse Variation

In direct variation, $y = kx$, where k is a nonzero constant. In direct variation, the variable y changes directly as x does. If a unit of Currency A is worth 2 units of Currency B, then $A = 2B$. If the number of units of B were to double, the number of units of A would double, and so on for halving, tripling, etc. In inverse variation, $xy = k$, where x and y are variables and k is a constant. A famous inverse relationship is $rate \times time = distance$, where distance is constant.

Imagine having to cover a distance of 24 miles. If you were to travel at 12 miles per hour, you'd need two hours. But if you were to halve your rate, you would have to double your time. This is just another way of saying that rate and time vary inversely.

71. Domain and Range of a Function

The domain of a function is the set of values for which the function is defined. For example, the domain of $f(x) = \dfrac{1}{1 - x^2}$ is all values of x except 1 and -1, because for those values the denominator has a value of 0 and is therefore undefined. The range of a function is the set of outputs or results of the function. For example, the range of $f(x) = x^2$ is all numbers greater than all or equal to zero, because x^2 cannot be negative.

COORDINATE GEOMETRY

72. Finding the Distance between Two Points

To find the distance between points, **use the Pythagorean theorem** or **special right triangles.** The difference between the xs is one leg and the difference between the ys is the other.

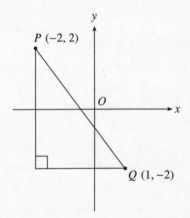

In the figure above, $\overline{PQ}$ is the hypotenuse of a 3-4-5 triangle, so $\overline{PQ} = 5$.

You can also use the **distance formula:**

$$d = \sqrt{(x_1 - x_2)^2 + (y_1 - y_2)^2}$$

To find the distance between $R(3, 6)$ and $S(5, -2)$:

$$d = \sqrt{(3 - 5)^2 + [6 - (-2)^2]}$$
$$= \sqrt{(-2)^2 + (8)^2}$$
$$\sqrt{68} = 2\sqrt{17}$$

73. Using Two Points to Find the Slope

$$\text{Slope} = \frac{\text{Change in } y}{\text{Change in } x} = \frac{\text{Rise}}{\text{Run}}$$

The slope of the line that contains the points $A(2, 3)$ and $B(0, -1)$ is:

$$\frac{Y_A - Y_B}{x_A - x_B} = \frac{3 - (-1)}{2 - 0} = \frac{4}{2} = 2$$

74. Using an Equation to Find the Slope

To find the slope of a line from an equation, put the equation into the **slope-intercept** form:

$$y = mx + b$$

The **slope is m.** To find the slope of the equation $3x + 2y = 4$, rearrange it:

$$3x + 2y = 4$$
$$2y = -3x + 4$$
$$y = -\frac{3}{2} + 2$$

The slope is $-\frac{3}{2}$.

75. Using an Equation to Find an Intercept

To find the y-intercept, you can either put the equation into $y = mx + b$ (slope-intercept) form—in which case b **is the y-intercept**—or you can just **plug $x = 0$** into the equation and **solve for y.** To find the x-intercept, **plug $y = 0$** into the equation and **solve for x.**

LINES AND ANGLES

76. Intersecting Lines

When two lines intersect, **adjacent angles are supplementary and vertical angles are equal.**

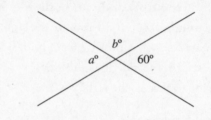

In the figure above, the angles marked $a°$ and $b°$ are adjacent and supplementary, so $a + b = 180$. Furthermore, the angles marked $a°$ and $60°$ are vertical and equal, so $a = 60$.

77. Parallel Lines and Transversals

A transversal across parallel lines forms **four equal acute angles and four equal obtuse angles.**

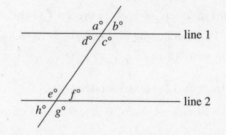

In the figure above, line 1 is parallel to line 2. Angles a, c, e, and g are obtuse, so they are all equal. Angles b, d, f, and h are acute, so they are all equal.

Furthermore, **any of the acute angles is supplementary to any of the obtuse angles.** Angles a

and *h* are supplementary, as are *b* and *e*, *c* and *f*, and so on.

TRIANGLES—GENERAL

78. Interior and Exterior Angles of a Triangle

The three angles of any triangle **add up to 180 degrees.**

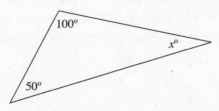

In the figure above, $x + 50 + 100 = 180$, so $x = 30$.

An exterior angle of a triangle is equal to the **sum of the remote interior angles.**

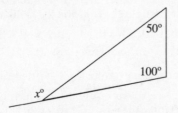

In the figure above, the exterior angle labeled $x°$ is equal to the sum of the remote angles: $x = 50 + 100 = 150$.

The three exterior angles of a triangle add up to 360 degrees.

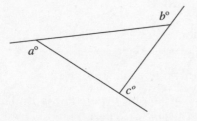

In the figure above, $a + b + c = 360$.

79. Similar Triangles

Similar triangles have the same shape: **corresponding angles are equal, and corresponding sides are proportional.**

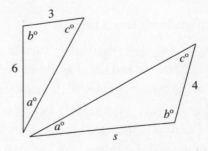

The triangles above are similar because they have the same angles. The 3 corresponds to the 4, and the 6 corresponds to the *s*.

$$\frac{3}{4} = \frac{6}{s}$$

$$3s = 24$$

$$s = 8$$

80. Area of a Triangle

$$\textbf{Area of Triangle} = \frac{1}{2}(\textbf{base})(\textbf{height})$$

The height is the perpendicular distance between the side that's chosen as the base and the opposite vertex.

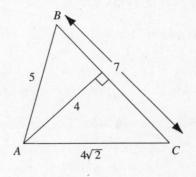

In the triangle, 4 is the height when the 7 is chosen as the base.

$$\text{Area} = \frac{1}{2}bh = \frac{1}{2}(7)(4) = 14$$

81. Triangle Inequality Theorem

The length of one side of a triangle must be **greater than the difference and less than the sum** of the lengths of the other two sides. For example, if it is given that the length of one side is 3 and the length of another side is 7, then you know that the length of the third side must be greater than $7 - 3 = 4$ and less than $7 + 3 = 10$.

82. Isosceles and Equilateral Triangles

An isosceles triangle is a triangle that has **two equal sides.** Not only are two sides equal, but the angles opposite the equal sides, called **base angles,** are also equal.

Equilateral triangles are triangles in which **all three sides are equal.** Since all the sides are equal, all the angles are also equal. All three angles in an equilateral triangle measure 60 degrees, regardless of the lengths of sides.

RIGHT TRIANGLES

83. Pythagorean Theorem

For all right triangles:

$$(\text{leg}_1)^2 + (\text{leg}_2)^2 = (\text{hypotenuse})^2$$

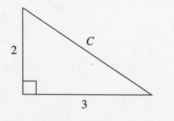

If one leg is 2 and the other leg is 3, then:

$$2^2 + 3^2 = c^2$$
$$c^2 = 4 + 9$$
$$c = \sqrt{13}$$

84. The 3-4-5 Triangle

If a right triangle's leg-to-leg ratio is 3:4, or if the leg-to-hypotenuse ratio is 3:5 or 4:5, it's a 3-4-5 triangle and you don't need to use the Pythagorean theorem to find the third side. Just figure out what multiple of 3-4-5 it is.

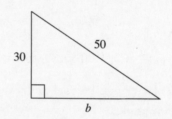

In the right triangle shown, one leg is 30 and the hypotenuse is 50. This is 10 times 3-4-5. The other leg is 40.

85. The 5-12-13 Triangle

If a right triangle's leg-to-leg ratio is 5:12, or if the leg-to-hypotenuse ratio is 5:13 or 12:13, then it's a 5-12-13 triangle and you don't need to use the Pythagorean theorem to find the third side. Just figure out what multiple of 5-12-13 it is.

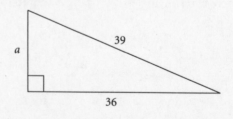

Here one leg is 36 and the hypotenuse is 39. This is 3 times 5-12-13. The other leg is 15.

86. The 30-60-90 Triangle

The sides of a 30-60-90 triangle are in a ratio of $x : x\sqrt{3} : 2x$. You don't need the Pythagorean theorem.

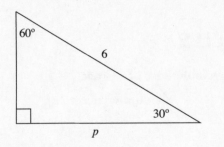

If the hypotenuse is 6, then the shorter leg is half that, or 3; and then the longer leg is equal to the short leg times $\sqrt{3}$, or $3\sqrt{3}$.

87. The 45-45-90 Triangle

The sides of a 45-45-90 triangle are in a ratio of $x : x : x\sqrt{2}$.

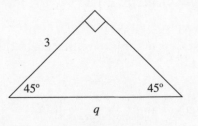

If one leg is 3, then the other leg is also 3, and the hypotenuse is equal to a leg times $\sqrt{2}$, or $3\sqrt{2}$.

OTHER POLYGONS

88. Characteristics of a Rectangle

A rectangle is a **four-sided figure with four right angles.** Opposite sides are equal. Diagonals are equal.

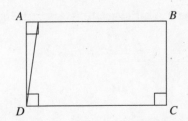

Quadrilateral *ABCD* above is shown to have three right angles. The fourth angle therefore also measures 90 degrees, and *ABCD* is a rectangle. The perimeter of a rectangle is equal to the sum of the lengths of the four sides, which is equivalent to 2(length + width).

Area of Rectangle = Length × Width

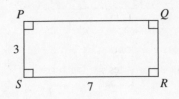

The area of a 7-by-3 rectangle is $7 \times 3 = 21$.

89. Characteristics of a Parallelogram

A parallelogram has **two pairs of parallel sides.** Opposite sides are equal. Opposite angles are equal. Consecutive angles add up to 180 degrees.

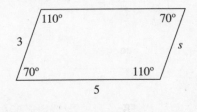

In the figure above, *s* is the length of the side opposite the 3, so $s = 3$.

Area of Parallelogram = Base × Height

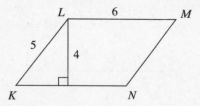

In parallelogram *KLMN* above, 4 is the height when *LM* or *KN* is used as the base. Base × height = 6 × 4 = 24.

90. Characteristics of a Square

A square is a **rectangle with four equal sides.**

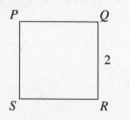

If *PQRS* is a square, all sides are the same length as $\overline{QR}$. The perimeter of a square is equal to four times the length of one side.

Area of Square = (Side)²

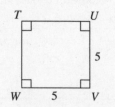

The square above, with sides of length 5, has an area of $5^2 = 25$.

91. Interior Angles of a Polygon

The **sum of the measures of the interior angles of a polygon = $(n-2) \times 180$,** where *n* is the number of sides.

Sum of the Angles = $(n-2) \times 180$

The eight angles of an octagon, for example, add up to $(8-2) \times 180 = 1{,}080$.

CIRCLES

92. Circumference of a Circle

Circumference = $2\pi r$

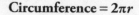

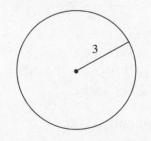

In the circle above, the radius is 3, and so the circumference is $2\pi(3) = 6\pi$.

93. Length of an Arc

An **arc** is a piece of the circumference. If *n* is the degree measure of the arc's central angle, then the formula is:

Length of an Arc = $\left(\dfrac{n}{360}\right)(2\pi r)$

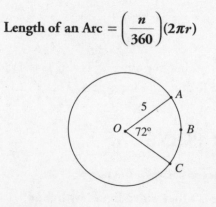

In the figure above, the radius is 5 and the measure of the central angle is 72 degrees. The arc length is $\dfrac{72}{360}$, or $\dfrac{1}{5}$ of the circumference:

$$\left(\frac{72}{360}\right)(2\pi)(5) = \left(\frac{1}{5}\right)(10\pi) = 2\pi$$

94. Area of a Circle

Area of a Circle = πr^2

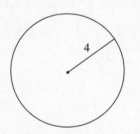

The area of the circle is $\pi(4)^2 = 16\pi$.

95. Area of a Sector

A **sector** is a piece of the area of a circle. If n is the degree measure of the sector's central angle, then the formula is:

$$\text{Area of a Sector} = \left(\frac{n}{360}\right)(\pi r^2)$$

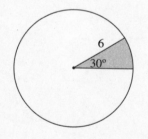

In the figure above, the radius is 6 and the measure of the sector's central angle is 30 degrees. The sector has $\frac{30}{360}$ or $\frac{1}{12}$ of the area of the circle:

$$\left(\frac{30}{360}\right)(\pi)(6^2) = \left(\frac{1}{12}\right)(36\pi) = 3\pi$$

96. Tangency

When a line is tangent to a circle, the radius of the circle is perpendicular to the line at the point of contact.

SOLIDS

97. Surface Area of a Rectangular Solid

The surface of a rectangular solid consists of three pairs of identical faces. To find the surface area, find the area of each face and add them up. If the length is l, the width is w, and the height is h, the formula is:

Surface Area = $2lw + 2wh + 2lh$

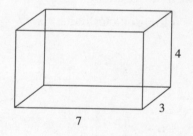

The surface area of the box above is:
$2 \times 7 \times 3 + 2 \times 3 \times 4 + 2 \times 7 \times 4 = 42 + 24 + 56 = 122$

98. Volume of a Rectangular Solid

Volume of a Rectangular Solid = lwh

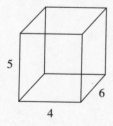

The volume of a 4-by-5-by-6 box is:

$$4 \times 5 \times 6 = 120$$

A cube is a rectangular solid with length, width, and height all equal. If e is the length of an edge of a cube, the volume formula is:

Volume of a Cube = e^3

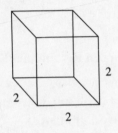

The volume of this cube is $2^3 = 8$.

99. Volume of a Cylinder

Volume of a Cylinder = $\pi r^2 h$

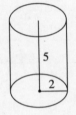

In the cylinder above, $r = 2$, $h = 5$, so:

Volume $= \pi(2^2)(5) = 20\pi$

100. Finding the Midpoint

The midpoint of two points on a line segment is the average of the x-coordinates of the endpoints and the average of the y-coordinates of the endpoints. If the endpoints are (x_1, y_1) and (x_2, y_2), the midpoint is $\left(\dfrac{x_1 + x_2}{2}, \dfrac{y_1 + y_2}{2} \right)$. The midpoint of $(3, 5)$ and $(9, 1)$ is $\left(\dfrac{3 + 9}{2}, \dfrac{5 + 1}{2} \right)$.

WRITING AND VOCABULARY REVIEW

PUNCTUATION REVIEW

COMMAS

1. Use Commas to Separate Items in a Series

If more than two items are listed in a series, they should be separated by commas. The final comma—the one that precedes the word *and*—may be omitted. An omitted final comma would not be considered an error on the SAT.

> Example: My recipe for buttermilk biscuits includes flour, baking soda, salt, shortening, and buttermilk.

> ALSO RIGHT: My recipe for buttermilk biscuits includes flour, baking soda, salt, shortening and buttermilk.

Be watchful for commas placed **before** the first element of a series or **after** the last element.

> WRONG: My recipe for chocolate cake includes, flour, baking soda, sugar, eggs, milk and chocolate.

> WRONG: Flour, baking soda, sugar, eggs, milk and chocolate, are the ingredients in my chocolate cake.

2. Use Commas to Separate Two or More Adjectives before a Noun

> Example: I can't believe you sat through that long, dull movie three times in a row.

It is incorrect to place a comma after the last adjective in a series.

> WRONG: The manatee is a blubbery, bewhiskered, creature.

3. Use Commas to Set Off Parenthetical Clauses and Phrases

If a phrase or clause is not necessary to the main idea expressed by a sentence, it should be set off by commas.

> Example: Phillip, who never had any formal chef's training, bakes excellent cheesecake.

The main idea here is that Phillip bakes an excellent cheesecake. The intervening clause merely serves to further identify Phillip; it should therefore be enclosed in commas.

4. Use Commas after Introductory Phrases

> Example: Having watered his petunias every day during the drought, Harold was disappointed when his garden was destroyed by aphids.

Example: After the banquet, Harold and Melissa went dancing.

5. Use Commas to Separate Independent Clauses

Use a comma before a conjunction (*and, but, nor, yet,* etc.) that connects two independent clauses.

Example: Marta is good at basketball, but she's better at soccer.

SEMICOLONS

Like commas, semicolons can be used to separate independent clauses. As we saw above, two related independent clauses that are connected by a conjunction such as *and, but, nor,* or *yet* should be punctuated by a comma. If the words *and, but, nor,* or *yet* aren't used, the clauses should be separated by a semicolon.

Example: Whooping cranes are an endangered species; there are only 50 of them alive today.

Example: Whooping cranes are an endangered species, and they are unlikely to survive if we continue to pollute their habitat.

Semicolons may also be used between independent clauses connected by words like *therefore, nevertheless,* and *moreover.* For more on this topic, see the section on "Sentence Structure" in this chapter.

COLONS

In standard written English, the colon is used only as a means of signaling that what follows is a list, definition, explanation, or restatement of what has gone before. A word or phrase such as *like the following, as follows, namely,* or *this* is often used

along with the colon to make it clear that a list, summary, or explanation is coming up.

Example: This is what I found in her refrigerator: a moldy lime and a jar of peanut butter.

Example: Your instructions are as follows: Read the passage carefully, answer the questions, and turn over your answer sheet.

THE DASH

The dash has two uses. One is to indicate an abrupt break in thought.

Example: The alligator, unlike the crocodile, will usually not attack humans—unless, that is, she feels that her young are in danger.

The dash can also be used to set off a parenthetical expression from the rest of the sentence.

Example: At 32° Fahrenheit—which is zero on the Celsius scale—water will freeze.

THE APOSTROPHE

The apostrophe has two distinct functions. It is used with contracted verb forms to indicate that one or more letters have been eliminated:

Example: The **boy's** an expert at chess. (The boy is an expert at chess.)

Example: The **boy's** left for the day. (The boy has left for the day.)

The apostrophe is also used to indicate the possessive form of a noun.

Example: The **boy's** face was covered with mosquito bites after a day in the swamp.

GRAMMAR REVIEW

SUBJECT-VERB AGREEMENT

The form of a verb must match, or agree with, its subject in two ways: person and number.

1. Agreement of Person

When we talk about person, we're talking about whether the subject and verb of a sentence show that the author is making a statement about himself (first person), about the person he is speaking to (second person), or about some other person, place, or thing (third person).

- First Person Subjects: I, we

  Example: I am going to Paris. We are going to Rome

- Second Person Subject: you

  Example: Are you sure you weren't imagining that flying saucer?

- Third Person Subjects: he, she, they, it, and names of people, places, and things

  Example: He is driving me crazy.

2. Agreement of Number

When we talk about number, we're talking about whether the subject and verb show that one thing is being discussed (singular) or that more than one thing is being discussed (plural). Subjects and verbs must agree in number. Subjects and verbs that don't agree in number appear very frequently on the SAT.

WRONG: The **children catches** the school bus every morning.

RIGHT: The **children catch** the school bus every morning.

Be especially careful of subject-verb agreement when the subject and verb are separated by a long string of words.

WRONG: **Wild animals** in jungles all over the world is endangered.

RIGHT: **Wild animals** in jungles all over the world **are** endangered.

PRONOUNS

A pronoun is a word that is used in place of a noun. The antecedent of a pronoun is the word to which the pronoun refers.

Example: <u>Mary</u> was late for work because
      ANTECEDENT

<u>she</u> forgot to set the alarm.
  PRONOUN

Occasionally, an antecedent will appear in a sentence after the pronoun.

Example: Because <u>he</u> sneezes so often, <u>Arthur</u>
        PRONOUN   ANTECEDENT

always thinks <u>he</u> might have the flu.
        PRONOUN

1. Pronouns and Agreement

In clear, grammatical writing, a pronoun must clearly refer to and agree with its antecedent.

Number agreement of pronouns is more frequently tested on the SAT than person agreement, although you may see a question that tests person agreement.

	Number and Person	
	Singular	**Plural**
First Person	I, me	we, us
	my, mine	our, ours
Second Person	you	you
	your, yours	your, yours
Third Person	he, him	they, them
	she, her	
	it	
	one	
	his	their, theirs
	her, hers	
	its	
	one's	

NUMBER AGREEMENT

Pronouns must agree in number with their antecedents. A singular pronoun should stand in for a singular antecedent. A plural pronoun should stand in for a plural antecedent.

> WRONG: The bank turned Harry down when he applied for a loan because **their** credit department discovered that he didn't have a job.

What does the plural possessive *their* refer to? The singular noun *bank*. The singular possessive *its* is what we need here.

> RIGHT: The bank turned Harry down for a loan because **its** credit department discovered that he didn't have a job.

PERSON AGREEMENT

Pronouns must agree with their antecedents in person too. A first-person pronoun should stand in

for a first-person antecedent, and so on. One more thing to remember about which pronoun to use with which antecedent: Never use the relative pronoun *which* to refer to a human being. Use *who* or *whom* or *that*.

> WRONG: The woman **which** is standing at the piano is my sister.

> RIGHT: The woman **who** is standing at the piano is my sister.

2. Pronouns and Case

A more subtle type of pronoun problem is one in which the pronoun is in the wrong case. Look at the following chart:

	Case	
	Subjective	**Objective**
First Person	I	me
	we	us
Second Person	you	you
Third Person	he	him
	she	her
	it	it
	they	them
	one	one
Relative Pronouns	who	whom
	that	that
	which	which

WHEN TO USE SUBJECTIVE CASE PRONOUNS

- Use the subjective case for the subject of a sentence.

Example: **She** is falling asleep.

WRONG: Nancy, Claire, and **me** are going to the ballet.

RIGHT: Nancy, Claire, and **I** are going to the ballet.

- Use the subjective case after a linking verb like *to be.*

Example: It is **I.**

- Use the subjective case in comparisons between the subject of verbs that are not stated, but understood.

Example: Gary is taller than **they** (are).

WHEN TO USE OBJECTIVE CASE PRONOUNS

- Use the objective case for the object of a verb.

Example: I called **her.**

- Use the objective case for the object of a preposition.

Example: I laughed at **him.**

- Use the objective case after gerunds and infinitives.

Example: Asking **him** to go was a big mistake.

Example: To give **him** the scare of his life, we all jumped out of his closet.

- Use the objective case in comparisons between objects of verbs that are not stated but understood.

Example: She calls you more than (she calls) **me.**

3. Who and Whom

Another thing you'll need to know is when to use the relative pronoun *who* (subjective case) and

when to use the relative pronoun *whom* (objective case: *whom* goes with *him* and *them*). The following method is very helpful when you're deciding which one to use.

Example: Sylvester, (*who* or *whom*?) is afraid of the dark, sleeps with a Donald Duck night-light on.

- Look only at the relative pronoun in its clause. Ignore the rest of the sentence.

(Who or whom?) is afraid of the dark.

- Turn the clause into a question. Ask yourself:

Who or whom is afraid of the dark?

- Answer the question with an ordinary personal pronoun.

He is.

- If you've answered the question with a subjective case pronoun (as you have here), you need the subjective case *who* in the relative clause.

Sylvester, **who** is afraid of the dark, sleeps with a Donald Duck night-light on.

If you answer the question with an objective case pronoun, you need the objective case *whom* in the relative clause.

Try answering the question with *he* or *him*. *Who* goes with *he* (subjective case), and *whom* goes with *him* (objective case).

SENTENCE STRUCTURE

A sentence is a group of words that can stand alone because it expresses a complete thought. To express a complete thought, it must contain a subject, about which something is said, and a verb, which says something about the subject.

Example: Dogs bark.

Example: The explorers slept in yak-hide tents.

Example: Looking out of the window, John saw a flying saucer.

Every sentence consists of at least one clause. Many sentences contain more than one clause (and phrases too).

A **clause** is a group of words that contains a subject and a verb. "Dogs bark," "The explorers slept in a yak-hide tent," and "John saw a flying saucer" are all clauses.

A **phrase** is a group of words that does not have both a subject and a verb.

"Looking out of the window" is a phrase.

1. Sentence Fragments

A sentence fragment is a group of words that seems to be a sentence but which is *grammatically* incomplete because it lacks a subject or a verb, or which is *logically* incomplete because other elements necessary for it to express a complete thought are missing.

WRONG: Eggs and fresh vegetables on sale at the farmers' market.

This is not a complete sentence because there's no verb to say something about the subject, *eggs and fresh vegetables*.

WRONG: Because Richard likes hippopotamuses.

Even though this contains a subject (Richard) and a verb (likes), it's not a complete sentence because it

doesn't express a complete thought. We don't know what's true "*because* Richard likes hippopotamuses."

WRONG: Martha dreams about dinosaurs although.

This isn't a complete sentence because it doesn't express a complete thought. What makes Martha's dreaming about dinosaurs in need of qualification or explanation?

2. Run-On Sentences

Just as unacceptable as an incomplete sentence is a "too-complete" sentence, a run-on sentence.

A run-on sentence is actually two complete sentences stuck together either with just a comma or with no punctuation at all.

WRONG: The children had been playing in the park, they were covered with mud.

WRONG: The children had been playing in the park they were covered with mud.

There are a number of ways to fix this kind of problem. They all involve a punctuation mark or a connecting word that can properly connect two clauses.

- Join the clauses with a semicolon.

RIGHT: The children had been playing in the park; they were covered with mud.

- Join the clauses with a coordinating conjunction and a comma.

RIGHT: The children had been playing in the park, and they were covered with mud.

(Coordinating conjunctions: *and, but, for, nor, or, so, yet*)

- Join the clauses with a subordinating conjunction.

RIGHT: Because the children had been playing in the park, they were covered with mud.

OR

RIGHT: The children were covered with mud because they had been playing in the park.

(Subordinating conjunctions: *after, although, if, since, while*)

- And, of course, the two halves of a run-on sentence can be written as two separate, complete sentences.

RIGHT: The children had been playing in the park. They were covered with mud.

VERBS

On the SAT you'll find items that are wrong because a verb is in the wrong tense. To spot this kind of problem, you need to be familiar both with the way each tense is used and with the ways the tenses are used together. English has six tenses, and each has a simple form and a progressive form.

	Simple	**Progressive**
PRESENT	I work	I am working
PAST	I worked	I was working
FUTURE	I will work	I will be working
PRESENT PERFECT	I have worked	I have been working
PAST PERFECT	I had worked	I had been working
FUTURE PERFECT	I will have worked	I will have been working

1. Using the Present Tense

Use the present tense to describe a state or action occurring in the present time.

Example: I **am** a student.

Example: They **are studying** the Holy Roman Empire.

Use the present tense to describe habitual action.

Example: They **eat** at Joe's Diner every night.

Example: My father never **drinks** coffee.

Use the present tense to describe things that are always true.

Example: The earth **is** round.

Example: Grass **is** green.

2. Using the Past Tense

Use the simple past tense to describe an event or state that took place at a specific time in the past and is now over and done with.

Example: Norman **broke** his toe when he tripped over his son's tricycle.

3. Using the Future Tense

Use the future tense for actions expected in the future.

Example: I **will call** you on Wednesday.

We often express future actions with the expression *to be going to:*

Example: I **am going to move** to another apartment soon.

4. Using the Present Perfect Tense

Use the present perfect tense for actions and states that started in the past and continue up to and into the present time.

Example: I **have been living** here for the last two years.

Use the present perfect for actions and states that happened a number of times in the past and may happen again in the future.

Example: I **have heard** that song several times on the radio.

Use the present perfect for something that happened at an unspecified time in the past.

Example: Anna **has seen** that movie already.

5. Using the Past Perfect Tense

The past perfect tense is used to represent past actions or states that were completed before other past actions or states. The more recent past event is expressed in the simple past, and the earlier past event is expressed in the past perfect.

Example: When I turned my computer on this morning, I realized that I **had exited** the program yesterday without saving my work.

6. Using the Future Perfect Tense

Use the future perfect tense for a future state or event that will take place before another future event.

Example: By the end of the week, I **will have worked** four hours of overtime.

ADJECTIVES AND ADVERBS

On the SAT, you may find an occasional item that's wrong because it uses an adjective where an adverb is called for, or vice versa.

An adjective modifies, or describes, a noun or pronoun.

Example: A woman in a **white** dress stood next to the **old** tree.

Example: The boat, **leaky** and **dirty**, hadn't been used in years.

An adverb modifies a verb, an adjective, or another adverb. Most, but not all, adverbs end in -*ly*. (Don't forget that some **adjectives**—*friendly, lovely*—also end in -*ly*.)

Example: The interviewer looked *approvingly* at the *neatly* dressed applicant.

STYLE REVIEW

PRONOUNS AND REFERENCE

When we talk about pronouns and their antecedents, we say pronouns refer to or refer back to their antecedents. We talked earlier about pronouns that didn't agree in person or number with their antecedents. But a different kind of pronoun reference problem exists when a pronoun either doesn't refer to any antecedent at all or doesn't refer clearly to one, and only one, antecedent.

Sometimes an incorrectly used pronoun has no antecedent.

POOR: Joe doesn't like what **they play** on this radio station.

Who are they? We can't tell, because there is no antecedent for *they*. On the SAT, this sort of usage is an error.

RIGHT: Joe doesn't like what **the disc jockeys play** on this radio station.

Don't use pronouns without antecedents when doing so makes a sentence unclear. Sometimes a pronoun seems to have an antecedent until you look closely and see that the word that appears to be the antecedent is not a noun, but an adjective, a possessive form, or a verb. The antecedent of a pronoun must be a noun.

WRONG: When you are painting, make sure you don't get **it** on the floor.

RIGHT: When you are painting, make sure you don't get **paint** on the floor.

Other examples of pronoun reference problems:

WRONG: I've always been interested in astronomy and finally have decided to become **one.**

RIGHT: I've always been interested in astronomy and finally have decided to become an **astronomer.**

Don't use pronouns with remote references. A pronoun that is too far away from what it refers to is said to have a remote antecedent.

WRONG: Jane quit smoking and, as a result, temporarily put on a lot of weight. **It** was very bad for her health.

RIGHT: Jane quit smoking because **it** was very bad for her health, and as a result, she temporarily gained a lot of weight.

Don't use pronouns with faulty broad reference. A pronoun with broad reference is one that refers to a whole idea instead of to a single noun.

WRONG: He built a fence to stop people from looking into his backyard. **That's** not easy.

RIGHT: He built a fence to stop people from looking into his backyard. The fence was not easy **to build.**

REDUNDANCY

Words or phrases are redundant when they have basically the same meaning as something already stated in the sentence. Don't use two phrases when one is sufficient.

WRONG: The school was **established and founded** in 1906.

RIGHT: The school was **established** in 1906.

RELEVANCE

Everything in the sentence should serve to get across the point in question. Something unrelated to that point should be cut.

POOR: No one can say for sure just how successful the new law will be in the fight against crime (just as no one can be sure whether he or she will ever be a victim of a crime).

BETTER: No one can say for sure just how successful the new law will be in the fight against crime.

VERBOSITY

Sometimes having extra words in a sentence results in a style problem.

WORDY: The supply of **musical instruments that are antique** is limited, so they become more valuable each year.

BETTER: The supply of **antique musical instruments** is limited, so they become more valuable each year.

WORDY: We **were in agreement with each other** that Max was an unsuspecting old fool.

BETTER: We **agreed** that Max was an unsuspecting old fool.

COMMONLY MISUSED WORDS

AMONG/BETWEEN

In most cases, you should use *between* for two items and *among* for more than two.

Example: The competition **between** Anne and Michael has grown more intense.

Example: He is always at his best **among** strangers.

But use common sense. Sometimes *among* is not appropriate.

Example: Plant the trees in the area **between** the road, the wall, and the fence.

AMOUNT/NUMBER

Amount should be used to refer to an uncountable quantity. *Number* should refer to a countable quantity.

Example: The **amount** of food he threw away would feed a substantial **number** of people.

AS/LIKE

Like is a preposition; it takes a noun object. *As*, when functioning as a conjunction, introduces a subordinate clause. Remember, a clause is a part of a sentence containing a subject and verb.

Example: He sings **like** an angel.

Example: He sings **as** an angel sings.

AS . . . AS . . .

The idiom is *as . . . as . . .*, **not** *as . . . than . . .*

WRONG: That suit is **as** expensive **than** this one.

RIGHT: That suit is **as** expensive **as** this one.

FEWER/LESS

Use *fewer* before a plural noun; use *less* before a singular one.

Example: There are **fewer** apples on this tree than there were last year.

Example: He makes **less** money than she does.

NEITHER . . . NOR . . .

The correlative conjunction is *neither . . . nor . . .*, **not** *neither . . . or . . .*

Example: He is *neither* strong *nor* flexible.

Avoid the redundancy caused by using *nor* following a negative.

> WRONG: Alice's departure was **not** noticed by Debby **nor** Sue.

> RIGHT: Alice's departure was **not** noticed by Debby **or** Sue.

ITS/IT'S

Many people confuse *its* and *it's*. *Its* is possessive; *it's* is a contraction of *it is*:

> Example: The cat licked **its** paws.

> Example: **It's** raining cats and dogs.

THEIR/THEY'RE/THERE

Many people confuse *their, there,* and *they're. Their* is possessive; *they're* is a contraction of *they are*:

> Example: The girls rode **their** bikes home.

> Example: **They're** training for the big race.

There has two uses: it can indicate place and it can be used as an expletive—a word that doesn't do anything in a sentence except delay the subject.

> Example: Put the book over **there.**

> Example: **There** will be 15 runners competing for the prize.

NOTES

NOTES

<u>**NOTES**</u>

NOTES